City Halls and Civic Materialism

The town hall or city hall as a place of local governance is historically related to the founding of cities in medieval Europe. As the space of representative civic authority it aimed to set the terms of public space and engagement with the citizenry. In subsequent centuries, as the idea and built form travelled beyond Europe to become an established institution across the globe, the parameters of civic representation changed and the city hall was forced to negotiate new notions of urbanism and public space.

City Halls and Civic Materialism utilizes the city hall in its global historical incarnations as bases to probe these changing ideas of urban public space. The essays in this volume analyze the architecture, iconography, and spatial relations that constitute the city hall to explore its historical ability to accommodate the "public" in different political and social contexts as the relation between citizens and civic authority has had to be revisited with the universal franchise; under fascism; after the devastation of the world wars; decolonization; and most recently, with the neoliberal restructuring of cities.

As a global phenomenon, the city hall challenges the idea that nationalism, imperialism, democracy, the idea of citizenship – concepts that frame the relation between the individual and the body politic – travel the globe in modular forms, or in predictable trajectories from West to East, North to South. Collectively the essays argue that if the city hall has historically been connected with the articulation of bourgeois civil society, then the city hall as a global spatial type – architectural space, urban monument, and space of governance – holds a mirror to the promise and limits of civil society.

Swati Chattopadhyay is a Professor in the Department of History of Art and Architecture at the University of California, Santa Barbara. She is the editor of the *Journal of the Society of Architectural Historians*, and the author of *Representing Calcutta: Modernity, Nationalism, and the Colonial Uncanny* (2005), and *Unlearning the City: Infrastructure in a New Optical Field* (2012).

Jeremy White is an architect and a lecturer in the Department of History of Art and Architecture at the University of California, Santa Barbara. He is currently working on a book manuscript on the politics of planning in 1930s Los Angeles, titled "Constructing the Invisible City: Planning and Politics of the 1932 Olympic Games in Los Angeles."

THE ARCHI*TEXT* SERIES

Edited by Thomas A. Markus and Anthony D. King

Architectural discourse has traditionally represented buildings as art objects or technical objects. Yet buildings are also social objects in that they are invested with social meaning and shape social relations. Recognizing these assumptions, the Archi*text* series aims to bring together recent debates in social and cultural theory and the study and practice of architecture and urban design. Critical, comparative and interdisciplinary, the books in the series, by theorizing architecture, bring the space of the built environment centrally into the social sciences and humanities, as well as bringing the theoretical insights of the latter into the discourses of architecture and urban design. Particular attention is paid to issues of gender, race, sexuality and the body, to questions of identity and place, to the cultural politics of representation and language, and to the global and postcolonial contexts in which these are addressed.

Framing Places
Kim Dovey

Gender Space Architecture
by Jane Rendell, Barbara Penner & Iain Borden

Behind the Postcolonial
Abidin Kusno

The Architecture of Oppression
Paul Jaskot

Words Between the Spaces
Thomas A. Markus & Deborah Cameron

Embodied Utopias
Gender, social change and the modern metropolis
Rebeccah Zorach, Lise Sanders, Amy Bingaman

Writing Spaces
Discourses of architecture, urbanism, and the built environment
C. Greig Crysler

Drifting – Migrancy and Architecture
Edited by Stephen Cairns

Beyond Description
Space Historicity Singapore
Edited by Ryan Bishop, John Phillips & Wei-Wei Yeo

Spaces of Global Cultures
Architecture Urbanism Identity
Anthony D. King

Indigenous Modernities
Negotiating architecture & urbanism
Jyoti Hosagrahar

Moderns Abroad
Architecture, cities and Italian imperialism
Mia Fuller

Colonial Modernities
Building, dwelling and architecture in British India and Ceylon
Edited by Peter Scriver & Vikram Prakash

Desire Lines
Space, memory and identity in the post-apartheid City
Edited by Noëleen Murray, Nick Shepherd & Martin Hall

Visualizing the City
Edited by Alan Marcus &
Dietrich Neumann

Framing Places 2nd edition
Kim Dovey

Re-Shaping Cities
How Global Mobility Transforms
Architecture and Urban Form
Edited by Michael Guggenheim &
Ola Söderström

Bauhaus Dream-house
Modernity and Globalization
Katerina Rüedi-Ray

Stadium Worlds
Football, Space and the Built
Environment
Edited by Sybille Frank & Silke Steets

Building the State
Architecture, Politics, and State
Formation in Postwar Central Europe
Virag Molner

Edited by
Swati Chattopadhyay and Jeremy White

City Halls and Civic Materialism

Towards a Global History of Urban Public Space

LONDON AND NEW YORK

First edition published 2014
by Routledge
2 Park Square, Milton Park, Abingdon, Oxon OX14 4RN

and by Routledge
711 Third Avenue, New York, NY 10017

Routledge is an imprint of the Taylor & Francis Group, an informa business

© 2014 Swati Chattopadhyay and Jeremy White

The right of Swati Chattopadhyay and Jeremy White to be identified as author of this work has been asserted by him/her in accordance with sections 77 and 78 of the Copyright, Designs and Patents Act 1988.

All rights reserved. No part of this book may be reprinted or reproduced or utilised in any form or by any electronic, mechanical, or other means, now known or hereafter invented, including photocopying and recording, or in any information storage or retrieval system, without permission in writing from the publishers.

Every effort has been made to contact copyright-holders. Please advise the publisher of any errors or omissions, and these will be corrected in subsequent editions.

Trademark notice: Product or corporate names may be trademarks or registered trademarks, and are used only for identification and explanation without intent to infringe.

British Library Cataloguing in Publication Data
A catalogue record for this book is available from the British Library

Library of Congress Cataloging in Publication Data has been requested.

ISBN: 978-0-415-81900-8 (hbk)
ISBN: 978-1-315-81368-4 (ebk)

Typeset in Frutiger
by Saxon Graphics Ltd, Derby

Printed and bound in Great Britain by
TJ International Ltd, Padstow, Cornwall

For Shaoni

Contents

List of Figures xi
Contributors xv
Foreword by Laura Kolbe xix

Introduction

1 City Halls: Civic Representation and Public Space 3
 Swati Chattopadhyay and Jeremy White

Civic identity

2 "A Laudable Pride in the Whole Of Us": City Halls and Civic Materialism 17
 Mary P. Ryan

3 Civic or National Pride?: The City Hall as a Communal "Hotel" in Scandinavian Capital Cities 56
 Laura Kolbe

4 Rebuilding City Halls in Postwar Germany: Architectural Form and Identity 78
 Jeffry M. Diefendorf

5 The Old Town Hall in Prague: An Unresolved Architectural Challenge 97
 Veronika Knotková and Hana Svatošová

Engaging the public

6 Town Halls in Australia: Sites of Conflict and Consensus 115
 Jenny Gregory

7	Courting the Council: The Municipal Palace and the Popular Petition in Morelia, Mexico, 1880–1930 *Christina M. Jiménez*	136
8	The Bombay Town Hall: Engaging the Function and Quality of Public Space, 1811–1918 *Preeti Chopra*	158
9	Los Angeles City Hall: Space, Form, and Gesture *Jeremy White*	177

Re-forming public space

10	Politics, Planning, and Subjection: Anticolonial Nationalism and Public Space in Colonial Calcutta *Swati Chattopadhyay*	199
11	Transformation of Public Space in Fascist Italy *Lucy Maulsby*	217
12	Moving Beyond Colonialism: Town Halls and Sub-Saharan Africa's Postcolonial Capitals *Garth Andrew Myers*	237
13	Jakarta's City Hall: A Political History *Abidin Kusno*	255
14	Seoul Spectacle: The City Hall, the Plaza and the Public *Hong Kal*	276

Epilogue

15	Public Space and Public Action: A Note on the Present *Jeremy White*	295

Index *301*

Figures

2.1	The Place d'Armes in 1803.	20
2.2	Second-floor plan of the Cabildo.	22
2.3	Municipal Hall in Lafayette Square.	25
2.4	Plan of the first floor, Municipal Hall, New Orleans.	26
2.5	New York's City Hall, 1826.	30
2.6	Interior stairway, New York City Hall.	31
2.7	Floor plan, New York City Hall.	33
2.8	Council Chamber, City Hall, New York, 1830–31.	34
2.9	Northern façade of Tweed Courthouse with its stairway removed.	38
2.10	View of the rotunda, Tweed Courthouse.	39
2.11	"Design for a Proposed Monumental Fountain in the City Hall Park."	41
2.12	Bird's-eye view of the San Francisco City Hall.	44
2.13	"New City Hall, San Francisco," c. 1896.	45
2.14	San Francisco City Hall.	48
2.15	The Sandlots of New City Hall (San Francisco).	52
3.1	*Stockholms-Tidningen* describing the June 1923 opening celebrations of the new City Hall.	57
3.2	The City Hall of Copenhagen (1905).	58
3.3	The Stockholm City Hall was located close to the crossroads of the sea and Lake Mälaren.	62
3.4	The City Hall of Helsinki was located in the Market Place.	63
3.5	The City Hall of Oslo was planned close to the sea and historic city centre.	66
3.6	The entrance façade of Oslo Town Hall.	68
3.7	Reykjavik's modern City Hall.	70
3.8	The Blue Hall (Blåa hallen) in Stockholm City Hall.	72
4.1	Aachen Rathaus, 1647.	80
4.2	Aachen Rathaus 1840.	81
4.3	Aachen Rathaus, today.	82

4.4	Cologne Rathaus, 2004.	84
4.5	Munich Rathaus and Marienplatz, 2006. Photo: David Iliff.	86
4.6	Berlin Rotes Rathaus, 2007. Photo: Olbertz.	88
4.7	Hannover Rathaus, 2005. Photo: Robert Friebe.	91
4.8	Stuttgart Rathaus Marktplatz, 1907.	92
4.9	Stuttgart Rathaus, 2006. Photo: Joachim Köhler.	93
5.1	Map of Prague, 1850, with Old Town Hall, highlighted.	99
5.2	Old Town Square, 1793.	100
5.3	Old Town Hall, 1904. 101	
5.4	Plan of the Old Town Hall, first floor, 1897.	102
5.5	Antonín Wiehl, design proposal for Old Town Hall, 1909 (first prize).	105
5.6	Josef Gočár, design proposal for Old Town Hall, 1909.	105
5.7	Jaroslav Fišer–Karel Fišer, design proposal for Old Town Hall, 1946 (prize winner).	109
6.1	Sydney Town Hall c. 1894–95.	118
6.2	Packed function in the Centennial Hall, Town Hall Sydney, c. 1890s.	119
6.3	Striking members of the firemen's union vote, Lower Town Hall, Sydney, 24 June 1955.	122
6.4	Melbourne Town Hall, c. 1880.	124
6.5	Interior view of Town Hall, Melbourne, c. 1892.	125
6.6	Matriculation and Civil Service Examination in the Great Hall of Melbourne Town Hall, 1873.	126
6.7	Toodyay Memorial Hall (Toodyay Town Hall prior to renaming in 1957), 2013.	129
6.8	Town anger: Toodyay residents gather in Toodyay Memorial Hall at a meeting to coordinate bushfire relief efforts, April 9, 2011.	132
7.1	Morelia's Municipal Palace at 403 Allende Street, refurbished in the 1850s.	139
7.2	The main entrance and façade of the Municipal Palace.	140
7.3	The front entranceway to the Municipal Palace with a central open-air patio surrounded by a covered arcade walkway.	141
7.4	The main interior stairway leads to the second level of the Municipal Palace.	141
7.5	A 1932 Circular in which the Secretary of the City Council of Morelia requests all the shoe shiners in the city gather for a meeting in the Municipal Palace.	142
7.6	Public scribe in Mexico (photographer active 1862–77).	146
8.1	Town Hall, Bombay, 1821–33, view of entrance, by Colonel Thomas Cowper.	159
8.2	Town Hall, Bombay, 1821–33, sketch of building by Colonel Thomas Cowper.	159
8.3	Plan of the city of Bombay, 1909.	162

8.4	Town Hall, Bombay, ground floor (basement) plan, redrawn in 1885.	163
8.5	Town Hall, Bombay, first floor plan, redrawn in 1885.	164
8.6	Statue of Sir Jamsetjee Jeejeebhoy and British worthies, Town Hall, Bombay.	167
8.7	Statue of Sir John Malcolm to the right and Lord John Elphinstone's statue in the background to the left, Town Hall, Bombay.	168
8.8	Jagannath Shankarshet's statue, Town Hall, Bombay.	172
8.9	Madhav Baug, Bombay. View from inside, looking towards gate.	173
9.1	Eviction of Occupy LA, November 2011.	177
9.2	City Hall captured shortly after construction was completed.	179
9.3	Spring Street steps: a familiar prop in advertisements, television shows and movies.	180
9.4	Location of City Hall in relation to the earlier no speech zone.	182
9.5	Miss LA: City Hall is depicted at the foot of the mountain representing the promise of growth.	185
9.6	The forecourt is enclosed by a colonnade sheltered by groin vaults, each bay punctuated by a mosaic representing industry.	187
9.7	Forecourt: the tower wall above the doors are adorned with a pediment and inscriptions.	188
9.8	Entry doors: each of the six panels depicts a moment in the city's history.	189
9.9	Under the rotunda: the two principal corridors intersect under the rotunda, its walls, floor and ceiling adorned in iconography.	191
9.10	Plan of Los Angeles City Hall, 1928.	193
10.1	Calcutta Town Hall.	199
10.2	Exhibits in the Lower Floor of Town Hall, Calcutta.	200
10.3	Map of Calcutta showing the location of Town Hall.	202
10.4	The Town Hall in Calcutta by Fredrick Fiebig, c. 1845.	203
10.5	Plan of Upper Floor of Town Hall, Calcutta.	204
10.6	Natmandir of Sobhabazar Rajbari.	207
10.7	Plan of Sobhabazar Rajbari showing location of Natmandir.	208
11.1	The Provincial Fascist Party headquarters, 1923–27 on Corso Venezia, Milan.	218
11.2	Map of Milan from 1932 showing the approximate location of the Fascist Party's provincial headquarters, 1923–43.	220
11.3	Office of the Secretary of the Provincial Federation, Corso Venezia.	221
11.4	Casa del Fascio, Paolo Mezzanotte, Via Nirone, Milan, 1926–27.	222
11.5	Plan of ground floor, Casa del Fascio, Mezzanotte.	223
11.6	Room of Honor (Salone d'Onore), Casa del Fascio, Mezzanotte.	225
11.7	Provincial Fascist Party headquarters, 1931–40.	226
11.8	Ground floor and site plan for the Sede Federale, 1940.	229

11.9	Portaluppi, model of Sede Federale, 1939–40.	230
11.10	Model of proposed reorganization of Piazza del Duomo showing Giovanni Muzio's Arengario exhibited at the VII Triennale, Milan, 1940.	232
12.1	Radio Zanzibar headquarters, Raha Leo, Zanzibar, 2012.	244
12.2	The ten Michenzani apartment blocks dominate the Ng'ambo skyline, 1991.	244
12.3	Raha Leo Civic Center, 1947.	245
12.4	Raha Leo Civic Center under repair, 2012.	246
12.5	Street scene in downtown Dodoma, 2008.	249
13.1	Analytical map of Jakarta (1938) indicating the locations of the city halls discussed in the chapter: (a) The *Stadhuis* of Batavia (1710); (b) The *Balai Kota* – City Hall – complex (1945, 1972) and the Governor's Office (1954).	256
13.2	Johannes Rach's Stadhuis, 1770.	257
13.3	The Stadhuis of Batavia, now Museum of Jakarta, January 2011.	258
13.4	The Stadgemeente Raadhuis of the Dutch colonial era became the "Balai Kota" (City Hall) in 1945 (picture 1956).	263
13.5	The office of the Governor, first used in 1954.	264
13.6	The emblem of the municipality of Jakarta with the national monument at the center.	266
13.7	The site plan of Independence Square indicating the *Istana* (the President's Palace) on the north and *DKI* (the City Hall of Jakarta) on the south.	266
13.8	The 24-floor Blok G, constructed in 1972 replacing the demolished "stadgemeenten raadhuis" used as "Balai Kota," 1950–72.	269
13.9	The cluster of the City Hall is identified by a series of "blocks."	270
14.1	The new Seoul City Hall built in 2012 behind the old City Hall.	276
14.2	The Seoul City Hall built in 1926 during the Japanese colonial period.	278
14.3	The crowd gathered in front of the City Hall to cheer for the Korean soccer team during the FIFA World Cup soccer tournament in June 2002.	281
14.4	A huge crowd of candlelight protesters gathered in front of the City Hall in 2008.	283
14.5	Seoul Plaza blocked by lining up police buses, 2009.	284
14.6	The Eco Plaza inside the new City Hall.	285
14.7	A plan of the new City Hall and the old City Hall.	286

Contributors

Swati Chattopadhyay is Professor in the Department of History of Art and Architecture at the University of California, Santa Barbara. She is the editor of the *Journal of the Society of Architectural Historians*, and the author of *Representing Calcutta: Modernity, Nationalism, and the Colonial Uncanny* (2005), and *Unlearning the City: Infrastructure in a New Optical Field* (2012).

Preeti Chopra is an Associate Professor of Architecture, Urban History, and Visual Studies at the University of Wisconsin, Madison. Chopra's research concentrates on architecture and urbanism in South Asia, with a focus on western and northern India in the colonial and postcolonial context. She is the author of *A Joint Enterprise: Indian Elites and the Making of British Bombay* (2011).

Jeffry M. Diefendorf is Professor of History at the University of New Hampshire. His publications include *In the Wake of War: the Reconstruction of German Cities after World War II* (1993), *Business and Politics in the Rhineland, 1789–1834* (1980), and edited volumes: *American Policy and the Reconstruction of Germany, 1945–1955* (1994), *Rebuilding Urban Japan after 1945* (2003), and *City, Country, Empire: Landscapes in Environmental History* (2005).

Jenny Gregory is Professor of History and Head of the School of Humanities at the University of Western Australia. Her most recent monograph is *City of Light: A History of Perth Since the 1950s* (2003). Her current projects include a critical analysis of the work of British town planner Gordon Stephenson and an examination of the history of "Energy Capitals."

Christina M. Jiménez is an Associate Professor in the Department of History at the University of Colorado, Colorado Springs. She is currently working on a monograph entitled *Making an Urban Public: How the City Revolutionized Citizenship in Mexico, 1880–1930*. She co-edited *The Matrix Reader: Examining the Dynamics of Oppression and Privilege* (2008).

Hong Kal is an Associate Professor of Art History in the Department of Visual Art and Art History at York University, Canada. Her research concerns the politics of exhibitions and socially engaged art practices in Korea. She is the author of *Aesthetic Constructions of Korean Nationalism: Spectacle, Politics and History* (2011).

Veronika Knotková has a Master's degree from Charles University, Prague, and is a historian at the Prague City Archives. Her research concerns the history of Prague's local administration in the nineteenth and twentieth centuries and Prague's system of education.

Laura Kolbe is Professor of European History in the Department of History at the University of Helsinki. Her research focuses on urban governance and finances, municipal policies, urban infrastructure, city building process, architecture and planning, and welfare systems. She has edited four volumes of *Suomen Kulttuurihistoria I–IV* [Cultural History of Finland I–V, 2002–2004].

Abidin Kusno is an Associate Professor at the Institute of Asian Research and Faculty Associate of the Department of Art History, Visual Art, and Theory at the University of British Columbia. He is the author of *Appearances of Memory: Mnemonic Practices of Architecture and Urban Form in Indonesia* (2010) and *Behind the Postcolonial: Architecture, Urban Space and Political Cultures in Indonesia* (2000).

Lucy Maulsby is an Assistant Professor in the School of Architecture at Northeastern University. Her scholarship focuses on the relationships between architecture, urbanism, and politics, with a particular emphasis on modern Italy. Her book *Fascism, Architecture and the Claiming of Modern Milan* (2014) explores Milan's urban and architectural transformation in the Fascist period.

Garth Andrew Myers is Paul E. Raether Distinguished Professor of Urban International Studies at Trinity College, Connecticut. He is the author of *Verandahs of Power: Colonialism and Space in Urban Africa* (2003), *Disposable Cities: Garbage, Governance and Sustainable Development in Urban Africa* (2005), and *African Cities: Alternative Visions of Urban Theory and Practice* (2011).

Mary P. Ryan is John Martin Vincent Professor of History at Johns Hopkins University. Her books include *Civic Wars: Democracy and Public Life in the City during the Nineteenth Century* (1997) and *Mysteries of Sex: Tracing Women and Men through American History* (2006). In progress is "Taking the Land to Make the City."

Hana Svatošová has a Ph.D. from Charles University, Prague, and is a historian at the Prague City Archives. Her research interests include the history of towns and cities, and the history of Prague's local administration in the nineteenth and twentieth centuries.

Jeremy White is an architect and a lecturer in the Department of History of Art and Architecture at the University of California, Santa Barbara. He is currently working on a book manuscript on the politics of planning in 1930s Los Angeles, titled "Constructing the Invisible City: Planning and Politics of the 1932 Olympic Games in Los Angeles."

Foreword

Laura Kolbe

This study of the town hall grew primarily out of an interest in how local or municipal power manifests itself in urban context. The development of town and city halls has been, and still is, dependent on the expansion of towns, cities, and municipalities. Although originally a European institution, the city hall has many global stories that complicate the picture. Physical and architectural organizations of the building type, its location in the city, and spatial practices have distinct traditions in North and South America, Asia, and Africa. What makes city and town halls interesting are these particularities within the building type's universalism, because it not only produces a diverse range of architectural responses, it also implies different urban configurations. One aspect remains common: the building type and its urban setting embraces the requirements and aspirations we normally describe as political power: administrative and political relationships, legitimacy and authority, as well as community feeling. In the best cases, town and city halls can play a vivid and revealing role within the local political community, fostering the feeling of civic pride. In the worst cases, the building becomes a symbol of the oppression and elite power politics of the non-local governing authority.

In many European countries the law provides for types of local government units to which the term municipality may be applied – as in France (*commune*), Italy (*comune*), the Low Countries (*gemeente*), and most Scandinavian countries. Several other European countries, notably Great Britain and Germany, have a diversified system of local government in which several different categories of governance exist. In Great Britain the term municipality is in general used only for the large boroughs (municipal corporations). In the United States a municipality is a political subdivision of a state within which a municipal corporation has been established to provide general local government for a specific population concentration in a defined area. A municipality may be designated as a city, borough, village, or town.

Municipal corporations are organized under the applicable state constitution and laws, with powers of government expressly or implicitly conferred by that constitution and laws, and also by charter. In Europe, municipalities have had since the early nineteenth century corporate status and usually powers of self-government. At the global level, there is a complex system of local government and laws regulating local government, but one thing is common: the local government usually needs a house for administration and policy-making: a town or city hall. Within the municipality, these powers are exercised by a governing body elected by the people. A municipality is basically the response of the state government to the need for certain public services (i.e. waste disposal, police and fire protection, water supply, health services) in addition to what is available from the county or other local governments in the area.

The city hall is a tool in the service of an urban historian who may see the building as a set of "symbolic" elements or view the building in relation to changes in social and economic history. As symbols of local government, some town hall buildings may have great significance as landmarks – for example the Guildhall, London, *das rotes Rathaus* in Berlin, and *das Wiener Rathaus* in Vienna. City halls may also serve as cultural icons that symbolize their cities as is the case with Stockholm and Oslo City Halls, Toronto City Hall, Brussels Town Hall, Philadelphia City Hall, and Los Angeles City Hall, which have all been featured in Hollywood films and television series. However, most city halls are ordinary buildings, only important to their local constituencies. Very little has been written on this building type, forming maybe the largest and most significant form of common, open, and public buildings in the world.

The modern concept of the town hall came about with the development of local or regional government. In the Middle Ages, wealthy cities asserted themselves against the prince and against the social order of aristocracy and church. Cities administered by a group of elected or chosen representatives, rather than by a lord or princely ruler, required a place for their council to meet. The grandest setting for such a council was created in Italian Renaissance cities, where commerce, wealth, power, and mercantile tradition met. The original purpose of the *Palazzo Pubblico* in Siena, Tuscany (1297–), for example, was to house the republican government. It soon became a model for other towns, and provided the vocabulary of this building type: a piazza in front, a campanile, and rich iconography in the interior meeting rooms. The whole building embodied a strong moral message of the secular values of the republican and local government, and contributed new elements to existing urbanity. In Germany, the early town halls were built to fulfill the needs of burghers. Commerce, legal matters, burghers' meetings and representation, both public and private, were the primary needs. The main features – meeting rooms and spaces for administration, archives, and representation – were developed already during the fifteenth and sixteenth centuries. In England commercial activities dominated. Town halls were easily accessible, with covered halls, and they served as market places and places of assembly. The grand festival hall, office rooms, municipal treasury, and a prison were essential parts of the spatial ensemble.

After Siena, the most important iconographical inspiration in northern Europe came from republican Amsterdam. The town hall (1648–65) was designed to be the showcase of the city's burgeoning prosperity. It was the largest governmental building in seventeenth-century Europe. This town hall set the material, visual, and iconographical pattern for similar municipal architecture in northern Europe. Rich marble sculptures adorn the western and eastern façades and the building's interior. Three iconographical elements dominate: personifications, allegories, and patrons of the city of Amsterdam (as the centre of the world). This semi-public space tells a story by using the history of ancient Rome, allegorical figures of ancient gods and goddesses, and biblical virtues as narrative iconographic elements in and outside the building.

In many growing nineteenth-century urban centers, city halls demonstrate the manner in which metropolitan development, architecture, and urban design were understood as genuine means of expressing political and social conditions. The emergence of "national" styles and modernism in the late nineteenth and early twentieth centuries was self-conscious of the break from elite history; city hall architecture was responding to the desire for a larger franchise, participatory in expressing local, urban, and middle-class values, as well as a multiplication of administrative needs. Political decision-making developed alongside party politics at the same time as "the public sphere" (*die Bürgerliche Öffentlichkeit*) was formed.

During the nineteenth century municipal government was liberated step by step from the magistracy and transferred to the new authority, the town council. The establishment of poor relief, building regulations and health care, plus schools, public libraries, and the management of local roads and fire-fighting were the major tasks of the towns during the first stage of modernization. This infrastructure created needs for special administrative and political bodies. The need for a municipal headquarters to accommodate administration, decision-making (the city council), and representation resulted in the separation of judicial decision-making and courtrooms from the town hall.

During the period from 1840 to 1945 the new bourgeois municipal politics was celebrated in many cities and towns by impressive town and city halls. Town halls became manifestations of local political history. They were planned in the period when municipal governance was in the hands of enlightened, liberal, creative, and even progressive citizens, many of them formidable urban reformers. The assembly room was a creation of the eighteenth century, linked with the political needs of the bourgeois class. The multi-purpose public hall (for entertainments and gatherings) and banqueting hall become new spaces of the town hall, now more as arenas of social life. Both reflected credit on the town as a political, cultural, and social whole. Town hall buildings could often include "reading rooms" to provide free education to the public, and it eventually became customary for the town or city council to establish and maintain a public library as part of its service to the community. With an expanding bureaucracy, extra space was needed for police and fire services, a restaurant, library, archives, and registry clerk. With all these elements included, the full-grown European city hall was a complex building. Its setting in the existing urban landscape became a major challenge. The task was to find a form for the modern city and its new social classes. All over Europe, local and national history was revised or written anew and the city hall became a site for expressing these views through iconographic and architectural means.

The role of the European city remains key, even if we view the city hall from a global perspective, as the events that revolutionized Europe and its cities in the nineteenth century also served to establish European dominance throughout the New World and beyond. Thus, the history of the city hall outside Europe continued to be linked to practices in Europe. The building type was the same, but the municipal message was transformed; now the city hall became the symbol of foreign power and non-local elite formation.

Today, most growing cities – metropolises and megalopolises – are in Asia and Latin America. The meaning and function of the city hall has changed both over time and with shifts in geopolitics; in the twenty-first century, the city hall attempts to accommodate a larger suite of civic and cultural activities than before, and is often completely removed from the administrative center. This is therefore a good moment to ask questions about the building as transformed through global use and as part of a global market.

Introduction

Chapter 1: City Halls

Civic Representation and Public Space

Swati Chattopadhyay and Jeremy White

The global landscape is an assemblage of metropolitan conurbations centered on the ideological and physical construct of the city. The roots of this construct are generally traced back to the mercantile towns of western Europe during the late Middle Ages, places of overlapping and competing spheres of governance. The autonomy of the city represented a shift away from older political obligations, the feudal lord and the church, and the ambition for self-determination was embodied in an urban-centered building, the town hall. As a secular public space it also afforded congregational functions inappropriate either in the guildhall or cathedral, buildings with which the town hall often competed for spatial privilege.[1] The town hall, or city hall in American nomenclature, was hitched to the fortunes and problems of economic exchange, especially that between city and country. As the space of representative civic authority it aimed to set the terms and extent of public space.

By public space we refer to not merely a space of gathering that is potentially open to all, but one that is inherently political, with the capacity to foster group or community identity. Historically, public space has been intimately tied to the power and limits of political representation. Globalization, spearheaded by colonialism and imperialism in the nineteenth and twentieth centuries, changed the parameters of civic representation and along with it the notion of cities and public space. This volume utilizes the city hall in its historical global incarnations as the base from which to probe these changing ideas of urban public space.

THE GLOBAL PRESENCE OF CITY HALL

The city hall is found all over the globe, and yet it is an understudied building in terms of both architectural history and typology. Despite the immense popularity and global reach of the city hall as an urban monument, there are only a few works that treat the subject from either an architectural or a historical perspective.[2] The existing scholarly works focus on discrete traditions, delimited geographically or temporally, or they conduct a survey that leaves little scope for analytic depth.[3]

While there are only a handful of essays on city halls in Europe and the United States, there is no work of note on the hundreds of city halls in Asia and Africa; and none that studies city halls across geopolitical domains.[4] Even though we know that the idea of the town/city hall traveled outside Europe along the path of modern colonialism and imperialism, we know very little of exactly how this happened or in what ways the form and the use of city hall changed (if at all) when it was transplanted in the colonial context.[5]

The global focus in this study of city halls allows us to investigate its promises and limits as a civic institution, that is, its historical ability to accommodate the "public" under different political and social contexts, an important dimension that has yet to be explored. This has to do with the city hall's role in the political life of cities: central yet inconsistent. It is usually understood as a house for local governance, a *domus civica*, but it is also an architectural stage with representational ambition – iconographic and political. More than a shell or stage, the city hall is perhaps the most public of public interior spaces, one with complex and complicated histories. The complexity resides in its foundation in divergent traditions of public space that defy a linear understanding of its formal invention. If the contemporary city hall in western Europe may be traced back to the economy and politics of the late-medieval city – in the town hall of England and the *palazzo pubblico* in Italian city states – it gathered new meaning as *rådhuset, rathus, stadshuset*, and *stadhuis* in northern Europe, while one can find in the city halls in nineteenth- and twentieth-century United States, conceptual vestiges of other buildings of public assembly such as New England meeting houses, parish halls, courthouses, and taverns.[6] The litany of institutions would increase if we move outside Europe and the United States, and the diverse rationales for adaptation of form and meaning are uneven at best. Understanding these rationales require viewing the city hall in terms of its specific location and conditions of production in the light of global processes.

When the idea of the city hall, along with some of its spatial components, was carried to the colonies by European merchant-administrators they used the institution to reinvent colonial-civic identity in terms of class, race, and gender. Its very claim as a "representative" institution (the idea for which it stood), however, would make it a site of political maneuver by the colonized elite and a focus of anticolonial nationalism. In the process it would split open the very idea of the citizen-subject upon which the city hall was premised. The city hall's spatial organization, its location in the city, and the practices it enabled or refused are important clues to understand this split, the gap that opens up between different constituencies – colonialist, nationalist, elite, subaltern, the governors and the governed. This is particularly important because the city halls in the European context and later in the colonial context were tied to nationalism and national identity, that assumed the integrity of the nation-state (or would be nation-state) as a premise, and yet paradoxically relied on elements of the building type's idea and form that were born in another (often foreign and rival) context.

Another dimension that lends significance to this examination of the city hall in the global context is the challenge to the idea of civic representation as a worldwide phenomenon. It is therefore not a surprise that the relation between citizens and civic authority had to be revisited as new ideas of the public and new parameters of citizenship emerged at different moments in the nineteenth and twentieth centuries: with the universal franchise, under fascism, after the devastation of the world wars, decolonization, and most recently, with the neo-liberal restructuring of cities. That in some cities the city hall continues to have an important role in the manifestation of civic pride, and in others it has become a fossilized institution, says something important about the relationship of this institution to the specificity of its political and spatial contexts. This is also to suggest that as a global phenomenon, the city hall challenges the idea that nationalism, imperialism, democracy, the idea of citizenship – concepts that frame the relation between the individual and the body politic – travel the globe in modular forms, or in predictable trajectories from the West to East, North to South, or that they are merely reproduced without substantial reorganization when instituted in a particular socio-political context.[7] If the city hall has historically been connected with the articulation of bourgeois civil society, then the city hall as a global spatial type – architectural space, urban monument, and space of governance – holds a mirror to the promise and limits of civil society.

We see in the city hall an opportunity to explore the relation between representation, building, and public space. The authors in this volume write with an awareness of the multiple connotations that the city/town hall bears as public space, as a space of local representative governance (irrespective of whether the idea is indeed materialized), and as social space. The city hall's uneven geopolitical manifestations preclude it from being straitjacketed into types. Collectively, we pose questions that move beyond typology, and a good number of the chapters investigate the city hall at the edges of its categorical identity.

CITY HALL AS A SPATIAL TYPE

Our emphasis on examining the city hall as public space and as an instance of *civic materialism*, to use historian Mary Ryan's phrase in her chapter in this volume, moves us away from the notion of the city hall as building type to the city hall as a spatial type. The idea of civic materialism directs us to the ordinary, everyday experience of citizenship produced in the process of negotiating the material constituents of public space. This includes the city's residents requiring or demanding access to physical spaces of the building that houses municipal governance, encountering the social and political gestures of the building and its urban setting, and debating the role of municipalities in setting the norms of public space.

We are foremost interested in exploring the city hall as spatial process that must move beyond the form-function linkage that dominates studies of building types, opening up the notion of typology to various factors that are both historically contingent and not of the architect's and patron's making. Here we are suggesting an important distinction between the city hall as a building type, which implicitly or explicitly assumes coherence between form and function, and what we are calling a spatial type, thereby foregrounding the linkages between a variety of social actors and spaces. These linkages may vary in scale and encompass the city, region, nation, empire, and the globe, and are transformative. To clarify the difference, the study of a building type may be conducted with or without reference to its location in the landscape or the social basis of its production. Indeed, Michael Guggenheim and Ola Söderström note that building types are "abstractions of both built form and human activities." They are formed by:

> detaching given features from existing, locally rooted buildings and condensing them into a non-local type. By this process formal features are identified and related to specific functions. The history of building types can then be written as a history of very specific local circumstances that give rise to new building types that are abstracted and reduced to a description of essential features, to make them reproducible.[8]

In contrast, a spatial type must not only take into account the specific "local" social and political contexts of its shaping, but needs to consider global pressures and processes that might have a significant impact in shaping these local conditions, as is very clearly the case in the colonial, postcolonial, and neoliberal situations that many of the chapters in this volume examine.

There are two issues here. First, the study of building types as a method of analysis is beholden to an Enlightenment episteme that locates its claim to authority in the dual move of classification and separation. The city hall as a building type has been subject to these formal interventions, and charting that history would give us a very limited and partial account of the historical import of the town hall as public space. As a global history, such tack would proliferate types: the English town hall vs. the Scandinavian city hall, the American city hall vs. the town hall of the British Raj, and so on, without necessarily addressing why these differences and similarities matter. Second, the form-function linkage privileges the intentions of architects and builders. Buildings are worth studying for the intentions of their makers as well as for the unintended effects in a spatial milieu, and indeed these unintended effects are the essential elements of civic materialism.[9] The intentions of the architects and authorities are appropriated, altered, and ignored in the process of investing space with meaning. A spatial type recognizes both the intentions of its makers as well as those effects that are products of claims by myriad constituencies; it helps to disperse intentions to encompass a larger landscape. It includes both the why and how of putting the artifact together, but crucially, it views the meaning of the building shaped by historical eventualities that were not within its original compass. The latter has to do with changes in a building in a particular location over time that we may gather from a longitudinal study, as well as the transformations that take place when the idea of a city hall moves from one geopolitical locale to another, producing particular histories of transplantation.[10] We are interested in the translation – changes in form, emplacement, meaning, and use of the building – that takes place in the process of transplantation.[11]

The objective of viewing the city hall as a spatial type, however, is not an end in itself. The goal is not typification in the form of generating sub-types; rather we seek to use it as a point of departure to explore the character of public space. Thus we pay particular attention to the physical (architectural) organization of the building, the location of the building in the city, and the spatial practices, both everyday and exceptional, that give it social and political meaning. Methodologically, it acts as the rabbit hole allowing us to enter a different world of ideas and social relations, opening up new ways to conceptualize a history of public space. This is especially important given that most discussions of the "public" and "public sphere" are remarkably non-spatial.[12]

CITY HALL AS PUBLIC SPACE

The idea of the "public" is historically tied to the ability and power of (self-) representation. Jürgen Habermas argued that the freedom of the bourgeois individual is mediated by access to public space, and this freedom was strictly limited to elite men until the late nineteenth century.[13] Access to public space was conditioned in planned and unplanned ways, neglecting those who have been left out of the imagination of the public. What or who constitutes the public is both contextually contingent, and underwent a sea-change over the course of the nineteenth century, as the boundaries of the public sphere expanded to include the working classes, blacks, women, minorities, and the ex-colonized in the ranks of those who have the power of self-representation.

While political theorists and geographers have neglected the political implication of city hall as public space, urban historians who often address public space as a physical construct, have neglected this "model" public space that has stood for centuries in the name of the citizenry, good government, and the "virtues" of the public. Consider the urban history legacy. In *The Culture of Cities* (1938), Lewis Mumford, summarizing the significance of the town hall in urban formation, noted its changing significance in the late Middle Ages as it became a privileged space for the elite. In it:

> the leading families, drawn chiefly from the wealthier circle of wholesale merchants, might – to the envy of the rest of the population – hold their dances and routs. It became, in fact, a sort of collective palace of the patriciate: hence it was often called a 'theatrum' or playhouse.[14]

Although he did not clarify, the context in which he placed his summary of the town/city hall suggests that he saw this elite influence as a departure from the cooperative genius of the town, an oligarchy thwarting the fuller possibilities of "democratic" politics. In so doing he suggested something important about the town/city hall as a building type and civic ideal, and the form of politics that finds its resonance in such an interiorized public space for civic decision-making.

Mumford, like many later scholars, saw the city hall as a key element in the cultural apparatus of the bourgeoisie, but did not pursue its conceptual and theoretical implications.[15] It is noteworthy that Habermas' historical exposition of the bourgeois public sphere as a concept and practice refers to a range of interior spaces of assembly, including the bourgeois salon, coffeehouses, taverns, playhouses, and voluntary associations, and even parliamentary assemblies, as he tries to locate the domain of the emergent public sphere in early modern Europe between the state and the family. Curiously, he is entirely silent on the subject of the town hall.[16] As a space marked by the competing demands of the citizenry – between the market and the municipality – one would imagine that it would be an ideal site for testing the promises and limits of the public sphere and its under-theorized relation to public space. Also, given subsequent critiques of Habermas' work, particularly in terms of its class, gender, and racial bias, how do we mobilize the idea of the public sphere to understand representative politics and public space in the present?[17] In what ways might the city hall as a spatial type enable us to do so? What happens when the limits of the bourgeois public sphere are exposed, as they have been in much of the world since the nineteenth century, as European ideas and concomitant views of racial privilege traversed and marked the colonial divide?

While city halls have continued to be built as emblems of "civic pride" across the world well into the present century, the historical evidence suggests that the institution has lost its place as a center of power politics, particularly in the ex-colonial world. This loss of centrality has a fairly direct correlation to the understanding of democratic politics and city governance in much of the world today. Given that democratic politics is no longer subject to a bourgeois public sphere, ideal or otherwise, and most of the population has inadequate access to civic institutions even in functioning democracies,[18] it is useful to think of the transformative moments in the lives of city hall in order to generate a better understanding of the politics of public space. How does the city hall operate as a figure in the cultural apparatus of its citizens, when it is placed under political pressure from a different constituency? What are its (remaining) promises and limitations as public space?

Collectively, we represent a wide methodological and disciplinary field: history, urban history and theory, geography, art and architectural history. The studies included in this volume address specific historical moments since the late eighteenth century to the present that test the validity of this urban concept. We are primarily concerned with the building as it is "brought to a crisis" – that is, it has to be justified, redesigned, re-signified, or bypassed, to realign the ideas of citizen-subject and public space. Indeed some of the essays in this volume examine historical moments when city politics or city governance move entirely out of the city hall, as in fascist Italy, twentieth-century India, and contemporary African cities.

Given so many of the city halls in the last two centuries have served as centerpieces of their urban plans that sought to refashion city centers – think of the magnificent Art Deco City Hall of Buffalo, New York (1932) built along the central axis of the Ellicott Plan[19] – we began this volume with a host of questions that relate the physical edifice of the city hall to the larger urban milieu.[20] How is the city hall delineated as a representative civic monument through its iconography, architectonics, and physical location in the urban fabric? How are they produced at the intersection of various scales – city, regional, national, global – and how do they communicate their scalar aspirations? How does the city hall harbor and produce contradictory and conflicting visions of the public and public space?

The essays in this volume focus on two conceptual modes of investigation: vocabulary and spatial practice. These modes can be elaborated as axes of power relations that are sometimes mutually supportive and sometimes in conflict. Vocabulary has to do with understanding the city hall as a didactic artifact, focusing on the building as a statement or language of images. It is remarkable that even with the advent of modernist formal ambition, in which decoration was deemed *passe*, the desire for iconographic and figural meaning in town halls retained vitality. This perhaps suggests that the volume and massing of architectural form itself is insufficient to express the idea of "the public," let alone a "democratic" or "socialist" public. Vocabulary also implicates the scales of community that the city hall represents. Although we may presume a purely local or city-wide role, the city hall is often given a regional, national, or imperial role as well. What task is the building intended to do, and who is in a position to do the intending? In other words, who plans, funds, and constructs the architectural edifice and determines its vocabulary?

The second mode, spatial practice, makes sense of the city hall as an everyday space of social contact, where questions of location in the larger urban context, or production of that context, are as relevant as the building's internal arrangement of rooms, corridors, desks, windows, and (especially) open and closed doors. Access is thus a primary concern – for whom and in what way is the building accessible? How does the city hall operate as a space of contact between citizen and municipal agent? Is it really a space of contact, or does it operate as an insulative barrier, keeping at arm's length all but the most well-placed and powerful citizens from meaningful interaction with government? How does the architectural organization of space and urban location of the building facilitate conformity or challenge to civic authority? This might include both subtle and overt spatial statements that give meaning to contact between citizen and municipal agent. Once the building is seen in terms of spatial practice, in which multiple actors negotiate space and agency, we begin to perceive other itineraries of the "public" that are not confined to the bourgeois imaginary alone.

The book is organized in three sections. Mary Ryan's article, here reproduced from the *American Historical Review*, sets the stage for discussion. She surveys city hall construction in what is now the United States, crossing national boundaries by examining the case studies of Spanish New Orleans and Los Angeles, and then the later United States versions in those same locales, as well as those in New York, Baltimore, and San Francisco. Paying particular attention to the contentious political machinations of the nineteenth century that resulted in the funding and construction of those buildings and their subsequent use, Ryan's account introduces our two key themes of vocabulary and spatial practice. The contributions by Laura Kolbe, Jeffry Diefendorf, and Veronika Knotková and Hana Svatošová under "Civic identity" are primarily concerned with the first category, architectural iconography as an expression of civic imagination, and the choices encountered in articulating competing imaginations, taking as examples the model of early modern and modern European city halls. While Kolbe traces the process through which city halls in Scandinavian capital cities became emblematic of the respective nations, Diefendorf examines the new desire for municipal autonomy in the wake of World War II and the troubling legacy of Nationalist Socialism. Knotková and Svatošová provide a vignette of a different nationalist project that the city hall in Prague was expected to emblematize. Here the nation, ethnically split, could not be easily reconciled by recourse to an imagined unified past – it remains, as they note, an "unresolved" architectural question. These authors study the intention of the politicians, city authorities, and architects in shaping the edifice and its urban meaning in Europe, emphasizing the historical understanding of the city hall as an urban symbol of the polity.

It is usually taken as a given that the city hall is a house of municipal government, and yet some of our chapters explore cases where it is a house of government in name only, or, where it served as the site of political contestation between competing constituencies, some better represented by municipal government than others. The studies in the next two sections reveal just how important the city hall can be as a symbol of a united civic elite, or as a tasteful repository of cultural lineage that bears little relevance to the values and ambitions of an ethnically diverse local population.

The second set of essays under "Engaging the public" focus on the modes of constituting public space, taking the city hall as an example and point of departure. Jenny Gregory and Christina Jiménez look at the city halls in Australia and Mexico respectively as the site for negotiations by different constituencies that gave rise to new publics. Jiménez argues that petitioning to the city council in Morelia, Mexico, enabled an otherwise disenfranchised and politically marginalized population the opportunity to participate in local politics and to bargain for rights and resources *as an urban public* by demonstrating their civic competence and sense of justice. Gregory explores three case studies in Australia in the late nineteenth and early twentieth centuries, focusing on the lengthy and politically charged process of constructing the city halls, and the lives of the buildings thereafter. We find problems of inclusion and exclusion, demonstrations of national unity and the elaborate negotiations between interest groups, and manipulation of the space of town hall as an attempt to control or influence the political life of the town. Preeti Chopra's and Jeremy White's essays analyze the city hall as public space in terms of architectural organization, access, and iconography in view of their multiple constituencies. Chopra traces the changing meaning of the town hall in colonial Bombay by examining its varied functions and the qualities of its public spaces. Utlilizing a controversy from the 1870s over the placement of the statue of an Indian merchant-philanthropist in the building, she assesses how the different groups among the city's residents viewed their ownership of the town hall as public space. Jeremy White examines the Los Angeles City Hall's gesture towards an imagined public, and the manner in which its iconographic assemblage attempted to adorn the points of contact between city authorities and residents, to dramatize and ennoble, and to create public memory, and thus, to help reinforce a civic identity based on place and a selective construction of history.

The third set of essays under "Re-forming public space" address the call to civic and political reform in the last two centuries to understand how the city hall's role changed and the manner in which its surrounding urban space and related urban institutions were implicated in new urban imaginations. The essays question the connection between public sphere and public space and test the limits of this relation. Lucy Maulsby studies the rising importance of the Party Headquarters in fascist Milan eclipsing the city hall's role as a civic institution, to argue that these buildings provide a critical point of departure for assessing fascism's effort to manipulate and transform the public spaces of the modern city. The chapters by Swati Chattopadhyay and Garth Myers address the process of bypassing the city hall as an ideal in the imagination of civic life in colonial India and postcolonial Africa respectively, and locate the roots of discontent in the founding of these institutions under colonial rule undergirded by racism. Abidin Kusno views the city hall in Jakarta in the long durée of colonialism and in tracking its long political history argues that the city hall has undergone a critical shift, from a site of the self-representation of power, to a place of intense contestation over the definition of city and citizenship in present-day Jakarta. Hong Kal's essay begins with the city hall in Seoul constructed under Japanese colonialism, and the process through which it became a site for the postcolonial elite and more recently as a site of popular protest defying the municipality's intention to treat the city hall as a site of cultural consumption under neoliberalism. These chapters discuss the "new" roles that the city hall is meant to support. The essays in this third section reflect on new models of urban sensibility in which the city hall, depleted of content, might survive on charisma alone. We conclude with Jeremy White's comments on the role of urban public space in the light of political unrest in cities around the world today. After all, between the Arab Spring, the fall of American discontent, and the Turkish Spring in progress, the question of urban public space now appears more important than ever.

NOTES

1 For a seventeenth-century example of this ambition to make the city hall the most prominent building, see Judi Loach, "The Hotel de Ville at Lyons: Civic improvement and its meaning in seventeenth-century France," *Transactions of the Royal Historical Society,*

Sixth Series 13 (2003), 251–79. For earlier examples see Robert Tittler, *The Town Hall and the English Urban Community, c. 1500–1640* (Oxford: Oxford University Press, 1991), and for later examples see Colin Cunningham, *Victorian and Edwardian Town Halls* (London: Routledge, Kegan and Paul, 1981).

2   Katharine Freemantle, *The Baroque Town Hall of Amsterdam* (Utrecht: Haentjens, Dekker & Gumbart, 1961); Gillian McIntosh, *Belfast City Hall: One Hundred Years* (Belfast: Blackstaff Press, 2006); Cunningham, *Victorian and Edwardian Town Halls*, op. cit.; Tittler, *The Town Hall and the English Urban Community*.

3   William L. Lebovich, *America's City Halls* (Washington: Preservation Press, 1984).

4   While there are plenty of references to city/town halls in the urban history of colonial Africa and South Asia, there is only one short article dedicated to the building type: Cordelia O. Osasona, "The Ile Nla: A colonial town hall in Ife-Ife," Nigeria, *African Arts* 34, no. 1 (Spring 2001), 78–82

5   As Anthony King notes, there are many ways to think of building types, but form and use are the two key criteria for identifying a building type. See "A global sociology of building types," in Michael Guggenheim and Ola Söderström, *Reshaping Cities: How Global Mobility Transforms Architecture and Urban Form* (London: Routledge, 2010), 26.

6   Kevin Sweeney, "Meetinghouses, townhouses, and churches: changing perceptions of sacred and secular public space in southern New England, 1720–1850," *Winterthur Portfolio* 28, no. 1 (Spring 1993), 59–93.

7   Here see Partha Chatterjee's critique of the modularity of nationalism in *Nation and its Fragments* (Princeton: Princeton University Press, 1993).

8   Michael Guggenheim and Ola Söderström, "Introduction," *Reshaping Cities*, 5–6.

9   Dell Upton, "Architectural history or landscape history," *Journal of Architectural Education* 44, no. 4 (August 1991), 195–99.

10 King, "A global sociology of building types," 35.

11 On the idea of *translation* in terms of architectural and spatial ideas moving across the colonial divide, see Swati Chattopadhyay, *Representing Calcutta: Modernity, Nationalism, and the Colonial Uncanny* (London: Routledge, 2006), Chapter 3.

12 This is partly due to the reluctance of political theorists after Machiavelli to locate political theory in a particular city or republic.

13 Jürgen Habermas, *Structural Transformation of the Public Sphere: An Inquiry into a Category of Bourgeois Society* (Cambridge, MA: MIT Press, 1991).

14 Lewis Mumford, *The Culture of Cities* (New York: Harcourt and Brace, 1938).

15 For an earlier study see Asa Briggs, *Victorian Cities* (London: Odhams Books Limited, 1963), and for a more recent work, see Simon Gunn, *The Public Culture and the Victorian Middle Class* (Manchester: Manchester University Press, 2000).

16 Habermas, *Structural Transformation of the Public Sphere*.

17 See for example, Craig Calhoun, ed., *Habermas and the Public Sphere* (Cambridge, MA: MIT Press, 1996). Mary Ryan, one of our contributors, was one of the authors represented in this volume.

18 Partha Chatterjee, *Politics of the Governed* (New York: Columbia University Press, 2003).

19 The Ellicott plan of 1804 anticipated the boom of this frontier town. For other examples of the centrality of city hall in the urban plan of the city, see the chapters by Ryan, Kolbe, Chopra, White, Chattopadhyay, and Kusno in this volume.

20 The book project began as an exploration of the concept of civic materialism and public space in a panel organized by Swati Chattopadhyay and Jeremy White at the 2008 Meeting of the International Planning History Society (IPHS) in Chicago. The panel was inspired by Mary Ryan's groundbreaking article on city halls in the United States, included in this volume, in which she problematized the idea of "civic virtue" and the materiality of civic space, and Laura Kolbe's presentation on Scandinavian city halls in Uppsala, Sweden, that focused on iconography and community imagination. The discussion that

ensued was followed by another panel at the 2010 Meeting of the IPHS in Istanbul organized by Chattopadhyay and White that pushed further the logic of public space that supports the idea of city halls. The chapters by Kolbe, White, Chopra, and Chattopadhyay are drawn from these conferences, while the rest were solicited for this volume. We thank Anthony King, Thomas Markus, and the anonymous reviewers for their critical feedback on this project.

Civic identity

Chapter 2: "A Laudable Pride in the Whole Of Us"

City Halls and Civic Materialism

Mary P. Ryan

The object of civic pride referred to in the title of this essay is a classic municipal building that still stands and serves a public purpose in the city of New Orleans. First opened in 1853 (and now called Gallier Hall, in recognition of its architect), it was designed as the place of government for the city's second municipal district, better known as the "American Quarter." Upon its inauguration, the Municipal Hall won accolades for serving such diverse public purposes as "affording employment to large numbers of citizens, the bone and sinew of society," and displaying "the progress of taste in our midst … increasing prosperity and of course … a laudable pride in the whole of us." This single and rather modest building proved to be a capacious civic symbol, expansive enough to satisfy both artistic standards and commercial values, to meet the needs of workers as well as merchants, and to inspire allegiance from those who claimed the United States as either their "native or adopted land."[1]

Like thousands of similar structures that dotted the American landscape in the nineteenth century, the Municipal Hall of the Second District of New Orleans also harbors rich evidence about civic life in the past; but, like all historical documents, its meaning remains complex and ambiguous. Even as the inhabitants of the American Quarter of New Orleans boasted of their new public accommodations, the city's sizable and equally proud minority, those of French descent, snubbed the new building and gathered downriver in their own public places in the French Quarter. Public attitudes toward civic buildings were fickle as well as diverse. Midway through the nineteenth century, residents of American cities tended to share New Orleans' pride in their public architecture. New Yorkers were so attached to their City Hall, for example, that when it was ravished by fire it provoked "universal grief" and poignant pleas to rebuild it for the sake of "the jostled, jammed and unsheltered public."[2] Under a democracy, however, the official occupants of civic residences were only tenants, never owners, and consequently the public reputation of the city hall could change as quickly as an annual election. In the last half of the nineteenth century, city halls across America came under a cloud of suspicion and became emblems more of "the shame of the cities" than the "pride of the whole of us." This essay will not resolve the longstanding dispute about the pride or shame of either cities or civic architecture but seeks to demonstrate that the protean passions public buildings inspired merit more attention from historians. Objects that provoked such intense public reaction, be it pride or scorn, are of interest both in their own right and as factors that contribute to the formation of civic culture and the course of historical events.

Although civic architecture is a tangible, obdurate, indeed monumental, form of evidence about the past, it is too seldom studied outside the field of art history. Yet scattered investigations of Italian Renaissance squares, imperial government houses, English town halls, and Beaux Arts courthouses offer convincing proof that architecture and the built environment are invested with historical significance of a very high order. We are told that public buildings in particular have "the power ... to shape and structure experience," to "represent ... power, authority, and legitimacy within the community." One scholar has shown that the public spaces of Paris played "a major role in defining the history of the city" and "in the creation and representation of the centralized state." Others have read English town halls as "statements in brick and mortar of urban consciousness and of pride and confidence in their towns," as "exponents of the life and soul of the city."[3] Taken in the aggregate, case studies such as these point to public architecture as a prime example of the interpretive promise of the "cultural landscape" as defined by Dell Upton: "The fusion of the physical with the imaginative structures that all inhabitants of the landscape use in constructing and construing it."[4]

This essay adapts these principles of architectural and landscape analysis as strategies for solving some quite conventional problems in urban and political history. It exploits the potential of the built environment not just to represent the cultural assumptions of its builders and architects but also to provide a three-dimensional form of evidence about history more generally. More than just a textual or visual imprint from the past, the built environment constituted the actual physical space in which people made history. Accordingly, the buildings constructed and used by a public body could be pivotal to historical developments. In the prudent formulation of architect and historian Peter Rowe, they can "without anthropomorphizing too much become actors, or at least significant stage sets for actors in a much broader play of sociopolitical forces." Rowe has demonstrated this power of public places through the exegesis of something he calls "civic realism."[5] This case study considers more vernacular material sources – American city halls – and will interrogate them for evidence about modern democracies rather than ancient republics or West European monarchies.

Before returning to these comparative architectural questions, this investigation will address a more specific and prosaic issue in the history of American urban politics. The history of the nineteenth-century American city has long been encased in a kind of reverse Whig interpretation, which charts a steep decline from republican civic virtue to the corruption of city machines, which provoked a warfare between bosses and reformers that has been waging in the history books and newspapers ever since.[6] Analysis of the architectural form of the American city hall injects a kind of civic materialism, if not realism, into this debate. What Americans colloquially imagine as "city hall" is a unique focal point of the everyday, ordinary experience of citizenship, a lay person's political practice that is seldom articulated in a formal or literary way. The term itself was conjured up in the public imagination in the nineteenth century when it anchored the idea of government in a social space and shaped political expectations around a public meeting place, a hall. This essay will examine these public buildings and their immediate surroundings for evidence of a vernacular political culture that complicates that all-too familiar descending plotline of American urban history.[7]

This material and vernacular evidence requires its own ad hoc methodology. What follows is, first of all, an exercise in institutional political history. It examines the decision-making process that led nineteenth-century American cities to invest, at times extravagantly, in public buildings. The city hall was the product of nitty-gritty political struggle: its planning and construction required decisive collective action, severely tested the public will, and taxed the pocketbooks of notoriously niggardly citizens. Once constructed, the city hall yields a second and especially resonant kind of material evidence for historians. The floor plans and spatial arrangement of the city hall literally set the path of citizens through their government. The way a municipal building was situated within the larger urban plan offers material answers to such vexing questions as: Where do public and private meet? How does civil society relate to the state? The third research strategy is a straightforward analysis of text and rituals, as well as stylistic and decorative features of buildings, in order to decipher the symbolic meanings ordinary citizens might have attached to their government. All told, vernacular architecture bespeaks more than the aesthetic intentions of architects: it testifies about a whole sequence of civic actions that involved politicians, bureaucrats, builders, voters, and anonymous citizens. Many fingerprints, in other words, can be found upon the marble and bronze of America's city halls.

The sites chosen for deploying these tools of civic materialism represent a range of cities, located in the north, south, and west of the United States. Over the course of the critical period of American political development roughly bounded by the nineteenth century, three locations – New York, New Orleans, and San Francisco – produced five exemplary public buildings.[8] The first research site is the seat of Spanish colonial administration in New Orleans, built between 1795 and 1799 and called the Cabildo. This structure, which occupies the very center of the French Quarter, served as the house of government until 1852, when the city offices were relocated to the Municipal Hall of the American Quarter, the second research location. The story of public architecture in New Orleans will be followed by tales of two buildings located in lower Manhattan. The first has borne the proper name City Hall since construction began in 1803. The second, its intended extension, soon took the name of County Courthouse, and its cornerstone was laid in 1862. The final location for this study, San Francisco, not only extends the regional scope of this story but also provides a chronological counterpoint. For decades, San

Franciscans made their civic home in the secondhand quarters of the Jenny Lind Theater. They did not lay the cornerstone for a proper city hall until 1872, and the project was not completed until 1892. San Franciscans made up for their tardiness with an ornate and massive construction project: it would fill four acres of public space. The historical meaning of these city halls did not terminate when construction ended. The buildings themselves framed the subsequent thought and behavior of leaders and citizens, sometimes for well more than a century.

The first examples of municipal building in the New World serve to remind political historians that North American cities hosted a great variety of governmental systems. This catalog of civic architecture begins in the city of New Orleans with a building that testifies to both the multiple national heritages and the imperial ancestry of the American political tradition. The first house of government in Louisiana goes by the generic Spanish title Cabildo, dates from 1769 in the reign of Charles IV, and was erected on a French town plan designed in 1721 for Louis XIV. The dual pillars of the ancien regime, military power and religious uniformity, were built into the urban plan for New Orleans, which placed the hall of government in the central square, beside St. Louis Cathedral and facing a military parade grounds, the Place d'Armes. The central square was decorated with such symbols of state power as a pillory, arsenal, and jail. To this day, the alliance of church and state is symbolically central in the city of New Orleans, where the symmetrical triad of St. Louis Cathedral, the Presbytere, and the Cabildo stand sentinel over the tourists and street musicians of Jackson Square[9] (Figure 2.1).

The first modest Cabildo burned down in 1788, clearing the way for the landmark public building that still stands in Jackson Square. The creation of a new house of government was not the simple fiat of the Spanish throne but rather an act of local administration, which augured a new regime in public architecture. The

Figure 2.1
The Place d'Armes in 1803 by J. S. Boqueto de Woiserie. Shown are the Cabildo, St. Louis Cathedral, the unfinished Presbytere and Almonaster's buildings, which then flanked the square. Courtesy of the Historic New Orleans Collection, Museum/Research Center, New Orleans.

Cabildo was the initiative of Don Andres Almonester y Roxas, who had made his fortune by converting land grants from the crown into lucrative real estate in the trading post on the Gulf of Mexico. Almonester parlayed colonial success into a knighthood, a place on the colonial council, and the authority to plan public space. According to the minutes of the colonial council, it was agreed in 1785 "to let this gentleman proceed to reconstruct [the Cabildo] under the terms he had proposed, giving him sufficient authority to carry it out." Almonester's *noblesse oblige* bore a certain taint of self-interest. His contract called for reimbursement from the government coffers with the sole proviso that the sums expended would never be so large as to deplete the treasury. Nor was the financing of this early American civic building without the petty rancor that would mark the history of American public spending. The philanthropist's widow would be bickering with the city fathers about the bill for the Cabildo as late as 1803, four years after its completion.[10]

The hybrid process of constructing the Cabildo, equal parts colonial decree and New World mercantile enterprise, was reflected in the completed building, as designed by a French engineer named Gilberto Guillemard, who was under the hire of the Spanish military. The Cabildo provided a fitting stage for the top-down administration of colonial power. The majority of the space was set aside for the corps de garde, and its signature architectural feature, a five-gabled arcade fronting the square, was adapted from the design of an earlier military structure. The entire two-story rectangular edifice was encased in thick brick and stucco walls and trimmed with Roman embellishments, which lent a sense of enclosing authority to the whole building. The floor above this military fortification was laid out for the more polite aspects of colonial administration. The offices of local administrators were fronted by reception rooms and a handsome arcaded gallery. The largest room on the second story, the Sala Capitular, was the only space in the architecture of authority whose arrangement suggested public deliberation and the interplay of citizens and officials. The beamed ceiling, the fireplace, and comfortable furnishings created an environment conducive to polite conversation about public concerns. The Governor's Council ordered twelve seats, which were probably grouped around a small table like that found in later restorations of the room. A nest of plain benches was placed a few paces away, at a distance that suggests the patience of colonial supplicants who awaited the adjudication of disputes by the crown's agents in New Orleans.

The Cabildo's interior space carefully contained any more active and widespread political participation. The entrance to the house of colonial government was through a vaguely marked arch roughly in the center of the arcade. It did not lead to a clear civic destination within. Doorways to both the left and right of the entryway led to the rooms assigned to the corps de garde. Beyond the former was a rugged stone stairway providing access to a second-floor gallery fronting the Place d'Armes and affording a narrow space for courtly reception. At the center of the second story was a block of undistinguished rooms, among them a council chamber set rather recessively toward the side of the building. As if to interrupt this broken, halting access to the Sala Capitular yet again, the architect provided an alternative, more direct but more secretive access to the office of the executive authority, a small stair at the rear of the first floor room, which was assigned to the lamplighter. In sum, the internal space of this early American governmental building paid some respect to grand neo-classical spaces found in eighteenth-century royal houses (the arcade and the gallery) and resembled the halls of state in Renaissance republics with a council chamber on the second story. Still, the Cabildo offered ordinary citizens limited access and failed to provide anyone a very direct or inviting path to some center of civic assembly or deliberation (Figure 2.2).

The decorative features of the Cabildo also denoted a government insulated from the general population. The walls were graced with the portraits of Charles IV and his family; the tympanum of the pediment presented the Spanish coat of arms to the rustic population that lounged in the Place d'Armes. Just below that symbol was a second-floor balcony lined with intricate iron railings. This final architectural characteristic of the *ancien regime* in the Americas, the balcony, provided an elevated space from which colonial authorities might issue proclamations and enact the proper protocol of absolutism. Rather than inviting the people into the public house, this architectural feature was designed for dispensing edicts from the citadel of authority.[11]

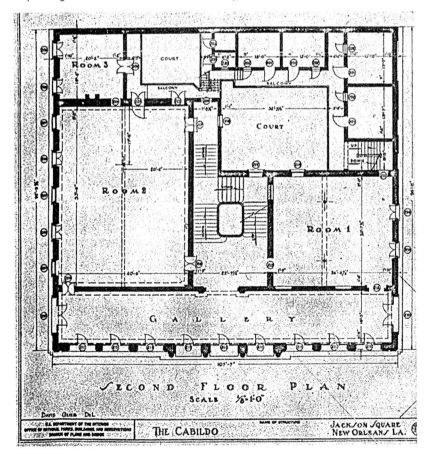

Figure 2.2
Second-floor plan of the Cabildo. Drawn for the Historic American Building Survey. Reproduced from the Collections of the Library of Congress.

The political ideology implicit in the architecture of the Cabildo was also displayed in the ceremonies performed around it and in the impressions it made on contemporaries. The galleries of the Cabildo and the space of Place d'Armes became the stage on which to mimic the pomp of European courts. Events in the history of the royal family or military victories were commemorated in an almost feudal manner, with a proclamation in the Cabildo, a Mass in St. Louis Cathedral, and a procession of officials through the Place d'Armes. Almonester's knighthood, for example, occasioned a reenactment of Old World pretensions.

> He was enveloped in the great mantle of the Order and his train was carried by three lackeys in red. An immense crowd followed him as he went in state from the Cathedral to his dwelling. He placed himself in his mantle, at the door of his drawing room, where he affectionately kissed on both cheeks all who approached to greet him, to the number of more than three hundred.

This procession passed by the Cabildo, which was then under construction at the behest of the new knight. It would stand for some time to come as a symbol of the brief and shabby reign of feudal absolutism in North America. A visitor in 1813 was still moved by the symmetry of the north side of the Place d'Armes: "quite an imposing aggregate of law, religion and punishment." A few years later, another visitor from the North was shocked when the deliberations in the Sala Capitular were interrupted by shrieks from the corps de garde below, emitted by slaves being whipped at their masters' behest for a fee of 25 cents. The ground outside the Cabildo maintained a pillory for slaves until 1847, twenty years after it had been abolished for free white criminals. Nothing in the manner of erection, the spatial organization, or the vernacular uses of the Cabildo gave any suggestion of incipient democracy in North America.[12]

A visit to the Cabildo at the midpoint of the nineteenth century would find it only slightly updated, despite some major political changes in the Crescent City, by 1850 a booming commercial town in the jurisdiction of the United States of America. A city hall handed down from a colonial oligarchy still served as the mayor's office until 1852. Although the Spanish coat of arms was removed from the pediment in 1804, soon after the Louisiana Territory was purchased by the United States, it was not replaced with an American eagle until 1819. The Sala Capitular was converted to a city council chamber and refurbished in 1825 to serve as the quarters of visiting dignitary General Lafayette. Only with the reorganization of the city into three municipalities in 1836, a time when city elections had become more contested and partisan, was this chamber enlarged to accommodate the popularly elected legislature. By then, the reinvigoration of commerce as well as politics was apparent in the grounds around the Cabildo. The daughter of the Cabildo's original benefactor, Micaela, Baroness de Pontalba, contributed the major improvement of the Place d'Armes, the elegant brick structures laced with iron balconies that frame the two sides of the square perpendicular to the cathedral block. The First Municipality rewarded Pontalba by exempting her from taxes for twenty years and went on to finance additional improvements in the square. The Place d'Armes was fenced and landscaped, and the Cabildo was crowned with a third story and a mansard roof. The last piece of remodeling, which dates from the 1840s, completed the symmetry of the square by complementing the roof of the Presbytere and the Pontalba Apartments. A renovated entryway beckoned citizens into the public gallery, which spanned the entire third floor. The democratization of civic space extended to the plaza outside the Cabildo, which would soon be renamed and presided over by an equestrian statue of Andrew Jackson.

These alterations in the Cabildo were relatively minor, however, both structurally and in civic consequence. As of 1850, Jackson Square played host primarily to residents of the First Municipality, most of them of French ancestry and language. The ethnic division of urban politics was especially brazen in New Orleans, where the government itself was divided into separate units anchored by separate "French" and "American" city halls. In fact, the architectural improvements in the French Quarter were in large part an attempt to compete with the more dramatic innovation in public architecture then under way in the Second, "American," Municipality.[13] The American district quickly proceeded to mirror itself in a public building. The district council resolved to appropriate $120,000 for a new city hall in 1845, and when the cost climbed to over $340,000 a few years later, there was no great public outcry. The boosters of the Second Municipality stipulated: "It is distinctly understood no defective marble is permitted."[14] They spared no expense in choosing the location of this civic project: the high-priced residential area of Lafayette Square. The exceptions to the private façades around the square were the Oddfellows Hall, a school, and a Presbyterian church, all sites and symbols of Yankee culture and the enterprising voluntary spirit that suffused the commercial economy and civic life in general.

Commercial associations pervaded the new public architecture. The City Council employed the trusted local architect James Gallier, who had already designed many of the spaces they frequented, including the Merchant Exchange and the St. Charles Hotel. Coincidentally, Gallier had accumulated a real estate fortune of his own. The architect, who seems to have been given a free hand in the design of the new city hall, chose to enshrine the commercial republic in Greek Revival casings, modeling some aspects of his design on the Erechtheum atop the Acropolis, perhaps not incidentally the citadel of another slave republic.[15] In keeping with Greek Revival style and in deference to the public importance of his project, Gallier designed a lofty exterior with a sixty-foot portico and towering Doric columns. The elevation of the narrow stairs and depth of the portico placed the inner sanctum of public life at a greater distance from the bustle of the street than was the case in Gallier's commercial buildings. Yet a *naïve* observer of the New Orleans skyline would easily mistake nearby places of business for the city hall. The St. Charles Hotel and the Merchant Exchange, but not Municipal Hall, were crowned with domed rotundas in the style of the United States Capitol[16] (Figure 2.3).

"A Laudable Pride in the Whole Of Us"

Figure 2.3
Municipal Hall in
Lafayette Square.
Courtesy of the Historic
New Orleans Collection,
Museum/Research
Center.

The interior space of Municipal Hall is also a curious mixture of commercial and civic elements. The portico opens into a long, wide central hall that is lined with spacious, square chambers and an even larger reception room. Stairways midway down the hall rise to the second story, which is divided into large quadrants that served as the mayor's reception room, a dining room, ballroom, and city council chamber (Figure 2.4). On the third floor, Gallier opened up the most dramatic space, a grand hall with a ceiling that arched a full eighty-five feet and was set with a stage and galleries. This space was called a lyceum and, like the assembly room atop the Cabildo, seems designed to gather citizens together and promote public intercourse. The lyceum of Municipal Hall was a somewhat poorer cousin to the grand public space of the St. Charles Hotel, which clustered generous public spaces all around its wide rotunda.[17] Gallier crowned the classic face of the municipal hall with the insignia of public architecture that had become standard in Washington, D.C., as well as locally: a pediment on which was sculpted the figure of "Liberty supporting justice and commerce." By adding Commerce to the more familiar republican deities, Gallier introduced a fitting contemporary element into the architecture of the public. But its precise meaning is as opaque as the plaster of which it was cast. Should we read this grouping as money-changers entering the house of Liberty? As civil society merging with the state? Had commercial prosperity replaced the mixed constitution as the safeguard of republican virtue?[18]

One can conclude at least that the New Orleans Municipal Hall presents a contrast with its predecessor in the French Quarter that is suggestive of a transfiguration of the blueprint for urban politics. First, while the circulatory spaces are more open than the Cabildo, they still project a rather daunting monumentality,

City Halls and Civic Materialism ■

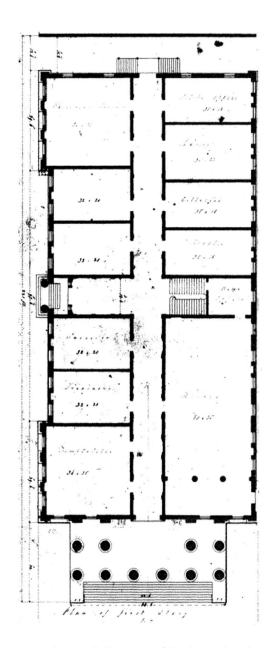

Figure 2.4
Plan of the first floor, Municipal Hall, New Orleans. Courtesy of the Sylvester Labrot Collection, Southeastern Architectural Archive, Tulane University Library.

a pompousness that might well discourage faint-hearted or low-status citizens from entering. The scale of the portico and the narrow, recessed stairways announce the importance of this public space more boldly than they welcome pedestrians within. The ten columns raised sixteen steps above the entryway form a gauntlet of shadows as they obscure and darken the doorway. Those citizens who did enter, however, would find quite an array of commodious spaces. Most of them were called reception (not meeting) rooms, indicating their function was to foster genteel sociability rather than to facilitate the deliberative aspects of an elected legislature. These kinds of spaces were a familiar habitat for merchants accustomed to gathering in hotels and clubrooms of the American Quarter. By setting aside a capacious space in which select citizens could socialize, or study in the lyceum, the municipal government opened its house to polite civil society, and seems to have made the city hall more analogous with other buildings in the neighborhood, like the St. Charles Hotel and the Oddfellows Hall. The Second District of New Orleans at mid-century resembled a spatial model for the bourgeois public sphere as formulated by Jürgen Habermas. It suggests a place where public opinion might be shaped by rational discourse, but it also put severe, if seldom spoken, limits on who might participate in such august proceedings.

The public ceremonies and literary texts that inaugurated Municipal Hall delivered a similar message about changes in the practice of urban politics. Although there appears to have been no formal ceremony laying its cornerstone, the organ of communication for the literate public of the American district, the *New Orleans Picayune*, swelled with pride on the day the council room opened for business in 1853. "The worthy fathers of the second municipality met last evening in solemn enclave for the first time in the new council room. The place is beautiful indeed and in every way worthy of the purpose for which it is to be used." The press praised spaces like the mayor's room as a tribute to the "taste and good judgment of those in charge" and proclaimed Municipal Hall an architectural wonder. The *Picayune* boasted: "The citizens of the second municipality may well be proud of owning the handsomest municipal hall in the United States. The stranger will find in few cities on this continent more to command his admiration or invite his scrutiny than the public and private edifices of New Orleans."[19]

Even a superficial look at the public architecture of this one southern city reveals decisive changes in the fundamental principles of government. A spirit of enterprise, civic engagement, voluntary energy, and urban ambition suffused the vaulted spaces of Municipal Hall. The apertures were widened just far enough to permit a thriving middle class to enter its opulent reception rooms and grand lyceum, under whose high ceilings merchants who were habituated to socializing in the Merchant Exchange and St. Charles Hotel were most likely to feel at home. The council room, that space where elected representatives deliberated about the "common good," was hard to distinguish from all the other rooms and buildings that displayed the robust commercial enterprise of the American Quarter. In antebellum New Orleans, political participation was skewed by ethnicity and race as well as class. The rather narrow and recessed entry to the haughty Municipal Hall was particularly restrictive for those who lived downriver in either the French Quarter or the immigrant sector further to the east. Slaves and free men and women of color were certainly not invited across the classical portico of Municipal Hall. Nonetheless, when the government of New Orleans was consolidated in 1852, the Municipal Hall of the American Quarter became its only "city hall." It would remain so until 1957, at which late date its daunting classical façade and off-center location still presented an apt metaphor for the obstacles to equal citizenship in a segregated city.

North of the Mason-Dixon Line, America's civic materialism tells quite another story. While the architectural heritage of New Orleans bore traces of the European monarchies that adapted easily to American slave society, the citizens of New York City erected their city hall on a freestanding republican foundation. Even during the colonial period, New York's public buildings had more in common with an English borough than a bastion of empire. The Corporation of the City of New York made its eighteenth-century headquarters first in a tavern and later in a building just north of Wall Street, the far outskirts of the city at the date it was built, 1698. The latter structure featured a tall façade, cupola, and central balcony that presented a rather haughty face to the citizen-pedestrian. Entry to a modest public chamber was through a narrow and secluded passage hidden behind an arcade that ran the front of the building. This colonial construction served briefly as the national capitol during George Washington's presidency, and the structure was remodeled in 1789 by Pierre Charles L'Enfant. The entryway to the building, rechristened Federal Hall, was still relatively constricted, but those citizens who found their way within enjoyed a commodious public space, whose republican improvements included vaulted chambers for both the Senate and the House of Representatives and lavishly appointed galleries that rose two full stories.[20]

When the federal government was transplanted to Washington in 1800, the environs of Federal Hall reclaimed a local, but still proudly republican, civic identity. The area bounded roughly by Chambers Street, Broadway, and Park Row was landscaped and renamed City Hall Park.[21] A few years later, the park was raked clean of the symbols of Old World authority like the jail, armory, almshouse, and the old government house. The almshouse had been converted to the New York Institute, a city-owned building made available to philanthropic and educational societies. The less coercive and more voluntaristic inscription on New York's public space befit a city government that was now entrusted to a single, popularly elected deliberative body, the Common Council. With an appointed mayor, nominal property restrictions on the franchise, and ingrained habits of deference, however, the city corporation was far from a pure democracy. Rather, citizens of some property and their chosen representatives ran the city corporation as a rather plebeian facsimile of a classic republic. Soon, they set about redesigning public space in their own image. In 1802, at a time when two public buildings, the old "State House" as well as "Federal Hall," were vacant, the ordinarily parsimonious Common Council voted to construct a civic building all their own. This proud new edifice would become the archetypal "City Hall."

The aldermen of New York City took upon themselves the responsibility of overseeing the entire process of designing and constructing their new workplace. The "City Hall Building Committee," like other specialized city commissions, was composed of members of the Common Council, that is, directly elected, not appointed, officials. The Common Council empowered the committee to select an architect but specified that they "take the opinion or advice of such mechanics, artisans or other persons as shall be deemed useful and make suitable compensation." An open competition elicited proposals from a range of Manhattanites, including a doctor, a painter, carpenters and builders, as well as professional architects. The committee reviewed the plans, made a recommendation to the council, secured a majority vote ratifying their choice, and proceeded to put the winning plan on public view at a nearby confectioner's shop. The republican procedure had a rather democratic outcome. The chosen architects, John McComb, Jr. and Joseph François Mangin, were relatively humble practitioners of their art, each with only a few modest buildings to their credit. In their choice, the councilmen rebuffed a more renowned and pretentious architect, Benjamin Latrobe, who became contemptuous of such competitive public commissions. Latrobe railed against the humiliation of being "preferred to the workman who may enter the lists against me" and dismissed McComb and Mangin as a "New York bricklayer and a St. Domingo Frenchman," each of meager formal education. The public officials of New York seemed to subscribe to more vernacular architectural principles. McComb's local connections, including his familiarity to the Common Council as a one-time city surveyor, won out over Latrobe's pedigree and the patronage of Aaron Burr. The new city hall was built on a sturdy foundation of small-town familiarity, civic pride, and the simple processes of representation and consultation. Such chaste republican practices augured some innovations in the civic landscape.[22]

This project proceeded at a lackadaisical pace, taking eight years to complete. While McComb was commissioned to oversee the actual construction of the plan he co-authored, he was only the agent of the Building Commissioners and obliged to confer regularly with the Common Council and consult with elected officials about such minutiae as the selection of marble, the hiring of stonemasons, and the laying of bricks. By 1808, McComb reported that the walls had advanced up to the windowsills of the second story and had nearly exhausted the quarter-million dollars of the original appropriation. The council demanded and received a close and frugal accounting from McComb, who kept the final expenditure down to an acceptable $500,000. The tone of this cumbersome but civil process was set in the first official exchange between the republican government and the builder-architect, dated March 21, 1803: "The committee feel impressed with the magnitude of this undertaking, and they assure the Board that in all their determinations, they have endeavored to combine durability, convenience and elegance with as much economy as the importance of the object will possibly admit."[23]

In this decorous manner, New Yorkers crafted a modest building that, in the regard of ordinary citizens and architectural critics alike, is a landmark in public architecture. The sight of it evokes a pervasive and palpable sense of welcome into civic space. A newspaperman ambling through City Hall Park in 1834 captured the everyday civic lessons that the municipal improvements of the young republic would convey. He greeted his place of government as a "sight that rejoices our eyes."[24] Late in the next century, writer Phillip Lopate echoed these sentiments when he recalled entering City Hall for the first time at the age of twelve: "I looked up at the graceful relic and my heart swelled with pride."[25] Just how this relatively humble building acquired its timeless civic power remains an architectural puzzle and political marvel. The Common Council set out only the first vague parameters of republican civic materialism. They gave the project, first of all, a prescient name, calling it not a government house but a "city hall." Next, they specified a central location, in the public commons, with its wings aligned with nearby public buildings. From the earliest sketches and engravings, City Hall stands as the beckoning focal point of a public landscape, situated not on the edge of a martial parade ground but right in the middle of a place of casual social mingling.[26] This welcoming ambiance was carried into the building itself by the stunning sequence of architectural features that create an unobstructed public processional: broad, gradually ascending steps proceed through an open line of graceful arches and glide effortlessly upward along a circular stair to the chambers of representative government (Figure 2.5).

This masterful blueprint for public space bears no simple architectural signature. No clear precedent is found in either L'Enfant's Federal Hall, the English mansion-house, the French hotel de ville, or the oeuvre of McComb or Mangin. The best approximation of its pedigree is the vernacular process whereby a hands-on, homegrown citizen-architect sifted through the ideas of his French partner, his English pattern books, the directives of the city council, and his own experience in the urban polity.[27] Out of this process emerged the unique architectural features that beckon citizens inside New York's republican sphere. The wide, gently elevated exterior stairs that rose to a single-story portico were probably designed by Mangin, selected by the Building Commission, ratified by the Common Council, altered and engineered by McComb, executed by artisan citizens, and subjected to revision at every turn. The finished building created a remarkable civic effect: it converted virtually the whole front of the central wing of City Hall into a commodious, readily accessible public space. Between 1803 and 1812 (when the project was finally finished), the builders of New York's City Hall systematically

Figure 2.5
New York's City Hall, 1826. Drawn by William Guy Wall, engraved by John Hill. Prints Collection, Miriam and Ira D. Wallach Division of Art, New York Public Library.

rejected the architectural elements of previous civic projects: they eschewed the narrow internal passages of the Cabildo, the daunting portico of Gallier Hall, and the insulation of L'Enfant's remodeling of Federal Hall. A similarly unspoken but decisive process of selection carved out generous public pathways inside New York's City Hall: a wide rotunda, open stairway, and easy passages to public rooms on the second floor. This almost magic combination of openness and elevation suited the virtuous citizens of a republic better than Gallier's commercial style or Latrobe's rejected plan, whose narrower vestibule and squat form were modeled after his design for the Bank of Pennsylvania.[28] In building their hall, the representatives of the citizens of New York happened upon an architecture all their own. The commodious circulatory features of New York's City Hall – the stairs, entrances, and hallways – were the earmarks of a vernacular republican style. It proved in retrospect to be the standard by which all the previous municipal buildings seemed narrow, constricted, and exclusive (Figure 2.6).[29]

The same unspoken political and architectural standards informed the allocation of space within City Hall. The instructions to architects authored by the Common Council specified only the most basic requirements, each associated with different governmental functions: eight courtrooms, six juror rooms, and "one for the common Council." Architects and builders translated the blueprints into elegant but comfortable accommodations for the people and their representatives. The rotunda and stairway pointed to destinations on the second floor, where, above the office and courtrooms, stood three major public spaces for which the council would determine the exact use. The central space just opposite the top of the stair became the Governor's Room and was flanked by two large chambers, approximately thirty-six by forty feet, one of which was reserved for sessions of the municipal legislature. When, for a brief period in the 1830s, the city charter divided

Figure 2.6
Interior stairway, New York City Hall, Historic American Building Survey. Reproduced from the Collections of the Library of Congress.

the municipal legislature into two chambers, one of these assembly rooms housed the Board of Aldermen, the other the Board of Assistants. It was the southwestern chamber, however, that became enduringly associated with the legislative process central to a small republic (Figure 2.7).[30]

The interior decoration of the Common Council chamber suggests further idealized architectural conditions for governing a republic. The furnishings conferred considerable importance and high definition on the central figurehead, usually a mayor, who presided over the legislature. His accoutrements included an ornate podium, a throne-like seat, a canopy, and a place at the front of the room. At the other end of the spectrum, visiting citizens shared simple benches, placed in an elevated gallery space and separated by a railing approximately four feet in height. In between the people and the presidency stood a simple circle of desks and seats for the legislators. This arrangement compelled both the mayor and the citizens to respectfully observe the central political drama, the deliberations of popularly elected councilmen.[31]

If the interior decorations are to be believed, civic virtue was a republican but hardly a spartan matter. The Common Council invested in antique furnishings valued at over $1,400, commissioned scores of official portraits of political leaders and military heroes, and stockpiled no less than thirteen works by John Trumbull, the Revolutionary War painter, in the Governor's Room. They also agreed to paint the ceiling of the City Hall chamber with a view called "New York Receiving the Tribute of the Nation." John McComb lovingly adorned the public rooms with fine woodcraft. At the highest elevation of City Hall perched a simpler but equally classic symbol, a statue of Justice. The icon the city fathers placed atop the cupola was a crude figure, executed in wood, lacking a blindfold, and holding a steelyard. Subsequent councilmen were embarrassed by Justice's rustic appearance and voted to add a blindfold and a more elegant scale to her accessories. The figurehead of justice was the object of considerable public attention, even identification. New Yorkers penned poems to this "emblem of dignity and durability" and recoiled in pain when she was "wrapped like a martyr" in the fire of 1858. Justice was part of a hodgepodge of political symbols that graced New York's City Hall, from personified power in the mayor's throne to specialized spaces for legislative, judicial, and executive branches of government.[32]

This physical evidence establishes a number of broad political principles that underpinned the design of City Hall and then structured the political life that transpired within the building. The first principle comes from that recurrent motif of invitation and openness that proclaims that city government is a public project. A simple contrast with Federal Hall or New Orleans's Cabildo, constructed less than a decade earlier, should suffice to establish this point. The second principle, that of a mixed constitution, seems equally transparent, clearly visible in the allocation of space for the judiciary, the legislature, and the executives (both the mayor and the governor). The official assignment of space in City Hall was the subject of considerable discussion by the Common Council in the first two decades in the building's life. The mayor's power was restrained architecturally by his distance from both the circle of legislators and the lobby of citizens. Local practice,

"A Laudable Pride in the Whole Of Us" ■

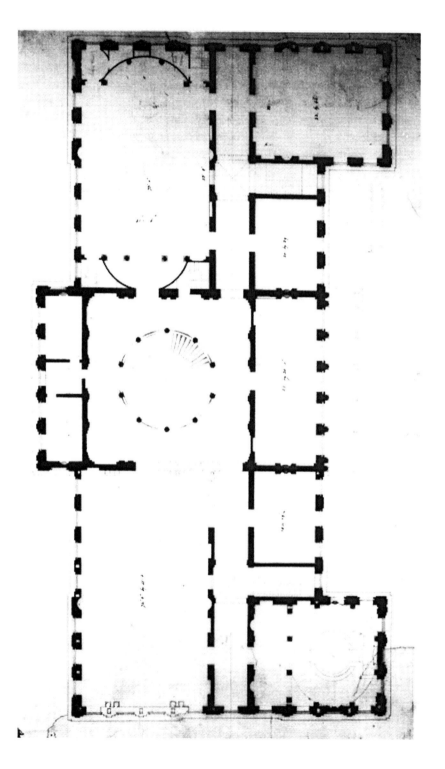

Figure 2.7
Floor plan, New York City Hall. Drawn by John McComb, 1802. Collection of the New York Historical Society.

City Halls and Civic Materialism

as prescribed by state and municipal constitutions and inscribed on the floor plan of City Hall, also disdained pure democracy. Deference to the judgment of social betters was inscribed in elevated and decorous architectural features and enacted in politics. An electorate of propertied, overwhelmingly white men sent their social betters to fill the ornate seats of the Common Council chamber, while the vast majority of the citizenry remained respectfully in the lobby.

Although this classic balance of a mixed constitution was maintained until at least 1830, both architecture and its usage gave a privileged position to the representative branch of city government. The chamber of the Common Council was both the busiest public space and the focus of public attention. As one city directory put it in 1817: "It is fitted up in an elegant and commodious manner for the meetings of the corporation which are open at all times to the citizens."[33] A sketch attributed to C. Burton and dated 1830 focused the eyes of his contemporaries on this same civic space and directly toward the circle of councilmen. Burton etched images of electors in the gallery and posed them leaning over the railing that bordered the legislative space, straining, it would seem, to share in the deliberative process. This artist even found a place for women, or their bonnets at least, in the republican circle. These fashionable ladies were also stationed in the lobby but further to the rear and at a safer distance from the center of the republican drama (Figure 2.8). Architects, councilmen, and observers seemed to concur in representing politics as a functionally differentiated process that modulated both executive power and democratic participation. Yet the governmental decisions were worked out in a house of government whose public spaces had become conspicuously more open and inviting than its classic republican antecedents.

Figure 2.8
Council Chamber, City Hall, New York, 1830–31. Drawn by C. Burton, engraved by H. Fossette. Prints Collection, Miriam and Ira D. Wallach Division of Art, New York Public Library.

The interior of New York's City Hall ushers the public into spaces designed expressly for the interaction of citizens with one another. The magnetic circle of the Common Council chamber with its surrounding galleries was the most obvious and official arena for mutual engagement and deliberation. Ordinary citizens were invited to participate in direct public discourse elsewhere as well. They could meet with one another in the Governor's Room, whose elegant spaces were opened to the general public for a mayor's reception every New Year's Day. They could break bread and imbibe alcoholic beverages on the public ground of City Hall Park each July 4th. City Hall also accommodated some more sober and lofty public projects. The Common Council granted space in City Hall for meetings of the Medical Arts and Bible societies, and gave permission for Sunday School students to parade on the grounds. In New York in the first quarter of the nineteenth century, the city actually invested a considerable amount of financial resources and enthusiasm in providing space for this open and interactive public assembly, this material and architectural base of the widening, petit-bourgeois public sphere.[34]

While such architectural evidence about political culture is indirect, inferential, and tentative, contemporaries clearly subscribed to one incontrovertible assessment of City Hall. This building was cause for hearty public pride. Even an epidemic could not cancel the festivities planned to inaugurate the building project. The laying of the cornerstone of City Hall was preceded by a long civic procession that included representatives of New York's well-organized public sphere like the Mechanics' Society as well as the Common Council and other city officials. Much of the citizenry was enrolled in the ceremony as the procession filed along Broadway and through the park to the honored site, where a military salute was fired and the crowd regaled with "a supply of wine from the corporation." Once completed, City Hall became New York's major landmark, eclipsing the church spires and Wall Street businesses nearby. Blunt's visitors' guide proclaimed in 1817, "The City Hall is the most prominent and most important building in New York. It is the handsomest structure in the United States: perhaps of its size, in the world."[35]

Still, it is prudent to recall that these lofty civic sentiments were conjured up in a small city, perched at the outer reaches of European civilization, whose governmental tasks remained very prosaic. The Common Council sat amid those antique furnishings and ruled on such mundane aspects of public civility as the subject of this resolution dated August 15, 1814: "A presentment of the Grand Jury against the indecent practice of persons making water against the walls of the City Hall was read and referred to the City Inspector." We learn a few days later that the civic good was decisively served by the erection of a shed "to present the evil complained of."[36] Through the first half of the nineteenth century, such small gestures brought politics and place together in the everyday maintenance of republicanism.

This familiar quality of urban politics would not last for long. As the population of the city of New York passed half a million at mid-century and reached seven digits by 1875, city government outgrew its old quarters, and big city politics burst out of its republican constraints. Property restrictions on voting were abolished for white men by 1842, and the first populist mayor, Fernando Wood, was elected in 1850, making New York City government an aggressively partisan democratic project. Not coincidentally, Mayor Wood proposed that municipal government vacate the City Hall of the early republic and build new quarters uptown nearer the demographic center of the city. When the State Legislature finally approved the project in 1857, clouds of suspicion were beginning to gather over City Hall. Precipitated by charges that Mayor Wood pandered to constituents, especially the foreign-born, this cynicism was given an architectural grounding in the "tea room" on the first floor of old City Hall. In the 1850s, this space was used for the refreshment of the Board of Aldermen, which ran up bills as high as $9,000 annually. The *New York Tribune* reported in 1852 that the city fathers would soon be returning from recess to "the broad steps of the City Hall and the sacred porches of the Tea Room" and then added sardonically that, until then, there was "no bribery, no bullying, no vote-buying, no juggling of contracts, no fun whatsoever to enliven the sultry hours." A new political climate, the first winds carrying germs of municipal shame, had begun to erode the foundation of public architecture.[37]

A new political culture required a new architecture. By the time ground was broken for the new city hall in 1862, the project had been reconstituted as a county courthouse. This alteration in the civic building program was more than a simple administrative expedient. It was symptomatic of a restructuring of governmental practice in the late nineteenth century. Increasing suspicion of big city governments and their diverse and intensely partisan electors brought close surveillance from the state level. A series of institutional reforms, often introduced into the state legislatures by middle-class business and rural interests, hamstrung the city council – the local domain, that is, of representative democracy. In New York, that meant that the legislature in Albany transferred major public power from City Hall to the County Board of Supervisors, the governing body that was to be accommodated with a new public building.[38] The municipal reforms of the period also complicated the financing of any major civic project. Construction could not commence until the State Assembly and Senate had authorized the Supervisors to sell stock in a public or "sinking" fund in the initial amount of one million dollars. By going into debt and embracing the methods of finance capitalism, New York's public officials would eventually secure as much as eleven million dollars for their county courthouse. The process of paying out these astronomical sums proved even more cumbersome than its appropriation. While making contracts for materials and construction was entrusted to the three members of the Building Commission, their actions were constantly scrutinized by the Board of Supervisors, the State Legislature, and the court of public opinion as convened by the press. At the very least, thirty different companies would contract for everything from iron to awnings before the new courthouse was completed. This intricate and expensive process has left a trail of financial documents that still bewilders historians. We may never know the true cost of New York's County

Courthouse, yet we can be assured that its construction inched forward ensnarled in a skein of red tape and public suspicion.[39]

The byzantine process began with the selection of an architect. The commissioners' original choice was John Kellum, who came recommended for his previous work on such local landmarks as Stewart's Department Store. Kellum defined the basic spaces of the new building and oversaw the construction of the interior over halfway to its conclusion, when he was replaced by Leopold Eidlitz, whose previous credits included a number of churches and banks as well as parts of the State Capitol building. Kellum and Eidlitz bore little resemblance to McComb and Mangin, the builder-designers of old City Hall. The second generation of civic builders put themselves before the public as professional architects with well established reputations, thriving offices in New York City, and considerable professional and aesthetic pretensions. Eidlitz's practice in particular was a far cry from the artisan mode of building design. An author of architectural treatises and a central figure in the Gothic Revival, Eidlitz was acutely conscious of the artistic merit of buildings and relatively indifferent to the taste or needs of the general public.[40]

The people's representatives gave these architects *carte blanche* in designing the courthouse. The major contribution of the Common Council was to specify the site, just to the north of City Hall on Chambers Street. This decision was based on the administrative convenience of being close to the other courts and official functions clustered around City Hall Park, which by the 1860s had become a more specialized governmental space. Indeed, this municipal building project was conceived more as a service to public employees who required expanded office space than as a site of civic interaction. By the 1850s, the business of public building had become perfunctory to say the least, calculated in terms of square footage and cost estimates. The *New York Times* was contemptuous of pleas to save the trees in City Hall Park and invoked the "Manifest Destiny" of expanding office space.[41] Given this scant attention to architectural (as opposed to financial) details on the part of city officials, Kellum and Eidlitz went quite freely about their work. The public space that they composed seemed, in some respects, to carry forward the commitment to openness and accessibility begun by Mangin and McComb. Kellum's original plan invited the people into public space by way of broad steps leading up to a classic portico (Figure 2.9). In fact, his design called for two such staircases, only one of which was ultimately built. The flow of public space continued well inside the building, where two stairways radiated up a full three-and-a-half stories through a grand rotunda topped with a tinted glass skylight. Combined with contiguous lobbies, the stairs and rotunda created a very generous public space. They accounted for nearly a quarter of the courthouse's total footage and greeted New Yorkers with a first impression of democratic possibilities (Figure 2.10).[42]

Yet that impressive pair of stairways and rotunda did not lead to a central civic destination. The floor plans failed to mark off a path to some focal public place (like the Common Council chamber of the old City Hall). Neither did the

Figure 2.9
Northern façade of Tweed Courthouse with its stairway removed, Historic American Building Survey. Reproduced from the Collections of the Library of Congress.

building plans reserve a large space in which the public might assemble (such as the lyceum in Gallier Hall). When Eidlitz replaced Kellum as architect in 1876, he blocked the civic passageways further by separating the rotunda from the office wings with massive brick walls. The space beyond the stairs and lobbies was carved up into a monotonous honeycomb of rooms layered up six floors (counting the basement and mezzanines). Within this warren of offices and courtrooms, it is hard to locate the representative element of county government, the chamber of the Board of Supervisors. A sketch dated 1868 does reveal, however, a chamber fitted with some of the old architectural props of representative government, including the familiar circle of desks and chairs, a podium for the presiding officer, and an elevated lobby.[43]

The decoration of this and other interior spaces of the County Courthouse suggests further alterations in the use and meaning of public space. The legislative chamber, much like the courtrooms, was invested with relatively opulent architectural detail: intricate moldings, frescos, pediment windows, and ornate chandeliers. Beyond these more public rooms lay a labyrinth of relatively unadorned halls and offices. By contrast, both Kellum and Eidlitz expended an immense amount of artistry and public funds decorating the circulatory spaces under the rotunda. Kellum favored detailed iron and marble, Eidlitz polychromatic brickwork; together, they created a gallery of visual stimulation. This formal and abstract aesthetic was bereft of more explicit political representations (like the icons of civic virtue and portraits of civic leaders found in City Hall). Reviews of the new building were mixed: while some praised the awesome spectacle of the stairway and rotunda, others dismissed the interior of the County Courthouse as "the darkest hallways in New York."[44] The interior design, like the spatial composition, of the New York courthouse is subject to various interpretations. Some features seem to

"A Laudable Pride in the Whole Of Us" ■

Figure 2.10
View of the rotunda, Tweed Courthouse, Historic American Building Survey. Reproduced from the Collections of the Library of Congress.

beckon the people inside and to flatter them with opulent display. Other spaces seem politically hollow, without civic intention, public meaning, or invitation to stop and socialize, much less debate with fellow citizens. New York's new courthouse sent an ambiguous message to the citizenry; its spaces suggested an uneasy cohabitation between democratization and atomization.

What looks like ambiguity in the architecture reads like cynicism in the accounts of the public commemoration of the new municipal structure. The cornerstone ceremonies for New York's new courthouse were at best perfunctory.

The indifference cannot be explained entirely by the date, 1862, in the midst of the Civil War, for after all, New Yorkers had braved an epidemic to celebrate the old City Hall fifty years earlier. The press notices of the event of 1862 were uncommonly laconic in their prose. Most of the dailies devoted a short paragraph to describing the truncated procession of officials across from City Hall to the foundation of the courthouse, where they were met by what was variously described as "a large assembly of citizens," "several hundred persons," or "a number of spectators." The oratory was lethargic, if not downright gloomy. It featured a tedious account of the difficulties of winning legislative approval for this undertaking and judicial complaints about the ventilation in the old quarters. The usually flamboyant Mayor Wood damned the whole project with this faint and backward-looking praise: "it gives an importance to the building and thus to some extent imparts a dignity to the purpose for which it is intended." In conclusion, Wood allowed, "I cannot forebear the hope that the historical associations of the new building may be no less auspicious than those which belong to its predecessor." Wood's modest expectations were mocked by the disgruntled editorial in the *New York Times*. Of all the speakers at the cornerstone ceremony, the editor noted, "We do not see in anyone of them a very satisfactory explanation of their reasons for throwing on the city the burden of this enormous additional expenditure just at this present time, or any estimate of the rate of taxation to submit to within the next few years according to present appearances." The editorial closed with this taunt: "unless we are greatly mistaken we shall soon see a movement for effective financial reform in our city affairs."[45] Still, by 1865, the *New York Times* was susceptible to the charms of public architecture, as it boasted that the noble marble pillars of the County Courthouse façade resembled St. Paul's Cathedral.[46]

Only two years later, the *Times* had changed its critical position back again. The headline bellowed, "The County Court House – extravagance and plunder." Within five years, the *Times* would paint those same marble pillars as tawdry symbols of financial mismanagement and municipal graft. The façade became a mantle of political shame covering a public building renamed the Tweed Courthouse. Its namesake, William M. "Boss" Tweed, was intermittently a member of both the Board of Supervisors and the Building Commission during the period when the courthouse was constructed. Although hardly the sole catalyst of the campaign against political machines, the Tweed Courthouse was more than just a convenient symbol of corruption. It served as the ledger in which journalists recorded how Tammany Hall misspent the taxes paid by the frugal middle class. The Democratic municipal government was driven from office by a barrage of audit sheets published in the daily press. The charges included such inflated expenditures as $100,000 for furniture, carpets, and painting and the veiled bigotry of gratuitous comments about hastily naturalized laborers who took six weeks to complete one day's work.[47] The most legible political symbolism of the courthouse was not carved on its pediment or mounted on its cupola but etched in *Harper's Weekly*. This sketch of a fountain outside the courthouse showed a demure Liberty being presented with the bill of expenses for the construction. At her feet lay an open moneybag spilling filthy lucre into the coffers of Boss Tweed (Figure 2.11). This masterful political iconography articulated a new vernacular civics lesson, that politics is a dirty business operated by venal men. The cynical attitude toward politics at least brought some cognitive order to the confusing state of municipal government in the Gilded Age. It did not, however, encourage further investment in public architecture.

Figure 2.11
"Design for a Proposed Monumental Fountain in the City Hall Park."
Cartoon by C. G. Parker, *Harper's Weekly*, October 7, 1871, p. 932.

To this day, this major architectural monument to public life in a democratic city is known as "the house that Tweed built;" its civic identity and architectural repute are still tainted by association with the corruption of big city politics. The Tweed Courthouse had hardly been completed when it was dubbed an architectural "monstrosity" and threatened with demolition. Its drapery of shame was not unique among American public buildings. The City Hall of Philadelphia set a particularly high standard of graft and gaudiness, and attempts to build a new City Hall in Chicago were thwarted by similar political cynicism. Across the country in San Francisco, municipal reformers compared another costly public building project to a cesspool and proposed that public funds would be better spent on a sewage system. Civic materialism would seem to have descended from the pristine symbolism of the classic rotunda to the architectural gutter. At this juncture in the story of city halls, the correspondence between public building and public confidence seems a chimera. How could the same marble pillars evoke civic pride in one instance and public shame but a few years later?

Before surrendering the history of public architecture to the cynicism of the Gilded Age, one more example of civic materialism merits consideration. A look westward to the upstart city of San Francisco indicates that the civic architecture of the late nineteenth century had some redeeming features. Although San Franciscans did not make a major investment in public architecture until 1870, at a time of growing disillusionment with urban politics elsewhere, their belated civic enterprise exuded something of the exhilaration as well as the tension of urban democracy. By this date, city government had democratized to an extent that complicated major public projects. The proposal for a new city hall was initiated by the Board of Supervisors of the County and City of San Francisco, a legislative body that had been elected directly by an active, partisan, and relatively broad citizenry. (It included white and African-American males but still excluded women and immigrants from Asia.) In 1870, however, in San Francisco, as in New Orleans and New York, urban government was held in ill repute at the state level, and the residents of big cities were losing control over their own affairs and finances. The tight-fisted taxpayers of California would not permit any deficit spending whatsoever and required the Board of Supervisors to resort to special revenue-generating activities, such as selling public lands or making special annual assessments. Hence it is understandable that it took twenty-two years to complete the city hall whose cornerstone was laid in 1870. Nonetheless, San Francisco would ultimately commit at least four million dollars to this public project, testimony to considerable civic largesse as well as fortitude.[48] In 1873, Mayor William Alvord explained the tenacious commitment to public architecture in the city of San Francisco: "It is difficult to estimate the full influence on public taste, and the full value as a source of pleasure, of a handsome architectural pile elegantly exposed and surrounded. It is cheap and mean to deny ourselves and our posterity an advantage of this kind which we can secure so easily."[49]

This extravagant civic enterprise was undertaken with popular enthusiasm and press approval. The *San Francisco Chronicle* riveted public attention on the plans for building a new city hall and reported regularly on a nationally advertised design competition. At their editorial suggestion, the San Francisco Commissioners carried the democratic aspects of city planning a step further: they put the entries on public display. The *Chronicle* was pleased to report that "the Art Gallery of the Mechanics Pavilion is now being prepared for the display of the plans in such a way that all those who are interested may examine them at their leisure, make suggestions and propose changes and improvements." The commissioners selected the plan that the *Chronicle* had judged "the most beautiful," the design of Augustus

Laver, whose credits included a cathedral in Montreal and the Albany statehouse. Public surveillance did not end with the selection of a trusted architect: the Commission and the Board of Supervisors retained the right to oversee the process of construction and insisted on reviewing all contracts. The volatile political climate of the city also penetrated the construction site and in one instance replaced Laver with an apparent charlatan who was well connected with Denis Kearney, popular leader of the Workingmen's Party. Despite all the vicissitudes of urban politics and the inefficiencies of the democratic process, San Francisco's City Hall Commissioners finally completed their task in 1892 and bequeathed to the city the public building first visualized in Laver's plan but subject to copious vernacular remodeling thereafter.[50]

That plan is unfortunately lost, taking with it almost all physical traces of the ill-fated public building, which was destroyed during the earthquake and fire of 1906. Only a few sketches and incomplete published records of "old city hall" remain extant to suggest the outlines of what was an indubitably distinctive example of public architecture. We do know that the planners were determined to make their city hall central to everyday public life. It was located neither on cheap land at the outskirts of the city nor in the old civic center of Portsmouth Plaza but up Market Street near such hubs of the expanding commercial city as the Hibernian Bank and Mechanics Institute. Unlike the similarly situated New Orleans structure, however, San Francisco's City Hall was not designed to blend in with commercial architecture. A grand domed tower, far higher than any surrounding buildings, boasted the importance of the public sphere. City boosters fought repeatedly to retain funding for this arrogant civic symbol, this "grand and imposing structure" whose size was variously estimated as 57 to 90 feet in diameter and as high as 453 feet. At the same time, the elevation of San Francisco's City Hall was not set at so high an angle that it was aloof from the everyday comings and goings of the people. Both the Commissioners and Board of Supervisors took precautions to make this towering new city hall accessible to citizens. They specified "the erection of a Corinthian portico in the center of the Larkin street front and of two entrance porches on each side of the porticos," added a set of stairs for the use of neighbors, and rejected a location on less expensive land in a more remote part of the city. Engravings and photographs from the turn of the century show a permeable structure, with multiple points of entry for a stream of pedestrians, carriages, bicycles, and trolleys. The entry to the hall of records fronted along a wide landscaped boulevard that afforded a particularly gracious invitation to the citizens who regularly promenaded down Market Street. One bird's-eye sketch of the finished building indicates that the people of San Francisco could access their city hall from a variety of locations, not just one grand stair or portico but multiple portals, on each of the many sides of a building described as an inverted "f." Flush with the street in some places, irregularly broken with indentations at others, the City Hall seemed like a porous maze that, while open, required some ingenuity to navigate. Moreover, citizens could find ample space for navigation within as well as outside, in serpentine hallways and a grand interior piazza. It was as if the usual city hall was turned inside out, replicating the streets and squares in the intricate and fluid pattern of interior space (Figure 2.12).[51]

The original instructions to architects specified some of the intended uses to which these interior spaces would be put: "the different Courts and Boards of City and County, Hall of Records and also offices for the various officers of the said City and County." A directory of the completed building confirmed this rather bureaucratic cast of public space, which was cut up into scores of offices ranging from the 4,000 square feet allotted the tax collector to the 200 square feet reserved for witnesses, segregated into chambers for males and females. The plan as finally approved granted the largest and most central space of the whole building, some 7,200 square feet directly under the dome, to a "hall of records," shelter, that is, for the sacred objects of an expanding city bureaucracy. Spaces for the citizens themselves and their representatives, while dwarfed by the hall of records and greatly outnumbered by administrative offices, were still prominent in the floor plan. San Franciscans, like New Orleanians before them, were invited to assemble within City Hall, in a space of 6,000 square feet called variously the Public Assembly

Figure 2.12
Bird's-eye view of the San Francisco City Hall, *Harper's Weekly*, March 30, 1872. Courtesy of Bert Hansen.

Hall or Grand Hall. A chamber of 1,800 square feet accommodated the Board of Supervisors in greater comfort than earlier legislative bodies, and was placed, as customary, on the second or main floor with easy access to the stairs. A sketch of this chamber in the published reports reveals a familiar picture of a central semicircle of desks, the elevated lobby to the rear and along two sides, podium to the front, all overlaid with classic details. The major difference from the chamber of New York's Common Council, furnished more than half a century earlier, was the provision of separate desks and chairs for each legislator, a reflection perhaps of the replacement of corporate virtue by partisan conflict among the people's representatives.[52]

A paucity of documentation also leaves such questions as specification of the furnishings and decoration of San Francisco's City Hall to speculation. There is little comment in the public records about any central representative symbols, impersonations of Liberty, Justice, or Commerce on the face of this city hall, which is nonetheless a riot of decorations. (A statue erected just in front of City Hall in the 1880s was piled high with civic symbols, featuring robust forty-niners and winsome goddesses, but this was a monument to the private enterprise of industrialist James Lick.) The jagged façades and splayed wings of the public building were planted with Corinthian forests, five turrets, and that haughty hybrid, a towered dome, each blossoming with pediments, balconies, and statuary. In the dim light of this limited historical record, the premier city hall within the Golden Gate seems like a civic fantasyland (Figure 2.13).

A look at the ceremonies with which San Franciscans celebrated their new city hall does not dispel this phantasmagoric interpretation. On February 22, 1870, an estimated 20,000 people gathered to participate in the laying of the

Figure 2.13
"New City Hall, San Francisco," c. 1896.
Copyright B. C. Turnbull, courtesy of the California Historical Society, FN-18773.

cornerstone. This moment in the city's civic history was marked by a procession of city officials and military regiments into the excavation site, where the parade passed through a white-washed arch of triumph, onto a stage set in an amphitheater of sand piles. The foundation of the domed tower was laid out as a banquet table spread with two barbecued oxen and gallons of beer and "native wine." In word and deed, this festival bespoke an exuberant public spirit that made earlier and eastern ceremonies seem morose by comparison. The official orators trumpeted civic pride into imperial hubris, all symbolized by the plan of the new city hall. One declared the project "worthy of San Francisco, and which will stand for ages, the symbol of the resources, the grandeur and taste of the metropolis of the Pacific." Another proclaimed, "here is the universal empire. It knows neither tropical nor political limits." The grand master mason who laid the cornerstone invested imperial pretensions in the local city hall:

> within its walls as beneath its lofty dome, through ages let us trust shall be administered the vast and complicated interest of the queenly city where Orient and Occident under the inspiration of a nobler and more progressive civilization and reaching up to each other over continents and across seas clasp hands in fraternal grasp.

These breathless civic boasts elicited cheers of assent from a vast assemblage of the population, from fair ladies to rugged working men.[53]

The applause in San Francisco echoed and amplified the earlier cornerstone ceremonies in New York and New Orleans and seemed to celebrate an unflappably popular and democratic architecture. San Francisco in many ways carried forward and expanded the political ideology implicit in New York's republican architecture. The orderly entryways of a single stair and portico had, with the triumph of partisan party politics, proliferated into multiple points of access to the civic center. This progression from staid and deferential republicanism toward popular, mass democracy was not, however, the only axis of change in the architecture of the city hall. By comparison with its predecessors, San Francisco's City Hall also gave a smaller ratio of space to the deliberative, face-to-face, interactive element of politics. Simultaneously, the space devoted to administrative government had grown disproportionately to places for the open discussion of political issues – bureaucracy was overtaking public debate.

The alterations of urban politics reflected in this sequence of city halls are too complex, however, to be contained in a pat narrative of bureaucracy and interest group politics advancing fast on the heels of mass democracy (the basic narrative of such influential works as Habermas's *Structural Transformation of the Public Sphere*). Some of the complications in the basic meaning of politics were connoted by the novel political terminology that seeped into the oratory at the cornerstone ceremony. Leonidas Pratt, the grand master mason quoted above, boasted that San Francisco's City Hall would be the place where "political economy and the science of Government shall attain perfection." Even more portentous than his deference to government by experts and imperialists was Pratt's expectation that

City Hall would be a place where "the vast and complicated interest" of the city of San Francisco would "be administrated." This intimation of what would be known as interest-group politics was more than fortuitous; it reflected the conflicts that inevitably emerge when major and costly public projects are opened up for democratic discussion.[54]

In fact, from the very outset, the construction of a new city hall for San Francisco was associated with palpable, specific, and contentious interests within the city. Soon after the cornerstone was laid in place, amid the prolonged depression of the 1870s, 2,000 workers had gathered at Yerba Buena Park to apply for construction jobs. The *San Francisco Chronicle* championed their needs, saying: "There is no harm in making the necessities of the laboring man known and at this time in particular to the representatives of the people assembled in Sacramento."[55] Those who debated the City Hall Bill before the State Assembly concurred on one rationale for the project: "that a large number of citizens of San Francisco needed employment."[56] This particular species of interest-group politics, a recourse to government to meet the basic economic needs of disadvantaged citizens, can be seen as a laudable harbinger of social democracy or as vulgar pleading for special treatment. The more unseemly side of interest-group politics was written into the City Hall appropriations in 1876 as something known colloquially as the "antiMongolian clauses," which prohibited the employment of anyone but white men on this public works project. If the interests of unemployed white workers were the most clearly expressed in the debate about City Hall, those of more affluent San Franciscans were not entirely invisible. This class of citizens, who most often represented themselves simply as taxpayers, had a penchant for dismissing such expensive civic improvements as "public waste."

But for the time being, in San Francisco at least, the various factions of the citizenry came together and agreed to build lavishly for a public purpose. Some good-hearted opposition to the city hall project surfaced in the press in the form of chagrin at the unruly behavior of the workers, who were ceremonially feasted after the cornerstone dedication. (Their table manners did leave something to be desired as they devoured the meat of two oxen and allegedly threw their tin plates at the women and children who ringed the crowd.) As late as the 1870s, in San Francisco at least, there was still material evidence to support a thriving if disheveled democracy. The language of ceremony, the architecture of public space, and the process of enacting public works projects all conspired to welcome a slowly widening range of different groups and interests into the public realm.[57] As late as the 1890s, neither the cynicism of civic reformers nor the distaste of latter-day architectural critics had much currency in San Francisco. The ephemera collections of local archives are stocked full of engravings, postcards, and photographs that confer pride of place on City Hall. During public holidays, its dome and tower were illuminated or draped in laurels. Family portraits were snapped in front of City Hall, and the edifice remained a favorite civic backdrop for fine engravings complete with representations of fashionable men and women (Figure 2.14).

City Halls and Civic Materialism ■

Figure 2.14
San Francisco City Hall.
Courtesy of the
California Historical
Society, FN-31674.

By the close of the nineteenth century, however, the civic stigma associated with the Tweed Courthouse would be affixed to San Francisco's City Hall and much of American political culture. When, in 1906, the once-proud structure collapsed under the strain of the great earthquake and fire, local historians and architectural critics alike saw some poetic justice in this aspect of the disaster. Few published commentaries mourned the passing of what they now regarded as a monument to bad taste and corrupt politics. The standard narrative of urban politics and public architecture is written from this perspective, and colludes in slandering City Hall as a waste of the taxpayer's money. Public architecture would not be redeemed in San Francisco until 1917, when yet another City Hall would gain legitimacy through the sponsorship of Progressive reformers and their architect partners from the City Beautiful movement.[58]

Historians have good reason, both architectural and political, to question this chronicle of civic decline, which relies on the written testimony of the most articulate and over-represented historical informants: middle-class reformers, professional architects, and highly educated cultural critics. Public buildings themselves point to some ways of picturing the politics of the past that contradict this assessment. To begin with, this material evidence extends and complicates a history of urban politics that is too often foreshortened and flattened. The architectural record that extends from the podiums of imperial authority like the Cabildo, monuments to republican propriety like Gallier Hall and New York City Hall, and the rugged edges of the Tweed Courthouse and San Francisco City Hall has left landmarks of a finely differentiated political history. Taken together, they denote a halting, erratic development from imperial absolutism to republican polities to a tenuous and imperfect democracy. In their materiality and three-dimensionality, these public buildings served as both the schoolhouses and the theaters of political change. They opened up, and sometimes closed down, access to municipal government on a prosaic, everyday basis – in legislative chambers, administrative offices, and in the stairways, parks, and promenades outside.

As they evolved over the course of the nineteenth century, American city halls introduced some distinctive new elements into the catalog of civic architecture. Understandably, the young republic that had led the expansion of suffrage and invented a two-party system would quickly outgrow authoritarian spaces like the New Orleans Cabildo. The municipal architecture of the early republic was more homologous with the British town halls (described so alluringly by Asa Briggs). New York's City Hall and the Municipal Hall of New Orleans resembled the town halls in both their architectural elements and in their narrow political base, the suffrage limited to the propertied middle class. Still, the eclecticism of American civic architecture does not fit snugly within the West European architectural tradition, as seen for example in the acute and telescopic vision of Richard Sennett. While, on the one hand, Gallier Hall resembled the Victorian town hall, it was also like a throwback to the authoritarian floor plan of a Roman basilica, a style that is not entirely incongruous with the modern slave republic of the antebellum South. The homespun architects of New York City, on the other hand, practiced another form of pragmatic eclecticism: they blended French style with the functional and political exigencies of municipal representative institutions. The resulting structure served as an enduring material bridge between republican civic responsibility and the openness of a rapidly expanding plebian democracy. The civic landmarks of the Gilded Age, including such grandiose conceits as the domed tower that rose in San Francisco's civic center, gave exuberant expression to American popular democracy during years of fervid partisanship and high voter turnout. To find facsimiles of its mélange of porticos, colonnades, and assembly halls, one would have to look back to the Greek polis, whose complex of civic buildings provided multiple spaces for public debate but only for a tiny proportion of the population. When such debates engaged a mass electorate in the ethnically diverse and class-divided city of the nineteenth century, classic standards of public decorum were inevitably violated. No sooner had American citizens created a distinctive democratic architecture than their creation became an object of suspicion and then scorn.

These ambiguous meanings and ironic twists in the history of the American city hall can only be understood on native ground, in the particular political history of the nineteenth-century American city. From this second perspective, the evidence of civic materialism suggests some revisions in one prominent chapter in American urban and political history, the standard account of corrupt urban machines. The record of municipal architecture demonstrates that indictments of political graft are not a very sensitive historical barometer. The cost of public buildings like the house that Tweed built, or of San Francisco's City Hall, was shockingly high and inflated far above the original estimate. But so, too, were their august predecessors, like the stately New York City Hall, whose construction also created lucrative public contracts for friends of patrician council members. (Benjamin Latrobe, for example, had boasted of his friendship with Aaron Burr, whose "interest procured me all the votes of the corporation save one," only to lose his bid to a crony of the Federalist majority.) Without discounting the excesses of building projects like the Tweed Courthouse, one can concede that financing civic building has seldom exemplified tidy book-keeping. The new urban historians have calculated that the founding fathers and Mugwump reformers also had difficulty balancing budgets, and, conversely, city bosses could be stingy with the taxpayer's money. Furthermore, the charges of corruption can actually be read as symptoms of democracy: neither the Spanish viceroy nor patrician benefactors were subject to such a contentious popular review of their building projects. What had changed over the course of the nineteenth century, however, was the degree to which literate and elite spokesmen trusted city officials and were willing to make these inevitably costly, long-term investments in public projects.[59] Popular deference to the elite leaders in the small city of the early republic had given way to more plebeian, democratically elected officials and a more contentious electorate. All this is to suggest that, rather than prompting historians to ratify the rantings of reformers about the corruption of city bosses, the municipal buildings of the late nineteenth century should inspire some appreciation of the political determination to create costly public places even at a time of political conflict, economic hardship, and middle-class cynicism.

The architectural and spatial features of buildings like the Tweed Courthouse and San Francisco City Hall also speak up through the static of charges of corrupt urban machines to bear testimony to a stubborn and robust urban democracy. The sketches that remain of San Francisco's Old City Hall as well as the standing testimony of Tweed Courthouse – which still flanks New York's City Hall on Chamber Street (clipped of its portico and stair but saved from the bulldozer of urban development czar Robert Moses, thanks to vigilant preservationists) constitute an entirely creditable architectural record. The city builders succeeded in keeping up with the rapidly growing administrative needs of the big city. The increasing number and complexity of tasks assumed by the public sector required the expansion of the public payroll, the specialization of services, and a concomitant increase and renovation of public buildings. At the same time, cities like San Francisco continued to build for public accessibility and assembly, and gave an honored place to the heart of representative democracy, the council chamber. Voters still spent freely and architects labored diligently to create the legislative chambers wherein the people's representatives, now elected by a broader and more demanding franchise than ever, met, put their minds and interests together, and tried to fashion a civic whole. Public architecture had not yet become "a huge filing cabinet" (architect Charles Moore's phrase for San Francisco's Federal Building) but remained something of a palace of the people. The Tweed Courthouse and San Francisco's Old City Hall deserve an honored place in the pantheon of public architecture. They expressed and carried forward the same ineluctable historical process inaugurated in New York's City Hall in 1803, that of creating space in which to imagine and to practice representative government. The city halls of the Gilded Age, with their playful architectural gestures of welcome to the public, also served such pragmatic functions as putting people to work during hard times, thereby adding a small but laudable dose of social democracy to the political ideals implicit in vernacular republican styles of building. Because they opened up public space, acknowledged social differences, and housed a democratic, deliberative government, city halls provide material refutations of narratives of decline in public architecture and public life. In an architectural history stock full of cathedrals, chateaus, and museums, the city hall claims attention and respect as a modest monument to democracy.

Regardless of their conformity to high aesthetic standards, the buildings created for and by a large and active citizenry can contribute mightily to civic vitality. San Francisco's City Hall, for example, became the staging ground of a major social movement even before the structure was completed. In the late 1870s, the Workingmen's Party of California conquered local politics from its base at the "Sandlots," mere mounds of dirt created by the excavations for City Hall (Figure 2.15). The remarkable steps of New York's City Hall have served as the stage for protest and occasional riot for close to two centuries. All the political struggles that took place just outside formal political spaces like the mayor's office or conference rooms serve as a reminder that the value of public space should not be measured simply as a contribution to good civic comportment in elegant chambers. Late in the twentieth century, when Mayor Rudolph Giuliani threatened to restrict the use of that precious civic resource, the steps of City Hall, he was bluntly informed that "people come to this beautiful building to raise their concerns and express their opinion. We're here today to say that City Hall belongs to the people, and we want it back." Even at the end of the twentieth century, the battle for, at, and on the steps of City Hall was still in process.[60]

This tenacious defense of the civic architectural heritage suggests a final reason to pursue the three-dimensional study of political history yet further. City halls enliven and revise the conventional conception of the historical timeline. The documents of civic materialism do not exit the stage of history on the usual cue but can endure and influence the course of events for centuries. In fact, four of the five buildings studied here still survive; two of them (both in New York City) still serve the same civic purposes for which they were designed. Thousands of New Yorkers congregate every working day in City Hall Park. They come to serve on juries, sue in court, claim social services, get married, or visit the municipal archives. Some of them enter the city council chambers to participate directly in making public policy. When they do, their prosaic acts as citizens are infused with a sense of history. Performing a bureaucratic errand in an older public building is invested with quiet grandeur when a citizen climbs a classic staircase that is the bequest of the early republic to the contentious democracy of our day. When the New York Preservation Society was lobbying to award City Hall landmark status, they surveyed city officials about the architecture they inhabited. At least one public servant replied. Paul O'Dwyer, then president of the Board of Estimate, which met in the old Common Council chamber, wrote: "There is something especially democratic about having the meetings of the Board of Estimate in that room. We have found that people get somewhat disillusioned and discontent when they have to attend public hearings at Police headquarters, although the space there is much more spacious and new and can with greater comfort accommodate all of the people who come there."[61] Even in the waning days of the twentieth century, New York's "City Hall" inspired popular movies and a television series. This is faint praise compared to the florid rhetoric that emanated from cornerstone ceremonies over a century ago. But it demonstrates that public architecture is more than an inert by-product of governmental processes; it can affect the quality of civic life, and for generations. Much as Michael Schudson has argued from the written records of citizenship, the evidence of civic materialism bespeaks an eclectic repertoire of constitutional, republican, and democratic elements that have sustained self-government over the long haul of American history.[62] The city halls of the

Figure 2.15
The Sandlots of New City Hall (San Francisco), *The Wasp*, 1880. Courtesy of the Bancroft Library, University of California, Berkeley.

nineteenth century continue to offer incentives to build, if not for "the whole of us," at least in the hopes of continually expanding and diversifying the circle of civic life.

NOTES

> This essay has benefited immensely from the careful reading of my colleagues at the University of California at Berkeley and two groups in particular: first, the American Studies reading group, including Paul Groth, Richard Hudson, Margaretta Lowell, Donald McQuade, and Kathleen Moran, and, second, the Townsend Humanities Seminar and its director, Randolph Starn. Michelle Bogart offered an acute and instructive critique of an early draft. I am indebted to Dell Upton of the Department of Architecture for his erudition, shrewd advice, and correction of my architectural blunders. My Berkeley colleague David Henkin gave his usual incisive and kind reading. I have also to thank Robin Bachin and the American Studies faculty at the University of Miami for their helpful reading of an earlier version.

1 *New Orleans Picayune*, October 13, 31, 1853.
2 *New York Times*, December 22, 1858.
3 Katherine Fischer Taylor, *In the Theater of Criminal Justice: The Palais de Justice in Second Empire Paris* (Princeton, NJ: Princeton University Press, 1993), xx; Robert Tittler, *Architecture and Power: The Town Hall and the English Urban Community, c. 1500–1640* (Oxford: Oxford University Press, 1991), 4; Colin Cunningham, *Victorian and Edwardian Town Halls* (London: Routledge, Kegan and Paul, 1981), preface; Hilary Ballon, *The Paris of Henry IV: Architecture and Urbanism* (Cambridge, MA: MIT Press, 1991), 12; Asa Briggs, *Victorian Cities* (London: Odham Books, 1964); Richard Sennett, *Flesh and Stone: The Body and the City in Western Civilization* (New York: W. W. Norton, 1994).
4 Dell Upton, "Architectural history or landscape history?," *Journal of Architectural Education* 44, no. 4 (August 1991): 195–9. He postulates that "publicly accessible spaces can have and should have a civic orientation that is direct, palpable, and there for the purposes of reminding us both of who we are and who we might become." While Rowe's words echo the sentiments of the editor of the New Orleans Picayune in 1853, the examples he offers, the Piazza Del Campo in Sienna, the New York City Plan of 1803, and Francois Mitterand's grand projects for Paris, are drawn from the pantheon of Western architecture.
5 Peter G. Rowe, *Civic Realism* (Cambridge, MA: MIT Press, 1997), 9.
6 Terrence McDonald, "Constructing the Liberal Subject: Re-reading the Narrative of Urban Political Corruption in Twentieth Century America," Paper presented at the Meeting of the Organization of American Historians, 1997.
7 Charles T. Goodsell, *The Social Meaning of Civic Space: Studying Political Authority through Architecture* (Lawrence, KS: University of Kansas Press, 1988); Amos Rappoport, "Vernacular architecture and cultural determination of form," in Anthony D. King, ed., *Buildings and Society: Essays on the Social Development of the Built Environment* (London: Routledge and Kegan Paul, 1980), 283–306; Daniel Bluestone, *Constructing Chicago* (New Haven, CT: Yale University Press, 1991), esp. chs. 5–6; Upton, "Architectural history or landscape history?," 195–9; Dell Upton, "Another city: The

urban cultural landscape in the early republic," in Catherine E. Hutchins, ed., *Everyday Life in the Early Republic* (New York: Winterthur Museum, 1994).

8 For more background on these cities, see Mary P. Ryan, *Civic Wars: Democracy and Public Life in the American City during the Nineteenth Century* (Berkeley, CA: Univeristy of California Press, 1997).

9 Samuel Wilson, Jr. and Leonard Huber, *The Cabildo on Jackson Square: The Colonial Period, 1723–1803* (1970; Gretna, LA: Pelican Publishing Company, 1973), iv, 1.

10 Wilson and Huber, *The Cabildo on Jackson Square*, 27–40.

11 *Historic American Building Survey*, New Orleans, Louisiana. All references to the survey are to the Collection held by the Library of Congress, reproduced and microfiched and arranged by location.

12 Wilson and Huber, *The Cabildo on Jackson Square*, 30, 50, 64.

13 Wilson and Huber, *The Cabildo on Jackson Square*, 59–75.

14 *Historic American Building Survey*, New Orleans, Gallier Hall.

15 James Gallier, *Autobiography of James Gallier, Architect* (New York: Da Capo Press, 1973); *Historic American Building Survey*, Gallier Hall; *New Orleans Architecture, Vol. 2: The American Sector,* text by Samuel Wilson, Jr., compiled by Roulhac Toledano and Sally Kittridge Evans (Gretna, LA: Pelican Publishing Company, 1974), 93, 119, 204-05.

16 Gallier, *Autobiography*, plates 5–10, pp. 1–17.

17 *Historic American Building Survey*, New Orleans, Gallier Hall, 6–7.

18 *Historic American Building Survey*, New Orleans, Gallier Hall, 7–8; *New Orleans Architecture*, 2: 205.

19 *New Orleans Picayune*, May 11, 12, 1853; *Daily Crescent*, October 15, 1849.

20 Louis Torres, "Federal Hall revisited," *Journal of the Society of Architectural Historians* 29 (1970): 327–38.

21 I. N. Stapes, *The Iconography of Manhattan Island, 1498–1909* (New York: Robert H. Dodd, 1915–28), plate 57.

22 Minutes of the Common Council of New York City, December 17, 1802; Evan Cornog, "To give character to our city: New York's City Hall," *New York History* 69 (November 1988): 388–423; "Some Architectural Designs of Benjamin Latrobe," *Library of Congress Quarterly Journal of Current Acquisitions*, 13 (May 1946).

23 Minutes of the Common Council, March 21, 1803.

24 "City Hall as seen in 1834," *New York Times*, June 13, 1934.

25 Phillip Lopate, "Unpretentious mirror for the metropolis," *New York Times*, October 30, 1998: B38.

26 For a full demonstration of the cultural and social meaning of this space, see Michelle Bogart, "Public space and public memory in New York's City Hall Park," *Journal of Urban History* 25 (January 1999): 226–57.

27 Clay Lancaster, "New York City Hall stair rotunda reconsidered," *Journal of the Society of Architectural Historians* 29 (1970): 33–9.

28 Damie Stillman, "New York City Hall: competition and execution," *Journal of the Society of Architectural Historians* 23 (October 1964): 129–40.

29 *Historic American Building Survey*, New York, New York, 234, pp. 1–5; Goodsell, *Social Meaning of Civic Space*; William L. Lebovich, *American City Halls* (Washington, D.C.: Preservation Press, 1988).

30 Mary T. Flannelly, "City Hall" (typescript), New York Historical Society, Fall 1975.

31 Goodsell provides an excellent description and analysis of council chambers such as this, but I dispute his interpretation, which gives emphasis to the authoritarian meanings of the space and its furnishings.

32 Flannelly, "City Hall;" Stopes, *Iconography of Manhattan Island*, 587.

33 Blunt's *Stranger's Guide to the City of New York* [1817], quoted in Flannelly, "City Hall."

34 See Minutes of the Common Council, April 6, 1812, November 9, 1804; September 2, 1811; May 13, 1816; April 5, 1819.
35 Blunt's *Stranger's Guide*, quoted in Flannelly, "City Hall," 45.
36 Minutes of the Common Council, August 15, 1814.
37 Barbara S. Peterson, "The Corporation Tearoom" (typescript), vertical file, Municipal Records Room, Municipal Archives, New York City.
38 See Jon C. Teaford, *The Unheralded Triumph: City Government in America, 1870–1900* (Baltimore, MD: John Hopkins University Press, 1984).
39 "The Tweed Courthouse: Historical Structure Report," prepared by the Landmarks Preservation Commission, New York City: Preservation Commission Archives, New York, n.d., Appendices B and D.
40 "The Tweed Courthouse," 29–41; Robert A. M. Stern, Thomas Mellins, and David Fishman, *New York 1880: Architecture and Urbanism in the Gilded Age* (New York: The Monacelli Press, 1999).
41 *New York Times*, January 18, 1859.
42 "The Tweed Courthouse," report of the Landmarks Preservation Commission, provides a complete pictorial and blueprint record of the spatial composition of the courthouse.
43 Donald M. Reynolds, *The Architecture of New York City* (New York: Wiley, 1984). See blueprints in "The Tweed Courthouse."
44 "The Tweed Courthouse," 61.
45 *New York Herald*, *New York Tribune*, *New York Times*, December 27, 1861.
46 *New York Times*, December 26, 1865.
47 *New York Times*, April 22, 1868; October 11, 1870.
48 A. T. Spotts, "History and Report of the Construction of the New City Hall from April 4, 1870 to November 1889" (San Francisco, 1886), pamphlet, Bancroft Library, University of California, Berkeley.
49 Spotts, "History and Report," 9.
50 Spotts, "History and Report"; Harold Kirker, *Califomia's Architectural Frontier: Style and Tradition in the Nineteenth Century* (San Marino, CA: The Huntington Library, 1960), 97–9; *San Francisco Chronicle*, September 22, November 18, 16, December 2, 1870.
51 Spotts, "History and Report," 19, 25.
52 San Francisco Board of Supervisors, Municipal Reports, 1871, 403–15, frontispiece, 1877–88.
53 *San Francisco Call*, *San Francisco Chronicle*, and *San Francisco Daily Alta*.
54 *San Francisco Daily Alta*, February 23, 1870.
55 *San Francisco Chronicle*, April 4, 1870.
56 *San Francisco Daily Alta*, April 2, 1870.
57 *San Francisco Chronicle*, April 5, 1870; *San Francisco Daily Alta*, April 2, 1870; *San Francisco Call*, February 23, 1872.
58 Judd Kahn, *Imperial San Francisco: Politics and Planning in an American City, 1897–1906* (Lincoln, NE: University of Nebraska Press, 1979).
59 Terrence McDonald, *The Parameters of Urban Fiscal Policy* (Berkeley, CA: University of Californai Press, 1986); L. Ray Gunn, *The Decline of Authority: Public Economic Policy and Political Development in New York, 1800–1860* (Ithaca, NY: Cornell University Press, 1988); Sennett, *Flesh and Stone*.
60 *New York Times*, November 15, 1999: A27.
61 A copy of Paul O'Dwyer's letter is appended to the Flannelly report cited above, n. 30. It is dated October 28, 1975.
62 See Ryan, *Civic Wars*; Michael Schudson, *The Good Citizen: A History of American Civic Life* (1998; rpt. edn., Cambridge, MA: Harvard University Press, 1999).

Chapter 3: Civic or National Pride?

The City Hall as a Communal "Hotel" in Scandinavian Capital Cities

Laura Kolbe

Stockholm's City Hall was inaugurated on June 23, 1923. It was Midsummer Eve, the most Swedish of all holidays, celebrating the 400th anniversary of King Gustav Vasa's entry into Stockholm – the historical foundation of the Swedish nation-state.[1] The most impressive event of the day was the procession of citizens through the city to the courtyard of City Hall. The procession emphasized the democratic and liberal elements in Swedish history. The iconographic narrative of the building was closely linked to local and royal history and to Sweden's general historical development. In keeping with the royalist approach to the festivities, King Gustaf V opened the new building. In his speech, Allan Cederborg, chairman of the city council and one of the leading figures in the local bourgeois community, praised the beauty of the building, auguring a long and peaceful development. The building symbolized the strong political links between state authorities and local government (Figure 3.1). Stockholm, as capital city, was the seat of this national consensus, and this new building, dubbed "The Queen of Lake Mälaren," would guarantee the durability of the nation into a prosperous future.[2]

    The city hall project in Stockholm shared many features with city halls in Northern Europe. Between 1880 and 1950 in other Scandinavian capital cities – Copenhagen, Oslo, Helsinki and Reykjavik – the municipal authorities explored the possibility of building a new city hall, studied locations and invited proposals for its design, but only three were realized, namely in Copenhagen in 1905, in Stockholm in 1923, and in Oslo in 1950. The City Hall in Copenhagen was a great source of inspiration to Stockholm, while Oslo looked to both Copenhagen and Stockholm (Figure 3.2).[3] In Helsinki the city authorities bought in 1901 an old hotel by the Market Place and sought to plan a city hall on the site. An architectural competition in 1914 revealed ambitions to monumentalize the plan, but it was not realized due to economic circumstances. Instead, the city authorities rebuilt the old hotel and its surroundings into a city hall precinct in phases, beginning in the 1920s.[4] In Reykjavik, the idea of a city hall was as old as in the other four cities, dating back to 1918, when the first committee was established by the Mayor to discuss the building of a city hall. However, it took

Civic or National Pride?

Figure 3.1
Stockholms-Tidningen describing the June 1923 opening celebrations of the new City Hall.

nine decades to plan the edifice and the new city hall was finally inaugurated in spring 1992.[5]

The planning of city halls in Nordic capital cities was related to the larger European phenomenon of bourgeois nation-building during the nineteenth and twentieth centuries.[6] In accordance with the central and southern European examples, the Scandinavian city halls were planned in the center of the growing city, in close communication with governmental buildings and state administration. The location had a communicative message: the building was placed either at a point of historical interest or it marked a geopolitical centrality in the city's urban development. In Copenhagen, the site selected for the proposed city hall was situated on the city's old rampart, immediately south of the historical Western City Gate with surrounding fortifications. It was demolished in 1859, and declared

57

City Halls and Civic Materialism ■

Fig. 22. Rådhuset i Köpenhamn av Martin Nyrop.

Figure 3.2
The City Hall of Copenhagen (1905) was located in an area, which was a lively, urban meeting place, close to the main railway station, urban amusement park Tivoli, and governmental buildings. Source: Beckett, *Kjobenhavns Raadhus,* 1908.

municipal property in 1870. The new City Hall Square was planned at the site of Copenhagen's old Haymarket, now transformed into an exhibition area that played host to the Nordic Exhibitions of 1872 and 1888. In Stockholm, Oslo, Helsinki, and Reykjavik the water element was central: in Stockholm the city hall was located on the inland waterway at Lake Mälaren. In Oslo the city hall faced the old harbor and in Helsinki the old harbor and market place. In Reykjavik the beautiful urban environment of Lake Tjornin was considered a worthy setting for a building intended to symbolize the city's status as the capital of Iceland.

In each of the capital cities, the project of nation-building and city governance became aligned to produce a particular pattern of design that influenced how the city hall functioned as an urban public space. This process was facilitated by the close connection between municipal expansion and state formation in Scandinavia, and the principle of centrality that created an urban system, with a large dominant capital city ruling a mass of minor towns and villages. The city hall, together with state buildings, constituted central elements in the self-images and urban landscapes of all five capital cities.

The location of the city hall reflected the centrality of local government in the Scandinavian political system and in capital city planning.[7] Originally during the seventeenth century, the capital cities in Scandinavia were designed chiefly as seats of royal/imperial and national government, but later they began to serve as economic, political, and social centers of a growing bourgeois society. This comprehensive historical development became an essential part of the iconographic narration of the city halls. Several points can be made about how cultural and political meanings were related to each other by this spatial relationship in and to the urban core, communicating both the local municipal tradition and modern needs of city governance and representation.[8] First, the city hall was planned to become the main symbol of the city, a political "hotel." Second, it was the seat of civic management and local politics. Third, and originally, it was a place for representation, civic activities, and national rituals for the enlightened, wealthy, and even progressive bourgeois class. The members of this class were usually engaged in the new industrial professions, especially banking, insurance, services, and the public sector. Many of them were inspired by internationalist movements.[9]

In the mid-nineteenth century, the juridical and "constitutional" development of local self-government was similar in all Scandinavian countries, due to their common historical roots. Municipal government was one of the key factors in stabilizing societies as lay and ecclesiastical communes were separated.[10] In Norway the first municipals reforms were made as early as in 1837. In 1840, Denmark gained a new municipal constitution, which was expanded in 1849. In the local histories of Sweden and Finland, the most important milestone was the passing of the local urban government statutes in 1862 and 1875. The city council became the city's supreme decision-making body. Municipalities were given the authority to undertake activities that aimed to satisfy the common needs of their inhabitants.[11] As Gunnar Bolin, Keeper of the Records to the City of Stockholm, put it in 1923:

> this created the need for special premises for the new body which should be of a representative kind. The idea of a 'hotel,' where guests of the city should be received, and where festivals could be held, had long been floated before the mind of citizens.[12]

The growth in commerce and industry meant that Scandinavian capital cities became by far the largest cities in their countries, and also "true national capitals" in the commercial and cultural sense.[13]

The extensive local governmental reforms introduced between 1910 and the 1920s made local governance more democratic and stable. "One-man-one-vote" opened the municipal bodies to socialist and social democratic parties. Their power grew not only in financial and commercial circles, but also in politics and administration.¹⁴ The history of independent self-government has been presented as part of an ancient Scandinavian democratic heritage whose roots go back to medieval times. This legacy gave a social interpretation of the local past, with a strong nation-building paradigm.¹⁵

In what follows I want to discuss the communicative aspects of these Scandinavian city halls as they were intended to operate within the larger civic realm. The motives behind the construction of town and city halls were rather similar, indicating comparable levels of urban development. In Scandinavia, the German influence was still strong. Council (*rådet*) buildings developed along continental lines and the council house (*rådhuset*) in cities and towns housed local and central administration and functioned as courts of law. When the modern city hall of the nineteenth century was developed, the old name continued to be used. When cities grew, both names: *stadshuset* (town/city hall) and *rådhuset*, were, and still are, in use, both for those housing courts of law and those without.¹⁶

PLANNING THE CITY HALL

In Scandinavian cities the dream of a city hall was propelled by municipal reforms and all cities experienced a long planning process. There was a strong wish to put an end to the long-standing problem of overcrowding in the law courts and offices for city administrators. A series of architectural competitions took place for the design of the city hall. In Copenhagen an open free competition was announced in the summer of 1888, in two stages. In Stockholm the competition was held in 1902, in Helsinki 1914 and again 1958, in Oslo in 1917–18 and in Reykjavik as late as in 1986. The entries in all cities were rather monumental, spanning the full breadth of historical styles, and drawing inspiration from monumental buildings like French castles, Flemish warehouses, and Gothic churches – or in Reykjavik's case, from modernist architecture. One or two architects were chosen as the winners: in Denmark Martin Nyrop, in Stockholm Ragnar Östberg, in Oslo Arnstein Magnusson and Magnus Paulsson. In Helsinki the jury was not satisfied with the first competition, and no first prize was given. Later, the work was given to architect Aarno Ruusuvuori. In Reykjavik the winners were architects Margret Hardardottir and Steve Christer.¹⁷

The planning of the city hall became a long-term municipal project. In Copenhagen it took 13 years, and in Stockholm some 20 years. In Helsinki and in Oslo it took over 40 years and in Reykjavik 70 years. Building costs and location were discussed and municipal needs, ideological matters, and aesthetic values analyzed. As a political process it was consistent with the municipal decision-making tradition in Scandinavia: important projects must be communicative, open, and have the support of the political majority. In all cities, the work was controlled locally by a special building committee. Politically, the committee was an independent body, responsible only to the city council. The studios and workshops used for sculpture, painting, iron forging, woodcarving, and textiles were located close to the building site or in the building area. Different kinds of specialists and professionals worked with the project, sharing a common goal and developing a strong sense of devotion. The finished products became the sum of each worker's contribution – and above all stood the heroic figure of the architect. In all cases, city halls immortalized their architects.[18]

The setting in the city center was considered to be political, reflecting the high status of urban communality, social participation, and citizenship in the Nordic countries. In Copenhagen, the building of Martin Nyrop was the sixth city hall. After a lengthy political discussion the building was planned so that its main façade is at the spot where the old West City Gate was situated. This gate was the "zero stone," the starting point of all road distances on Zealand, stretching out towards "the whole wide world." In the early days of the twentieth century the area was a lively urban meeting place, close to the main railway station, the urban amusement park Tivoli, and governmental buildings at Slotsholmen. While excavating the foundations of the building, it was discovered that the ancient sea bottom had originally extended to this area. Later here on the night of February 10, 1659 the Swedes, the "old enemy" of Denmark, made their main assault on Copenhagen. These historical, symbolic, and maritime aspects are seen in the decorative program of the edifice.[19]

In Stockholm, the city administration started to grow in improvised quarters in the Old Town of the Vasa era. Ragnar Östberg was one of the many architects trying to place the new city hall within the traditional and dense Old Town in the early 1890s. He made his first drawings for a "Hotel de Ville" in Stockholm as early as in 1893. After a worldwide study tour during the 1890s he returned home, having his thoughts still "in ... the building question ... examining the problems of a monumental project, that [would] liberate the imaginations from daily drudgery." The crucial point came in 1901 when city court judge Richard Öhnell asked Östberg's advice. The task was to be split: first a courthouse would be planned, then a building for city administration. The question of location was unsolved and Östberg made the proposal for a new site at Kungsholmen, a royal island in Lake Mälaren, "right on the water, so typical for Stockholm, and with enough additional land for future expansion."[20] According to the architect, the location even had some historic meaning; it was "a quarter of the town which arose during the seventeenth century, when Sweden was a great power" (Figure 3.3).[21]

In Stockholm, closeness to the sea and historic trade routes and waterways were essential aspects of the setting of city hall. Kungsholem reflected the local bourgeois and trade history. St. Erik's bridge was built to connect the island to the Old Town. The open waterside location placed the city hall, the royal palace, the bourse and the parliament building – traditional symbols of the capital city – all close to one another, but only from a bird's-eye view. A location separate from the old urban center was one of the major aims of the project. As Knut Agathon Wallenberg, one of leading figures behind the planning, pointed out, "the municipal building will gain a location worthy of its noble duties (and) of representing the city, without competition from any other monumental building."[22] After a long discussion in the city council, a decision was made to erect two different buildings. The municipal building (*stadshuset*) was placed on the Eldkvarn site and the courthouse (*rådhuset*) in the Fruktkorgen area.[23]

City Halls and Civic Materialism

Stadshuset från Söder Mälarstrand.

Figure 3.3
The Stockholm City Hall was located close to the crossroads of the sea and Lake Mälaren. Source: *Stockholms stadshus vid dess invigning sommarafton 1923*.

In Christiania/Oslo the final planning of a new city hall started in 1916, when leading local politician and chairman of the city council (*byrådet*), Justice Hieronymus Heyerdahl, presented an idea for a new modern urban planned area. The aim was to combine the construction of a new town hall (*storstue*) with the restoration of the old city slum area close to the harbor at Pipervika. Heyerdahl came up with the idea of placing the future city hall close to the sea. As he indicated, during the last decades of the nineteenth century, the city had developed into one of Northern Europe's central ports. The chosen area was centrally located, partly to underline the role of the city as a "maritime city," partly to communicate with the central streets of the capital city. Close to the area were *Universitetsgaten* and *Karl Johangade*, the main streets, having the royal castle, main building of the university and national parliament (*Stortinget*) in close context. A further basic need was national representation – 1914 had been a great jubilee year, the centenary of the Norwegian constitution (1814). The Norwegian capital city was lacking suitable festive and banquet spaces.[24]

In Helsinki the functions of a town hall were transferred in 1913 to a former hotel in the city *Societetshuset*, located most centrally between the two main public spaces, the Senate Square and Market Place. An architecture competition for a new city hall was held in 1912–13 but without any successful results. The main issue was how to keep the aesthetic balance between the "imperial" Senate Square and the "bourgeois" market place. The winning entries, like Armas Lindgren's design, awarded second prize, proposed the demolition of the old buildings in the block. The First World War and Civil War (1918) dispelled any dreams of a new city hall. The issue of a city hall remained pending until 1932 when the old hotel *Societetshuset* was officially inaugurated as the city hall of Helsinki.[25] The second planning competition for a modern city hall within the boundaries of the old central quarter was won by architect Aarno Ruusuvuori in

Civic or National Pride?

the late 1950s. His plan showed an attempt to retain fragments of the old buildings with imposing new reception and meeting facilities and administrative areas. The plan was based on the idea of *sanering*, meaning that inner parts of buildings were demolished and replaced with modern interiors. Outside walls were left intact. The wish was now to protect and preserve façades in the area around Senate Square, Helsinki's "Old Town." The banqueting room and auditorium of the former city hall was preserved. The second phase of rebuilding was carried out in the 1980s when a new modern meeting room for the city council was added. Some repairs were carried out to revive the historical atmosphere of the area on the northern side. Eventually Helsinki's City Hall became a symbol of post-war modernism and the ideals of efficient town planning (Figure 3.4).[26]

In 1929 the Reykjavik city council offices were moved to a temporary location and the Executive City Council voted to allocate funds for the construction of a city hall. The first design competition in 1946 offered three site options, one on the northern shore of Lake Tjornin and two on the slope overlooking the old city center. None of the proposals won the first prize. Later the City Planning Coordination Committee proposed locating the city hall on the northern end of the lake after having studied 16 sites and the City Council agreed unanimously to locate the city hall on the southern side of *Vonarstraeti* (facing the northern end of the lake). In 1986 the second design competition took place for a city hall on the northern shore of the lake. The first prize was awarded to the architects Margret Hardardottir and Steve Christer and they were commissioned to design the building. The location does not allow any place or square in front of the house, nor any direct or urban communication with central state buildings, like *Althingi*, the parliament or the cathedral. The building's context is the lake: "stark and modern, it is the nerve center of Reykjavik, connecting nature, water and bird life to the center of town."[27]

Figure 3.4
The City Hall of Helsinki was located in the Market Place, and the main façade opens towards the sea. Source: The City Museum of Helsinki.

63

During their construction, all city halls grew to become major national projects. Inauguration ceremonies, the press publicity surrounding them, and their coverage in architectural publications show the kind of reactions these buildings provoked in the public. The main aim was to create a "hotel," "public home," a political place, a ceremonial core and a symbolic place for the capital city – and indeed for the nation and civil society at large. The inauguration of the city halls was commemorated in all three cities by magnificent publications. The jubilee books and architects' articles of the times show that the lofty reputations of these buildings were already in place during the planning process, created mainly by other artists and architects writing in important national venues.[28] One of the foremost Danish artists, architect Peder Vilhelm Jensen-Klint, described Copenhagen's city hall in *Nordisk Tidskrift* in 1903. Swedish architect Ragnar Josephson analyzed Stockholm's city hall in *Ord och Bild* in 1923. In Oslo the leading architectural journal, *Byggekunst*, dedicated a whole special issue to the city hall in 1950.[29] The motivation was clear: city halls were built to symbolize the role of the capital city in a national context.

CIVIC REPRESENTATION

During the early years of the twentieth century, the modern Scandinavian capital city hall was considered to be an attractive new type of building, because it could at the same time express the "character of a nation," be a worthy representation of the "ethnic Scandinavian race," and be the modern "soul of [the] capital city."[30] In 2000 Barbara Miller Lane described the Nordic city halls as a new kind of public building. According to her, the Copenhagen city hall set the tone: "Nyrop's city hall and the buildings of his followers gave the impression of a new town within the city, one that contrasted strongly not only with the cramped streets and tiny buildings of the oldest part of Copenhagen but also with the solemn-looking neoclassical buildings around the Amalienborg."[31]

The city hall carried a communicative element, and served as a medium for expressing the social values of the ruling urban class and ideas of history linked to the local and national framework. Design guidelines and a detailed town-planning program were drawn up for the first time in Copenhagen, when the municipality issued invitations for a design competition in 1888. The principal stipulations concerned costs, technical details, and the building material to be used (natural stone or brick). The design was to include a covered courtyard, a banqueting hall, rooms for the city councilors and the magistracy, as well as offices for the four departments of the magistracy and the city archive. There was also a request for a garden and open space in front of the building. The total floor space required was specified precisely. In Stockholm, the city's building department had prepared a building agenda for the new city hall as early as 1892 and in Oslo in 1915.[32]

Several points can be made about this agenda and the larger process. First, in all city halls many elements of European continuity were present, including the three historical functions: meetings, markets, and magistracy. The assembly room was a creation of the eighteenth century, linked to the needs of the bourgeoisie, but the multi-purpose public hall (for entertaining and gatherings) and the banqueting hall were something new. Both reflected the idea of the town as a cultural and social place. The expanding bureaucracy brought an increase in the volume of office and meeting space. Extra space was needed for police and fire services, a restaurant, and library, archives, and a registry clerk. With all these elements included, the full-fledged city hall was a complex building.[33]

Second, the significance of the city hall is in the variety of ways in which the vocabulary of traditional European city hall architecture was transferred to Scandinavia to express the distinct personality of these cities. The early twentieth-century architects were familiar with the historical role of great town halls such as the *Palazzo Ducale* in Venice, the city hall of Siena, Lübeck's *Das rote Rathaus,* the *Hotel de Ville* in Paris and Amsterdam's *Stadhuis*. The central elements of these buildings were their location in the city center and/or in the market place, urban monumentality and rich decoration. Germany gave to Scandinavian city halls picturesque details, the festive hall, a tavern, and courtyards. France and Belgium gave balconies and weathercocks. Italian architecture inspired the bell tower or *campanile* in Copenhagen, Stockholm, and Oslo (Figure 3.5).[34]

Third, the general impression given by the location of the city halls of Copenhagen, Stockholm, Oslo, and Reykjavik is one of heaviness and enclosure, alluding to old fortresses, extended and rebuilt many times. Façade and its material played an important role in communication. Brick, considered to be an "honest" European material, was used in Copenhagen, Stockholm, and Oslo, concrete in Reykjavik. Both materials give a feeling of unity. Brick architecture had a long tradition as a building material in the Netherlands, Denmark, England, and north Germany, countries with mercantile middle-class, bourgeois values. In all three city halls brick symbolized medieval unity, or as architect R. Josephson noted, "gave a feeling of the romantic, picturesque tradition of both former local aristocratic milieus and medieval cities with their brick castles."[35]

Politically, brick was alien to the tradition of imperial classicism used in Helsinki. Classicism was the style adopted by the European aristocracy and imperial elite, well fitted to the community as a whole in "Emperor's Helsinki."[36] It was considered a supranational style with strong roots in state architecture. In Reykjavik during the latter part of the twentieth century, concrete became a symbol of modern industrial building. The chosen material, together with aluminum and glass, was clearly linked to the message of European modernism, opposing the more traditional local materials such as turf, wood, and Icelandic rock: "Belgian white cement and Danish sand together with a hard blue indigenous aggregate was used to achieve the palest color for the concrete (even when wet), and large custom plywood forms were specified to minimise surface blemishes." Light in color with a sandblasted surface, the concrete was chosen to ensure that the building remains dignified as it ages. The characteristics of light, water, and vegetation were as important as the solid building material itself in creating the City Hall's external and internal aspect.[37]

City Halls and Civic Materialism

Figure 3.5
The City Hall of Oslo was planned close to the sea and historic city centre.
Source: *The Oslo City Hall*, 1953.

Not only the material but also the location of the Copenhagen, Stockholm, and Oslo city halls showed the eternal longing of the northerner for southern climes. Copenhagen's winning entry reflected the council's image of the city, inspired by medieval European urban history – solid, wealthy, and looking forward to future growth. Stockholm and Oslo's city halls are also "Mediterranean buildings," comparable to the public buildings of Italian city-states. These port cities saw themselves as being a "new Venice of the North." The tower, the strongest medieval European element of communicating civic power, was the signature of the city halls in Copenhagen, Stockholm, and Oslo. In Italian towns the tower was a manifestation of civic protection against landlords, belligerent nobles, and other undesirables.[38] At the end of the nineteenth century it was transformed into a symbol of bourgeois pride and self-esteem, elevated above the urban horizon and welcoming visitors. In Copenhagen the public followed the building of the 350-foot tower with great enthusiasm. In Stockholm, Östberg devoted most of his time to planning the tower. In Oslo, the tower motif was modernized from a single tower to a skyscraper with two high sections on each side of the building. Still, the asymmetry of the towers (the clock in the eastern tower and the astronomical clock in the western tower) suggests medieval sources.[39]

The artworks on the façades were central tools of communication; they combined both local and European tradition. The main idea was to depict the intellectual culture of the city. In Copenhagen, detailed decoration around the main doorways of the façade underlined the value of national flora and fauna, beloved motifs in the National Romantic style. In Stockholm, the classical Greek gods Bacchus and Mars were placed as statues on the northern façade and important figures of the Arts (Painting – Sculpture – Music – Architecture) were located on the southern façade. A Civic Tree, an oak, was planted in the Civic Courtyard. In Oslo the city's emblem, the swan, is repeated as a motif. The four seasons, and sea horses, symbolizing the maritime nature of the city, were prominent themes in the façade decoration.[40]

In Copenhagen, "urban work" was symbolized by the guards of the city; six watchmen, representing the feudal police, flank the flagpole on top of the roof of the front building. The eastern façade of Stockholm city hall was decorated with 23 gilded figures that depict the different professions important to the city's history. In the Civic Courtyard both statesmen and local politicians were represented, from King Gustav Vasa, to the first elected chairman of the city council, Sigurd von Friesen. In Oslo the themes of the common people and everyday urban life were developed further with a series of sculptures on the façade depicting forest workers, fishermen, and a builder. Statues and stone engravings of everyday life, including the corner relief *Albertine*, portraying two men and a prostitute, are located all around the building.[41]

The communicative message of these city halls was meant to be seen in the iconographical elements of the façade: urban virtues, local legends, and town emblems, allegorical figures symbolizing ancient virtues, gods and goddesses, as well as patrons and great men of the city and state.[42] Such imagery in the city hall façades attempted to unite the city and the community of each capital. Other themes of the city halls' decorative program were nature (the sea in all three cases), animals, flora, Christian symbols and people (mother and child motif), as well as Nordic and Viking mythology and urban folklore. The written word, too, played an important role in the buildings' architecture in the form of names, proverbs, and folk songs (Figure 3.6).[43]

Finally, the most important element of the planning of the city halls was the accessibility to the building. The best of classical European city halls front onto an open square and communicate intimately with the urban environment. In Copenhagen, the location of the city hall is the most urban and central of the five and the city hall deals more directly with the street life of the city. The *Rådhuspladsen* (the Town Hall Square) is one of the busiest meeting points in Copenhagen, an urban place for citizens and tourists, with many hotels, shops, cafés, and restaurants nearby. In Stockholm, Östberg's city hall was meant to be

Figure 3.6
The entrance façade of Oslo Town Hall. *Yggdrasilfriesen* in the Civic Courtyard symbolizes the ancient virtues of the nation.
Source: *The Oslo City Hall*, 1953.

viewed from a distance. It is clearly a monumental, independent work of art, and thus less accessible than the old city hall in the medieval Old Town of Stockholm. It was planned to be separate from the crowded center of the city, and to be viewed from the sea or from the city. No public space was planned in front of the building – on the contrary, heavy traffic passes the building, being close to the main railway station. In Copenhagen and Stockholm, the open inner space, a courtyard (*Borgargård*) in the city hall, was planned to be a castle-like courtyard rather than an open, urban public space.[44]

In Oslo, a bird's-eye view of the city reveals that the open waterside location puts the city hall, the royal palace, the bourse and the parliament building – traditional symbols of the capital city – all close to one another, with a clear communicative idea behind the arrangement. The setting of the building is somewhat different to that in Copenhagen and Stockholm; it derives its monumentality by pulling itself away from the most central parts of the city, but it communicates with the harbor area and creates its own spaces for urban participation, walking, and entertainment.⁴⁵ A monumental and symmetrical, semi-circular square (*Fridtjof Nansens plass*) was planned on the city-side of the city hall and the harbor area reshaped as a monumental park area. These open places on both sides of the city hall resembled medieval Italian urban and public piazzas and have been used as central political space for local and national gatherings.⁴⁶

In Helsinki the site of the former hotel and new "hotel," specifically City Hall, had dual connotation. In 1911 the wish was to ensure that the place remained in the heart of the city center though the city was in practice expanding in northward, westward, and eastward directions. The new city hall compound was to be designed in-between the main Senate Square and old Market Place and South Harbour; the Square stands for national government and political manifestation in the same way as the Market Place stood for commerce and seafaring. However, the main entrance to the City Hall was on the side of the Market Place.⁴⁷ In Reykjavik the proximity of the lake and its surrounding natural environment has greatly influenced the quality of the building. A small pond was created at the corner of Tjarnargata and Vonarstraeti, fronted by a moss-grown wall that underlines the proximity and interaction of the City Hall and the lake. The narrow frontal area and opening towards the street does not allow any public gatherings in front of the edifice.

The planners' particular admiration for Italian and German cities is seen in how the building became part of everyday urban life. In Copenhagen, Oslo and Helsinki an essential part of the building's identity is its relationship to the public space fronting city hall. The area is experienced as being cohesive and strong, both due to its connection to the urban landscape and in its everyday urban use. This communication takes place in the form of public and private traffic and pedestrian exploit. The square is frequently used for specific political demonstrations and cultural celebrations.

In Helsinki the market place area had gained new importance already in the early years of the twentieth century, and its transition towards a central urban element was sealed with the competition of some splendid business headquarters, Esplanade Park, and the city's first fountain statue of *Havis Amanda*. The spot had become more urbanized and more suitable for pedestrians. Today, the City Hall and the Market Place create one of the main touristic images of the city and a popular meeting place for locals and visitors. In Oslo the *Rådhusplassen* links the City Hall to the maritime image, but in front of the main entrance of the City Hall is the urban Fridtjof Nansen's Square, a traffic line and a collective and political meeting place of Oslo people. The square is surrounded on the north side by office buildings shaped as a circle, created at the same time as the City Hall. The square's name invokes the Norwegian explorer, scientist, and diplomat Fridtjof Nansen, a figure of national pride.

In Copenhagen the City Hall Square (*Rådhuspladsen*) is a successful public square in the center of the city (Figure 3.7). Due to its large size, its central location

Figure 3.7
Reykjavik's modern City Hall communicates both with the urban water element, and forms a central part of the city's central walking route.
Source: City of Reykjavik.

and its affiliation with the City Hall, it is a popular venue for a variety of events, celebrations, and demonstrations. It is often used as a central datum for measuring distances from Copenhagen. This commercial and political spot is linked to the eighteenth-century royal city by the popular pedestrian street Strøget. H. C. Andersens Boulevard, Copenhagen's most heavily trafficked street, and Vester Voldgade passes the square on each side of the City Hall. Notable buildings around the square include Palace Hotel and Politikens Hus, the headquarters of the national daily *Politiken*, and Industriens Hus, the headquarters of Danish industry.

In Stockholm and Reykjavik the specific character of the City Hall is marked by the formal relationship between the building and the water. In Stockholm, there is no space in front of the City Hall for public gatherings; inside, the great halls are frequently used for local, academic, national, and royal celebrations, most popular of these being the international Nobel Price Gala Dinner. Immediately after its construction, Stockholm's City Hall became a symbol of the city, a postcard motif admired from afar as a monumental work of art. Reykjavik presents a contrary scenario. As its architect noted, "[t]he City Hall is a touch-plate between the water and the city and shares in their interaction. It extends beyond its physical boundary along the banks of the Lake as a continuation of the building."[48]

CIVIC CENTER OR MONUMENTAL WORK OF ART?

The central purpose of a modern city hall is administration. The building's core is shaped by the council offices for administration and governance, and this part is usually closed to outsiders. All Scandinavian city halls have two main sections for open or semi-open communication with citizens – the spaces for meetings and state rooms for receptions and banqueting. In-between is the third space, the civic hall, planned to accommodate great crowds of people on ceremonial and political occasions. It is here that civic expression and a desire for monumentality come together.

The main civic space inside the building in Copenhagen is the Civic Hall (*Rådhushallen*) and in Stockholm the Blue Hall (*Blåa Hallen*). The ambitious, monumental, ceremonial main hall in Oslo, *Rådhushallen*, on the first floor, is the heart of the building. All three spaces welcome visitors. These regular-shaped grand main halls interweave ornaments, sculpture, paintings, and decorative elements, emanating civic pride. In Reykjavik the ground floor of the building is organized around the walking routes between the West and the town center and continued via a bridge to the theatre Idno. Formed as it is, the ground floor is in effect a direct extension of the street. As the official introduction to the City Hall says, "this space enables the city authorities to practice their role as an informing source and stimulators of cultural activities within the City."[49] On the ground floor citizens can find a place to relax close to the lake, study the typographical model of Iceland, or simply mingle, socialize, and have a cup of coffee. In Helsinki the main entrance hall is open to the public as a conventional exhibition and information space.[50]

In an iconographic sense, these halls represent the urban past. The materials for the façade of the Copenhagen Civic Hall come from all around Denmark. This collection of national materials was used to create a Mediterranean piazza, with façades, balconies, open gateways, and *loggias*. In this Italian hall, civic histories are told. Busts of famous Danes are placed here, including sculptor Bertel Thorvaldsen, an honorary citizen of Copenhagen, the writer Hans Christian Andersen, the nuclear physicist Niels Bohr, winner of the Nobel Prize, and architect Martin Nyrop. A line of inscription encircles the room, describing the main events in the history of Copenhagen. The hall is used as a polling station during municipal and parliamentary elections. It is also used for official celebrations, exhibitions, concerts, and receptions hosted by the city council.[51]

The Blue Hall in Stockholm is regular in form and is the biggest space in the building (Figure 3.8). It is called "blue" although it is a room of red brick. The floor and the stairs are of Kolmråden white marble. The unpainted red brick, "something quintessentially Swedish," was considered by the architect to be more suitable than marble. Blue has national connotations, blue being the color of the Swedish flag. This hall was inspired by Italian urban architecture in the same manner as the hall in Copenhagen. Both have balconies, open walkways (*loggias*) and monumental staircases. On the rooftop terrace of the Blue Hall there is a bust of the architect Östberg, portrayed as a proud local artist holding the first version of the City Hall in his hands.[52]

In Oslo City Hall one enters straight into the Main Hall, which combines the functions of civic hall and banqueting hall. It is monumental space, in 1950 one of the biggest civic halls in Europe (38m x 31m). As the City Hall of Oslo is seen as "hele nasjonens storsue" (the monumental home of the whole nation), this space combines both civic and national elements. The main flooring material, marble, is rich in ornamentation and stairs placed along the long wall indicate the influence of the country's former capital, Stockholm. Although the Italian elements are evident (staircase, balconies) the Main Hall's decoration tells the story of Norway's national past.[53]

City Halls and Civic Materialism

Figure 3.8
The Blue Hall (Blåa hallen) in Stockholm City Hall, with its arcades, represent a courtyard. It derives its name from the architect's original design. Source: *Stockholms stadshus vid dess invigning sommarafton 1923*.

In all city halls, the council offices and banqueting floors are reached by monumental staircases. According to the European tradition, the true wealth and civic pride of a city was to be seen in its banqueting halls. In Copenhagen the Banqueting Hall communicates with the same interior design as the Council Chamber, with a heavy ceiling and white walls. Nyrop's ideas came from the ballrooms of Renaissance, a "period of joy and festivities."[54] On the wall facing the Town Hall Square there is an inscription commemorating "a splendid period when not only Greenland and the Faroe Islands, but also Iceland and the former Danish West Indies (The Virgin Islands) considered Copenhagen capital of the realm."

In Stockholm the Golden Hall (*Gyllene Salen*) is the effective climax of the communicative function of the city hall: a grand space combining the local and the national to form the history of the capital city. It is covered with gold mosaic tiles inspired by Sicilian church interiors and the Byzantine tradition. The north-facing main wall is dominated by a huge image of the Queen of Mälaren holding her crown and sceptre, while the midsummer sun shines on her. The most important city buildings are on her lap, and she receives praise from the representatives of the regions of Sweden. The south wall is dedicated to the history of the city, with pictorial representations from medieval times to the modern day. Episodes from the nation's history are represented in the window niches, starting with Bishop Ansgar christening the Swedes at Birka around 830CE, and continuing with monarchs such as Magnus Ladulås, Erik XIV, Queen Christina, and Gustav III. Above this history lesson are representations of the seven virtues: faith, hope, charity, prudence, justice, fortitude, and temperance, and the seven ages of man, from the cradle to the grave. Seven doors lead from the hall to the balcony. The pictorial illustrations on the eastern wall are dedicated to culture and the arts, nature, and engineering.

In Oslo the equivalent of the Golden Hall is the *Det Lange Galleriet* (Long Gallery). Close aesthetic allusions to Florence are evident, such as the colorful ceramic relief work. In Oslo city hall, themes from everyday life are emphasized. Gender equality, industrialization, and the presence of the working class were new features in local politics. The representation of contemporary political history is another novelty in the city hall of Oslo. The large murals in the Civic Hall illustrate the history of Norway, its political development, its economy and commerce, and its mythology and influential personalities. The main fresco is named *Work–Administration–Festivities*, and is clearly influenced by the nationalist spirit of the post-war era. It is thus more modern, political, and impressionistic than the paintings in Copenhagen and Stockholm.

CONCLUSION

City halls in Scandinavian countries are central elements in understanding how bourgeois, liberal, and the soon-to-be democratic and modernist messages became visible in these capital cities. The buildings were expressions of political, social, and cultural conditions, and the changes in these conditions, specifically the effort to bring the working classes within the fold of bourgeois values. The city hall became a tool in the larger nation-building project; its architects required to help construct a national identity as well as facilitate the necessities of municipal administration. The particularities of topography, urban planning, and milieu became the material for a larger historical and geographical claim that presented itself as civic virtue. The decorative programs of the city halls in particular, sought to assert the historicity of the nation and its capital city. Recourse to history enabled the architects to interpret the source and nature of municipal pride, and urban historians were needed to tell this story. City hall communicated with, and even manipulated, citizens, as the jubilee publications and inauguration ceremonies show, to bring about their participation in city building as nation building. City hall architecture in Scandinavian capitals must in this sense be seen as a narrative element in the townscape, one in which the story of the nation-state became deeply intertwined with the municipal self-presentation of the city itself.

NOTES

1. During the reign of Gustav Vasa (1523–60) the church was turned into a national institution, the crown confiscated its estates and the Protestant Reformation was introduced in several stages. At the same time the administration was organized along German lines, and power was concentrated in the hands of the king. The position of the crown was strengthened further in 1544 when a hereditary monarchy was introduced. All this is considered in Swedish historiography to be the founding of modern Sweden.
2. A detailed description of the celebrations is *Stockholms stadshus vid dess invigning sommarafton 1923* (Stockholm: AB Gunnar Tisells Tekniska Förlag, 1923), 313–39. See also Swedish newspapers of the day June 25, 1923 (*Svenska Dagbladet, Dagens Nyheter, Stockholms Tidningen*). There is a vast literature on the City Hall of Stockholm, which still is a central tourist attraction, with daily guided tours and a special city hall shop. See for example Elias Cornell and Ivar Sviestins, *Stockholm Town Hall* (Stockholm: Byggförlaget, 1992); Martin Wickman, *The Stockholm City Hall*, (Stockholm: Sellin & Partner, 1993); Henrik Eklund, *Ur Stadshusets historia 1901–1923* (Stockholm: Stockholms stadsmuseum, 2003).
3. To celebrate the 1000th anniversary of the city of Oslo (before 1924: Christiania) a monumental book of the City Hall was published: Ulf Gronvold, Nils Anker, and Gunnar Sorensen, *Det store loftet. Rådhuset i Oslo* (Oslo: Oslo kommune, 2000). See also: *The Oslo City Hall* (Oslo: City of Oslo, 1953) and Mari Lending, ed., *Rådhus som monument* (Oslo: Norsk Form, 2001). The two main books on the Town Hall of Copenhagen are Francis Beckett, *Kjobenhavns Raadhus* (Kobenhavn: F. Hendriksen, 1908) and Ida Haugsted and Hakon Lund, *Kobenhavs Rådshus* (Kobenhavn: Bøger & Kuriosa, 1996).
4. Laura Kolbe and Pekka Puhakka, *Helsinki City Hall. History and Fine Food* (Helsinki: Otava Publishing Company Ltd, 2008), 50–5.
5. Peter Armansson, *The City Hall of Reykjavik*, (Reykjavik: Reykjavikurborg, 2004), 1–2.
6. Leonardo Benevolo, *The European City* (Oxford: Blackwell, 1993), 160–69, Niel Kent, *The Soul of the North: A Social, Architectural and Cultural History of the Nordic Countries, 1700–1940* (London: Reaction Books, 2000) discusses the specific aspects of cultural development in Scandinavia.
7. Denmark and Norway formed a Union 1380–1814, Sweden and Norway in 1814–1905. Finland was part of Sweden from medieval times until 1809. In June 1905 the Norwegians declared the Union dissolved. The Grand Duchy of Finland, as a part of the Russian Empire from 1809, became independent in December 1917, as a part of the Russian Revolution. Ulf Östergaard, "The geopolitcs of Nordic identity – from composite states to nation states," in Øysten Sørensen and Bo Stråth, ed., *The Cultural Construction of Norden* (Oslo: Scandinavian University Press, 1997), 20–30.
8. This aspect is to be seen in the popular presentations of the city halls in today's tourists' reading, promoting and giving tips on "what to see" – places of interest in urban areas. In researching this article, the following websites were all accessed on May 27, 2007. For Copenhagen, the story of the city hall is told, for example, at http://travel.yahoo.com/p-travelguide-2773855-kobenhavns_radhus_copenhagen-i. In Stockholm the city's official website praises the city hall at http://www.stockholm.se/Extern/Templates/Page.aspx?id=115225. For Oslo's part we may read http://www.answers.com/topic/oslo-city-hall. These websites are also, respectively, the sources of the three quotations presented here (26 III 2012).
9. A good general survey on the new middle class groups is Jürgen Kocka (Hg.) *Bürger und Bürgerlichkeit im 19. Jahrhundert* (Göttingen: Vandenhoeck & Ruprecht, 1987). See even contemporary literature, Peter Ashley, *Local and Central Government. A Comparative Study of England. France, Prussia, and the United States* (Hong Kong: Forgotten Books,

2013; original work published in London, 1906), 1–2, "in all European nations, whatever may have been the previous course of their constitutional history, the persistent and rapid growth of the functions of the state, and the constant assumption of new and onerous duties and responsibilities in the last century, have rendered some attempts at decentralisation and some grants of self-government absolutely necessary, if the national administrations is to be carried on with success" and John A. Fairlie, *Essays in Municipal Administration* (New York: Macmillan, 1908), 2–3, "This increase in urban communities and urban population has meant much more than a corresponding increase in the work and importance of municipal government …; it has brought about new conditions which demanded the exercise of new functions to make life in the cities even as satisfactory as life in the country."

10 Andreas Sävström and Niels Andrén, "Det folkliga självstyret," in *Nordisk samhörighet en realitet*, (Stockholm: Åhlen & Söners Förlag, 1946), 59, 76.

11 *Kommunalförvaltningen i Norden 2000. En rapport om kommunalförvaltning i olika nordiska länder.* Finlands Kommunförbund (Helsingfors: Finland Kommunalförbud, 2000), 5–10. A general presentation is Jan Kanstrup and Steen Ousager, ed., *Kommunal opgavelosning 1842* (Odense: Odense University Press, 1990). Historical contribution: C. G. Hammarskjöld, *Bidrag till tolkning af K. Förordningarne den 21 mars 1862 om kommunalstyrelse på landet och i stad samt om kyrkostämma med ledning af prejudikat* (Stockholm: Norstedt, 1888).

12 *Stockholms stadshus vid dess invigning*, 334.

13 Lars Nilsson, *Staden på vattnet, del II* (Stockholm: Stockholmia förlag, 2002), 198–206; Jan Eivind Myhre, *Oslo bys historie fra 1814 til 1900, Bd. 3*, (Oslo: Cappelen, 1990), 285–9; Synnove Veinan Hellerud and Jan Messel, *Oslo – A Thousand-Year History* (Oslo: Aschehoug, 2000), 14–16; and Matti Klinge and Laura Kolbe, *Helsinki – The Daughter of the Baltic Sea* (Helsinki: Otava, 2007), 55–65 analyze the central elements of urban growth in Nordic capital cities. These elements are the explosive growth, financial ascendance, as well as city's geographical location in the country, being central in all ways. This made the capital city a midpoint of social and cultural activities.

14 Anthony Sutcliffe, *Towards the Planned City* (Oxford, Basil Blackwell, 1981), 162–5; Pieter Rietbergen, *Europe, A Cultural History* (London: Routledge, 1998), 352–5. A good general survey on the new middle-class groups is Jürgen Kocka, ed., *Bürger und Bürgerlichkeit im 19. Jahrhunder* (Göttingen, 1987), 38–41 and Simon Gunn and Rachel Bell, *Middle Classes. Their Rise and Sprawl* (London: Routledge, 2002); Graeme Morton, Bourdien de Vries and Robert J. Morris, *Civil Society, Associations and Urban Places. Class, Nation and Culture in Nineteenth-Century Europe* (London: Ashgate, 2006), 2–13. Also see, Tom Ericsson, Jørgen Fink and Jan Eivind Myhre, *The Scandinavian Middle Classes 1840–1940* (Oslo: Oslo University Press, 2004).

15 Peter Aronsson, "Local politics – the invisible political culture," in Sorenson and Strath, eds., *The Cultural Construction*, 174–81. Also Gerd Bloxham Zettersten, *Nordisk perspektiv på arkitetur. Kritisk regionalisering i nordiska snstadtshus 1900–1950* (Stockholm: Arkitektur, 2000), 52-54.

16 Wickman, *The Stockholm City Hall*, 22–3; Bloxham Zettersten, *Nordiskt perspektiv på arkitektur*, 54–5.

17 Beckett, *Kjobenhavns Raadhus*, 221–2; Roosvaal, *Stockholms stadshus*, 334–8; *The Oslo City Hall*, 5–6, Kolbe and Puhakka, *Helsinki City Hall*, 65–71; Armannsson, *The City Hall of Reykjavik*, 2–3.

18 The detailed description of the planning and building process is carefully described in Beckett's and Roosvaal's "jubileumbooks," published already during the first years after the inauguration.

19 Beckett, 221.

20 Wickman, *Stockholm City Hall*, 13–15; Ragnar Östberg, *The Stockholm Town Hall* (Stockholm: P.A. Norstedt, 1929), 15–17; Eklund, *Ur Stadshusets historia 1901–1923* (Stockholm, 2003), 13–24.
21 Östberg, *The Stockholm Town Hall*, 11–12.
22 Wickman, *Stockholm City Hall*, 17–23; Östberg, *The Stockholm Town Hall*, 18–20; Westman started to work with the *rådhuset* plan and Ragnar Östberg with *stadshuset*.
23 Östberg, *The Stockholm Town Hall*, 21–2.
24 *Rådhuset i Oslo*, 83–4, 148–51; Grönvold and alii, *Det store löftet*, 44–5.
25 Kolbe & Puhakka, *Helsinki City Hall*, 46-56.
26 *Kaupungin Leijona-sydän, Stadens leijonhjärta*, in Sinikka Vainio, ed., *The Lionheart of the City* (Helsinki: The City Museum of Helsinki, 1998) describes the history of the old Lion quarter in the heart of Helsinki, which today occupies the city's central administration.
27 Introduction to Reykjavik City Hall, http://www.nat.is/travelguideeng/plofin_city_hall.htm (26 III 2012). The quotation is in http://www.visitreykjavik.is/desktopdefault.aspx/tabid-166/371_read-1395/ (read in 26 III 2012).
28 See note 26.
29 Peder V. Jensen-Klint, "Köpenahvns rådhus, opfört 1893 af arkitekt Martin Nyrop," in *Nordisk Tidskrift för vetenskap, konst och industri* (1903) 293–314; Ragnar Josephson, "Stockholms stadshus," *Ord och Bild*, illustrerad månadskrfit, 30, årgången 1923, 337–51; *Byggekunst*, nr 9–10 (1950), "Oslo Rådhus."
30 Josef Strzygowski, "Indoardisches und Nordisch-Sachliches in Östbergs Bau," in Johnny Roosval, ed., *Stockholms Stadshus vid dess invigning Midsommarafton 1923*, (Stockholm: AB Gunnar Tisells Tekniska Förlag, 1923), 148–57.
31 Barbara Miller Lane, *National Romanticism and Modern Architecture in Germany and the Scandinavian Countries* (New York: Cambridge University Press, 2000), 180–1.
32 Beckett, *Kjobenhavns Raadhus*, 206–8; Roosvaal, *Stockholms stadshus*, 52; *Oslo City Hall*, 5–7.
33 Colin R. Cunningham, *Victorian and Edwardian Town Halls*, 3–7; I. Sármány-Parsons, "Rathausbauten," 100. Many model books on the architecture of public buildings were published during the late nineteenth century. In German speaking areas – relevant to Scandinavian architects – the series *Gebäude für Verwaltungszwecke*, Grundriss-Vorbilder von Gebäuden aller Art: Gebäude für Verwaltungszwecke: Handbuch für Baubehörden, Bauherren, Architekten, Ingenieure, Baumeister, Bauunternehmer, Bauhandwerker und technische Lehranstalten (Leipzig: Baumgärtner's Buchhandlung, 1885) Bd IX, included plans for city halls.
34 Paul Clemens, "Das Stadthaus zu Stockholm und die Europäische Monumentalbauten in alter und neuer Zeit" and Marcel Aubert, "La persistence du type des anciens Hotels de Ville de France dans L'Hotel de Ville de Stockholm, " in Roosvaal, *Stockholms Stadshus;* A. Reinle, *Zeichensprache der Architektur. Symbolen, Darstellung und Brauch in der Baukunst des Mittelalters und der Neuzeit* (Zürich: Verlag fur Architektur Artemis, 1976), 61–8.
35 Sixten Ringbom, *Stone, Style and Truth. The Vogue for Natural Stone in Nordic Architecture 1880–1910* (Vammala: Suomen Muinaismuistoyhdistys, 1987) discusses how the question of the facade material was raised in Nordic countries already during the 1840s. In the 1890s brick and natural stone were the two materials architects preferred; Josephson, "Stadshuset och stadsplanen," 131.
36 Matti Klinge, *Pääkaupunki. Helsinki ja Suomen valtio 1808–1863* (Helsinki: Otava Kustannus, 2012), 101–2.
37 Armannsson, *The City Hall of Reykjavik*, 7.
38 Aino Katermaa-Ottela, *Le casetorri medievali in Roma* (Helsinki: Societas Scientiarum Fennica, 1981), describes how the Italian city towers played an important role in the urban landscape and mentality.

39 Reinle, *Zeichensprache der Architektur*, 183–7; Beckett, *Kjobenhavns Raadhus*, 56–67. Five bells, four small ones for quarter-strokes and one big one for striking the hours, mark the urban time. The bells rang for the first time at New Year 1900. This tradition is now televised nationwide every year. Östberg, *En arkitekts anteckingar*, 99–111, devoted a chapter in his book to analyzing the function and aesthetics of the city hall tower. *Rådhuset i Oslo*, 148–68: in the first building programme of the city hall of Oslo was a wish for a separate tower inspired by the medievalism of Copenhagen and Stockholm. Several drawings during the 1920s show how, due to the rather narrow location, the idea of the tower was reduced and two modern and high elements were linked closely to the building's body.

40 *The Oslo City Hall*, 38–9.

41 Beckett, *Kjobenhavns Raadhus*, 223; Roosvaal, *Stockholms stadshus*, 335–8.

42 In Copenhagen the central element is the coat of arms depicting three towers, an anchor, and a heart. The founding father of the city, Absalon, Bishop of Roskilde and Archbishop of Lund, is represented in the center of the city hall's facade by a gilt statue. According to legend, he founded the city in 1167. By the main door there is a relief inspired by the shape and decoration of medieval cathedrals, with figures from *Byens aeldste Råd* (the old city council) and 25 members of various urban craft guilds. The motto on the building, *Saa er Byn som Borger* (S:B:B), "A city is what its citizens are," is a saying often repeated. It is accompanied by the city coat of arms.

43 Here is not the place to present the artistic programmes, artists and designers of the city halls. The same pattern was repeated in all cities: a committee was established to plan the decorative scheme. Competitions were arranged to find the best artists and designers to realize these programs. All this was done together with the architect. In all cases, the result was the same: city halls became the show rooms for the best local and national art and design. Either the artists were already famous or this work made them immortal at national level. There is not the space here to name all the eminent artists. The decorative scheme is presented in great detail in the books of Beckett, Roosval and Just.

44 Beckett, *Kjobenhavns Raadhus*, 222.

45 See Aronsson, "Local politics – the invisible political culture," 174–81; Zettersten, *Nordisk perspektiv på arkitetur*, 52–4. Communal reforms were seen as an invention of the (liberal) state. This perspective focuses on the role of central government and on the inventiveness of local municipalities.

46 Just, *Rådhuset i Oslo*, 253-62. Josephson, 'Stadshuset och stadsplanen', in Roosvaal, *Stockholms stadshus*, 116-33.

47 Kolbe and Puhakka, *Helsinki City Hall*, 46–8.

48 P. Armannsson, *The City Hall of Reykjavik*, 1.

49 Introduction to Reykjavik City Hall, see http://www.nat.is/travelguideeng/plofin_city_hall.htm (12 I 2013).

50 Wickman, *The Stockholm City Hall*, 109–12; Beckett, *Kjobenhavns Raadhus*, 224; Kolbe and Puhakka, *Helsinki City Hall*, 76–8.

51 Beckett, *Kjobenhavns Raadhus*, 162–9. Nyrop had asked the keeper of the public records, Mr Adolf Ditlev Jorgensen to make a suggestion for these texts, "de vigtigste haendelser i Kjobenhavs Historie." Many sculptural details represent people and animals that were involved in building the city hall.

52 Roosvaal, *Stockholms Stadshus*, 93–6.

53 *The Oslo City Hall*, 12-20. . The main fresco is named *Work – Administration – Festivities* (by H. Sorensen). Many outstanding Norwegian artists participated and later were involved in the decoration of the City hall, like painters Henrik Sörensen and Alf Rolfsen (Main Hall/*Rådhushallen*), Axel Revold (Main Festive Gallery) and Johan Wilhelm Midelfart (Banqueting Hall).

54 Beckett, *Kjobenhavns Raadhus*, 221.

Chapter 4: Rebuilding City Halls in Postwar Germany

Architectural Form and Identity

Jeffry M. Diefendorf

For centuries, the city hall (or Rathaus) has played a central role in defining the character of German cities. City halls were once the focal point of German political life, but there were enormous variations in the degree of independence that cities enjoyed. Some cities, such as Hamburg and Cologne, functioned as free city-states from the Middle Ages into the nineteenth century, whereas others, like Berlin and Munich, were the sites from which monarchies ruled their states. Moreover, as part of its struggle against Napoleon, Prussia – the largest German state and the one which led the unification of Germany in 1871 – first encouraged local political initiatives but then increasingly emphasized self-administration of policies and laws determined elsewhere as opposed to full self-governance in its cities.

The architecture and ornamentation of city halls and the activities they housed embodied the efforts of the citizens to set themselves apart from other dominant secular and religious institutions, such as royal dynasties and the Catholic and Protestant churches. City halls were the sites of local governance or administration and also sites of festivals and rituals that helped construct a sense of collective or shared identity while also legitimizing the authority of those individuals or groups that actually exercised some measure of power in the cities. Sculptures on façades celebrated local notables alongside important dynastic or national figures. The buildings thus linked civic authority with the performance of civic pride.[1]

The bombs and artillery shells that rained down on Germany's cities during World War II destroyed or badly damaged nearly all of the country's city halls. As city residents emerged from the ruins, returned from shelter in the countryside or from prisoner-of-war camps, they longed for the familiarity of old civic buildings, buildings that served as acceptable sites of collective memory. In 1945, the fate of German nationhood was uncertain, and the vast destruction, the total defeat of National Socialism, and the Allied occupation of Germany posed enormous challenges for the cities. The Nazis had taken over local government and put it under the direction of central authorities. The western Allies, however, first allowed a measure of political life to emerge only on the local level, and they sought to encourage democracy in the cities. Two new German states were created in 1949. West Germany was a democratic, federal state; East Germany was a communist, centralized state. How would city halls fit into this changing political and physical landscape? Should they be restored or rebuilt in their prewar forms or should they be built in modern forms? Should they represent the past glories of the cities or should they represent new political practices?[2] Given the urgency of repairing the urban infrastructure and building new housing, should a city give a high priority to reconstructing a historic city hall and providing space for city bureaucrats? If these buildings were to embody local identity, should only local architects be considered qualified to design new city halls or rebuild city halls?

The history of German cities and city halls is so varied and complex that it defies easy generalizations. However, an examination of a few examples of postwar reconstruction can illuminate some of the many issues faced by local authorities and the citizenry. For this purpose it is useful to distinguish between city halls built during the period of the Holy Roman Empire and those built in the nineteenth and early twentieth centuries. During the first half of the twentieth century, including the early postwar years, there was widespread agreement that pre-nineteenth century architectural monuments merited preservation as part of local, national, or European cultural heritage. There was no such agreement about nineteenth-century architecture that had taken historicist forms: neo-Gothic, neo-Renaissance, neo-Baroque, and neo-Classical.[3] Reconstructing these later town halls was thus open to question.

One must not, however, assume that the pre-nineteenth century town halls were in their original condition just before World War II. They had been modified for many reasons. Built for small towns with small governments, they originally provided space for mayors, city councils, and official festive occasions. As the cities and the tasks of running them grew during the industrial age, it became necessary to find more space for city officials. This might mean acquiring neighboring buildings or constructing new ones, and cities did not necessarily find it important to give these office buildings representative forms. Moreover, past disasters such as fires had commonly necessitated rebuilding, and this had often brought changes in the architectural form of the original town halls, something which further complicated decisions about rebuilding after 1945. Only one thing was certain: Nazi symbols, such as swastikas or portraits of Hitler, if still present, had to be removed.

In all cases, the postwar scarcity of funds and building materials meant that it took several years, even decades, before rebuilding the town halls could be completed. The hyperinflation after the war and the bomb damage to local businesses and residences combined to keep city treasuries empty. The currency reform of 1948 and the beginning of the Marshall Plan in that year stimulated the economic recovery of West Germany, but Marshall Aid was not directed toward urban reconstruction. Cities had to rely on their own resources to rebuild their city halls and decide on how to rebuild.

City Halls and Civic Materialism

THE ANCIENT CITY HALL

Aachen

Located close to the borders of both Belgium and the Netherlands, Aachen is a city that chose to rebuild its city hall to evoke, if not perfectly replicate, its medieval form. The city had gained fame twelve centuries earlier as the capital city of Charlemagne's Holy Roman Empire. Charlemagne died in Aachen and was buried in its cathedral. Subsequent emperors received the imperial crown from the pope but were coronated as kings of Germany in Aachen until 1572, when that ceremony was moved to Frankfurt am Main. Aachen's city hall was erected near the cathedral in the mid-fourteenth century.[4] A monumental building in Gothic style with two main floors and towers on either end, its façade was decorated with statues of 30 kings and emperors. Inside, in addition to rooms for city officials, the building boasted a huge (45 by 20 meter) hall (variously called the Reichssaal, Kaisersaal, or Krönungsfestsaal) with a vaulted ceiling used to celebrate royal coronations (Figure 4.1). The city hall and cathedral were Aachen's dominant architectural features and embodied in stone its identity as a place of royal history.

A major fire in 1656 destroyed much of the city and badly damaged the city hall. In rebuilding, the medieval proportions were retained, but the façade and tops of the two towers were given Baroque rather than Gothic form (Figure 4.2). Starting in 1841, and reflecting the romantic interest in the Middle Ages, the city

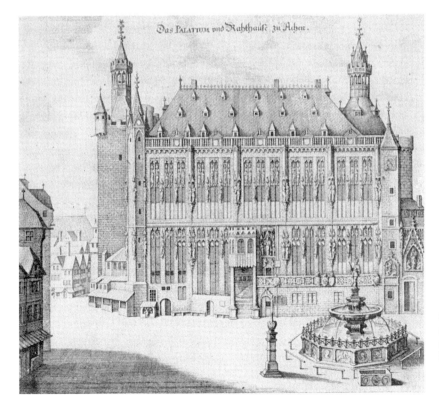

Figure 4.1
Aachen Rathaus, 1647, etching by Matthäus Merian the Elder.

council began a program that lasted 60 years to renovate and re-Gothicize the building. A neo-Gothic façade replaced the Baroque façade on the north side. It featured 44 new statues of various emperors plus a large ensemble of Christ flanked by Charlemagne and Pope Leo III above the main entrance. Sculpted reliefs honored the city's guilds, the liberal arts, various disciplines taught at the polytechnical academy (which later became the city's university), and emblems or coats-of-arms of various royal families, important bishops and abbots, and four other imperial cities – Frankfurt, Nuremberg, Worms, and Cologne. The city also commissioned a series of new frescoes for the Kaisersaal, painted by Alfred Rethel, to depict events in the life of Charlemagne and subsequent emperors. In 1883, another fire destroyed parts of the city hall, including the roof and tops of the towers. The latter were rebuilt with large neo-Gothic spires and the main roof received Gothic form with dormers. The northern Rhineland became part of Prussia in 1815, and Prussia led the establishment of a new German empire in 1871. Aachen honored its Hohenzollern rulers with paintings in the council hall. Under the Nazis, the city added a bust of Hitler and swastika flags but otherwise maintained its existing decorative program.

Bombing raids in July 1943 and in April 1944 brought severe damage to the city hall, destroying the tower tops, much of the roof, and parts of the Kaisersaal. This was an assault on the city's ancient identity, and with Germany's defeat, city officials immediately turned to its reconstruction, but this took many years. On the first floor, the arched vaults and the council hall were rebuilt by 1951. In this room, about 70 percent of the original wood paneling survived and the damaged sections were replicated. The original paintings were put back in place. In the so-called "White Hall," four-fifth of the Baroque decoration was recreated following photographs. On the second floor, a local artist had begun in November 1945 to remove and preserve those Rethel frescoes in the Kaisersaal that had not been totally destroyed, salvaging five of the original eight. The rebuilding of the great

Figure 4.2
Aachen Rathaus 1840, etching by Henry Winkles.

Figure 4.3
Aachen Rathaus, today.

hall was finished in 1957, with a new floor and windows in a simple modern style. Little of the Baroque or nineteenth-century neo-Gothic decoration in the hall was retained, though the Rethel frescoes were reinstalled between 1953 and 1957. Between the mid-1960s and 1982, following the design of a local architect, much of the exterior of the building was renovated, and new tops evoking the Gothic character of the restored building were installed on the towers (Figure 4.3).

This city hall, then, underwent several episodes of destruction and rebuilding over the centuries, but it has remained, along with the cathedral, the dominant building in the city center and one that defines its identity for its citizens and for outsiders. Just as Charlemagne had been both a Frankish king and Roman emperor, this border city sought a way to reclaim its position as a city of note in Europe. Starting in 1950, the city awarded the International Charlemagne Prize for contributions to the culture of Western Europe. This is awarded in a ceremony in the Kaisersaal, with coats of arms representing the old empire, the city itself, and Charlemagne behind the podium. Prize recipients are also heralded before crowds in front of the city hall.

Cologne

In contrast to Aachen, Cologne chose to rebuild with a mixture of old and new. Cologne's city hall evolved over centuries. In the early Middle Ages, Cologne was ruled by an archbishop, and the dominant buildings were Romanesque churches. The great Gothic cathedral, the building that became the city's symbol, was begun in 1248. Work on it continued through the fifteenth century and then mostly stopped, leaving its huge towers unfinished until the mid-nineteenth century. In 1288, the city won its independence from the archbishop at the battle of Worringen, and

Cologne's growing civic spirit took shape in the city hall.[5] The initial building for the city's leaders was constructed in the mid-twelfth century, but this was destroyed by fire and a more impressive two-story structure with a large meeting hall, the Hansasaal, took shape by 1360. In the early fifteenth century, a 180-foot Gothic tower was added on one end, giving the city hall an imposing presence, its silhouette rivaling the unfinished cathedral and the towers of the Romanesque churches. On the city hall square, a two-story loggia in the style of the Renaissance was constructed as a new entry portal in 1569–73. The seventeenth century saw a further addition in late-Renaissance style that later became known as the "Spanish Building." By the 1790s, the original statuary decorating the tower had deteriorated so badly that they were removed. Extensive renovations took place during the second half of the nineteenth century. New statues decorated the tower, but in contrast to Aachen, the eclectic architecture remained intact up until World War II. The bombing raids then destroyed almost all of the city hall except the Renaissance loggia, leaving only fragments of other sections remaining.

Already in July 1945, Hans Vogts, the head of the city historic preservation office, submitted to the mayor a proposal to rebuild the tower, the Hansasaal, the loggia, and a courtyard (the Löwenhof) in their historic forms, but to rebuild the rest of the city hall complex following the precepts of modern architecture. Acting quickly, however, was impossible because of the dire shortages of funds, building materials, and labor. In this city, it was also the case that repairs on the cathedral, the Romanesque churches, and the Gothic Gürzenich meeting hall had priority over the city hall. In 1950, work began on the tower, which Hanna Adenauer, Vogt's successor and niece of former mayor and now Federal chancellor Konrad Adenauer, called "the biggest and most important secular tower [of its kind] in Europe." The design called for a slightly simplified base and top but otherwise the tower was to regain its "historic form" with its five floors with windows.[6]

In 1960, an architectural competition was held for the design of the rest of the city hall complex. Nine local architects and five outsiders were invited to submit proposals to a jury made up mostly of local architects and officials but including a few notable outsiders. The competition announcement stipulated that certain historic spaces, like the Hansasaal, be restored as best possible, and that historic elements that could be salvaged should be incorporated into the rebuilt structure. The east side of the building facing the Alter Markt should reflect the proportions and rhythm of buildings there. On Rathausplatz, the building containing the Hansasaal should be clearly distinct from other wings. Also a "clear distinction" should be made between those parts that were to be "representative" and those that would house administrative offices. Chief officials should be located in the "representative" building because:

> a city hall is a building which, above and beyond all functional needs, should allow the citizenry spiritually to represent itself in the building. In this sense, the authentic representative tasks [of the city hall] must not take the form of conventional facades found on buildings of business.[7]

The winner of the competition was Karl Band, a Cologne architect who had been an active participant in postwar rebuilding.

A dozen years were needed to complete reconstruction. At its inauguration in August 1972, Lord Mayor Theo Burauen declared that the building must represent the citizenry and should not "foreground splendor" but instead "mirror community accomplishments," "aspirations and self-consciousness." It was important to retain as much ancient substance as possible, since the site and building was "a highly visible, undeniable part of Cologne's proper identity" ["unübersehbare, unübergehbare Substanz des eigenen kölnischen Ichs"]. Moreover, he said that "a democratic city hall must be a *space* ... a place for bounteous and wide-ranging encounters, activities, and meetings of the citizens, not just petty, dreary offices of bureaucrats" (Figure 4.4).[8]

That the city hall was a centerpiece of the identity of Cologne's citizens was reinforced by a new program of statuary for the exterior of the tower. The tower and its connections to the city hall were completed in the mid-1970s. The 124 new statues were commissioned from local sculptors and the last mounted in 1995. The statues on the ground floor are of rulers from ancient Rome and the Holy Roman Empire and on the top level are of "patron saints" from the ancient world and Middle Ages, but also Adolf Kolping, the founder of a Catholic charity for workers in the nineteenth century, and Edith Stein, a Jew who converted, became a nun, and was then murdered by the Nazis. The three levels in between contain figures

Figure 4.4
Cologne Rathaus, 2004.

of artists, writers, church leaders, businessmen, and politicians who shaped the city's history. These range from the medieval painter Stefan Lochner to the Nobel-Prize-winning novelist Heinrich Böll, the theologian Meister Eckhart, Joseph Cardinal Frings (cardinal 1942–69), the perfume manufacturer Johann Maria Farina, the inventor of the modern internal combustion engine Nicolaus Otto, the 1848 revolutionary leaders Robert Blum and Karl Marx, and Lord Mayor and Chancellor Konrad Adenauer.[9] Citizens of all religious and political backgrounds could thus find historic figures here with whom they could identify.

Munich

Munich is an interesting case because it was home to both an old and a new city hall, both located on the Marienplatz, the city's main square. The old hall, on the east side of the square, was built in the fifteenth century, and the city government also used the adjacent Thalburgtor tower. Baroque modifications were made in the following two centuries, but then the exterior regained its Gothic facade between 1861 and 1864.[10] Three years later, the city began construction on a large, new town hall on the north side of the square. In Gothic revival style, this building boasted an 85-meter tall tower and a Glockenspiel with life-size figures that, three times daily, reenact a sixteenth-century royal marriage, a joust, and a popular dance. The height of the tower is only 13 meters less than the towers of the nearby Frauenkirche (the Cathedral of Our Lady) and the chief symbol of the city. Construction on the new Rathaus lasted until 1908, but the mayor, town council, and many city officials moved to the new building in 1874. The revolution of 1918 saw the end of Bavaria's Wittelsbach dynasty. Munich was still the capital of Bavaria, but it now had greater responsibilities for administering the large city and surrounding administrative district. In the late 1920s, the city erected a 12-story office building in the southern part of the old city center to house much of the city bureaucracy. Designed by Hermann Leitenstorfer, an architect in the city building offices, this skyscraper was for three decades the only such building in Munich. It was considered an example of the "new architecture" (Neues Bauen) because of its height, flat roof, and lack of decoration on its facades, though Leitenstorfer bowed to the characteristic colors and materials of historic buildings in the old city rather than featuring lots of glass and a visible steel frame.[11]

Both city halls were damaged in the war, the older one most severely, with the tower and southern half of that building having been totally destroyed. The men in charge of planning the city's reconstruction, including Helmut Fischer and Leitenstorfer (now head of the building office), wanted to demolish the old town hall entirely, freeing up that end of the square to provide a smoother flow of traffic. They wanted the city to use the opportunity created by the bombing to rebuild in new and modern rather than in traditional forms. (At the same time, they were also urging that Munich make a break from its close association with National Socialism.) In contrast, Munich's residents vocally favored recreating the old city hall, and in the end they prevailed. The northern part of the old Rathaus was rebuilt between 1952 and 1957, the old tower rebuilt in Gothic form between

City Halls and Civic Materialism

Figure 4.5
Munich Rathaus and Marienplatz, 2006.
Photo: David Iliff.

1971 and 1974. However, the city's mayor, council, and much of its bureaucracy continued to be located in the "new" town hall and office skyscraper, where war damage was repaired without controversy.[12] The neo-Gothic "new" town hall so dominates the main square that visitors and residents seldom notice the much smaller original hall at the end of the square (Figure 4.5).

"NEW" CITY HALLS OF THE NINETEENTH AND TWENTIETH CENTURIES

The cases discussed above illustrate many of the central issues faced in deciding how best to reconstruct the physical presence of city government and administration in cities with very old city halls. These same issues are also evident when we turn to the second category of town halls, the imposing Rathäuser of the nineteenth and early twentieth centuries in cities like Berlin, Hannover, and Stuttgart.

In his book on Rathaus architecture, Martin Damus demonstrated that, during this period, town halls did have a common type as representative of "bourgeois class dominance."[13] The typical nineteenth-century town hall was mostly symmetrical in form (though a clock tower is sometimes off-center or set back) and often located on a "market" square – even though a market was no longer necessarily there – because this site signified the central place of a city. The buildings adapted and elaborated the forms of German Romanesque, late Gothic, and north-German or Flemish Renaissance palace architecture.[14] This architectural historicism sought to derive values from the past rather than breaking from it. There were often richly ornamented windows to identify the main council hall and ceremonial balconies over the main entryways. In the early twentieth century, this type continued, but there were also some adaptations of neo-classical palace forms capped with a dome rather than tower and also some attempts at "'modern' monumentality."[15] Hannover's town hall is the best example of this type.

Ornamental iconography served to connect the citizenry with local traditions, civic ideals, and make the buildings worthy locations for city business. Damus argues that "historical references were indispensable. They guaranteed readability and aimed beyond a historically anchored legitimization of the new city administration and representational buildings to the legitimization of the bourgeois elite's domination of the city" at a time when the bourgeoisie could not contest the power of monarchies.[16] Common historicist models, however, also posed a challenge to the display of local civic authority. Ornamental decoration with clear references to local history was also a way of distinguishing one historicist city hall from another as well as to set the city halls apart from other historicist structures, such as theaters, police stations, or commercial buildings. It also helped "localize" city halls designed by architects from other cities. Most of these city halls were designed and built during the period of the Second Empire (1871–1918), and officials in charge of the decorative programs had to find a balanced way to represent long city histories, respect for more local royal dynasties like the Welfs (or Guelphs) in Hannover or Wittelsbachs in Bavaria, and the Hohenzollern dynasty of Prussia and the new empire.[17]

In her 2009 book on city architecture in the Wilhelmine period, Maiken Umbach complicates the usual picture of traditionalism versus modernism, arguing that the bourgeoisie, in asserting its position in the cities, sought to configure city buildings and public spaces in ways that were simultaneously technically or functionally modern and closely tied to the particular historic milieu of the city. This was a modernism, then, that did not seek a complete break with past forms, as did the international modernism of the Bauhaus and other modernisms of the 1920s which revealed themselves in commercial buildings.[18] Instead, civic values and civic authority could be made visible and anchored to specific central places through historicist or vernacular architecture, and the bourgeoisie could assert its role as the caretaker of collective memory and identity.

In the 1920s, modernist architecture and its emphasis on the primacy of function over form challenged the idea that a distinctive form was suited for civic buildings. As city governance became more identified with bureaucracy rather than an elected council, it was not evident that offices for city bureaucrats should differ from those of office workers in the private economy. Moreover, because cities during the Weimar Republic both lacked resources to erect new civic buildings and placed highest priority on supporting housing construction, very few modernist town halls were built.[19] The Nazis, of course, strongly believed in neo-classical forms for state and party buildings, and they showed relatively little interest in structures that would house city government. After the wartime bombing of German cities had begun, some planners advocated rebuilding in ways that combined modernizing the infrastructure with repairing or reconstructing important historic monuments, including city halls, but in practice the Nazis were more interested in building new cities in the conquered territories in the East. Moreover, preparing for and then fighting the war meant that most Nazi construction projects were put on hold and never realized. The tension between modernism and traditional, historicist architecture re-emerged during postwar reconstruction.

Berlin

Because old Berlin and its surrounding villages grew so rapidly in the nineteenth century, that city saw the construction of several large town halls. The Rotes Rathaus (Figure 4.6) and the Charlottenburger Rathaus provide examples of town halls built in a historicist form that were badly damaged in the bombing and then restored in their prewar form. The Altes Stadthaus is also a good example of a historicist administrative building rebuilt in its prewar form.

It is worth noting that rebuilding the authority of city government in Berlin was extraordinarily complex. Berlin had been the capital of Prussia, then simultaneously capital of the Wilhelmine empire, then of the Third Reich. In 1945 it was divided by the Allies into four sectors which did not match the prewar city districts, and in 1947 the Allies formally abolished the historic state of Prussia. In 1961, the city was physically divided by the building of the Wall. East Berlin functioned as the capital of the DDR, while West Berlin functioned more or less as if a city-state. The East Germans sought to erase symbols of most kinds of prewar

Figure 4.6 Berlin Rotes Rathaus, 2007. Photo: Olbertz.

authority, whether monarchical or Nazi, by demolishing many restorable buildings like the imperial palace and the Reich chancellery. Here the authority of the new socialist state was to be paramount. That was not the case in West Berlin, where the various districts, which had derived from the villages that had made up the city, had their own governmental institutions. It is sometimes forgotten that at the time of the Berlin Blockade (1948–49), one of the most contested issues was the location of Berlin's city government. In 1945 the city had a single city government, located in the Red Town Hall, or Rotes Rathaus, so named for the color of its brick not its politics, which was in the Soviet sector. In 1948, the city government split, with the mayor and other parts of officialdom moving to the undamaged town hall in the district of Schöneberg in West Berlin. The Red Town Hall continued to house city offices for East Berlin, but everyone knew that real authority was not in the hands of the city but the Socialist Unity Party and the central government. By 1969, the symbol of the new East Berlin was not the town hall but the new television tower on Alexanderplatz, with its café and observation deck rising 207 meters and the broadcast antenna 368 meters above the central city, dwarfing the towers of the town hall and churches.

The original town hall of central Berlin had been built around 1300, enlarged in subsequent centuries, and demolished in 1865 for a new building. The style of this building was late Italian Renaissance. Built of red brick, it occupied almost an entire block. There were polygon towers the height of the roof on the corner, large round windows on the middle floors containing rooms for the city parliament and ceremonial functions, and heavy external decoration in terracotta. The central tower rose 74 meters and on its sides were sculptures of the Berlin bear. There were strong differences about whether decoration on the façade and interior should feature the city's history, the various trades and institutions in the city (like the university), dynastic representations, or great events, like the wars of liberation against Napoleon. This process became more complicated with the wars of unification and the creation of the new empire between 1866 and 1871. Top city officials wanted to honor the empire, but the more liberal city assembly preferred to honor the achievements of the citizenry. Finally in 1876–79, a series of 36 reliefs in terracotta were commissioned for the facade and featured the life of the citizens: workers, craftsmen, scientists, artists. Little attention was given to the nation's rulers or wars, and of the latter, the wars of liberation were most favored, although in 1873, gilded bronze statues of Elector Friedrich I and Wilhelm I were installed at the entry to the meeting hall of the city parliament.[20] These honored the rise of Prussia and the newly created empire, but the overall impression made by the building was to celebrate the authority of the city government.

The building was badly damaged in the war. Some interior spaces were quickly repaired for use, but overall reconstruction took place between 1950 and 1958. The prewar external form was recreated, but inside extensive changes were made to what had become more a seat of bureaucracy than representative government. On the square in front, two new bronze sculptures by Fritz Cremer of a man and a woman clearing rubble were added in 1954, presumably to connect city administration with the working class that was celebrated for rebuilding the city.[21] That this connection worked, however, is doubtful. These sculptures were erected shortly after the city's construction workers had sparked a near revolt against the communist regime on June 17, 1953.

The rapid growth of Berlin in the late nineteenth century through the incorporation of adjacent towns and the migration of industries and laborers brought with it an expansion of the city bureaucracy that exceeded the capacity of the Rotes Rathaus. Between 1898 and 1911, the city constructed a new building near the town hall – the Altes Stadthaus – to accommodate around 70 percent of the city's officials, including some of the city police. Designed in an Italianate Renaissance style by the city's building director, Ludwig Hoffmann, this monumental building was intended to represent the authority of the city and featured an 80-meter tall tower topped with a dome and a statue of the goddess Fortuna.

The building was damaged both in the bombings and in the siege of the city by the Soviet army in the last months of the war. The first postwar city government, appointed by the Soviets, moved into another building, because of the damage to both the Stadthaus and Rathaus. Minor repairs were made to the Stadthaus, but major work only began in 1950. When rebuilding was complete in 1955, it was not the city government but the council of ministers of the German Democratic Republic that took occupancy. The authority of the city government of East Berlin, of course, was already vastly diminished. (After the collapse of the GDR in 1989–90, several of the prewar features of the Altes Stadthaus, such as the mansard roof and the statue on the dome, were restored, and several agencies of the united Berlin city government reoccupied the building. Once again it represents civic authority.)[22]

The Rathaus of Charlottenburg, a village only incorporated into Greater Berlin in 1920, is another interesting example. Because Charlottenburg grew from 10,000 inhabitants in the mid-nineteenth century to 180,000 by 1900, its earlier town hall was too small for its governmental needs. A competition for a new building was announced in 1897, with winners among the 52 entries adapting "historicist styles" of the late Gothic and Renaissance. The prize jury declared that the winning entry suggested a "moderate, dignified splendor which symbolizes the fortunate situation of Charlottenburg and the powerful aspirations of its polity."[23] As was typical of this type of Rathaus, there was a symmetrical 70-meter-wide front façade and a clock tower 88 meters tall. In fact, the tower was taller than the cupola of the nearby royal Charlottenburg Palace, much to the irritation of Emperor William II. Above the main entry was a relief sculpture combining the city's coat of arms and an image of Pallas Athena, thus equating Charlottenburg with the ancient home of democracy. Inside there were appropriate spaces for the town council, the mayor, reception halls, and administrative offices.

By the war's end, one-fourth of the building had been totally destroyed by bombing and fire and the rest so badly damaged as to be unusable. Restoration began in May 1945 on a small scale and accelerated after the 1948 currency reform. External rebuilding was completed by 1952, the interior in the next couple of years. The exterior, including the tower, was rebuilt in its original form, as was the case with many internal features. Rebuilding this representative, symbolic structure was clearly very important for both West Berlin and the district of Charlottenburg.

Hannover

Hannover built the largest new neo-classical city hall between 1903 and 1913 (Figure 4.7). Instead of erecting it on the main square in the old city center, this structure was placed in a large park on the edge of the central district, and it dominates the site. The project was spearheaded by Heinrich Tramm, a National Liberal politician who wanted the city hall to embody the history of the city, including its years as the residence of the Welf (or Guelph) dynasty, and also the new German empire.[24] The interior ended up being quite eclectic. The entry to the great hall featured larger-than-life bronze statues of Emperors Wilhelm I and II. Under the windows there were busts of Bismarck and Martin Luther, thus honoring both the creation of the Reich and the Reformation. Of special note, the main meeting hall featured a huge wall painting by the Swiss Jugendstil painter Ferdinand Hodler entitled "Einmütigkeit" (unanimity or concord). Here Tramm took advice from the Jewish avant-garde impressionist painter Max Liebermann of Berlin, who urged breaking from historicism and moving in a more modern direction. The painting, which gave the large meeting hall the name Hodlersaal is 4.75 meters high, 15.17 wide, and portrays Dietrich Arnsborg, the spokesman of the citizenry, leading an avowal to the Reformation in 1533, with more than 60 citizens raising their right hands and arms in agreement. When William II came to the city to celebrate the opening of the building, he supposedly stood speechless

Figure 4.7
Hannover Rathaus, 2005.
Photo: Robert Friebe.

before the painting, and others were critical, though the press was largely supportive. Although hostile to modern art, the Nazis, surprisingly, did not destroy the painting. It was taken down to protect it in 1941 and hence survived, and was reinstalled after the war.[25]

The building was damaged but not destroyed in the bombing. Since the building was still functional, an impoverished city, which faced the enormous task of rebuilding the central city, had to use it even though the building was not much loved.[26] Rudolf Hillebrecht, the chief city planner, disliked its eclectic architecture and pretentiousness and found the layout unsuited for efficient city administration. However, a small city government remained in part of it in 1945, while British occupation officials temporarily took over much of the other space. In 1946, the new state government moved in for a year. Repairs of bomb damage on the exterior continued throughout the 1950s, with interior restorations continuing through the 1980s. Meanwhile, in the 1950s, in order to house city bureaucrats, Hillebrecht oversaw the construction of a large office building in a modern style next to the city hall.

Stuttgart

Finally, Stuttgart's postwar city hall is a prime example of a city deciding not to rebuild a historicist structure of the nineteenth century in favor of a modern design. That city's small fifteenth-century city hall had been replaced after an 1884 competition that drew 202 entries from across Germany (Figure 4.8). The winning entry came from a Berlin firm and featured a massive building in mixed neo-Gothic, neo-Renaissance style, with a 68-meter tall clock tower, and a 58-meter wide front façade on the market square.[27] Completed in 1905, its tower was 7 meters taller than the main tower of the Stiftskirche, the chief Protestant church in the city center, and taller than any royal buildings, thereby giving civic authority a predominant place in the city.

Figure 4.8
Stuttgart Rathaus Marktplatz, 1907.

The bombing badly damaged the town hall, though its tower remained mostly unharmed. The side wings, which housed the city administrative offices, were quickly rebuilt. In July 1949, the city council decided to rebuild the front section of the town hall and staged a design competition, limited to architects from the Stuttgart area and with the city's forceful Lord Mayor Arnulf Klett chairing the jury. In 1952 Mayor Klett got the town council to decide upon a design tending toward the modern, which he felt was the appropriate form to represent both the city and the new democracy.[28] The new building, completed in 1956, was clad in whitish limestone, asymmetrical in layout, with large, square, standardized windows and a starkly rectangular tower that replaced the old tower but retained some of its main features – a clock, sundial, Glockenspiel, and balcony over the main entrance (Figure 4.9).

The city's official gazette described the new town hall in these terms: "forever it will be clear that this building is not a place where orders are issued but a place for counsel, that no authority that issues decrees is housed here but instead citizens among citizens and for citizens propose, discuss, persuade, and decide."[29] In his study of Stuttgart's 1950s architecture, Gilbert Lupfer rightly argues that the new "tower embodied the traditional claims on power and self-consciousness of the citizenry." Moreover, the building was "an authentic expression of the times and its desire to conceal the deep political, cultural, and moral shock [of the Nazi era and war] behind an orderly facade."[30] Civic authority in Stuttgart was anchored in a modern building of monumental solidity.

Figure 4.9
Stuttgart Rathaus, 2006.
Photo: Joachim Köhler.

CONCLUSION

Whatever their architectural form, their large size and central location give German city halls and administrative buildings a prominent place in the urban landscape. Rebuilding after World War II was an urgent task because these buildings were important for the identity of the citizenry at a time when national identity was uncertain. In what became West Germany, city halls also were the location for a revival of political life on a democratic basis and a repudiation of the legacy of Nazism. Reconstruction, however, was challenging, and not only because of the degree of destruction and poor economic conditions immediately after the war. Decisions varied from city to city on whether to rebuild the city halls in their prewar form, whether to retain alterations made during previous eras, how to salvage and incorporate surviving historic remains, what sort of decorative sculptural or pictoral program to follow, and what events and people from past periods should be represented. Similar decisions had been made in previous centuries when rebuilding after earlier fires, when renovations were required because the buildings had deteriorated over time, or when the city halls had become too small and new space was needed.

In the twenty-first century the city halls are the sites where local democracy takes place, where local civic authority is exercised, and where important events can be celebrated. As the demographic makeup of German cities change, however, the extent to which city halls still shape local identity and function as primary sites of memory is uncertain. Large immigrant populations in cities like Berlin, Cologne, and Stuttgart have no particular connections with the glories of the ancient Holy Roman Empire, the rise of Prussia or other German states, the short-lived Second Empire, or the elites that first built and then reconstructed the city halls. Since many Germans themselves, especially in the immediate postwar period, often sought to think of 1945 as a "zero-hour" when connections with the recent past ceased and the country started over, there are surely many Germans who view the rebuilt city halls as both objects for tourists and offices of bureaucrats rather than vital markers of local identity. Cities change over time – demographically, culturally, and economically – and the perception of the city halls will undoubtedly change as well.

NOTES

1. On performing city pride, see Adelheid von Saldern, "Einleitung," in Adelheid von Saldern, ed., *Inszenierter Stolz. Stadtrepräsentation in drei deutschen Gesellschaften (1935–1975)*, (Stuttgart: Franz Steiner Verlag, 2005), 11.
2. One attempt to determine similarities and differences between the two German states is Ute Fendel's, *Wiederaufbau nach dem 2. Weltkrieg in Deutschland Ost und West: ein Vergleich anhand kommunaler Repräsentativbauten*. (Dissertation, Rheinische Friedrich-Wilhelms-Universität, Bonn, 1996). Fendel examines examples of city halls, concert halls, and cultural buildings, detailing the results of architectural or bureaucratic decisions but not probing deeply into the reasons for those decisions.

3 For historic preservation in Germany, see Jeffry M. Diefendorf, *In the Wake of War. The Reconstruction of German Cities after World War II* (New York: Oxford University Press, 1993), chapter 4, and Rudy Koshar, *Germany's Transient Pasts. Preservation and National Memory in the Twentieth Century* (Chapel Hill: University of North Carolina Press, 1998).
4 The following material has been drawn from Georg K. Heig and Jürgen Linden, *Vom Kaiserglanz zur Bürgerfreiheit. Das Aachener Rathaus – ein Ort Geschichtlicher Erinnerung* (Aachen: Shaker Verlag, 2006). See also Mathilde Röntgen, "Das gotische Rathaus zu Aachen," in *Das alte Aachen, seine zerstörung und sein Wiederaufbau*, Aachener Beiträge für Baugeschichte und Heimatkunst (Aachen: Aachener Geschichtsvereins, 1953), vol. 3.
5 For the history of the city hall, see the essays in Peter Fuchs, ed., *Das Rathaus zu Köln. Geschichte, Gebäude, Gestalten*, 2nd edition (Cologne: Kreven Verlag, 1994).
6 Hanna Adenauer, "Das Schicksal des Kölner Rathauses vor, während und nach dem Zweiten Weltkrieg," in Fuchs, ed., *Das Rathaus zu Köln*, 133–5.
7 Heinz Kleppe, "Ideenwettbewerb für den Wiederaufbau des Rathauses," in Fuchs, ed., *Das Rathaus zu Köln*, 162–3. The outsiders included the famed Alvar Aalto of Helsinki, Arne Jacobsen of Copenhagen, H. M. Kraaijvanger of Rotterdam, Ernst Zinsser of Hannover, and Sepp Ruf of Munich. Bartmann and Aalto declined to participate because of other commitments. The jury was chaired by Hannover's chief planner, Rudolf Hillebrecht.
8 Theo Burauen, "Wieder ein Haus der Bürger," in Fuchs, ed., *Das Rathaus zu Köln*, 210–11.
9 Hiltrud Kier, Bernd Ernsting, Ulrich Krings, eds., *Köln, der Ratsturm: seine Geschichte und sein Figurenprogramm* (Cologne: J. P. Bachem, 1996). The figures can also be viewed at http://de.wikipedia.org/wiki/Liste_der_K%C3%B6lner_Ratsturmfiguren (accessed June 2011).
10 Hartwig Beseler and Niels Gutschow, *Kriegsschicksale Deutscher Architektur. Verluste–Schäden–Wiederaufbau* (Neumünster: Karl Wachholtz Verlag, 1988), vol. 2, 1396–7.
11 Bayerischer Architekten- und Ingenieur-Verband, *München und seine Bauten nach 1912* (Munich: Bruckmann, 1984), 431.
12 See Diefendorf, *In the Wake of War*, 92–3, and Nina A. Krieg, "München leuchtend und ausgebrannt … Denkmalphlege und Wiederaufbau in den Nachkriegsjahren," in *Trümmerzeit in Münichen. Kultur und Gesellschaft einer deutschen Großstadt im Aufbruch 1945–49*), ed. Friedrich Prinz (Munich: Verlag C. H. Beck, 1984), 77–8. See also Gavriel Rosenfeld, *Munich and Memory: Architecture, Monuments, and the Legacy of the Third Reich* (Berkeley: University of California Press, 2000), chapter 2.
13 Martin Damus. *Das Rathaus. Architektur- und Sozialgeschichte von der Gründerzeit zur Postmoderne. Schwerpunkt: Rathausbau 1945–1986 in der Bundesrepublik Deutschland* (Berlin: Gebr. Mann Verlag, 1988), 24.
14 German historicism rejected the idea that civic buildings must be based on the classical models of ancient Greece. Roman classicism was another matter, and Byzantine domes could likewise serve as models.
15 Ibid., 46, 61ff.
16 Ibid., 30.
17 For essays on a number of cities during this period, see Ekkehard Mai, Jürgen Paul, and Stephan Waetzoldt, *Das Rathaus im Kaiserreich: kunstpolitische Aspekte einer Bauaufgabe des 19. Jahrhunderts* (Berlin: Gebr. Mann Verlag, 1982).
18 Maiken Umbach, *German Cities and Bourgeois Modernism, 1890–1924* (Oxford: Oxford University Press, 2009). Umbach devotes considerable attention to the city hall of Hamburg.
19 For a study of state-sponsored architecture during Weimar, see Christian Welzbacher, *Die Staatsarchitektur der Weimarer Republik* (Berlin: Lukas Verlag, 2006.)

20 Christa Schreiber, "Das Berlinische Rathaus–Versuch einer Entstehungs- und Ideengeschichte," in Mai, Paul, and Waetzoldt, *Das Rathaus im Kaiserreich*, 115–21, 135–6.
21 *Die Bau- und Kunstdenkmale in der DDR. Hauptstadt Berlin*, ed. Heinrich Trost, and Kollektiv der Abteilung Forschung, Institut für Denkmalpflege der DDR (Munich: C. H. Beck, 1983), vol. 1, 30–5.
22 See Wolfgang Schäche, ed., *Das Stadthaus. Geschichte, Bestand und Wandel eines Baudenkmals* (Berlin: Jovis Verlag, 2000.) There is a good description of the history of this building at http://de.wikipedia.org,wiki/Altes_Stadthaus, accessed November 21, 2010.
23 Irmgard Wirth, *Die Bauwerke und Kunstdenkmäler von Berlin. Stadt und Bezirk Charlottenburg* (Berlin: Gebr. Mann, 1961), vol 2, part 2, *Stadt und Bezirk. Textband und Tafelband of Bauwerke*, 140. See also the official description of the building by Gisela Scholtze, "Die drei Rathäuser der Stadt Charlottenburg," (1986, revised 2006 by Monika Thiemen [Bezirksbürgermeisterin] and Karl-Heinz Metzger [Pressesprecher], accessed at: http://www.berlin.de/ba-charlottenburg-wilmersdorf/bezirk/lexikon/textscholtze.html).
24 Charlotte Kranz-Michaelis, "Das Neue Rathaus Hannovers–ein Zeugnis der 'Ära Tramm,'" in Mai, Paul, and Waetzoldt, *Das Rathaus im Kaiserreich*.
25 Wolfgang Steinweg, *Das Rathaus in Hannover. Von der Kaiserzeit bis in die Gegenwart* (Hannover: Schlütersche Verlagsanstalt, 1988), 91–4.
26 Ibid., 7. Steinweg calls it "an architectural fossil."
27 See Bernhard Sterra, *Das Stuttgarter Stadtzentrum im Aufbau: Architektur und Statplanung, 1945 bis 1960,* Stuttgarter Studien (Stuttgart: Silberburg-Verlag, 1991), vol. 2, 243–4.
28 Paul Sauer, *Arnulf Klett: ein Leben für Stuttgart* (Gerlingen: Bleicher, 2001), 150, and Sterra, 298. It is interesting that the new town hall did not become the primary symbol of the city. That honor went to the new television tower, built in 1954–55, on a hill overlooking the city.
29 *Amtsblatt der Stadt Stuttgart* (May 3, 1956), 1, quoted in Gilbert Lupfer, *Architektur der fünfziger Jahre in Stuttgart* Stuttgarter Studien (Stuttgart: Silberburg-Verlag, 1997), vol. 10, 251.
30 Lupfer, 250, 252.

Chapter 5: The Old Town Hall in Prague

An Unresolved Architectural Challenge[1]

Veronika Knotková and Hana Svatošová

The contemporary 50 CZK coin of the Czech Republic carries the inscription *Praga mater urbium* (Prague, mother of cities).[2] Above a Renaissance window next to the entrance to the Old Town Hall in Prague is a conspicuous inscription *Praga caput regni* (Prague, head of the Kingdom). Both of these traditional designations of the capital of the Czech Republic, former Czechoslovakia, and earlier the capital of the Bohemian/Czech[3] Kingdom, originate in the Middle Ages.[4] The first inscription appears approximately in the first half of the fifteenth century, while the use of the other had been documented and confirmed by the sovereign in 1316.[5] They both symbolically express Prague's status as an administrative, political, cultural, and economic center of the Czech state from its beginnings in the ninth century as "a city which is mythologically and functionally the oldest in Czech lands."[6] The self-confident motto *Praga caput regni* appeared on the Town Hall in 1525, when Prague faced the resistance of the Czech royal cities against the noble estate and later against the sovereign. Moreover, the motto *Praga mater urbium* was used in official charters as a symbolic expression of the city's central position as well as an expression of an indirect opposition to the king, who after the unsuccessful revolt of the burghers in 1547 radically restricted the former self-administrative liberties of the Czech cities.

The relationship between central government and local government within Central Europe is marked by the strong continuity of the idea of local self-administration since the Middle Ages.[7] The burghers projected their privileges, power, representation, wealth as well as their sense for justice onto the arts in the town halls: "The consciousness of the difficulties encountered on the way of gaining the city privileges was easily manifested in the efforts of constructing a town hall as a building of the most imposing architecture and beauty that would document the wealth and status of the city."[8]

Czech lands became part of the multinational Habsburg monarchy in the sixteenth century; they were its most developed region. After the abovementioned unsuccessful revolt of 1547, the self-administrative possibilities of the towns became significantly limited. The effects of the sovereign's absolute rule, and subsequent centralization of power within the monarchy, deepened this negative development. Greatly influenced by the revolution of 1848–49, full-fledged self-administrative life was somewhat renewed. But only in 1860 did the local administration become almost fully emancipated from monarchical control.[9] However, the actual character of local government was also shaped by multi-ethnic dialogue or conflicts. This was especially the case in both of the Czech lands and Prague, in which members of two ethnic groups, Czechs and Germans, have lived since Middle Ages. National rivalry, connected with the formation of a modern nation,[10] "accompanied by self-confirming rituals of all sorts," was projected onto the architectural form of town halls: unlike Western European cities, where town halls represented the wealth and prestige of a city in competition with rivals, in the Czech lands they additionally represented national ideology inflected by ethnicity.[11]

The architectural appearance of the Old Town Hall in Prague from the Middle Ages to the modern period recorded this development. Prague was a conurbation of four independent towns, Old Prague Town, New Prague Town, the Lesser Town, and the Castle Town, all tightly bordering each other. Old Prague Town also contained the Jewish Town, autonomous in its administration. Each of the four principal towns had its own town hall until 1784 when the Emperor Joseph II united them into one administrative unit, creating the Capital City of Prague (excluding the Jewish Town). The oldest and the most important of them became a seat of the united administration. The Old Town was most closely bound with the sovereign's power and it fulfilled special tasks for the crown. The same role was applied to the Old Town Hall, which itself became a place of key events in the history of the city and the country. For example, in 1458, the election of the Czech king took place here.

Both the real and symbolic significance of the Old Town Hall has been enhanced by its location in the Old Town Square (Figure 5.1). Historically it was one of the most important and psychologically the most delicately perceived places within Prague.[12] The historical, political, and cultural importance of this space was confirmed in 1962, when the Ministry of Culture declared it "a national cultural monument." Older generations were known to refer to the Town Hall and its Square, a bit emphatically, as "victims of our glory and our humiliation."[13] The building and its square have been linked together, the architectural fate of one tied to the other.

THE OLD TOWN HALL FROM THE MIDDLE AGES TO 1848

This architectural story began in 1338, when the Old Town burgesses bought up the most palatial burgher house within the square. The Old Town Hall was not created at once as were the town halls of other cities: the building was expanded as neighboring houses were purchased for the purpose. From its beginnings, the construction proceeded with a generosity appropriate to the first city of the

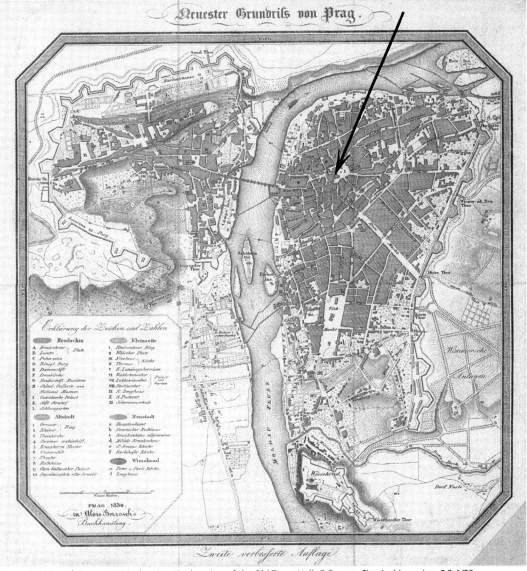

Figure 5.1 Map of Prague, 1850, showing the location of the Old Town Hall. © Prague City Archives, sign. P 2 A/33.

construction phase is possibly connected with the workshop that had also constructed St. Vitus's Cathedral and Charles Bridge. As construction of the Town Hall proceeded, the opposite side of the square saw the building of a central civic church, whose new Gothic structure was initiated by the Emperor. These two imposing buildings built on almost parallel lines symbolized two ideologies representing the spiritual and secular powers (Figure 5.2).

After unification in 1784, the other town halls lost their administrative function. The Old Town Hall housed the new administration of the larger city, a building subjected to more or less radical reconstructions and adaptations. The state administration made these decisions up until the first half of the nineteenth century, when self-administration was suspended by the monarchy. Over the years, architectural alterations completely transformed the way the building functioned, and often these changes were made with little sensitivity to the building's august past. For example, soon after unification, the great Gothic hall

Figure 5.2 Old Town Square, 1793. Left: Old Town Hall; right: Church of Our Lady before Týn/Týn Church. © Prague City Archives, sign. G 127A.

where the king had been elected was converted into office space, a second floor built inside the double-height space.

During the 1820s and 1830s, the state administration proposed to turn the Old Town Hall into a jailhouse. The project included a provision to preserve the Old Town Hall's tower and some Gothic elements. Additional office space within the building and the jailhouse were supposed to be constructed, one right next to the other. The state finally decided to build the jailhouse in another location. However, in 1838 the reconstruction of the Old Town Hall began under the leadership of Vienna's court architect, Peter Nobile.

Nobile designed the building according to the then contemporary and much favored Gothic Revival style. He approached the project with the objective of conferring an impression of grandeur and dignity as was considered to be appropriate for a town hall of such an important town.[15] The eastern wing of the Old Town Hall, adjacent to the square, was demolished along with the former great Gothic hall. The unveiling of the first part of the new construction in 1841 met with horror among Prague's cultural public. Protest was even directed toward the Habsburg Emperor. The construction was interrupted, thanks to the representatives of two important patriotic societies, the Society of the Patriotic Museum in Prague and the Society of Patriotic Friends of Arts in Bohemia, who were prudently joined by the city's administration.[16] Their efforts preserved the southern wing of the Town Hall with the abovementioned Renaissance window with the inscription *Praga caput regni*. The struggle to preserve this southern wing produced sharp debate about the building's construction. A century later, this protest was interpreted by the public as the first victory of the Czech people against Viennese rule.[17] Those early-nineteenth-century societies, however, were populated by Bohemian nobility, learned members of the bourgeoisie, and both Czech and German ethnicities, driven by patriotic, not nationalist sentiment.

The adaptation of Nobile's project was entrusted to another Viennese court architect, Paul Sprenger. The changes ultimately involved only modification to the façade fronting the Old Town Square. The city's administration was not about to entirely demolish an existing construction that had already swallowed up considerable financial resources. The east wing of the building that was finished in 1848 received two faces: one, ornamental and delicate, faced the square, while the second, rather ponderous, respected the original project of Nobile and led to the back-street (Figures 5.3 and 5.4). The outer iconographical decoration of the Town Hall's new façade was not exceptional in comparison to the contemporary standard of similar buildings. It consisted of sculptural depictions of rulers, as well as a broadly representative iconographic program that incorporated the Empire's many coats of arms, including the coats of arms of the four Prague cities, of state and city notables, and clerical dignitaries belonging to the noble estate. The building thus expressed all those powerful constituencies publicly active during the

Figure 5.3 Old Town Hall, 1904. Front façade (east wing, left): Paul Sprenger, side façade (north wing, right): Peter Nobile. © Prague City Archives, sign. VI 42/13.

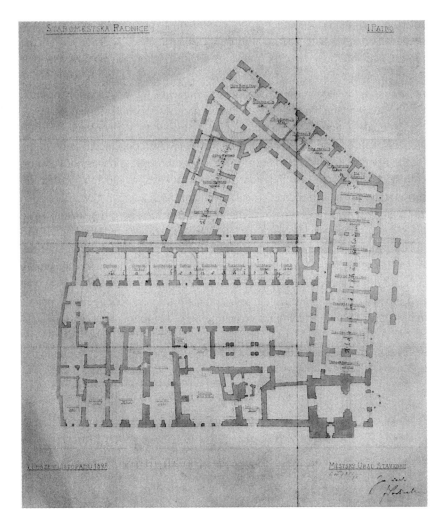

Figure 5.4
Plan of the Old Town Hall, first floor, 1897. © Prague City Archives, sign. MAP P I 3/373.

period of construction. Here, according to art historian Taťána Petrasová, was created "the first 'genealogy' of Prague's contemporary municipal authorities […], the first evidence of the growing self-confidence of the city council which had itself represented on the façade next to a number of Bohemian kings."[18] Contemporary representatives of the city here followed their medieval predecessors who had left their heraldic coats on the façade of the old wing of the town hall.[19] By resorting to Gothic revivalism, the inner decoration and equipment of the building were to correspond with its outer face. Plaques embedded in the façade attested to the growing sense of Czech nationalism. They recorded the start and end dates of the building's construction, but this data were not inscribed in the official language of German. Instead, they were written in Czech.

The new building was accepted by Prague inhabitants but not without reservations, although the general public got used to it over time. Well into the twentieth century, however, Czech art historians and other experts remained dissatisfied with the architectonic qualities of the building. Moreover, the building was judged from the positions of national ideology as a German or Viennese piece of work, lacking the expression of a more appropriate local (Prague's) architectural tradition. According to Petrasová, Nobile's project is now evaluated as "an initial construction of the romantic Gothic Revival," and Sprenger's adaptation as the most important piece of work of romanticism among Prague's architecture.[20] Nobile brought to Prague a monumental solution to the town hall's frontage that later influenced the design of Vienna's town hall by Friedrich von Schmidt in the 1860s. Nonetheless, the new building was of an excessive capacity, ignoring the building tradition and scale of the Old Town Square. It was only the beginning of the negative interventions within its urban form.

FIRST THREE TENDERS 1899–1909

The next chapter of the Old Town Hall's history began at the end of the nineteenth century. By then, the administration of the capital was firmly in the hands of emancipated Czech bourgeois citizens. Prague's communal election system remained unchanged during the half century until the end of World War I. This strict system meant that the multinational city was governed in turns only by two Czech middle-class parties with similar national programs. Prague Germans had left the corporation during the 1880s and deputies of the new (predominantly Social Democratic) parties had a much-reduced chance to share in the administration of the city. National and political conflicts gradually paralyzed both the Czech lands and even the Habsburg monarchy, but did not significantly limit the execution of Prague's city administration.

The ambition of Czechs to elevate Prague to the level of other developed European cities, and particularly not to fall behind Vienna, resulted in a demand for an expensive project of modernization, financed from the city budget. The most widely discussed project was the sanitation of the Jewish Town along with the Old Town. This measure remains controversial. The reason for undertaking this work was the drastically poor sanitary conditions in these areas. The historically valued part of the city was totally demolished, only synagogues, churches, and a part of the Old Jewish Cemetery were kept.[21] According to the pattern of Hausmann's Paris and other big cities, a new city centre grew there with modern apartment buildings designed in historicist style, reshaping a new street network. The sanitation project directly affected a part of the Old Town Square, i.e. the vicinity of the Old Town Hall. Thus the emptied areas in its neighborhood enabled the corporation to decide on the remodeling and enlarging of the Town Hall in 1899.

The so-called Nobile's Town Hall was not able to fit the needs of the developing city, nor was it suitable to the ruling bourgeoisie and the representation of the city at the end of the nineteenth century. The city offices were too large for the building, and they had been dispersed throughout the neighborhood. The rooms in the Old Town Hall, including the representative rooms, were cramped and they lacked modern technical equipment. Furthermore, it was expected that the planned unification between Prague and its suburbs (creating Greater Prague) would increase the demand for office space. In 1899 Prague's city representatives tackled this problem by scrutinizing the architectural examples of Vienna, Munich, Paris, and Berlin, as well as lesser Czech and Moravian towns, including suburbs of Prague.[22] They made preparations for the reconstruction of the Old Town Hall, initiating what has become a centuries-old debate over what functions that building should house and what historical and architectural references it should express.

The first architectural tenders for design proposals to remodel and enlarge the Old Town Hall were invited in 1899–1901, again in 1903–04 and once more in 1909, but none led to an unambiguous result.[23] Only the oldest part of the building was to be preserved (the southern wing), and both Nobile-Sprenger's new construction and the medieval houses neighboring the Old Town Hall were supposed to be demolished. This ongoing project prompted a discussion about the problems of regulation and urban planning in this area. Engaging in this discourse were the deputies of the city, as well as professional architects and urban planners. Modernizing the street system to accommodate newer modes of traffic and patterns of movement was the key point of argument. Traffic modernization was held to be superior to landmark preservation but emerging public opinion imposed the desire to preserve monuments of a perceived historical significance, including the architecture of the Old Town Hall and its square. In a few years, the city administration sought to save key landmarks from demolition.

Resistance against the sanitation project, dubbed *Bestia triumphans*, was loud enough to force city leaders to listen and engage in debate. The Club for the Old Prague representative was even invited to take part in drafting the third tender. The tenders to expand and renovate the Old Town Hall offer an opportunity to observe in microcosm the larger debate about the historical landscape of the City of Prague.

Although the idea of how the building should look differed in all three tenders, they all strived to create a monumental representative building, worthy of the city. The building was supposed to bear witness to the development of the Czech nation and its technological skills. The decisive moment for the course and results of the tenders was the fact that Prague's Town Hall was ruled only by Czech political parties of a national and conservative orientation. These tenders only allowed the participation of Czech architects. The third tender in 1909, however, gave room for the input of architects from other Slavic nations, which corresponded with the basic line of contemporary Czech polities, oriented to Slavic reciprocity. It discriminated against the ethnic Germans. The tenders were limited even for the architect-modernists because the city representatives doubtlessly preferred construction in a historicist style derived from Prague's architectural traditions.[24] In the third tender, we see a clear change: a direct confrontation between historically based work of an older generation of architects and a younger generation influenced by Art Nouveau or the modernism of Otto Wagner. The first prize from this tender was given to the strongly anachronistic project in the style of the Bohemian Renaissance (Figure 5.5). This proposal has been long forgotten, while a provocative project by a young architect Josef Gočár, that presented the reconstruction of the Old Town Hall as a new Tower of Babel, provokes emotion even now (Figure 5.6).[25]

Figure 5.5 Antonín Wiehl, design proposal for Old Town Hall, 1909 (first prize), in *Architektonický obzor* VIII, 1909, appendix no. VIII/47.

Figure 5.6
Josef Gočár, design proposal for Old Town Hall, 1909. Rear view; Old Town Hall's tower and the Church of St. Mary before Týn are on the right side, in *Styl* II, 1910, p. 57.

The debate hit deadlock. Reactions to the tenders were varied but acute, and even derisive, particularly where German nationals were concerned. The strongest opposition came from members of the younger generation of Czech architects, who predominantly criticized the absense of modern vocabulary in the proposed solutions. The problem was partly due to the poor quality of the tenders; they were more like improvisations than well-prepared documents. The city administration's conservatism, as well as that of the older generation on the juries, bent the debate towards a defense of the principles of the national neo-Renaissance that they had founded some 20 or 30 years previously. The debate over the representative character of the Old Town Hall struck a deep nerve. It had already been played out in other cultural genres. According to art historian Jindřich Vybíral, the "conflict between 'national' and 'modern' architecture in Bohemia around 1900 [...] had been preceded by a similar controversy in the field of literature." The poles of this debate were observed even inside the traditional political parties.[26]

Functional problems ultimately crippled the debate, exacerbating the extremely sensitive question of an ideal solution for such a historically significant location. In order to create access to the square from a newly created boulevard, a house sandwiched between the Old Town Hall and the Church of St. Nicolas, the chef-d'oeuvre of Prague's Baroque architecture, was demolished. The action set off cries of historical insensitivity, as critics claimed that its removal inappropriately (and inelegantly) exposed the church on the square in a manner that marred the intimate character of both the church and the public space it adjoined. The action led to a heated argument about the open and closed nature of the square, as well as the appropriate level of traffic accessing the square, an argument that divides architects to this day.

A certain fecklessness among the competitors and juries brought some experts to the proposals to construct a modern new town hall at an alternative location as was the case in other European cities, e.g. in Copenhagen and Stockholm. Defending the historical potency of the Old Town Hall and its square, this alternative was strenuously opposed by the members of the city administration.[27] Although rejected, the idea prompted a compromise that split the town hall program into two parts. The existing site was too saturated with historical meaning to be abandoned, and yet it could not adequately accommodate the increased demands for office space necessary to run a twentieth-century city administration. The decision was thus made to separate the representative and administrative parts of the town hall. A New Council House was constructed between 1908 and 1911 to provide office space, situated in close proximity to the Old Town Hall. Its monumental and ornate façade occluded its administrative function, but it satisfied the constituency keen to honor the neighboring baroque buildings (the Jesuit college Klementinum and the Clam-Gallas palace).

Simultaneously, with the construction of the New Council House, the city constructed the Municipal (Representative) House of the Capital City of Prague. This expensive and multifunctional building was constructed generously, but it was not to replace or to compete with the Old Town Hall. While the task of a town hall is to represent the city administration and community, the Municipal House was to represent Czech national society. Built on the outskirts of the quarter, which was inhabited mostly by Prague Germans, and in the vicinity of their representative seat, the German Casino (the Deutsches Casino), the pompous appearance of the Municipal House with rich decorations inside and out, was intended to be a "beacon of the Czechness of Prague."[28]

At the turn of the twentieth century, many Czech town halls were rebuilt or newly constructed, most in historical styles. In those towns dominated by a Czech majority, and this included Prague itself, the buildings were mostly arranged in the Bohemian Renaissance style, perhaps as a reminder of the "golden age of the Bohemian towns" of the sixteenth century (see Figure 5.5). However, in German-majority towns, those in Bohemia and Moravia, another stylistic tradition was expressed in the new architecture, that followed the architecture prevailing in Germany (for example the Saxon Renaissance style).[29] The town of Liberec (Reichenberg) was a special case. Considered to be the unofficial capital of the Bohemian Germans, its town hall was built in 1888 and completed in 1893 under the direction of a Viennese architect strongly inspired by Vienna's Town Hall on the Ringstrasse.[30] This happened as a result of a design competition presided over by none other than the architect of Vienna's Town Hall. Since it was to be a monument expressing German pride and ability, only German builders were contracted.[31] Liberec's Town Hall was partly funded by a local bank and industrial financiers.

THE OLD TOWN HALL IN THE TWENTIETH CENTURY

The Old Town Hall as well as Prague's public had to wait almost 30 years for another design competition. Meanwhile a key political change took place when the Habsburg monarchy broke up at the end of World War I and Prague thus became capital of the democratic Czechoslovak republic. In comparison with the previous tenders, the new tender celebrated both the six-hundredth anniversary of the Town Hall and the twentieth anniversary of the republic's founding in 1938; so lack of office space or that of a place of representation was not the issue at hand. Shortly before that another new office building (the New Official Building) had been finished close to the New Council House and a very attractive new residence in the Art Deco style was constructed for Prague's mayor within the palace of the Municipal Library (1928). The role of Nobile's Town Hall was reduced, as it became rather a decorative backdrop.

Unlike the previous tenders, this one was rather symbolic and it did not produce a satisfactory result either. Contrary to its predecessors, this tender preserved Sprenger's neo-Gothic Town Hall façade along with the old houses in the neighborhood that were supposed to have once been demolished to enable better traffic flow. Between the third and fourth tenders archaeological research in the Old Town Hall's area deepened both expert and public knowledge, thus increasing its historical value. An absolutely new social aspect of the Town Hall building had also entered play, for the design created a great inner courtyard, which would allow for gathering of people in numbers.[32] Thus, a part of the public life that had taken place at the square up until then would have been moved to the seat of the city's administration. This was a completely different approach in comparison to the beginning of the twentieth century, when a great "popular hall" was rejected as part of the program, with the rationale that large political gatherings would allegedly spoil the "peace and order within the Town Hall."[33]

The condition for the preservation of Sprenger's frontage met the contemporary prevailing architectural concepts – modern classicism and functionalism. Even though the architects accepted this, they did so in such a flippant manner that the outcome of the tender was an embarrassment. In response, the jury insisted on another round, but the project ground to a halt due to external political circumstances in 1938–39 and the Nazi occupation of Czech and Moravian lands in 1938–45. The German Nazi administration of the capital also attempted to create a solution for the Old Town Hall; however, their idea was absolutely contradictory to local building tradition. Fortunately, the project was never carried out due to a halt in construction during the war.[34] The German occupational representative at least wanted to create a restaurant in the old Gothic wing of the Old Town Hall, a common architectural function in town halls found within the German-speaking regions (Rathauskeller). Czech deputies managed to avert this with the explanation that it would be considered a "profanity of the building" by the wider public.[35]

The problem of Sprenger's frontage was finally resolved in a drastic manner. On May 8, the last day of World War II, *Waffen-SS* intentionally destroyed the eastern wing of the building. According to a leading contemporary Czech art historian, "the Germans in their fury rid Prague of the most disgraceful German-made element ever to see light in the city across the ages."[36] The remaining ruins of the Nobile wing were dismantled, leaving only the old south wing. The complex social and political climate of the state and administration of the city changed, culminating in 1948 with the communist coup that lead to the suppression of the self-administrative and decisive powers of the city's administration.

The Communist Party took over the whole state administration, absolutely controlling all aspects of life in the country. The planned economy produced five-year directives for the whole state economy, including the building industry. Preceding this, in 1946 a new tender to rebuild the Old Town Hall and the Old Town Square was launched. The new Old Town Hall was only to serve as a place of city representation, which had resulted from the pre war tender.[37] It was possibly the most radical one, dominated by functionalism and by a very insensitive interpretation of the area of the square.[38] This may have been the cause of its failure. The tender selection process was cut short by the communist coup and large-scale reorganization of priorities (Figure 5.7).

The New Council House was reconstructed for the needs of the management of the city and for self-administration, while the torso of the Old Town Hall, the building's oldest fragment, retained only a symbolic and occasional representative

Figure 5.7 Jaroslav Fišer–Karel Fišer, design proposal for Old Town Hall, 1946 (prize winner). © Prague City Archives, not signed.

function. During the next 40 years, another three architectural competitions for the reconstruction of the Old Town Hall and its square took place (1963, 1966–67, 1987–88), all of which were staged by the city administration in cooperation with professional institutions.[39] The 1966–67 tender was stopped by the 1968 Soviet occupation. The last of these tenders was inspired by the approaching fortieth anniversary of the communist coup. The tenders can be better understood as an opportunity for the new generations of architects to try to deal with this space. The urban solution of the square seemed to be more important than the sole reconstruction of the historical artifact itself, the Old Town Hall. Program and function were not always clear. The competition of 1946 considered the Town Hall as a seat of self-administration, whereas the competitions that followed struggled to attach an ideological badge to any future project; the inner function of a completed town hall remained unclear. During the 1960s, the programmatic goal of the Town Hall was to serve the higher political, representative, and cultural purposes of the city; towards the 1980s this direction had changed and the Town Hall was seen more as a multifunctional building to be used by a wider public, a "Cultural Palace" for the city. The excessive demands to the planned building of a Town Hall (planned spaces for representation, concerts, exhibitions, a restaurant, and other functions), without any ideological anchor, made for disaster. This, however, was countered by the large number of competitors taking part. Another coup, this time anti-communist, rendered this a dead project.

The latest competition, announced as the election theme by the previous mayor Pavel Bém (2002–10), has not brought hope to those invested in an Old Town Hall as a symbol of the city's rich past, or as a working and vibrant house for municipal government. Designers, authorities, experts, and the public are still groping for solutions to Nobile's replacement or reconstruction. That the city administration is no longer housed in that building or its square exacerbates the problem. What is happening, in fact, is the conversion of sovereign territory into a political vacuum, as there is no agency ready to physically occupy this space and restore the function, sense, and glory to this most important town hall building in the Czech Republic.

There are only a few present-day inhabitants of Prague still able to remember the Old Town Hall and its closed square. The overwhelming majority is unable to compare it with the building of the distant past, and thus the present state of the building is taken for granted. Here we have a tug-o'-war. On the one side, the general distrust of the decision makers and contemporary architecture, and on the other a nervy reaction which helps preserve the current status quo – i.e. the constructional gap and a little park – or to build a replica of the destroyed wing of the Old Town Hall, either Nobile's or medieval Gothic. The current city administration leans towards the medieval Gothic replica. A negative reaction from the architects is only to be expected. The scepticism among architects is also worrisome. The Dean of the Faculty of Architecture would rather leave the solution of this location to the next generation and the Chancellor of the Academy of the Arts reminded us of the words of Czech architect Jan Sokol: "sometimes it is a great architectural act not to construct anything in a certain place."[40]

To make a surgical analogy, the unsightly scar on the façade of the Old Town Square requires and demands the skilled hands of a fine cosmetic surgeon. One can only hope that its history, a litany of failure, destruction, and sheepishness will serve to inspire architects and urbanists to put their heads together and resolve the specific task with the appropriate humility and necessary vision. As a closing note, let us cross our fingers that such an effort shall not be slowed or prevented by future political interference either passive or aggressive. We are, after all, dealing with a building not only exceptional in itself, but one of political, psychological, and emotional importance for the entire country.

NOTES

1 Dedicated to Dr. Václav Ledvinka on his 65th anniversary.
2 During 1926–64 the inscription (in the Czech version) was a part of the coat of arms of the City of Prague.
3 The use of the word Czech/Bohemian *usually* varies without regards to its significance. Within the context of the period of formation of the modern nations during the nineteenth and early twentieth century *Czech* relates to the nationally Czech ethnic group, whilst *Bohemian* refers to the whole multinational country.
4 From the fourteenth to the seventeenth centuries Prague was a residential city of the Emperors of the Holy Roman Empire of the German Nation.
5 We would like to express our thanks for providing us with information and above all for reviewing the text to the director of the Prague City Archives, Dr. Václav Ledvinka.
6 Jiří Pešek, "The role of history and historical heritage in the development of Prague as a metropolis in the 19th and 20th centuries," in Jacek Purchla, ed., *The Historical Metropolis: A Hidden Potential* (Cracow: International Culture Centre, 1996), 153. For the newest history of Prague see Václav Ledvinka and Jiří Pešek, *Prag* (Praha: Nakladatelství Lidové noviny, 2001 [German edition]).
7 Jacek Purchla, "Mayors and city halls", in Jacek Purchla, ed., *Mayors and City Halls: Local Government and the Cultural Space in the Late Habsburg Monarchy* (Cracow: International Cultural Centre, 1998), 7.

8   Karel Kibic, *Historické radnice Čech, Moravy a Slezska*, 1 (Praha: Libri, 2009), 9.
9   See Peter Urbanitsch, "Functions and tasks of the municipal government in the monarchy," in Purchla, ed., *Mayors and City Halls*, op. cit., 11–23.
10 On the topic of the modern nation see: Miroslav Hroch, "From national movement to the fully-formed nation: The nation-building process in Europe," in Gopal Balakrishnan, ed., *Mapping the Nation* (New York: Verso, 1996), 78–97; for Czech-German relations see Jan Křen, *Die Konflikt-Gemeinschaft: Tschechen und Deutsche 1780–1918*, 2nd edition (München: Oldenbourg, 2000); for Prague Germans see Garry B. Cohen, *The Politics of Ethnic Survival: Germans in Prague, 1861–1914*, 2nd edition (West Lafayette: Purdue University Press, 2006).
11 Jindřich Vybíral, "The Bohemian town hall around 1900," in Purchla, ed., *Mayors and City Halls*, op. cit., 179.
12 About the Old Town Square see Cynthia Paces, *Prague Panoramas: National Memory and Sacred Space in the Twentieth Century* (Pittsburg: Pittsburg University Press, 2009), 25–36, 74–99; Cynthia Paces, "The battle for public space on Prague's Old Town Square," in John J. Czaplicka, Blaire A. Ruble and Lauren Crabtree, eds., *Composing Urban History and the Constitution of Civic Identities*, (Washington: Woodrow Wilson Center Press, 2003), 165–91.
13 Jan Teige and Jan Herain, *Staroměstský rynk v Praze* (Praha: Společnost přátel starožitností českých, 1908), 1.
14 Václav Ledvinka, "Staroměstská radnice," in *Revitalizace Staroměstské radnice a okolí: Možnosti a limity* (Praha: Hlavní město Praha, 2009), 39.
15 Teige and Herain, op. cit., 63.
16 Ibid., 73–6.
17 Prague City Archives, Magistrate of the Capital City of Prague, Department I. C, sign. 2/10, carton 57 (a letter of December 29, 1947).
18 Taťána Petrasová, "The history of the Town Hall in Prague in the 19th century," in Purchla, ed., *Mayors and City Halls*, op. cit., 187.
19 Rostislav Nový, "Nejstarší heraldické památky Staroměstské radnice v Praze," *Pražský sborník historický* 22 (1989), 33–70.
20 Taťána Petrasová, "Romantické přestavby pražské Staroměstské radnice (1836–1848) a jejich význam pro počátky pražské neogotiky" in Marie Mžyková, ed., *Sborník k romantickému historismu – Novogotice* (Sychrov: Zámek Sychrov, 1997), 138, 146; Václav Hlavsa, *Staroměstská radnice v dějinách pražského města* (Praha: Státní tělovýchovné nakladatelství, [1956]), 12.
21 See Cathleen M. Giustino, *Tearing Down Prague's Jewish Town: Ghetto Clearance and the Legacy of Middle-class Ethnic Politics Around 1900* (Boulder: East European Monographs, 2003); Rudolf Wurzer, "Die 'Assanirung' der Josefsstadt in Prag," *Die alte Stadt: Vierteljahreszeitschrift für Stadtgeschichte, Stadtsoziologie und Denkmalpflege* 20 no. 2 (1995), 149–74.
22 See Prague City Archives, Minutes of the City Corporation and of the City Council 1897–99; records of the Magistrate of the Capital City of Prague, Magistrate, Dept. I.C, sign. B 2/10, carton 57; *Administrační zpráva královského hlavního města Prahy za rok 1897, 1898*, (Praha: Hlavní město Praha, 1899, 1901).
23 See ibid., Minutes 1900–1911; Magistrate, Dept. I.C, sign. 2/10; *Administrační zpráva 1901–11* (Praha 1904–19).
24 Jindřich Vybíral, "Contest of ideas or conflict of interest? Architectural competitions in Prague around 1900," *Centropa* 5 no. 2 (2005), 105.
25 Prize-winning or interesting projects for all of the tenders were issued in: Eva Skalická, ed., *Srdce města: Historický, ubanistický a architektonický vývoj Staroměstského náměstí a soutěže na dostavbu a přestavbu radnice 1899–1988* (Praha: Útvar rozvoje hlavního města Prahy, 2008), 159–257.

26 Vybíral, "The Bohemian town hall around 1900," op. cit., 182, 181.
27 Prague City Archives, Magistrate, Dept. I.C, sign. 2/10 (Minute of the presidial committee, January 9, 1904).
28 Prague City Archives, Magistrate, Dept. B, 1901–10, sign. 60/317 (Minute of the city committee for Municipal House, October 3, 1903, the speech of mayor Vladimír Srb). See also Hana Svatošová and Václav Ledvinka, eds., *Město a jeho dům: Kapitoly ze stoleté historie Obecního domu hlavního města Prahy (1901–2001)* (Praha: Obecní dům, 2002).
29 See Kibic, op. cit., 234–83.
30 The basic source of inspiration for the Town Hall of Vienna was the mediaeval Town Hall in Brussels – Hannes Stekl, "Vienna's municipal architecture and infrastructure 1848–1914," in Purchla, ed., *Mayors and City Halls*, op. cit., 48.
31 Libuše Bílková, Hana Chocholoušková, Miloslava Melanová, and Jan Mohr, *Liberecká radnice* (Liberec: Město Liberec and Nakladatelství Dialog, 1993), 31, 34.
32 *Podmínky veřejné soutěže na vypracování náčrtků na úpravu Staroměstské radnice t.j. na její přestavbu, přístavbu a novostavbu* ([Praha], 1938), 11.
33 Prague City Archives, Magistrate, Dept. I.C, sign. 2/10 (Minute of the commision, March 6, 1902).
34 Miloš Hořejš, Protektorátní Praha jako německé město. Nacistický urbanismus a Plánovací komise pro hlavní město Prahu (Praha: Mladá fronta and Národní technické muzeum, 2013), 189–192.
35 Prague City Archives, Magistrate, Dept. I.C, sign. 2/10, (Minute of the commission, September 10, 1940).
36 E. P. [Emanuel Poche] books' cover to Bohumil Hypšman, *Sto let Staroměstského rynku a radnice* (Praha: Pražské nakladatelství, 1946).
37 *Podmínky veřejné soutěže na vypracování náčrtků na úpravu Staroměstského náměstí a radnice* ([Praha], 1946).
38 Zdeněk Lukeš, "Krátké zamyšlení nad soutěžemi na Staroměstskou radnici v Praze," in *Revitalizace Staroměstské radnice a okolí*, op. cit., 47.
39 See Skalická, ed., *Srdce města*, op. cit., 215–57; Karel Kibic, "Poválečné soutěže na dostavbu Staroměstské radnice," *Staletá Praha* 8 (1977), 129–44; *Umění* 36 no. 5 (1988), 385–480.
40 Zdeněk Zavřel, "Pět důvodů ke skepsi," in *Revitalizace Staroměstské radnice a okolí*, op. cit., 53; Jiří Kotalík, "Proč mezinárodní konference?," ibid., 14.

Engaging the public

Chapter 6: Town Halls in Australia

Sites of Conflict and Consensus

Jenny Gregory[1]

> The old Town Hall … the ancient home of the liberties of the people, how marvellously it combines energy and strength with beauty and grace, and how expressive it thus is of the very soul of republican Florence![2]

So wrote Walter Murdoch, Professor of English and noted essayist regularly published in Australian newspapers from the 1920s to the mid-1960s. How relevant is this, his description of the fourteenth-century town hall of Florence, to town halls in Australia, a continent colonized by the British in the late eighteenth century and a nation only in 1901?

In Australia, town halls are emblematic of the role of local government, the nation's third arm of government after federal and state governments. Most local governments, whether defined as a city, town, shire, or roads board, have a town hall. They were among the first public buildings constructed in Australia and more than 300 are heritage listed.[3]

Town halls have received little attention in Australian historiography. They stand somewhat uneasily between heritage and historical studies, with the former noting their civic and social values but emphasizing their architectural qualities. Historical studies, on the other hand, have not focused on the town hall, but on activities that have taken place within and around town halls as indicators of wider trends, noting the building only in passing as a focal point of civic administration and a large public space. This is not the place for a detailed literature review of the approach to the town hall in Australian history, though that may be a valuable exercise for the future. Suffice to say that town halls frequently appear in city and suburban biographies, but as bit players with the main emphasis elsewhere. Hence this foray into the role of town halls is indebted to larger studies where they exist, supplemented by extensive on-line newspaper research.

This chapter takes a case study approach to the history of the town hall in Australia. It discusses both the iconography and function of three town halls, providing examples of the way the town hall has functioned in its community.

Ranging from the magnificent capital city town halls of Sydney and Melbourne to the humble town hall of Toodyay in rural Western Australia, all have played an important role in their communities. They have provided a working space for local government officials, a space for public meetings and for community events that have varied from symphony concerts to amateur theatricals. They thus play a role in building community consensus. Equally, however, they have been heavily politicized sites of bitter community conflict.

SYDNEY TOWN HALL

The development of the Sydney Town Hall was an extraordinarily long and fraught process, taking 46 years from the selection of the site to the completion of the hall. It was beset by the competing egos of individuals, political maneuvering within local government, and power struggles between local and state governments.

The battle over a site for a town hall lasted for over 25 years, pitting municipal and state authorities against one another. In 1843, the newly created City of Sydney Council advised the State Government that it planned to build a town hall on the Old Burial Ground, no longer in use. The Government rejected the proposal, citing the inappropriateness of building a secular structure on a sacred site. The Council was not deterred, holding a competition for the design of a town hall to be situated on the Old Burial Ground and then submitting the two winning designs to the Government plus another request for the land. It again refused. Numerous sites were then considered. Shirley Fitzgerald has pointed out that all the sites proposed by the Council were close to the city's commercial centre, framing this as a move by the Council to "strengthen the municipal precinct and create a symbol of city government in the heartland of commercial Sydney."[4]

The Council eventually got its way in 1869, finally obtaining a portion of the Old Burial Ground to build its Town Hall.[5] It had manipulated public opinion in favor of the site by arranging for HRH Prince Alfred, Duke of Edinburgh, and the first royal visitor to Sydney, to lay a foundation stone on the site. He had survived an assassination attempt only a few days earlier and this had gripped Sydney. It was not surprising then, that, as the *Sydney Morning Herald* reported on April 6, 1868, 1,500 to 2,000 people attended. The Council thus gained maximum publicity for its ambitions and an apparent royal seal of approval, even though negotiations with government were still underway.

The terms under which the Government conceded the site were stringent. The Council was required to spend at least £25,000 on construction, the grounds were to be designed according to the advice of the Director of the Botanic Gardens, the encompassing walls were to be approved by the Colonial Architect, and any remains of corpses were to be exhumed and reburied in the new cemetery. The Hall had to be completed by 1 January 1872. Failure to fulfil any of these terms would result in harsh financial penalties.

The Council did not bow to the government's authority. Construction of the hall had not even commenced by 1872. Indeed, the Sydney Town Hall would not be fully realized for another 16 years and the Council would continue to meet in temporary premises. On the matter of budget, in cavalier fashion, the Town Clerk airily told a parliamentary committee that the Council's estimate of £35,000 would be at least doubled. He failed to produce a detailed and accurate revised costing, and appeared indifferent to the government's concerns.[6]

Beyond these conflicts between municipality and state, internal tensions within Council surfaced during the Town Hall's construction. These became obvious in the scandals surrounding the activities of the architects and planners. The earliest arose in a rivalry between John Henry Willson and Edward Bell. Willson had convincingly won an 1867 competition to design the Town Hall, but his success was tarnished by rumours that he had bribed two aldermen. As a result the Council withdrew Willson's £250 prize, and enlisted Bell, the City Engineer, to modify the plans. Bell submitted his revision of Willson's "City" design, which he named "City Improved." Within a few months the Council had terminated Willson's contract, pushing Bell to the fore. Infuriated, Willson broke into Bell's office, stealing several plans and marking others with "J. H. Willson, architect." The Council re-evaluated matters. Considering Willson's perceived injustice at the theft of his work, and the apparently deteriorating mental health of Bell, in 1870 the Council set about dismissing Bell and reappointing Willson. Bell's response was to resign, writing a heated letter criticizing the Council for lack of support and overwork. Though Willson remained at the helm of the project for the next year, he died in early 1872.[7]

In 1873 Albert Bond was appointed City Architect. Elaborating upon Willson's simpler sketches, he designed costly interiors for the Town Hall. But when Bond resigned in 1877, his successor, David McBeath, opted for a frugal approach to the completion of the Hall. Another major debacle resulted. McBeath's construction work was structurally unsound. Referred to as "the foundation scandal," an architectural firm commissioned by the Council discovered that the work was defective. In 1880, McBeath resigned on the grounds of poor health and the following year court proceedings found both McBeath and the contractors at fault. It was also discovered that the contractors had been overpaid. Moreover, an investigation into the building's plasterwork, some of which had fallen off the ceiling, found that this was also faulty.[8]

It was largely due to this widely publicized blunder that the Council subjected the next City Architect, Thomas Sapsford, charged with overseeing the final stage of the Town Hall's construction, to continuous scrutiny. Appointed in 1881, Sapsford's plans were repeatedly rejected by the Council, despite general acclaim from the architectural community. In 1885, the Council dismissed him, expressing concerns over his excessive spending and poor bookkeeping but, in 1886, he was reappointed on a lower salary.[9] He died later in the year. The *Sydney Morning Herald* of January 6, 1887 reported that Mayor John Young said that "the harsh treatment [Sapsford] received both before and since his reinstatement no doubt caused him to lose heart, making him liable to illness, to which he eventually succumbed."[10]

City Halls and Civic Materialism

Figure 6.1
Sydney Town Hall
c. 1894–95,
photographed by
Charles H. Kerry. Image
courtesy of the National
Library of Australia.

On its eventual opening on November 27, 1889, the Sydney Town Hall was hailed by the *Sydney Morning Herald* as "one of the largest city halls in the world." There was no mention of the scandals surrounding its design and construction. The opening ceremony, reported in both city and country newspapers, was spectacular: traffic was stopped and government offices closed, with all attention focused on the new Town Hall. Following an address by Mayor Harris to dignitaries, including the Governor, the Premiers of New South Wales and the neighboring state of Queensland, Speakers of both Houses of the Legislature, religious and naval leaders, and 5,000 invited guests, and a choral performance, the Mayor's eldest daughter declared the hall open. A ball for 3,000 people was held that evening and the following Sunday a united religious ceremony was held in the great hall (Figure 6.1).

The total cost of the new Town Hall had been around £200,000, as noted by the *Sydney Morning Herald*, which provided a detailed description of the hall on December 5, 1889. It was constructed of local sandstone and was described as a striking composite of French Second Empire architecture, inspired by the Hotel de Ville in Paris and neo-classicism. Its great hall measured 192 feet by 85 feet with a 65-foot ceiling and it is reputed to be the first public space in Sydney with permanent electric lighting. At the western end a Grand Organ, said to have then been the world's largest pipe organ of its type, was soon to be installed at the back of a proscenium arch stage. In front of that was an orchestra pit (modeled on the Leeds Town Hall) that could accommodate 500 performers. The basement contained a lower hall of the same dimensions, except for the ceiling height (20 feet), which was used for banquets and meetings, as well as offices, storerooms, and kitchens.

Figure 6.2
Packed function in the Centennial Hall, Town Hall Sydney, c. 1890s, photographed by Charles H. Kerry. Image courtesy of National Library of Australia.

Despite its lengthy and scandal-ridden road to completion, the Sydney Town Hall – with its great hall named Centennial Hall to mark the 1888 centenary of New South Wales – was hailed as a celebration of unity at its opening ceremony (Figure 6.2). In the *Sydney Morning Herald* on November 28, 1889, "Excalibur" commented: "The people were there … In the wide galleries they were thronged, the poor as well as the rich, the unlettered as the lettered, the official and the unofficial." The newspaper also pointed out that "the masses" joined officials in singing a rendition of "Old Hundredth" (likely to have been the version also known as "All People that on Earth do Dwell" based on Psalm 134) suggesting that this demonstrated an alliance between citizens and municipal powers. The Town Hall sat at the heart of this alliance, a symbolic and tangible testament to the inclusion of citizens by their municipality. Such inclusion would be further reflected years later in changes to the building's architecture; in 1934, for example, the Council removed the fence surrounding the Hall and replaced its porte-cochere with a large set of steps where people could sit and meet, making the Hall far more accessible to the public. More than 50 years earlier, "Excalibur" had envisaged this civic inclusion, calling the opening ceremony "a ritual of citizenship," and affirming that the Town Hall "exalt[ed] the citizenship by presenting it with … a temple of Democracy."[11]

At times the Town Hall served as an official platform for the voice of "the people." Not long before its formal opening, upon the arrival of a ship carrying Chinese immigrants into Sydney harbour in 1888, public objections to the ship's landing were aired at a Council meeting in the Town Hall. Council decided that the Mayor would lead a march on Parliament House protesting against the

Government's action in permitting Chinese immigration. The Town Hall thus facilitated what Fitzgerald has termed the "populist democratic tradition" expected of the municipality but, in doing so, encouraged conflict between local and state governments.[12]

The City Council's actions typified the widespread racial intolerance that existed in Australia. Legislation to restrict Chinese immigration to New South Wales was first introduced in 1861 in reaction to the flood of Chinese gold seekers, and was followed by further legislation in 1881, 1887, and 1898. The latter applied to all non-Europeans. After the states came together to create a federal government, the first legislation the new nation enacted was the Immigration Restriction Act 1901. Known as the "White Australia" policy, it remained in place for much of the twentieth century.

There were limits to the Town Hall's role in enabling the views of the public to be expressed. In August 1931, for example, Joseph Lyons, later Australia's Prime Minister, held a political rally at the Town Hall that degenerated into a riot. In consequence the Council declared that any individuals or groups seeking to use the Hall could be denied the right on the grounds of potential disorder. Taking an increasingly right-wing stance, Council then proceeded to ban anti-war, union, and communist groups, while often allowing fascist groups such as the New Guard to use the Town Hall.[13]

After the Second World War, the prominence of Communists in the Australian trade union movement and their conspicuous role in several major strikes, including the Coal Miners' Strike of 1949, gave rise to considerable fear among conservative groups. When the conservatives, under Robert Menzies, swept into power at the 1949 federal election, they enacted legislation to dissolve the Communist Party of Australia. The Communist Party challenged the act in the High Court, which ruled that it was constitutionally invalid, whereupon the government put the issue to a referendum, which was unsuccessful. It was in this climate that Cold War issues emerged in the Sydney Town Hall.

In 1948, the Council resolved that neither the Australian Communist Party nor the Australian Russian Society would be permitted to use any portion of the Town Hall. The Australian Russian Society unsuccessfully protested this move as a violation of their democratic rights.[14] Others who were banned from using the Town Hall, according to the *Sydney Morning Herald's* report of June 13, 1949, included the Teachers Federation and Workers Educational Association and the Australian Railways Union. The latter objected "if people such as Menzies [Prime Minister] can obtain the Sydney Town Hall to condemn the Labor Movement generally, the least that a Labor Council can do is to allow the Sydney Town Hall to be open to all legalized organisations."[15] This alluded to the fact that the Council was heavily politicized. Nonetheless, in early 1949, several unions had their applications to hold peace meetings at the Town Hall rejected. The New South Wales Fire Brigade Employees Union complained, as the *Sydney Morning Herald* reported on April 5, 1949, "the hall was let to Mr Menzies, who saw fit to attack the Labor movement and call for the dropping of atomic bombs," and threatened to withdraw its members from patrol duty at Town Hall functions if the ban was not lifted. They protested "the Hall is not yours, but belongs to the People."[16] Members of the Democratic Rights Council, whose request to use the Town Hall for a public meeting to discuss banning the atom bomb had been denied, took action, crowding into the public gallery of the Town Hall and calling for a review of the decision. Such protests culminated in several thousand people gathering at the Town Hall steps, shouting to Lord Mayor Ernie O'Dea (1948–52): "Open the doors, Ernie." This was not reported in the local press, but in a neighboring state newspaper, the *Townsville Daily Bulletin* on August 10, 1950, suggesting the conservative nature of the Sydney press as well as censorship of a large protest gathering at a time of considerable unrest.

The Australian Women's Movement against Socialisation, however, was permitted to meet in the Town Hall on the afternoon of Wednesday July 20, 1949. According to a sensational press report in the *Sydney Morning Herald*, headlined "Women Fight at Meeting in the Town Hall," the meeting was attended by more than a thousand women, mostly elderly, who passed "resolutions condemning Communism and Socialism" and expressing "unrelenting hostility to the lawless and heartless coal strike." When well-known feminist and activist Mrs Jessie Street demanded the right to speak without invitation at the end of a stormy meeting, a group of angry women surrounded her shouting "Communist! Socialist!" and tried to eject her from the Town Hall, despite the fact that she was recovering from a broken leg and leaning heavily on a walking stick.[17] Another woman from the New Housewives' Association had a hand clapped over her mouth "by a woman in a brown fur coat" as she was speaking and was pushed to the back of the hall. According to the report, there were "many angry and bitter scenes when women scuffled with one another."

By November 1950, the Council's acts of exclusion had attracted the attention of Clive Evatt, the Chief Secretary of the Labor State Government. Evatt wrote to the Council to inform them that their licence to use the Town Hall as a public hall was under review, and to that no future applications for hire could be denied "on political, sectarian or other unreasonable grounds."[18] He also advised that any bans that breached these terms could be appealed through his Department. The Council replied that they had never denied groups based on political motivations, and that the Department was interfering in Council matters. Evatt then instructed the Council to permanently display a notice in the Town Hall entitled "Human Rights and the Theatres and Public Halls Act." It highlighted clauses of the Act that defined a public meeting as "an assemblage of persons for any public purpose of a political, religious, charitable or intellectual nature," and a public hall as a place where such meetings were held. Applications for hiring premises licensed under the Act were not to be rejected "on political, sectarian, or other unreasonable grounds." Articles from the 1948 Universal Declaration of Human Rights were included in the notice. "Denial of freedom of expression," it declared, "is not merely intolerant – it is intolerable." Despite instructions to "display this notice in a conspicuous place," Council filed it away, with a note on it written by the Town Clerk reading: "discussed with L. M. *Not* to be exhibited."

Figure 6.3
Striking members of the firemen's union vote, Lower Town Hall, Sydney, 24 June 1955. Image courtesy of State Library of New South Wales.

Nevertheless, Evatt's actions had results, with regular union meetings held in the lower town hall during the 1950s.

Officially the bans remained until 1982, when Alderman Robert Tickner moved for their removal. Tickner explained that he had come across the largely forgotten bans while investigating a recent one – that of "Aboriginal or allied groups" using the nearby Redfern Town Hall (which was under the jurisdiction of the Sydney City Council). This latter ban was particularly striking considering that in the previous year, the Council had raised the Aboriginal flag at the Sydney Town Hall and held a civic reception in honor of National Aborigines Week.[19] These were particularly significant events. Since the 1880s, government policies of protection and then assimilation had dictated almost every aspect of the lives of Aboriginal people. They had no rights, but gradually became more politicized, holding their first civil rights gathering – the Day of Mourning – in 1938, the year marking 150 years of white colonization. They were refused use of Sydney Town Hall for this protest meeting.[20] Raising the Aboriginal flag on Sydney Town Hall in 1981 symbolized progress towards the elimination of institutionalized racism.

The raising of various flags on the flagpoles of Sydney Town Hall often exposed political battles within the Council. But it also revealed loyalist divisions among the people of a nation that had only been created in 1901. Tension between loyalties – to Britain or to Australia – was symbolized by the flag. In 1921, for example, Sydney City Council attracted public criticism when it failed to raise a flag on Anzac Day, the anniversary of the first major military action fought by Australian and New Zealand troops during the First World War. April 25 was officially named Anzac Day in 1916, just a year after the campaign, and it is now one of Australia's most important national occasions. When the Australian flag was not flown on Sydney Town Hall on Anzac Day 1921, many citizens sent critical letters to the Council. One letter suggested that this "disgusting act of disloyalty" showed that the Council had lost touch with public values.[21] When questioned about the matter, Lord Mayor W. H. Lambert became hostile. He was a Labor man, who also held pacifist and anti-Empire views, and found himself not only at odds with the public, but also at odds with his fellow councillors on a number of occasions. One such struggle arose between Lambert and Town Clerk Thomas Nesbitt over the raising of the Union Jack, the British flag. The Lord Mayor decided that this flag should not be flown, but the Town Clerk regularly attempted to circumvent his directions by placing the Union Jack on the Town Hall's central flagpole, flanked by the Australian flag. At times this attracted "warm congratulations" from many citizens according to the *Sydney Morning Herald* of October 14, 1921, which reported that the Town Clerk had received numerous telegrams praising "the determined stand he took … in refusing to be party to the hauling down of the Union Jack from the main flag pole at the Town Hall."[22] Here, the Town Hall became a site in which tensions between citizen and municipal authority, and colonial municipality and Empire, were projected and played out.

Despite the tensions revealed by these incidents, they should not be overplayed. Sydney Town Hall is still the official home of the City Council. It still meets in the historic Council Chamber with its public gallery intended to keep its processes open and transparent. As Sydney's largest indoor venue until the Sydney Opera House was completed in 1973, the Town Hall has also provided a heart for the city's civic and cultural life. Its Centennial Hall was the home of the Sydney Symphony Orchestra hosting performances of local and international musicians. Civic receptions for royalty and visiting dignitaries, memorial services, political meetings, grand balls, debutante balls, graduations, school speech nights, and Christmas concerts have been held there for more than a century.[23]

MELBOURNE TOWN HALL

Melbourne was founded as a speculative settlement in 1835 and a Town Council established in 1842 to administer its affairs. The State of Victoria, of which Melbourne became the capital, was not created until 1851. Hence the creation of local government predated the formation of state government by nearly a decade, its authority was pre-eminent for this period and it maintained its considerable status for many years.

The gold rushes of the 1850s brought extraordinary wealth to Victoria and a dramatic increase in population largely created "Marvellous Melbourne," as it became known. A Town Hall was built in 1853 but to accommodate growing town business larger premises were found in 1867.[24] These were still inadequate and the Council resolved to erect a new building to be designed by architects Reed and Barnes, with construction commencing in 1868. The decision made, it was erected without any of the scandals that had slowed the construction of Sydney Town Hall (Figure 6.4).

Figure 6.4
Melbourne Town Hall, c. 1880. Image courtesy of National Library of Australia.

The Governor of Victoria opened the new Melbourne Town Hall on August 9, 1870, a full nineteen years before Sydney Town Hall was opened. The *Illustrated Australian News for Home Readers* of August 13, 1870, announced its completion with more than a touch of hyperbole: "The hoarding now being removed the public have now an opportunity of seeing this magnificent building, which has, comparatively, rivalled the fairy tales of the Arabian Nights in the wonderful speed of its construction." The Hall, designed in French Second Empire style, had cost £200,000 to construct and furnish. Its great hall was described as "so large and so magnificent that there are not many in Europe equal to it." Lord Mayor Samuel Amess personally hosted (and funded) a grand concert and fancy dress ball to celebrate the opening, which was reported in detail in *The Argus* on August 13, 1870.

> On Thursday evening it was filled to overflowing with the guests of the mayor of Melbourne, chiefly in fantastic or beautiful fancy dresses, and dance and promenade filled up the whole night most delightfully. No such scene was ever witnessed before on the south side of the equator, and the opening of the Melbourne Town-hall will always be remembered by three or four thousand Victorian colonists as the most brilliant affair at which they were ever privileged to assist.

The dimensions of the great hall, as described by the *Illustrated Australian News for Home Readers* on August 13, 1870, were 174 feet by 74 feet with a height of 63 feet. An organ loft occupied the back of the stage. There was a large gallery at the other end and narrow galleries, which rested on iron pillars embedded in stone pediments, on either side of the hall. The roof was divided into panels, decorated

Figure 6.5
Interior view of Town Hall, Melbourne, c. 1892, photographed by Fred Hardie. Image courtesy of National Library of Australia.

"in a style between the Arabesque and Pompeian," painted blue and white with "prettily devised scroll work" in each corner, and in the centre "an intricate and elaborately-executed design, in which blue and colours of a darker hue intermixed with gold are exquisitely blended, while stars are dotted about in great profusion." It was lighted by two rows of windows in the roof (Figure 6.5).

Melbourne Town Hall enjoyed considerable prestige. It wielded the authority of Empire; on November 20, 1867, Prince Alfred, Duke of Edinburgh, had led the celebrations in laying the Hall's foundation stone (just four months before he laid the foundation stone of Sydney Town Hall), and later, the Duke approved its name, Prince Alfred's Tower.[25] Beyond imperial affiliations, the Town Hall also assumed influence from its attachment to Melbourne City Council. David Dunstan and John Young have noted that until the 1970s, the Council maintained a reputation as a "respected institution of substance," boasting councillors and aldermen who held significant social and political clout and respect as members of Parliament, major businessmen, professionals, and community leaders in Melbourne, a number of whom were rewarded with knighthoods.[26]

Accordingly, the Town Hall was host to many displays of grandeur. William H. Newman has argued that the Town Hall lived up to the expectations suggested by *The Argus* on August 13, 1870 as "a hall that was used by the citizens for the 'greatest variety of assemblage.'"[27] In this sense, Melbourne Town Hall not only acted as a central building of assembly, but also as a shared space where ordinary civilians and municipal and imperial authorities encountered and interacted with one another.

Figure 6.6
Matriculation and Civil Service Examination in the Great Hall of Melbourne Town Hall, 1873, wood engraving published in *The Illustrated Australian News for Home Readers*. Image courtesy of the State Library of Victoria.

However, Newman neglected the occasions on which these encounters were less amiable. At times the Town Hall became a place where these authorities stood over and in opposition to the people of Melbourne; a site where class and wealth divisions were not overcome but thrown into conflict. Jeff Sparrow and Jill Sparrow have asserted that Melbourne Town Hall historically acted as a "display of municipal power ... when the authorities required an imposing symbol of authority around which to rally their forces."[28] They cite two events in particular as symbolizing this function: the 1890 maritime dispute, and the 1923 police strike. In both episodes, the Town Hall served as a muster station for municipal power under threat, enabling civil unrest to be quashed.

In August 1890, Melbourne shipowners refused maritime officers the right to affiliate with the Melbourne Trades Hall. Widely seen as a violation of trade unionism, this sparked a huge strike by the officers. The *Argus* reported that "[i]n these colonies is being waged what the Germans would call a world battle." The strike was to peak in a rally on the Yarra Bank, which up to 100,000 people attended. The authorities endeavored to police this crowd; the government dispensed 200 Mounted Rifles, the Victorian Rangers, and all available cavalry. As well, Council reinforced these troops with a group of "special constables," ordinary civilians employed as volunteer combatants for the authorities. These "specials" signed up at the Town Hall, with 200 men enlisting over the course of a day. Significantly, *The Age* noted that "most of those sworn in yesterday are not of the working class, but are men engaged in Flinders Lane and other city houses." Similarly, on September 1, 1890, the *Argus* reported:

> muster was held in the courtyard on the basement of the Town Hall which was dimly lit with kerosene lamps, and the whole scene was a most extraordinary one. Shortly after 8 o'clock the men were marshalled into six companies, according to pre-arrangement and each company elected its own lieutenant by vote … Glancing down the lines one saw many well known faces. The law had quite a number of representatives, both solicitors and barristers. A frequent practitioner of the City Court was there, ready to substitute the convincing argument of the baton for the more tedious procedure of legal formalities, and a rising young barrister stood near him, apparently by no means displeased at the prospect of laying down his brief … in order to take his place in the ranks of the special constables.

Thus, Melbourne Town Hall came to represent an assembly point and a stronghold for conservative forces from the middle and elite classes to suppress the working class and assert their power. The rally came to a halt when the Trades Hall yielded, leaving the maritime officers with a poor compromise, and delivering a major blow to the union movement.[29]

Similar patterns became apparent in 1923 when the Melbourne police force held a strike against inadequate pay, poor conditions, and in particular the supervision of street constables by plain-clothes "spooks." As a section of the Town Hall served as headquarters for the traffic division of the police force, and although the majority of men in this division were on strike, this space became an assembly point for loyalist constables. Upon retreating to the Town Hall, these loyalists were surrounded and called "scabs," "blacklegs," and "curs" by the striking constables. The *Argus* reported:

> Efforts were made by the crowd to break down the main door, and a smaller door, but the demonstrators were lacking in spirit, and the attempt soon ceased. For a time there was a period of comparative inactivity, then bottles and eggs were hurled at any person who evinced sympathy for the loyal policemen. Ten minutes later, the doors of the Town Hall swung open, and the force of police, numbering about 30, with the sub inspectors at the head, charged the crowd with batons and handcuffs flying.[30]

These baton charges continued through the night and a high-pressure hose was also employed. Numerous civilians were injured and a makeshift first-aid station had to be set up in the Town Hall's courtyard. By the following day, more extreme measures were employed: "specials" were once again enlisted. The *Herald* reported:

> There was an exodus from Melbourne and suburban picture theatres on Saturday night when the management flashed upon the screen – *The ministry ask all returned soldiers to rally around General ('Pompey') Elliott at the Melbourne Town Hall to enroll as special constables and assist in preventing further looting in the city*. A splendid response followed. From 8 o'clock Saturday night until midnight last night the Town Hall was a scene of activity. It was

reminiscent of the early days of the Great War when recruiting was in progress. Young, old and middle-aged men enrolled as special constables. Officials found it difficult to cope with the rush ... Among the volunteers were leading commercial and professional men. Several Victorian and interstate graziers who were visiting Melbourne for the Melbourne Cup also took the oath and marched out with the squads.

This time, 1,500 civilians signed up – a response so overwhelming that there were insufficient batons until those stored in the Town Hall since the maritime dispute more than 30 years earlier were rediscovered. These civilians formed a Special Constabulary Force (SCF). Although the SCF was able to quell some looting that resulted from the strike, there were considerable civilian casualties; 200 people were treated in hospitals, the majority of whom had head injuries. Municipal power thus directly and physically threatened civilian rights and welfare. The press named the SCF "brethren of the baton." Not surprisingly they were widely disliked by the public, particularly in working-class suburbs where, according to Sparrow and Sparrow, they were stoned, beaten up, and even shot at.

Throughout its history, Melbourne Town Hall has been the city's showpiece and its main cultural, social, and political venue. As a meeting place for political debate, it has also continued to be an assembly and rallying point, notably during the anti-Vietnam War marches of the 1970s. Like Sydney Town Hall it was the home of the city's symphony orchestra for many years and many famous visiting musicians performed there. This included rock musicians in the 1960s, with the Beatles given a civic reception there in 1964.[31] It was also host to a range of other events. In 1956, for example, Newman noted that a yearly average of 150,000 people came through the doors of the Town Hall for a diverse range of events, including flower shows, mayoral balls, royal occasions, and the 1981 opening of the Commonwealth Heads of Government meetings.[32]

THE TOODYAY TOWN HALL

A vast distance from the metropolises of Sydney and Melbourne, the foundation stone was laid for a town hall at Toodyay in 1910. Toodyay is emblematic of the myriad small towns in Australia. Located 53 miles (85 km) to the north east of Perth, capital city of the state of Western Australia, the town site was declared in 1833, just four years after the British colonization of the western third of the Australian continent. Its name is derived from the Aboriginal word "Duidgee" thought to have meant "place of plenty."[33] It is situated on the Avon River and, with more fertile soil for pastures and crops than the sandy coastal plain, the district developed into a rich sheep and wheat farming area.[34]

With increasing population, the town was declared a municipality in 1877 and a council established to administer the affairs of the town area, followed by a Roads Board in 1887 covering a larger district. In 1899 Municipal Council Chambers were erected and meetings of both the Council and Roads Board were conducted there. But the township was still tiny, with only 339 residents in the Municipal area and 2,964 in the Roads Board area in 1901. A decade later municipality and Roads Board were merged to administer the 650 square mile district.[35] It was in response to this merger that a town hall was built.

Located on the town's main street, the Toodyay Town Hall incorporates the original Municipal Council Chambers (1899), now the foyer (or Lesser Hall) and rest rooms, with the purpose-built Town Hall (1910) to the rear (Figure 6.7). A further rear extension was added in 1956–57 and a side extension in 1990–91, when the whole building was restored and renovated. The building is brick with a hipped iron roof; the front of the building has a Dutch gable style parapet and decorated elevation with a scroll motif and mouldings around the windows and entrance.[36]

The Toodyay Town Hall was officially opened on October 7, 1910, with a Grand Charity Ball to raise funds for the Toodyay Hospital. The 83 feet by 33 feet hall, with steps to a proscenium arch stage, seats 200. In her history of the hall, Beth Frayne notes that ventilation and six large outward opening fire escape doors were special features. An acetylene gas generator provided the lighting. Electric lighting was not installed until 1920. Two large anterooms were constructed at the rear of the large stage, and water was laid on in the kitchen. Toilets were included. A local painter painted the Hall's "artistic pressed metal proscenium."[37] There was no grand organ loft or space for a symphony orchestra in this country town hall.

The Toodyay Town Hall was used for a variety of purposes. Prominent among these were public meetings, with electoral meetings a regular feature. Typical was the first, which was fully reported in the state's daily morning newspaper, the *West Australian* on September 16, 1911. It was presided over by the Mayor, who

Figure 6.7
Toodyay Memorial Hall (Toodyay Town Hall prior to renaming in 1957), 2013, photographed by Jenny Edgecombe. Image courtesy of Toodyay Historical Society.

introduced the candidates. The electorate, which numbered 3,600, was a conservative stronghold, with the incumbent member, T. F. Quinlan MLA, having held the seat for fifteen years and holding the position of speaker in the Legislative Assembly.[38] Addressing a large and sympathetic audience in the Town Hall, his election speech was wide-ranging and tailored to his largely agricultural community. He noted, for example, the success of government policies in opening up and developing agricultural resources in the state, including expanding the railways and enabling the Agricultural Bank to "lend money at cheap rates for long periods" for agricultural development; and promised his support for a proposal to carry water by train to country areas affected by the dry season. He also noted that he had introduced a deputation to the parliament requesting financial assistance for the town, and this had resulted in a grant of £250 for the Toodyay Town Hall, while a request for another £250 for the main road was under consideration. This point was the only one that raised a cheer from the assembled crowd seated in the Town Hall, until the conclusion of his speech.

> Let him assure them that his interests were bound up in the welfare of the people of Toodyay. If they could not vote for him he wanted their respect … He was there before them in public and had held himself open for their opinions. With that there was much applause and cries of "Well done, Tim".

Ten years later in 1922, a town hall audience heard sitting Country Party member in the State Legislative Council, Vernon Hamersley MLC, open his election campaign and this too was reported in the *West Australian* on May 10, 1922. Profoundly conservative, he had held the seat for eighteen years. Declaring himself "a son of the soil," he called on primary producers to organize politically to protect their interests, alerting the audience to the rise of trade unionism as a political power, and the menace of trades unions which could call for work stoppages, bring railways and other transport to a standstill, and paralyze the community, place "black" bans on goods and businesses, and cause "the ultimate destruction of civilization."

Just a year later the Toodyay Town Hall was the site of considerable political disaffection. A major dispute between the Primary Producers Association (PPA) and its political arm the Country Party was extensively reported in the *West Australian*. It detailed discussions at meeting after meeting in the Toodyay Town Hall throughout 1923 in the lead up to the State Elections of 1924.[39] The PPA attacked the executive of the Country Party for its actions in permitting the pre-selection of a candidate to represent Toodyay by a district council in another country town. This resulted in a split of the Party into two; the Ministerial Country Party (MCP) and the Old Country Party (OCP). In a tightly fought election five candidates competed for the seat of Toodyay in the Legislative Assembly and J. C. Lindsay from the OCP defeated the sitting member A. N. Piesse from the MCP, who was also the government whip and had held the seat since 1911. The upheaval ultimately resulted in a change of government, with the Labor Party claiming power.

Matters of importance to the community were frequently discussed at Town Hall meetings. These ranged from lectures on stock disease, sheep husbandry, dairying, spinning and weaving, to adult education lectures. The Town Hall was also the place where residents met for a variety of purposes and many were reported in the *West Australian*. A public meeting that had been held to discuss the unemployment situation was detailed in the newspaper on July 10, 1930. There it was decided that the unemployed would be engaged to complete the footpaths in the main streets and a fund sent up for families in distress. Teachers at the local school agreed to contribute 2d. in every £1 from their salaries and the Road Board agreed to match public subscriptions £1 for £1. On February 14, 1939, months before the start of the Second World War, the *West Australian* noted a meeting that had been held to discuss the enrolment of volunteers in a platoon being raised at Toodyay – "36 men enrolled in quick time." While on June 7, 1944, it reported that the Department of Manpower had arranged a meeting of farmers interested in employing Italian prisoners of war.

Many exhibitions, bazaars, dances, and balls were also held in the Toodyay Town Hall. The district is known for the beauty of its wildflowers and the Town Hall regularly hosted spring flower shows. It also hosted the local finals of the Miss Westralia Quest in conjunction with Wool Week as reported in the *West Australian* on February 25, 1932, while on May 20, 1941 the *West Australian* noted that Mrs Rayner was crowned National Emergency Queen at a ball in the Town Hall. There were many fundraising dances and balls. One of the earliest was held in 1914 to raise funds to assist a soldier who had been seriously injured. A detailed report appeared in the *West Australian* on June 29, 1914. It drew attention to "the fine ballroom, with its absolutely perfect floor," the dance band which played "all the latest ragtime, and made dancing on the highly polished floor a pleasure indeed;" the supper, "home-made and daintily served;" the supper table decorations, "shaded rose carnations, geraniums, and gracefully trailing fern … calling forth much admiration from visitors;" and described "the many handsome dresses" worn by the ladies. Another major ball was held in 1933 to mark the Centenary of Toodyay, which the Lieutenant Governor, local Members of Parliament, and the Mayor attended. On October 25, the *West Australian* reported that the "Picturesque Period Ball" had been "a brilliant success," though the Town Hall, albeit "artistically decorated" with the walls covered with "hollyhocks and palms" and "baskets of wisteria" hanging from the ceiling, was "far too small" for the 500 attendees.

A regular column headed "Country News" appeared in the *West Australian* and this provided details of many other events held in Toodyay Town Hall. They included annual children's balls and dances during the interwar years, the Toodyay Follies in 1932, and other amateur theatricals. There were even boxing matches held in the Town Hall and movies were shown in the hall from the 1920s until the 1960s. Recent activities in the Toodyay Town Hall, reported by the *Toodyay Herald* in September 2012, have included the Toodyay Community Singers' Musical Memories, a "real tour de force" which played to an audience of more than 300; the Rocky Horror Show put on by the Toodyay Theatre Group; and a "Feed the Paws" Quiz Night, with "heaps of pawesome prizes" in aid of country dogs.[40]

The Toodyay Memorial Hall still represents the heart of this rural community. During the devastating bushfires that raged around the town just after Christmas 2009, a relocation point was set up at the Town Hall for residents forced to abandon their homes as flames advanced on the township.[41] The bushfire destroyed 38 homes, damaged another 200, and burnt out 7,166 acres of land. During the fire and in the days that followed, the hall acted as a shelter for victims until alternative accommodation could be found and it continued to function as an information center for many weeks. Two months after the fire, the Office of Energy Safety released its report into the cause of the blaze. The report was inconclusive, but said the fire was most likely to have been caused by a fallen timber power pole and that high voltage conductors ignited barley stubble in extreme temperature conditions and high winds. At an "emotionally-charged meeting" in the Town Hall, "angry locals confronted representatives from Western Power and the Office of Energy Safety" saying that "they don't trust the results of the report."[42]

The State Government established a $10 million assistance fund for victims of the bushfire, but 97 residents and the Toodyay Race Club sued Western Power, a state enterprise, in a class action. In an unprecedented step, the State Supreme Court held a "strategic conference" in the Toodyay Memorial Hall. The media was also allowed to film the proceedings, thus breaking a long tradition in which media were banned from court proceedings. It was reputed to be the first time that the Supreme Court had moved beyond its usual state circuit.[43] Western Power denied responsibility for the fire, but was later involved in confidential mediation with some of the victims whose homes were destroyed or damaged.[44] The cause of the Toodyay bushfire is still the subject of an ongoing investigation by a parliamentary committee, with some calling for a Royal Commission.

Figure 6.8
Town anger: Toodyay residents gather in Toodyay Memorial Hall at a meeting to coordinate bushfire relief efforts, *Sunday Times*, December 30, 2009. Photograph: Kerris Berrington. Image courtesy of Newspix.

CONCLUSION

It is clear from this foray into the history of town halls in Australia that the activities that have taken place and the matters discussed within them are second only to the activities and matters discussed in the parliament. This is not surprising as local government is the third arm of government in Australia. What is surprising is the range of activities that have taken place in the town hall, the deep level of community engagement, and the level of both consensus and conflict that has been played out within their walls. In nineteenth-century Australia the ties of empire were strong, and regal and viceregal connections were paramount, with the Town Hall emblematic of imperialism, but with the rise of Australian nationalism and the federation of the Australian states into a Commonwealth, the focus turned to competing interest groups within Australian society, and town halls truly became the "home of the liberties of the people." Major conflicts were played out in the town halls of Australia, though, as the largest public meeting space in the community, the myriad civic, cultural, and community activities that were hosted at the town hall, and their role in building community and consensus must not be forgotten.

NOTES

1. With thanks to Isabel Smith for her research assistance.
2. Walter Murdoch, "An Australian in Florence," *Loose Leaves* (Melbourne: George Robertson & Co, 1910), 31.
3. There are 562 local government areas in Australia. For details see the website of the Australian Local Government Association (accessed September 10, 2012; http://alga.asn.au/)
4. Shirley Fitzgerald, *Sydney 1842–1992* (Sydney: Hale & Iremonger, 1992), 88–9 and http://www.cityofsydney.nsw.gov.au/sydneytownhall/building-history.asp (accessed May 30, 2012).
5. Fitzgerald, *Sydney 1842–1992*, 89–91.
6. "SC on the Working of Municipalities," 114, cited in Fitzgerald, *Sydney 1842–1992*, 92.
7. CRS 21/22; CRS 9/3, 78-83, cited in Fitzgerald, *Sydney 1842–1992*, 84 and see 91–3.
8. Fitzgerald, *Sydney 1842–1992*, 84–86, 92–6.
9. Fitzgerald, *Sydney 1842–1992*, 96–97, 99.
10. Cited in Fitzgerald, *Sydney 1842–1992*, 86.
11. Fitzgerald, *Sydney 1842–1992*, 101.
12. Fitzgerald, *Sydney 1842–1992*, 102.
13. Fitzgerald, *Sydney 1842–1992*, 105.
14. Fitzgerald, *Sydney 1842–1992*, 105.
15. CRS 34/1248/48, Doc 24, cited in Fitzgerald, *Sydney 1842–1992*, 105–6.
16. CRS 34/1248/48, Docs 41, 45, cited in Fitzgerald, *Sydney 1842–1992*, 106.
17. Jessie Street had been the Australian representative on the United Nations Status of Women Commission in 1948.
18. This and the following quotations in this paragraph are from CRS 34/6496/50, cited in Fitzgerald, *Sydney 1842–1992*, 106–7.
19. Fitzgerald, *Sydney 1842–1992*, 107.

20 http://www.sydneybarani.com.au/themes/theme3.htm and http://www.sydneybarani.com.au/themes/theme6.htm#p_3 (accessed May 21, 2013).
21 *PC* 1920, 161–5, cited in Fitzgerald, *Sydney 1842–1992*, 104.
22 Cited in Fitzgerald, *Sydney 1842–1992*, 104–5.
23 Further information about the Sydney Town Hall at http://www.cityofsydney.nsw.gov.au/sydneytownhall/discover-and-learn.asp (accessed May 30, 2012).
24 Jeff Sparrow and Jill Sparrow, *Radical Melbourne: A Secret History* (Carlton North: The Vulgar Press, 2001), 59.
25 William H. Newman, *Melbourne: Biography of a City* (Melbourne: Hill of Content, 1985), 213–14.
26 David Dunstan and John Young, 'When "Clown Hall" really was Town Hall: The Melbourne City Council in the 1960s,' in Seamus O'Hanlon and Tanya Luckins, eds., *Go! Melbourne in the Sixties* (Beaconsfield: Circa, 2005), 203.
27 Cited in Newman, *Melbourne*, 214.
28 This quotation and others in the following paragraphs relating to the maritime strike are from newspaper reports cited in Sparrow and Sparrow, *Radical Melbourne*, 59–60.
29 Sparrow and Sparrow, *Radical Melbourne*, 61.
30 This and the following quotations relating to the police strike are from newspaper reports cited in Sparrow and Sparrow, *Radical Melbourne*, 62–3.
31 Graeme Tucker, "Melbourne Town Hall," *eMelbourne: the Encyclopedia of Melbourne on-line* (Melbourne: School of Historical Studies, The University of Melbourne), 2008; http://www.emelbourne.net.au/home.html (accessed September 2, 2012).
32 Newman, *Melbourne*, 214.
33 There is some disagreement over the meaning of Duidgee, the phonetic European spelling of a spoken Aboriginal word. Some believe it represents the sound of small birds chirping duidji-duidji. Others that it is the name of beautiful Aboriginal women called Toodyeep. See Ken McIntyre and Barbara Dobson, anthropologists, "Duidgee – a little bird's song," *Toodyay*, 2011 (accessed August 20, 2012).
34 The town of Toodyay was first located to the west but, because of flooding, was transferred to its present location in 1860 and renamed Newcastle. In 1910 the town's name was changed to Toodyay because of confusion with the town of Newcastle in New South Wales. See Beth Frayne (comp.), *The Long Toodyay Chronology: Events in Toodyay's History, Part 1, 1829–1900* (Toodyay: Toodyay Historical Society (Inc)), 2009.
35 The Toodyay Road District became the Shire of Toodyay on July 1, 1961 following state government legislation whereby all road districts became shires.
36 Toodyay Memorial Hall, Toodyay Municipal Heritage inventory, listed on State Heritage Office website, http://inherit.stateheritage.wa.gov.au/Public/Inventory/Details/aaac801c-5147-43a3-b96f-f5ebb6ddf173 (accessed August 30, 2012).
37 Beth Frayne, "The Toodyay Memorial Hall (1910): a short history," *Duidgeeana*, 20, March/April 2011, 7. The Toodyay Town Hall was renamed the Toodyay Memorial Hall in 1957 after the Returned Servicemen's League paid for repair and renovation of the hall.
38 The Western Australian State Parliament comprises of a lower house, the Legislative Assembly, and an upper house of review, the Legislative Council. Legislation must pass through both houses before it is enacted.
39 The Country Party was established in 1914. In 1923 the PPA split from its representatives in the conservative ministry of Sir James Mitchell, with unity only re-established after the party went into opposition. Lenore Layman, "Country (National) Party," in Jenny Gregory and Jan Gothard, eds., *Historical Encyclopedia of Western Australia* (Crawley: University of Western Australia Press, 2006), 248.
40 *Toodyay Herald*, vol. 306, September 2012.

41 "Bushfire emergency: homes lost in Toodyay," *Perth Now,* http://www.perthnow.com.au/news/residents-flee-wall-of-flame-in-badgingarra/story-e6frg12c-1225814480592 (accessed August 30, 2012).
42 ABC News, February 20, 2010, http://www.abc.net.au/news/2010-02-20/toodyay-fire-victims-demand-answers/337520 (accessed August 30, 2012).
43 "Bushfire compensation case to be heard in Toodyay," *Sunday Times,* April 9, 2011, http://www.news.com.au/bushfire-compensation-case-to-be-heard-in-toodyay/story-e6frg13u-1226036485165?from=public_rss (accessed August 30, 2012).
44 WA today.com.au, August 24, 2012, http://www.watoday.com.au/wa-news/politician-vows-to-use-privileges-to-reveal-toodyay-fire-payouts-20120823-24omj.html (accessed August 30, 2012).

Chapter 7: Courting the Council

The Municipal Palace and the Popular Petition in Morelia, Mexico, 1880–1930[1]

Christina M. Jiménez

Since pre-Columbian times, urban life in Mesoamerica has developed around central plazas and their surrounding streets and buildings, which represented the hub of political, commercial, social, and administrative activities. The Spanish grafted the center of their colonial empire onto the urban spaces of the indigenous *Mexica*,[2] an idea illustrated by the construction of Mexico City on top of the Aztec capital of Tenochtitlán. The Spanish ruled the countryside from the city-centered institutions of colonial power. They imprinted colonial order onto the landscape, particularly in the recognizable urban form of the Spanish city center. The main plaza (*plaza mayor*), cathedral, governor's palace (*palacio de gobierno*), and palace of justice (*palacio de justicia*) embodied the physical and literal center of Spanish government and colonial rule.[3]

In the wake of Independence in 1821, Mexico's newly founded national institutions encompassed a blend of colonial and republican conceptualizations of government, a blending illustrated by the practice of naming the seat of municipal government the *palacio municipal* (municipal palace). Under both liberal and conservative governments, the title likely evoked notions of monarchical legitimacy and colonial grandeur among the newly independent Mexican elite, many of whom were Spanish *criollos* (persons of Spanish parentage, but born in the Americas). Local city councils, or *ayuntamientos,* embodied Mexico's equivalent of the town hall. The form (the city council) and the space (the palacio municipal) of local government fused local and monarchical powers; it simultaneously positioned the city council as a legitimate entity and represented the continued relevance of the colonial *cabildos* (Spanish colonial municipal councils). During the early decades of Mexico's national period (1820s to 1860s), the municipal ayuntamiento, like state and federal administrations, became embroiled in endemic conflicts over political control, thereby undermining political stability at all levels. Despite, and perhaps because of, this political instability, the municipal government emerged as a vital center of local politics and social practices, mediating everyday issues for people living in their city. People communicated their needs and requests to the Municipal Palace typically in the form of petitions. This chapter examines the intersections between popular petitioning, the Municipal Palace, and everyday urban politics in Morelia, Mexico.

Traditional approaches to political citizenship, which tend to focus on the right to vote, formation of political parties, the expansion of the press, and the Habermasian public sphere rooted in the press, salons, and popular culture, typically fail to include alternative forms of political engagement such as the practice of petitioning.[4] Attention to political petitioning enables us to enlarge the scope of popular citizenship and political culture, particularly at a time of limited formal political citizenship among Mexicans. Based on my reading of thousands of petitions archived in the Palacio Municipal of Morelia between 1880 and 1930, I argue that the right to petition authorities opened channels for daily dialogue between the political authorities and city residents, which residents used to assert a range of claims. These public claims were often articulated and legitimated as basic rights to the city – meaning the right to participate in and benefit from the city's public spaces, its consumer and popular cultures, its modernized infrastructure, and its urban promise. I describe how residents used a range of conceptual frameworks (including the public good, competence, honesty, and public accountability) and articulated multiple social identities (namely those rooted in neighborhood, notions of honor, and public contributions) in their petitions to the ayuntamiento and the other agents of the Palacio Municipal. Petitions, and the identities articulated in them, were often used as leverage for broader claims, namely justice and political accountability, both values articulated as part of Morelia's civic identity. I explore how perhaps this civic ethos connected to, or was informed by, the city's built environment and architectural patrimony.

The site of this study is Morelia, the provincial capital of Michoacán, a notable Mexican city since the early Spanish colonial period. The colonial architecture of the central *Plaza de Armas*, later renamed the *Plaza de Martires* (Plaza of Martyrs), the Cathedral of Morelia, city parks, and the colonial aqueduct reflect this history. As a subnational city, Morelia embodied many of the internal social contradictions and emerging urban problems plaguing other Mexican cities in the late nineteenth century.[5] Morelia's population growth from 1880 to 1930 represents an average expansion for a Mexican provincial capital and its hinterland during this period.[6] Descriptive evidence indicates that a significant portion of this population increase resulted from rural to urban migration. The effects of the liberal laws on villages, the commercialization of agriculture, the modernization of cities associated with the rule of President Porfirio Díaz, also referred to as the *Porfiriato* (1880–1910), and the volatile decades of the Mexican Revolution (1910–20) consistently pushed rural inhabitants into provincial cities like Morelia.

Although revolutionary violence largely spared Morelia, fundamental realignments between municipal, state, and federal powers occurred during the Mexican Revolution.[7] These realignments prove particularly visible in state capitals, like Morelia, where the Municipal Palace sat only a few blocks away from the State Governor's office (Palacio de Gobierno). Paralleling broader changes in the city, control over the physical spaces, resources, and people in the urban center became a point of contestation between the municipality and state governments.

Several of Morelia's most prominent historic buildings, the Palacio de Gobierno and the Palacio de Justicia, surround the Plaza de Martires and Cathedral in the historic colonial footprint [*la traza*], which functions as the heart of Morelia's historical patrimony. In contrast, the Municipal Palace, home of the city council and mayor, sits a few blocks off the main square at 403 Calle Allende, a street which runs along the south border of the plaza. Unlike the wide girth of the city's main artery, Madero Avenue, which traces the plaza's northern border, Allende Street is fairly narrow.

The architectural design of the Municipal Palace, both interior and exterior, is a combination of styles, ranging from classical, neo-classical, baroque, and French eclectic designs, quite typical to Morelia's historic buildings (Figures 7.1, 7.2, 7.3). To this day, Morelians identify with this blending and layering of architectural styles across the centuries as core to their unique historical patrimony and civic identity. In a definitive work on the topic, Ramírez Romero explains that this "architectural patrimony" includes something "intangible which creates our culture, which is ultimately our identity, that which Morelians have expressed through the explicit form of stylistic variety."[8] Several Morelia scholars focus on the history of the city, its cultural inheritance, and civic identity as expressed through the historical details of its buildings and architecture, often emphasizing processes of cooptation, re-definition, and re-purposing.[9] The shift from colony to republic necessitated a re-purposing of religious buildings in liberal-stronghold Morelia, including seminaries, convents, rectories, and other confiscated urban property of the Catholic Church. Republican governments transformed these buildings into spaces of education, industry, medicine, commerce, and government during the nineteenth century. Notably, the Municipal Palace, built in 1766, was originally a tobacco factory. The municipal government acquired and re-purposed it in the 1850s.

Since that time, the Municipal Palace performed pivotal roles representing *both* a primary *space* of political dialogue between the urban public and the municipal government, and a primary *relationship* where the men and women of Morelia came to experience themselves as legitimate members of the public, partaking in the historical patrimony of the city. So, what can we infer from the spaces that affected both the relationships and the practice of petitioning? Approaching the Municipal Palace from the street, one is struck by the symmetrical lines of the façade and the wide entryway into the interior. Upon entering the doorway, narrowness diffuses into an ample sunken central patio surrounded by two stories of arcaded walkways. The thick columns are slightly tapered with ornamented spandrels and arches and square-shaped capitals supporting the spring of the arch. A wide stone stairway leading to the second floor opens directly from the ground-level central patio (Figure 7.4). Ornamented wrought-iron hand railings line the staircase and the upper-level balconies. As a structure, the Municipal Palace presented a balanced impression of both authority and accessibility. Reflecting this balance, doormen likely stood in the front entrance, both according or interdicting entrance.

Figure 7.1
Morelia's Municipal Palace at 403 Allende Street, originally built and used as a tobacco factory in the 1760s, was acquired by the municipal government and refurbished in the 1850s. Photograph by the author.

Figure 7.2
The main entrance and façade of the Municipal Palace. Photograph by the author.

Figure 7.3
Passing through the front entranceway, a visitor to the Municipal Palace would enter into the central open-air patio surrounded by a covered arcade walkway. The second level of the building is accessed via a central stairway, visible on the far side of the patio. Photograph by the author.

Figure 7.4
The main interior stairway leads to the second level of the Municipal Palace. At the top of this first flight of stairs, an elaborate wall monument and official seal commemorates the history of Morelia. At the center of the wall monument is a small water fountain. Note the ceilings of the arcaded walkways are covered with dark wooden beams, typical in Morelia. Photograph by the author.

City inhabitants regularly entered the Municipal Palace to conduct business with the municipal government; they settled their debts, submitted paperwork, and gathered upon the request of the city council. Written correspondence – petitions, circulars, and regulations – generated political openings for a wide range of urban residents to discuss a broad spectrum of issues of daily life with municipal and state officials. The city council regularly called together municipal employees (like policemen, gardeners, street sweepers, etc.), municipally licensed occupations (including shoe shiners, water carriers, porters, domestic servants, and prostitutes among others), and other groups of residents (like shopkeepers or neighbors around a certain plaza, etc.) to gather in the patio of the Municipal Palace to hear announcements and new regulations. Officials distributed "circulars" (Figure 7.5) requiring members of that group to sign the document before passing it on, attesting that they were informed of the meeting. Local officials regularly arranged gatherings of this sort, providing both an opportunity for dialogue between the municipal government and worker-residents as well as between the members of the group themselves.

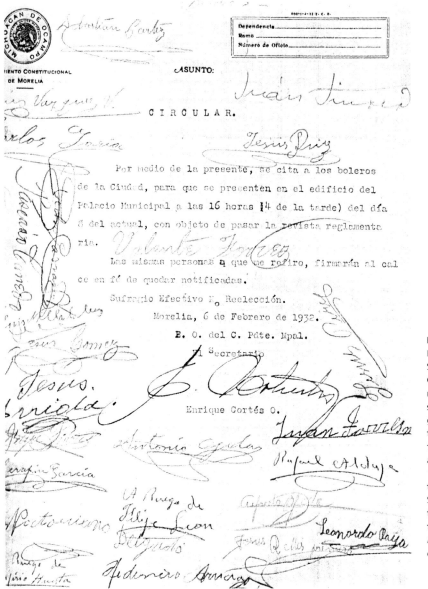

Figure 7.5
In this 1932 Circular, the Secretary of the City Council of Morelia requests all the shoe shiners in the city to gather for a meeting in the Municipal Palace at four o'clock in the afternoon on February 8, 1932 in order to review the revised regulations. Shoe shiners informed of the meeting have signed the circular. *Archivo Histórico del Municipio de Morelia*, c. 408.

Given these uses, the Municipal Palace, particularly its interior patio and walkways, represented the kind of accessible and publicly claimed spaces, like outdoor city plazas, emblematic of popular politics and protest in Latin America. As Anton Rosenthal suggests, "Analyzing public space, since its meaning or even its existence is situational, reveals changing relations of power, particularly between social classes."[10] In Morelia, traditional notions of honor and competency became tied to occupation and reputation within the community. People used their access to and dialogues with municipal authorities to document and to locate spatially their connections to the community. In this sense, the Municipal Palace came to embody a structure of historical patrimony as much as a place of public meanings associated with the political relationship it represented. These historical dynamics partially explain the continued efforts to defend and preserve Morelia's architectural patrimony as evidenced by the numerous laws and decrees to this effect: for example, in Morelia, Michoacán, the 1930 "Decree declaring the public utility of the vigilance and conservation of the structures determined to have historic and artistic value" and the 1931 "Law for the protection and conservation of monuments and natural beauty" were early versions of laws aimed to protect the colonial buildings (including the Municipal Palace) and to conserve the "typical colonial aspect" of the city.[11]

Generally, historians characterize the positivist orientation of the Porfirian state as both preoccupied with statistics, data-collecting, and record-keeping, and perpetuator of the marginalization and oppression of subaltern groups including indigenous villages, peasants, urban workers, the poor, and the uneducated. Researchers typically describe town halls as the stronghold of local elites set on containing, disciplining, and controlling the Mexican masses. Based on my archival research, Morelia's Municipal Palace challenges the uncomplicated nature of these assumptions. The administration did reflect the data-collecting, record-keeping generalization of the *Porfiriato*. And, members of the local elite sat on the city council and rotated as city mayor.[12] Nevertheless, the municipal government did not solely represent the interests of the elite, disregarding other urban constituencies. Archival records suggest a significant degree of sustained *engagement* with popular groups as well as a remarkable degree of *accountability* between residents and the municipal government, suggesting an alternative perspective to the typical depiction of people-state relations. Even people confined in the local jail communicated directly with the Supervisory Board of Prisons and the city council about the state of their trial or other issues.[13] In a remarkable example of this type, considering these general assumptions about Mexico's political culture during this period, prisoners at the local penitentiary successfully petitioned the Prefect in 1888. They requested to listen to music each day during visiting hours from 1 to 3 pm "as [they] had been accustomed during the preceding years."[14] The Prefect accepted.

As other contributors to this volume suggest, particularly those studying ex-colonial cities, after 1900, municipal governments gradually lost political power and leverage. The rise of the Mexican federal-state government structure in the 1910s and 1920s crystallized the shifting of revenue streams and political jurisdictions from the Municipal Palace towards state-level agencies and administrative branches. The ayuntamiento became financially impoverished and politically marginalized. Notably, "*municipio libre*" (liberated municipality) became a rallying cry of Mexican revolutionary forces after 1910, perhaps due, in part, to the accessibility and accountability associated with more autonomous municipal politics, public accountability, and popular engagement of the late nineteenth-century town hall.

POWER OF THE PETITION

Petitioning the Spanish King, Viceroy, Bishop, or other legitimate authority figure represented a primary mechanism for colonial subjects' appeal to the state's paternalism, justice, and protection. Indigenous populations under colonial rule were "quick to adopt the petitions, perhaps because petitions resembled oral or written appeals they were already familiar with."[15] The colonial practice of petitioning authorities, often associated exclusively with the emergence of constitutions, reminds us that earlier forms of government also generated mechanisms of accountability between rulers and subjects.

Popular petitioning persisted as a vital dynamic of the political culture of the city, blending traditional and modern practices into the city's historical patrimony. The republican practice of petitioning built upon and codified much older practices of pre-colonial and colonial communities in Mexico. After 1821, Mexico's republican constitutions embodied new versions of the paternalist colonial moral economy. Nineteenth-century regulations codified rights, responsibilities, duties, and obligations of government entities and individual Mexicans. Article 7 of the 1857 Constitution recognized the centrality of the petition to popular notions of legitimate government and enshrined the "right to petition local authorities and to get a response."[16] The proliferation of these legal codes also generated countless opportunities for residents to correspond with the state and establish micro-contracts regarding their rights and obligations as political subjects and community members. These obligations forced people into the political process by requiring them to engage in official correspondence, as residents, citizens, and nationals.[17]

Men and women used the petitioning process to demonstrate their competency, hard work, and honesty – positioning themselves as *vecinos* (neighbors or burghers) – and thus a part of the Mexican public with specific political rights, often invoking other specific guarantees – such as Article 124, "the right of free trade." This leverage of the petition was exclusive to neither Mexico nor Latin America. As Lex Heerma van Voss describes, for the European context and beyond, "[w]here petitions became an acceptable tradition, they could evolve into an institution which not only catered for the wishes of the individuals, but also was used to elicit general legislation."[18] In this way, "the right to petition easily brought about the right to assemble in order to draw up, discuss, and sign the petition."[19] In Mexico, petitioning also embodied a political act. The 1857 Constitution distinguished Mexican "citizens" from Mexican "nationals." Mexican parentage within the country guaranteed nationality, guaranteeing the rights and protections provided by the Constitution. However, the right to vote, to engage in formal politics and the duty of serving local governments hinged on the additional designation of "citizen." Mexican "citizenship" was granted only to men who qualified as "Mexican nationals," were eighteen if married, or twenty-one if single, and "possessed an honest way of making a living"[20] (the 1917 Constitution perpetuated this requirement in Article 34). The importance of demonstrating an honorable reputation and "honorable occupation" for working-class residents was likely linked to this subjective requirement that "citizens" possess an "honest occupation." This differentiation remained in force until the promulgation of the 1917 Constitution. Petitioning enabled otherwise disenfranchised and politically marginalized residents the opportunity to bargain for rights and resources as an urban public, and to demand political accountability in the city. The power of the petition built upon the colonial paternalist moral economy and subsequently served as a foundation for the expanded claims to Mexican "citizenship." By using their petitions to demonstrate their competence, civility, public contributions, and awareness of the obligations outlined in the Edict of Police and other urban regulations, petitioners revealed their understanding of the linkages between urban public space, petitioning, and political rights.[21]

Petitioning generated a two-way discussion around the municipal government's promise to protect the public; residents requested that the city council step in to protect their personal and collective interests. For their part, inhabitants of all classes invoked the promise of public protection in the case of dirty streets, leaky latrines, uncollected garbage, poorly constructed chimneys or houses, smoky ovens, flooded roads, police misconduct, abusive financial practices in the market, and unjust application of the law. Petitioners often conveyed their knowledge of the municipal council's responsibilities vís à vís the public, such as the duty of council members to respond promptly in writing to any popular request informing the petitioner of the outcome of his letter.

Historically, cultural, educational, socioeconomic class, and bureaucratic barriers to writing have disempowered and disenfranchised popular groups in Latin America. Angel Rama named this concentration of power around writing in Latin America – *la ciudad letrada,* "the lettered city."[22] Katherine Burns describes Rama's lettered city as "an urban concentration of men … wielding dominion over the official channels and instruments of communication."[23] Rama argues that writing, which was controlled by the *letrados* (lawyers or men who knew Latin and had studied for a law degree), held an "exclusive place" in Latin American societies "so revered as to take on an aura of sacredness."[24] However, in contrast to Rama's conclusion, my analysis suggests that learned and literate men were not the only people with access to writing. Popular appropriations of both writing, like the petition, and regulatory mechanisms in late nineteenth and early twentieth-century Mexico reveal alternative channels within or around the "lettered city."

While the state privileged print media as a means of official communication, face-to-face interactions certainly played a central role in the circulation of

City Halls and Civic Materialism ■

Figure 7.6
Public scribe in Mexico.
Photograph by Antioco
Cruces and Luis Campa
(active 1862–77),
well-known for their
photos of working
Mexicans.

knowledge in the city. Whether in the street, market, neighborhood plaza, or *cantina*, informal discussions and overheard conversations must have been a vital source of information for city dwellers. Ordinary men and women, who were likely aware of new local decrees, surely discussed these ideas with neighbors, family members, or co-workers. Nonetheless, given the high percentage of illiterate Mexicans in this period, many Morelians required the aid of an intermediary to engage in correspondence with the city council.[25]

Much of the documentation that historians use to write about non-elite actors forces us to rely upon sources generated through secondary actors, like scribes or notaries. Public scribes played an important role in the daily political participation of poorer residents, enabling illiterate or nominally literate men and women to engage in the political process (Figure 7.6). Unlike notaries or letrados, public scribes served poorer and working-class residents. They often worked in the accessible public spaces of the city: a small table in the main markets, the sidewalks of central avenues, under the arcaded walkways of the city central, or even inside the Palacio Municipal. For a few cents, illiterate or less-educated residents could hire a scribe to write or read their correspondence.[26] Informal conversations between scribes and petitioners became significant spaces for transmission of local knowledge. Scribes could have informed sellers of new laws or suggested how to couch arguments within legal frameworks or official rhetoric. Given the available sources, it is impossible to unravel the degree of influence a scribe (or other community member) had in determining the content of any given letter. Unfortunately, we know very little about public scribes, their level of education, their social background, or their daily functions in Mexico. While the urban public's dependence on the scribes certainly affirmed the persistence of the "lettered city" in Mexico, this legacy did not necessary perpetuate the exclusion of non-literate Mexicans.

THE POWER OF PAPERWORK AND NOTIONS OF ACCOUNTABILITY

From the late 1870s to the mid-1910s, the municipal city council of Morelia, headed by the Municipal President and approximately fourteen elected councilmen (*regidores*), received thousands of letters from a wide range of individuals, associations, groups, organizations, and businesses. Precisely how the petitions arrived is less clear. Some show the required stamp attached, presumably delivered through official channels. Others seem hand-delivered, either into the hands of the municipal secretary or to one of the councilmen, who were assigned to various city districts. The arrival of a petition to the Municipal Council set in motion an elaborate and well-documented administrative process of review, investigation, reporting, and response; this included internal memos or marginal notes in each petition's individual file archived with municipal records.

Once received by the municipal secretary, he delegated letters to the appropriate municipal commissions. These commissions, composed of three to five city councilmen, served as subcommittees of the general city council assembly. The number of commissions varied across the years. In 1880, the five core municipal commissions included: public works, water, gardens, public amusement, and food provisions (*abasto*). As the city grew in area and population, other commissions were established to oversee the expanding municipal bureaucracy. Once delegated, the commission deliberated about the course of action needed for the item at hand. Commissions often ordered an on-site inspection or investigation of the situation. If a neighbor wrote requesting to install new water piping to their house, they ordered an inspection to both confirm the proper location for the pipe's placement and note the state of the street pavement before the project began.

In most instances, city council members personally inspected locations involved in a complaint or dispute in the 1880s and early 1890s. After an inspection, the councilman would write a report (*informe*) with proposed responses to the petition. Council members regularly presented multiple voices on the matter in these reports. In some instances, commissioners' understanding of the issue at hand shifted following their inspection of the site. Often councilmen presented and discussed these reports either within the commission, or at a session of the city council. Municipal government files included brief summations of the city council's deliberations and the resulting decision. In most cases, the city council promptly responded to letters and petitions, although the turnaround time and overall response rate significantly declined through the 1920s.

Preserved documentation clearly illustrates a common concern of city councilors about resolving the matter while simultaneously upholding the law, protecting the "public," and not infringing upon individual rights. Petitioning created a paper trail of written dialogues evidencing city hall's administrative disposition to be a just arbiter. This evidence contradicts the typical generalizations of overt political favoritism among elites during the Porfiriato. Municipal officials in Morelia generally sought to disprove the notion that elite favoritism and "capricious" decision-making played into local governance. Through their detailed reports, municipal representatives defended their decisions invoking notions of municipal accountability to the public and the city's greater good.

Thorough municipal records produced a sense of administrative accountability, which came to be expected by residents. Basic requests, like those for a household water concession, illustrate this point. As a public resource, the municipal government managed the provision of water to urbanites; the allocation of specific amounts of water to different households; and the collection of water concession fees. Each water file in the Municipal Archives included information on both the amount and specific purposes of the water granted to each person. Files often contained other correspondence regarding the water grant including: changes in the amount of water needed, requests to begin piping the water, and letters officially renouncing the water grant. Jose Isla, an alfalfa farmer on the outskirts of the city, wrote to the city in November of 1883 requesting "*media naranja*" of water to irrigate his fields. Two years later he wrote again officially renouncing the water concession since he was "getting away from growing alfalfa and therefore no longer needed so much water." In one file the ayuntamiento had preserved his original letter outlining the terms of the grant; the notes and report of the water commission; and finally this letter renouncing the grant, thereafter deeming the file permanently closed.[27] Although a very common request, the city council scrupulously preserved all correspondence pertaining to Isla's concession in a single file.

The municipal archives maintained this type of meticulous record-keeping, particularly from 1880 to 1900, for most requests to the city council. Thorough documentation provided a foundation for administrative accountability and accuracy in municipal-resident negotiations. While the level of accountability of the municipal government is difficult to gauge, some of the most convincing evidence for administrative accountability appears in disputes between residents and the municipal treasury over billing charges. During these decades, residents seemed to rely upon and trust the thoroughness of municipal record keeping as it applied to records of debts owed to the municipal treasury.[28] Evidence indicates that the municipal treasurer was thorough and fair-handed in the collection of debt. Residents did not hesitate to write if they believed they were overcharged or wrongly charged for any type of municipal fee, debt, or fine. Even though the ayuntamiento continually experienced cash flow problems, it regularly reconsidered billing charges. For instance, when Lorenzo Campuzano Guerrero wrote to the council on July 22, 1884, he explained he had not been able to enjoy the two pajas of water granted to him for over 14 months since he had not been permitted to repair a leaky pipe, which crossed under the Plaza de Paz. He argued that he should not be charged for the lost water since the circumstances were beyond his control. The city council agreed with him and exempted him from paying the accumulated water fees.[29] Similarly, in 1896, Licenciado Jose Aldaiturrcaga wrote a forceful letter to the ayuntamiento claiming he was being overcharged for his household water supply. He wrote, "it is not fair, nor legal" to assess these charges.[30] The council agreed and corrected the problem. The effort to correct errors in the collection of water fees continued; by 1913, the municipal archive had a file designated "problems in billing mistakes in the municipal treasury." The treasury often readily acknowledged its mistake and promised to correct it, which usually required simply canceling someone's debt to the ayuntamiento.[31] In one case, Jose Trinidad Silva wrote an indignant letter of complaint about how the municipal treasury "had illegally ordered his water to be shut off." Before the council could investigate the matter, they received another letter from Silva explaining that the situation had been rectified the next day by the Municipal President, also the Commissioner of Water, who in a "kind-hearted" [*bondadoso*] way promised a prompt and efficient remedy, personally ordering the opening of the municipal outlet so he could access his water concession. Silva thus officially withdrew his complaint.[32]

Another example pertains to one of the most well-known foreign residents in Morelia, an Austrian engineer-architect named Guillermo Wodon de Sorinne. When he wrote to the city council in 1889 requesting six *pajas* of water for his large residence in the ex-convent of San Francisco, he sparked an internal debate among the council members. Two different reports were written for the consideration of the general assembly. One argued that his request should be granted. The second argued about the excessive amount of water requested: "he should not be granted more than any other vecino." In the end, Wodon de Sorinne received his six pajas of waters; the debate sparked by the request and the belief that he should not get any "more than any other vecino" indicates how liberal notions of rule of law and equality before the law were discussed at the local level.[33] While it is unclear who effectively could claim "vecino" status, the promise of equal access to and protection under the law for vecinos explains the desirability for many to claim this local identity for themselves.

Asserting the rule of law and public protection allowed the city council to deny many requests on the basis of their illegality, unconstitutionality, and/or potential harm to public interests. Municipal authorities appear particularly inclined to protect public interests, often invoking that specific language. In the city council's responses to individual petitions, the petition of Luis G. García, ex-Prefect and past Municipal President, one of the most politically powerful officials in Michoacán, illustrates this trend.[34] Despite his reputation, the councilors denied García's request for the rights to the run-off of the Fountains of Villalongin. He wanted to use the excess water to irrigate his gardens in the neighborhood of Capuchinas. The municipal commission denied the request, asserting that this run-off was already designated to irrigate the trees along the *Calzada* (cobblestone walkway) of Guadalupe. The cultivation of foliage in the city was central to the municipal beautification agenda. In the official response, the municipal secretary explained that the run-off from the Fountain was "destined to benefit and serve the public, therefore, they could not grant his request."[35] Public interest, in the form of tree beautification, thus trumped the private interests of this local notable.

Working-class petitioners likewise articulated notions of public good and public accountability in government. These letters came in the form of both individual and collective petitions. Language about competency and honor is often infused in these letters, especially when comparing the municipal council to the state government. In 1898, a dispute arose between the market stall sellers of San Augustine and the Administrator of Rents, a representative of the state government. The council stepped in to defend the local market sellers against the representative of the State of Michoacán. Sellers appealed to the council to defend their rights, intimating at their belief in the city council's accountability. In a letter signed by 27 women and men, they explained that while they were officially protesting the increase in rents, more importantly, they protested the fact that they had been given no explanation or logical appeal for the increase. They explained: the Administrator of Rents "did not let us know before about the increase in any way whatsoever, neither did he inform us of the motive of this increase." They requested that the ayuntamiento be the sole authority to collect their taxes "[s]ince, in our humble opinion, the City Council is alone competent, and not the Administrator of Rents." The council responded in writing, assuring the market sellers that "[t]here will not be an increase in rents for interior nor exterior market stalls of the Market San Augustine."[36] They also sent a memo to the Administrator of Rents informing him of the municipal council's decision. The municipality used this conflict, first, as leverage in its power struggle with the state government, and, second, to defend vendors' rights against a higher authority. These types of interactions were precisely what many local residents expected from their municipal government.

Another example arises in the 1894 dispute between a group of butchers and the Inspector of the division. The council launched an elaborate investigation after nine butchers demanded the dismissal of the Inspector of Provisions (*Abasto*) on account of his bad behavior and violation of Articles 5 and 6 of the Regulation on Meats. The butchers identified themselves as "vecinos and merchants" who were "making use of their right to petition which the law grants us." They explained, "for quite some time we have been suffering grave harm to our interests due to the poor service we received in the Department of Abasto under the supervision of Inspector Jose M. Caballero, who commonly treats us with very vulgar language, far from the honorable name of such an Illustrious Corporation." More specifically, the Inspector categorically prohibited the slaughter of cattle after 11 am; a request to do so led to "a barrage of insults." Inspector Caballero thus "violated their legal rights according to the regulations currently in effect." For these offenses, they solicited his dismissal. Accompanying the letter were not only signatures, but also short testimonies asserting that this information was, in fact, true. After investigating the complaint, the municipal commissioner determined that most of the workers in the slaughterhouse had no problem with the Inspector. Conversely, the people who submitted the complaint "had little to do with the Inspector," according to the commission's report. Therefore the council decided that "justice would not be served" by removing Caballero simply because "he has a strong character." Instead, Caballero was temporarily suspended, reprimanded, and warned "to be more courteous and moderate tempered in his dealings with people in the *Abasto*." The resolution also stipulated that the record book in the Department of Abasto be accessible to anyone who requested access. Although Caballero was not removed permanently from his position, the petitioners effectively denounced his abuses of power, got the city council on their side as watchdogs for possible future abuses, and demonstrated their expectation that regulations would be followed. Moreover, the incident affirmed that municipal records (Abasto record book, likely kept in the Inspector's office) be made open and accessible to members of the public. The council ordered that the resolution on this complaint be published in the *Official Newspaper of Michoacán*, presumably to make public these abuses of power, the assertion of public rights, and the council's "fair and just" actions.[37]

In both of these instances, petty merchants and working-class residents effectively argued for their rights as an honorable public, served by an honorable and competent city government. They grounded their arguments in claims based on their honorable behavior, honorable work, and by referencing the specific laws and regulations which the city council had a responsibility to uphold. By citing legal articles and principles, these men and women asserted their position as members of the public deserving protection. They successfully held the city council accountable for its legal standards and its promise of public protection, not only against administrative abuses, but also from violations to the everyday regulations that impacted their lives.

CONCLUSION

The emergence of new claims to "the public" transformed urban politics and spaces in nineteenth- and early twentieth-century Mexico. In this essay, I argue that one vital notion of the public emerged from the proactive stances of a wide range of urban residents in their official correspondence with the Morelian municipal government. Through the politics of petitions, these men and women claimed a right to urban public space as well as a right to a legitimate public and political identity in the city. Some residents adopted the specific language of rights and legal protections. Others invoked their claims to vecino identity. Still others presented themselves as competent, contributing members to the urban economy. All of these strategies resonated with the voiced promises of local authorities. In this sense, city inhabitants claimed the identity of the public for themselves and simultaneously asserted their expectation for public accountability on the part of local government. This righteous and just position of the "public" in Morelia became a powerful rhetorical mechanism for the continued assertion of rights and protections by Mexicans from popular classes throughout the nineteenth and twentieth centuries.[38] In the context of Morelia, the Municipal Palace (Mexico's version of the town hall) sat at the crux of these resident claims, local authorities, and notions of urban, civic patrimony.

Notions of honorable work and contributions to the public good resonated directly with older notions of community membership. Citizenship and notions of "the public" in Mexico were not just an outgrowth of nineteenth-century liberalism. As revisionists of Habermas have suggested, competing publics existed from the start, not just in the nineteenth century with the expansion of a specifically defined "public sphere." Competing public claims in Mexico can be traced throughout the colonial period, particularly, in popular and indigenous challenges to the racial, patriarchal hierarchy grounding Spanish claims to civility, discipline, rationality, and morality. Similarly, competing claims to the idea of "the public" helped constitute the bourgeois public sphere of the nineteenth century since the bourgeoisie's self-assertions of civility, education, and modernity positioned it against counter-publics, which were labeled as traditional, uneducated, uncivilized.[39]

The history of Morelia exemplifies this idea. Identities and customs of the urban community, far pre-dating 1800, laid the foundation for subsequent notions of the public and citizenship in the newly national (1821–1910), revolutionary (1910–20), and post-revolutionary (after 1920) periods of Mexican history. Local customs and earlier historical notions of community membership were key sources for alternate public (or counter-public) claims during the nineteenth and twentieth centuries. Most notable in the Mexican context were the notions of the *pueblo* [peasant village], *comunidad* [indigenous community], and the Spanish notion of *vecindad* [the neighborhood].[40] While historians have long acknowledged the importance of the pueblo and comunidad to peasant and indigenous identities in postcolonial Mexico, only more recently have studies emphasized the importance of vecindad to nineteenth- and twentieth-century notions of citizenship, nation, and the urban public.[41]

Vecino identity, a sort of proto-citizenship (similar to the notions of burgher or householder), required that a person perform certain duties and obligations for the community and establish an honorable reputation in order to justify their claim to membership therein. Although writing for an earlier period, Tamar Herzog explains, "[b]eyond its practical implications, vecindad denoted a social and cultural distinction. It identified people as both members of the community and civilized."[42] Notably, vecino membership was "extremely flexible, and linked to reputation."[43] The connection of honorable reputation to citizenship highlights the important overlap between vecino identity and citizenship, a slippage exploited by many Mexicans to position themselves as deserving members of the public. Petitions to the city council represented the primary space and relationship where residents actively worked this overlap to present themselves as vecinos of the city.

In nineteenth-century Mexico, the specific mechanisms allowing residents to move from "national" to "citizen" status depended largely on the locality. As Hilda Sabato notes, "[b]etween 1813 and 1855, for example, all the electoral laws in Mexico stipulated as a main requisite for potential voters that they be 'vecinos' of their locality." After 1857, however, "[t]he word (vecino) persisted in different contexts and probably referred to changing realities, but its usage always connoted the grounding of the abstract citizen in the particular territorial and social conditions of a concrete community."[44] Through their correspondence with local authorities, Morelians could assert their vecino status by asserting their rights guaranteed under the Liberal Constitution and by exploiting the slippage between colonial and postcolonial notions of vecino and citizen to position themselves as legitimate members of the urban community. The overlap between these two categories of subject representation enabled residents to claim the social and political rights associated with those identities, especially through courting the city council in their petitions. The Municipal Palace occupied the pivotal space of these petitions – connecting individual and collective identities of the city with legal rights and claims of the Mexican public.

In this essay, I have argued that Morelia's nineteenth-century political culture was more open to popular engagement than is often acknowledged. Exploring the practice of petitioning within the particular spatial politics of the historic colonial urban footprint reveals the essential role of historic patrimony as part of the city's civic culture. Contrary to common assumptions that local government and politics functioned as instruments of elite control, state repression, and economic exploitation during the Porfiriato, my research evidences a core dynamic of municipal accountability between the petitioning public and officials in the Municipal Palace. The form, tone, and rhetoric of these dialogues illustrate how the overlapping discourses of paternalism, liberalism, modernity, and regulation, at times, worked hand in hand to generate an ethos of political accountability and public protection to which city residents, including elites, were beholden. Public protection became a key element in the city's civic and historic patrimony of the city, centered on the petitioning culture of the town hall.

NOTES

1. Many thanks to my colleagues and graduate students in the History Department at the University of Colorado, Colorado Springs (UCCS) for comments on this manuscript, in particular Paul Harvey, Chris Hill, and Leah Witherow-Davis. Special thanks to Amanda King and Robert Sackett for their close reading of the manuscript. *Mil gracias* also to Dr. Luis Murillo for his timely help with photographs of the Palacio Municipal.
2. *Mexica* is the primary ethnic identity of the Aztec Empire. Please note: Spanish words will be italicized on their first use only.
3. On the urban orientation of Aztec and Spanish colonial societies, among many other works, see: Jay Kinsbruner, *The Colonial Spanish-America City: Urban Life in the Age of Atlantic Capitalism* (Austin: University of Texas Press, 2005); Charles Gibson, *The Aztecs under Spanish Rule: A History of the Indians of the Valley of Mexico, 1519–1810* (Stanford: Stanford University Press, 1964).
4. See Hilda Sabato, "On political citizenship in nineteenth-century Latin America," *American Historical Review* 106, no. 4 (2001): 1290–315; Carlos A. Foment, *Democracy in Latin America, 1760–1900* (Chicago: University of Chicago Press, 2003); Alicia Hernández Chávez, *La tradición republicana de buen gobierno* (México, D.F.: El Colegio de México: Fondo de Cultura Económica, 1993).
5. For an analysis of these processes in Morelia, see Lisette Griselda Rivera Reynaldos, *Desamortización y nacionalización de bienes civiles y eclesiáticos en Morelia, 1856–1876* (Morelia, Michoacán: Universidad Michoacana de San Nicolás de Hidalgo, Instituto de Investigaciones Históricos, 1996).
6. From the late nineteenth to early twentieth centuries, the urban population of the municipality increased from 23,835 in 1882 to nearly 60,000 in 1930. The larger territorial unit, the District of Morelia, increased from 111,000 in 1882 to around 200,000 inhabitants by 1930. See Gerardo Sánchez Díaz, *Pueblos, villas y cuidades de Michoacán en el Porfiriato* (Morelia, Michoacán: Universidad Michoacana de San Nicolás de Hidalgo, 1991); Enrique Florescano, ed., *Historia General de Michoacán,* vols. III and IV (Morelia, Michoacán: Instituto Michoacano de Cultura, 1989). Robert M. Buffington and William E. French note that "[b]etween 1877 and 1910, Chihuahua City's population grew from 12,000 to 30,000, Monterrey's from 14, 000 to 79,000. The Federal District more than doubled, to house in excess of 700,000 people, with nearly half its 1910 population originating from elsewhere in Mexico"; see Robert M. Buffington and William E. French, "The Culture of Modernity", Michael C. Meyer and William H. Beezley, eds., in *The Oxford History of Mexico* (New York: Oxford University Press, 2000), 425.
7. Many excellent studies of the Mexican Revolution could be referenced. A few seminal works addressing the experience of city residents include Alan Knight, *The Mexican Revolution, Vols. 1 and 2* (Cambridge: Cambridge University Press, 1986); John Hart, *Revolutionary Mexico: The Coming and Process of the Mexican Revolution* (Berkeley: University of California Press, 1987); Barry Carr, *El movimiento obrero y la política en*

México, 2 vols. (Mexico, D. F.: Ediciones Era, 1981); Adolfo Gilly, *La revolución interrumpida, México 1910–1940* (Mexico, D.F.: Ediciones El Caballito, 1971); or regional studies of export economies, political conflict, and political consolidation including Gil Joseph, *Revolution From Without* (Cambridge: Cambridge University Press, 1982); Aguilar Héctor Camín, *La Revolución Sonorense, 1910–1914* (Mexico, D. F.: INAH [Instituto Nacional de Antropología e Historia], 1975); Allen Wells, *Yucatan's Gilded Age: Haciendas, Henequen, and International Harvester, 1860–1915* (Albuquerque: University of New Mexico Press, 1985).

8 Esperanza Ramírez Romero, *Morelia en el espacio y en el tiempo: Defensa del patrimonio histórico y arquitectónico de la ciudad* (Morelia, Michoacán: Gobierno del Estado de Michoacán, 1985), xix.

9 Also see Gerardo Sixtos López, *Morelia y su centro histórico: Contribución a la historia urbana de la ciudad* (Morelia, Michoacán: Gobierno del Estado de Michoacán, Instituto Michoacano de Cultura, 1991); Jose Alfredo Uribe Salas, *Morelia: los pasos a la modernidad* (Morelia, Michoacán: UMSNH, Instituto de Investigación Históricas, 1993); Manuel González Galván, *Morelia: ayer y hoy* (Mexico, D.F.: UNAM, 1993); Ruben Murillo Delgado, *El centro historico de Morelia,* (Morelia, Michoacan: Talleres "Fimax Publicistas," 1990).

10 Anton Rosenthal, "Spectacle, fear, and protest: A guide to the history of urban public space in Latin America," *Social Science History* 24, no.1 (2000): 41.

11 "Decreto que declara de utilidad pública la vigilancia y conservación de los inmuebles cuyo valor histórico y artístico de determine," *Periódico Oficial*, tomo 1, no. 71, March 24, 1930, and "Ley de proteccion y conservacion de monumentos y bellezas naturales," *Periódico Oficial*, tomo LII, July 20, 1931, both reprinted in Ramírez Romero, *Morelia*, 117–43.

12 For biographical information on local elite and notable persons in Morelia, see Álvaro Ochoa Serrano, *Repertorio Michoacano, 1889–1926* (Zamora, Michoacán: El Colegio de Michoacán, 1995).

13 *Archivo Histórico del Municipio de Morelia* (Historical Archive of the Municipality of Morelia) (AHMM), *Caja* (Box) 255A, *Legajo* (Bundle) (Leg.) 7, *Expediente* (File) (Exp) 14, 1881 and Caja 255A, Leg 4, Exp 13, November 25, 1882. Also see various letters in Leg 9 of same box.

14 AHMM, Caja 264, Exp 11, December 11, 1888.

15 Lex Heerma van Voss, "Introduction," *International Review of Social History* 46 (2001), Supplement, 8. For specific discussion of writing petitions in colonial Latin America, see Steven J. Stern, "The social significance of judicial institutions in an exploitative society: Huamanga, Peru, 1570–1640", in George A. Collier, Renato I. Rosaldo, and John D. Worth (eds.), *The Inca and Aztec States, 1400–1800: Anthropology and History* (New York: Academic Press, 1982): 289–317; Matrin Lienhard, "Writing from within: Indigenous epistolary practices in the colonial period," in Rosaleen Howard-Malverde, ed., *Creating Context in Andean Cultures* (Oxford: Oxford University Press, 1997): 171–84.

16 Seventh Constitutional Congress, *Constitutión federal de los estados de México por el congreso constituyente el día de febrero de 1857* (Mexico City: Imprenta del Gobierno Federal, 1896).

17 For studies on urban citizenship and popular politics in Mexico, Escalante Gonzalbo, Fernando, *Ciudadanos imaginarios* (Mexico: El Colegio de Mexico, 1992); Andrés Lira, *Comunidades indígenas frente a la Ciudad de Mexico*; Carlos Illades and Ariel Kuri Rodríguez, eds., *Ciudad de México*; Claudio Lomnitz, *Deep Mexico, Silent Mexico: An Anthropology of Nationalism* (Minneapolis: University of Minnesota Press, 2001); Peter Guardino, *The Time of Liberty: Popular Political Culture in Oaxaca, 1750–1850* (Durham: Duke University Press, 2005); Antonio Annino, "Ciudadanía versus gobernabilidad

republicana en México: Los orígenes de un dilema," in Hilda Sabato, ed. *Ciudadanía política y formación de las naciones: Perspectivas históricas de América Latina* (D.F., Mexico: Colegio de Mexico, 1999), 62–93; Alicia Hernández Chávez, *La tradición;* Carlos Foment, *Democracy.*
18 Heerma van Voss, 3.
19 Ibid.
20 Seventh Constitutional Congress.
21 For an extended discussions of local negotiations around public plazas, see Christina M. Jiménez, "The networked city: Popular modernizers and urban transformation in Morelia, Mexico, 1880–1955," in Tim Edensor and Mark Jayne, eds., *Urban Theory Beyond the West: A World of Cities* (New York: Routledge, 2012).
22 Angel Rama, *The Lettered City* (Durham: Duke University Press, 1996). Also see Román de la Campa, "The lettered city: power and writing in Latin America," in Benigno Trigo, ed., *Foucault and Latin America: Appropriations and Deployments of Discoursive Analysis* (New York: Routledge, 2002), 17–43.
23 Kathryn Burns, *Into the Archive: Writing and Power in Colonial Peru* (Durham: Duke University Press, 2010), 3.
24 Rama, 29.
25 Ramon Eduardo Ruiz, *Mexico: The Challenge of Poverty and Illiteracy* (San Marino: The Huntington Library, 1963), 8. Ruiz estimates illiteracy rates in Mexican cities at around 85 percent and puts many rural villages closer to 100 percent in 1910. Regional literacy rates for Morelia during the late nineteenth and early twentieth centuries are not available.
26 For brief discussions of public scribes in Mexico, see Pablo Piccato, *City of Suspects: Crime in Mexico City, 1900–1931* (Durham: Duke University Press, 2001), 31, 38; and Susie S. Porter, *Working Women in Mexico City: Public Discourses and Material Conditions, 1879–1931* (Tucson: University of Arizona Press, 2003), 150, 190.
27 AHMM, Caja 254, Exp 44, November 13, 1883.
28 As a side note, the ayuntamiento usually did not collect interest on the personal debts owed by urban residents and they were not particularly demanding that debt was paid off immediately, often waiting for more than six months of accumulated bills before tracking down an individual for payment.
29 AHMM, Caja 253, Exp 186, July 22, 1884. For similar requests and decisions see Caja 254, Exp 72, November 21, 1890 (in box marked 1883–1884).
30 AHMM, *Libro* (Book) 330. Exp 106, April 14, 1896.
31 AHMM, Caja 23, Leg. 1, Exp 18, April 25, 1913.
32 AHMM, Caja 26, Leg. 2, Exp 87, January 17, 1913.
33 AHMM, Libro 304, Exp 40, November 19, 1889.
34 For another request by the Tena sisters that sparked internal debate within the ayuntamiento, between the municipal treasurer and the city council, see AHMM, Caja 27, Leg. 1, Exp 91, November 29, 1913.
35 AHMM, Libro 330, Exp 109, March 20, 1896.
36 AHMM, Libro 344, Exp 2, June 30, 1898.
37 AHMM, Libro 323, Exp 38, November 14, 1894. For newspaper article see Hermeroteca Pública Universitaria "Mariano Jesus Torres" ["Mariano Jesus Torres" Public University Newspaper Archive] (HPUMJT), "*Periodico Oficial*," vol. 104, December 30, 1894.
38 For expanded discussions of these ideas, see Christina M. Jiménez, "Performing their right to the city: political uses of public space in a Mexican city, 1880–1920," *Urban History*, 33, no. 3 (December 2006); and Christina M. Jiménez, "From the lettered city to the sellers' city: Vendors, politics and public space in urban Mexico, 1880–1920," in Gyan Prakash and Kevin Kruse, eds., *Cities: Space, Society, History* (Princeton, NJ: Princeton University Press, 2007).

39 For example, see Michael Warner, *Publics and Counterpublics* (New York: Zone Books, 2005).
40 For example, see Peter Guardino, *Peasants, Politics, and the Formation of Mexico's National State: Guerrero 1800–1857* (Stanford: Stanford University Press, 1996); Eric Van Young, *The Other Rebellion: Popular Violence, Ideology, and the Mexican Struggle for Independence, 1810–1821* (Stanford: Stanford University Press, 2001); Antonio Annino, "Ciudadanía versus," in Hilda Sabato, ed,. *Ciudadanía política*; Carlos Foment, *Democracy*; Claudio Lomnitz, *Deep Mexico*.
41 See note 17 above.
42 Tamar Herzog, *Defining Nations: Immigrants and Citizens in Early Modern Spain and Spanish America* (New Haven: Yale University Press, 2003), 7.
43 Ibid.
44 Hilda Sabato, "On political citizenship," 1296.

Chapter 8: The Bombay Town Hall

Engaging the Function and Quality of Public Space, 1811–1918[1]

Preeti Chopra

The Greek Revival Town Hall, designed by Colonel Thomas Cowper and completed in 1833, is one of the most notable buildings in Bombay from the British colonial period. Prominently located in the heart of the historic Fort district, the building demands attention with its wide flight of steps that dramatically rises above the raised basement (also referred to as "ground floor" in government records) to reach the main portico on the first floor (Figures 8.1 and 8.2). Today the building houses the Asiatic Society and its library, as it has done since the building's inception, and hosts lectures and conferences, while its large hall works as a public reading room. The contemporary uses of Bombay's Town Hall raise various questions about its function, construction, and reception among the public during the colonial era.

The Town Hall in colonial Bombay shared some similarities with the institution in Britain. Yet, its function and meaning were inflected by the local context and colonial rule in which the government of the Bombay Presidency, rather than the town of Bombay, controlled part of the building.[2] The Town Hall was begun at the behest of the British residents of Bombay and completed by the government to fulfill a variety of needs and uses for both these groups. However, even as the government completed the building there was a shift in the use of its public spaces: from the reservation of assembly rooms for the exclusive use of British inhabitants to utilization of the central hall and darbar room by the public, including the native public, at the discretion of the government. In this chapter, I will investigate what the institution of the town hall meant in colonial Bombay by examining its varied functions, and highlight the qualities of its public spaces. By "public," I do not mean to imply that all of Bombay's citizens constituted the public. Women, and especially Indian women, for example, would have rarely constituted the public. Instead, I show that the functions and qualities of spaces and points of access to the town hall indicate it catered to *differentiated publics*: while there were areas meant for a broader public, some spaces were meant for a "preferred" or "specific" public, distinguished on the basis of membership, race, status, or other criteria. By focusing on the controversy in 1871 over the placement of the statue of Jagannath Shankarshet (1802–65), a leading member of the native

The Bombay Town Hall

Figure 8.1
Town Hall, Bombay, 1821–33, view of entrance, by Colonel Thomas Cowper. Photograph by the author, 1998.

Figure 8.2
Town Hall, Bombay, 1821–33, sketch of building by Colonel Thomas Cowper. Courtesy of Bhau Daji Lad Sangrahalaya.

elite, in the town hall, my analysis reveals the specificities of the "public" that made claims to Bombay's Town Hall as a public space. Even though the "public" was invoked by native elites in making arguments in favor of the placement of Shankarshet's statue in the town hall, it was really a battle for the inclusion of native elites into the ruling oligarchy of British elites who controlled the town hall.

THE FUNCTIONS OF THE TOWN HALL IN BOMBAY

The Town Hall building in Bombay that was completed in 1833 was not the first to serve as town hall. Previous buildings that housed the functions of the town hall were originally built for other purposes. As early as 1675, a rented house, where judicial courts were accommodated, also functioned as the town hall. In 1677, the main room in the Court of Judicature (Mapla Por) of Bombay's governor Gerald Aungier, located in north Fort, served as the town hall. From 1720 to 1786, the court and town hall were moved to new rent-free quarters at Bazaar Gate in the "forfeited estate of Rama Kamati," also in north Fort. Here, a room served as the town hall even though by 1771 it was in need of repair. From 1786 and for a few years following this date, the principal room in a house rented from Mr Hornby (known as the Admiralty House, which was later the Great Western Hotel) served as the town hall. A government official by the name of Mr Henshaw was the first to propose the construction of a building for the town hall in 1793. This proposal was made again in a letter dated 10 October 1811 to the Bombay Government from Sir James Mackintosh, Chief Justice (Recorder) of Bombay. The government accepted this proposal in 1812. Messrs. Forbes and Co. and Messrs. Bruce, Fawcett and Co. asked and received the government's permission to hold a lottery to raise money for the building.[3] This account makes it clear that an institution known as a town hall that was linked to courts of justice existed in Bombay since the seventeenth century. While the functions of this institution remain sketchy, rather than a place of local self-government, the town hall represented the control of the state, in this case the East India Company, that governed Bombay from 1688 to 1858.

In 1811, the British residents of the city held a public meeting in Bombay at which a committee was appointed to raise funds and make arrangements for a new town hall's construction. Sir James Mackintosh noted the multiple purposes this new town hall was to accommodate: "a suitable building for public meetings and entertainments, and also to make a home for the library and museum of the Literary Society, and for the reception of statues and public monuments of British Art." The committee held lotteries in 1812 and 1823 to raise funds for this institution, having been granted a site for it by the East India Company in 1817. Work on the building was started in 1821.[4] At this initial stage in its conception and construction the town hall had three functions: first, to house the Literary Society, later the Bombay Royal Asiatic Society's Library; second, to provide a suitable setting for the location of statues of eminent men; third, to furnish a suite of public assembly and supper rooms.[5] The colonial Town Hall that was thus conceived in 1811, both as a building and institution, was decoupled from judicial courts and unlike town halls and civic halls in England in the sixteenth and seventeenth centuries, was never regarded "as the seat of … autonomous civic administration."[6]

These multiple uses and occupancy had something to do with the pattern of funding. In 1823, after having spent Rs 173,200 on the building, the Town Hall Committee found that it lacked funds to complete the structure. It then offered the unfinished building to the government to be completed by them and utilized for purposes of the state, while reserving the assembly and supper rooms rent-free for the use of British inhabitants. In November 1824, both the Government of Bombay and the Court of Directors of the East India Company considered the matter. Subsequently, the Government spent Rs 483,469 to complete the building. In other words, the government contributed roughly three-fourths of the cost and the Town Hall Committee one-fourth, not including the costs of the land, which belonged to the government.[7] The Bombay Branch of the Royal Asiatic Society contributed Rs 10,000 for the town hall, in return for which it received rooms in the north wing of the building "reserved for it and fitted up by Government."[8] In 1840, Maneckjee

Cursetjee, a Parsi, became the first member of the Bombay Branch of the Royal Asiatic Society but well into the 1860s the society had few Indian members.[9]

The Bombay Presidency was a province of British India that contained both British districts and native states with Bombay as its capital. Critical to the function and meaning of Bombay's Town Hall was the massive expansion of the territory of the Bombay Presidency that began just prior to the time of the institution's conception in 1811 and completion of the building in 1833. Later major additions to the presidency included the incorporation of native states through the doctrine of lapse; Aden in Yemen (1839), Sind (1843), and the Panch Mahals were leased from the Sindhias (1853). By 1910, the total area of the Bombay Presidency, including British districts and native states and excluding Aden in Yemen, was 188,745 square miles.[10] During the course of the Town Hall's history the building was used for the governance of the Bombay Presidency, not simply the town of Bombay. For example, the Bombay Legislative Council held its meetings here and both the Governor and the Commander-in-Chief "also had some rooms there for official purposes."[11]

How do these functions of the Town Hall compare with those in Britain with which its proponents were familiar? In the nineteenth and twentieth centuries, the town hall in Britain was associated with a variety of functions and spaces. The functions of pre-industrial town halls in Britain included meetings, markets, and the courthouse. The assembly room that emerged in the eighteenth century and was connected to the elevation of the middle classes, continued to be found in many nineteenth-century buildings and was also found in town halls. Strictly speaking, such rooms were only for the use of certain classes of society, or for certain activities. Other functions included corn exchanges, described as "a sort of cross between the assembly room and market," a multi-purpose public hall, banqueting hall, committee rooms, police and fire services; a reading room, sometimes for news, and subsequently a library; and living spaces for a caretaker, police, or fire-superintendent.[12] In light of this list of possible functions, and since it was the British inhabitants of Bombay, and not the government, who sought to found a building to house the town hall in Bombay, it is logical that they conceived of this institution primarily as a place of assembly and entertainment, which also accommodated a library.

The government's contribution to the construction of Bombay's Town Hall changed the meaning of the institution before the completion of its construction by stipulating that some government offices and storerooms be located here, adding a fourth function. Of greatest significance was the government's decision to allow the use of the hall for public purposes with government approval, which was the hall's fifth function. This opened up the use of the Town Hall to a broader public, including the native public, making it no longer largely an exclusive space for the town's [elite] British inhabitants.

The Town Hall became a middle ground for the holding of public meetings permitted by government, including meetings organized jointly by members of both British and native communities. It was an important venue and training ground for sections of Bombay's citizenry, particularly elite male constituency, in public modes of communication with the government of the presidency – by asking permission to hold a meeting for a particular purpose, through petitions signed at meetings, and reports of the assemblies published in newspapers – about its grievances or support of government through leadership and forms of assembly accepted by the government. The Town Hall then, was one of the institutions through which the government established its hegemony. At the same time it was an important social space for the British elite inhabitants to hold balls, banquets, and felicitate officials. Even as the Town Hall gave the city's local citizenry, both European and Indian, a space to voice opinion, the contained spaces of the town hall and hegemonic norms of correct procedure and decorum followed there in public meetings, spatially framed, bounded, and limited dissent.

Colin Cunningham points to the significance of town halls to the "developing townscape" of Victorian and Edwardian Britain: "Each of these buildings designed to be both a focus and a showpiece for its town as well as a functional creation."[13] With its Greek revival architecture and elevated main entrance, Bombay's Town Hall was certainly a "showpiece" for Bombay and located at a prominent site framing the center of the Fort, the nucleus of colonial settlement. In the 1860s, the Green fronting the Town Hall was transformed to become the Elphinstone Circle, Bombay's first major urban-design scheme. At this time, the Green was moved to center it with the line of Church Gate Street and the Town Hall.[14] In the 1860s, as

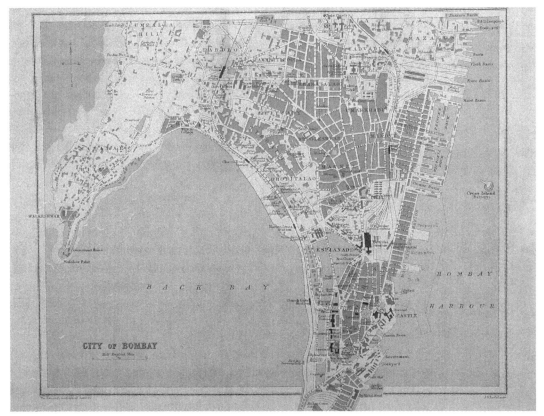

Figure 8.3 City of Bombay, 1909, plan. From *The Gazetteer of Bombay City and Island*, vol. 2, frontispiece.

the circle rose from the ground, the fort walls were pulled down. The city was re-centered as the destruction of the fort walls led to the creation of a new location for public buildings along the *maidan*, making the Elphinstone Circle the "old" center and shifting the heart of the city outwards, to a new frontier between the fort and the "native town" (Figure 8.3).

QUALITIES OF THE PUBLIC SPACES OF BOMBAY'S TOWN HALL

An analysis of Bombay's Town Hall's spaces reveals them to be public in varying degrees. Jürgen Habermas observed that we tend to "call events and occasions 'public' when they are open to all, in contrast to closed or exclusive affairs." However, this may not always be the case, as the term "public building" does not indicate that the building is open to the public. In actuality, according to Habermas, "'Public buildings' simply house state institutions and as such are 'public.' The state is the 'public authority.' It owes this attribute to its task of promoting the public or common welfare of its rightful members."[15]

Keeping the original intentions of the building in mind, in 1882, the government offices and storerooms in the basement/ground floor housed the Military, Medical, and Stationery Departments and by 1909, contained government offices of the Stamp, Stationery, and Income Tax (Figure 8.4).[16] On the first floor, the public was allowed the use of the central hall and darbar room for public purposes (Figure 8.5). The north wing of the first floor had been reserved free of rent for the use of the Asiatic Society of Bombay while, apart from the darbar room and the entry to it, the use to which the south wing on the first floor was put is not specified in the records.[17] Thus, the central hall and the darbar room were the *most public*. Public meetings were held here with the government's permission, but presumably could *also be occasionally reserved for a specific public* – the British inhabitants. By contrast, the rooms of the Asiatic Society were consistently reserved for its members or *reserved for a specific public*. Yet, the lobby/entrance to the Asiatic Society, where the statues were housed, was a public area. However,

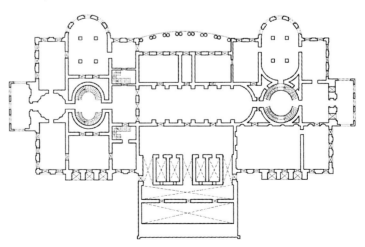

Figure 8.4
Town Hall, Bombay, ground floor (basement) plan, redrawn in 1885. North is to the left. Original plan courtesy of Maharashtra State Archives. Redrawn by Mukesh Negi, courtesy of Mandaville Designs Inc.

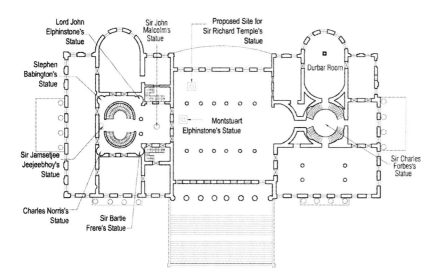

Figure 8.5
Town Hall, Bombay, first floor plan, redrawn in 1885. North is to the left. Original plan courtesy of Maharashtra State Archives. Redrawn by Mukesh Negi, courtesy of Mandaville Designs Inc.

through its location, placement of doors, and furnishings the lobby could indicate that it was a *public space for a preferred public*. Finally, the government offices and storerooms probably allowed *limited public access* to certain areas and not others.

The Town Hall offered multiple points of access, revealing a desire to make the building accessible to the public and gesturing to the diverse ways in which this building would have been approached and experienced. At the same time, the building's structure demonstrates a preference on the part of the British for self-contained distinct functions. An examination of the ground floor plan of the town hall drawn up in 1885 reveals a building that could be easily divided into three parts, each with its own entrance/s (see Figure 8.4). The wide steps led to the main entrance directly behind which was the central hall (see Figure 8.5). This was flanked by the north and south wings, which could also be entered from the ground floor through porticos on the north and south, perpendicular to the axis of the main entrance as well as through doors located at two porticos on either side of the main entrance. Compared to the building's main entrance, these access points were understated. The two porticos on the front façade, if used as entrances, led into government offices and not directly to the staircases. Perhaps this too was a device used to sort out different users, while at this same time making the government offices and staff as unobtrusive as possible. Members of the Asiatic Society could enter the building from the north portico or main entrance, while the natural entrance for those attending public assemblies would be up the impressive flight of steps of the main entrance, which may have intimidated non-elite members of the public.

In theory, sections of the Town Hall could easily be closed off. For example, by closing the main entrance to the building and the connecting doors to the north and south wings of the building, it was possible to block access to different sections. Although I have not seen an example of where this was done, my point is that these were contained spaces. By having the ability to give permission or block passage, the colonial government exercised control over the kinds of activities that took place in the Town Hall, while the very limited size of the public spaces physically cut off the vast majority of Bombay's citizenry from participating on a mass level in the meetings held here.

Steps to the main entrance of the building were far more than an access point, but instead, could also become a space for public assembly and expression. This stepped space was used on occasion for public announcements. In doing so, it allowed new audiences to be brought into the sphere of influence of the Town Hall and extended its public space. Following the Sepoy Revolt or the First War of Independence in 1857–58, an event that threatened British control over the subcontinent, the steps of the Town Hall became the site for the reading of the Queen's Proclamation on November 1, 1858. Following this, "a thanksgiving was offered" in all religious institutions on the island and every section of the public reportedly participated in the celebration of British victory.[18] In this case, the steps of the Town Hall – a symbol of the colonial government – with its impressive façade as a backdrop, were an effective location, a podium so to speak, from which a representative of the government could address a larger public, many of whom were unlikely to participate in meetings conducted in the building.

The control over space, both permanent and ephemeral, exhibited in its design, was a reflection of the tight control the government wished to have over its subjects. This, as well as a demonstration of belief in the rule of law, can also be seen in the five purposes of the Hall, which were considered distinct and non-negotiable. In case a new set of institutional arrangements were proposed, provision had to be made to find accommodations for those functions, excluded from the proposed arrangements, elsewhere. This is illustrated in the proposal to move the Town Hall. For example, in 1882–83 the government considered the transfer of the Town Hall to the municipality under certain conditions. These included the use of the Town Hall for public purposes with government approval, the continued possession by the Royal Asiatic Society of the rooms it occupied, and the ongoing use of government public offices until alternative arrangements for their accommodation had been made. The Municipal Commissioner was not agreeable to allowing the Asiatic Society to remain on the premises. All the same, it is interesting to note that, "it appeared to His Excellency the Governor in Council that a public building like the Town Hall of a city should properly belong to the Municipality of the city."[19] Clearly, at this point in history, the colonial state recognized the incongruity of state control over an institution that was supposed to be a symbol of local self-government. In the case of the Bombay Town Hall, the negotiations fell through and a plot of land was offered for the proposed Municipal Hall.[20] Even though the purposes of the Town Hall were non-negotiable, the Town Hall did temporarily house additional functions. One example is the room given to professors of the Elphinstone Institution in 1836 in the Town Hall.[21] At least two exhibitions of the Bombay Art Society, founded in 1888, were held in the Town Hall by ca. 1909.

Points of access and movements, in the form of the staircase, were the focal points of the three sections of the Town Hall. At the heart of the north and south wings of the building were elliptical and circular staircases respectively. The first floor of the north wing, occupied by the Royal Asiatic Society, opened into the central hall through a wall with openings (see Figure 8.5). The transverse central hall consisted of a double row of elegant Corinthian columns that ran parallel to the sturdy exterior Doric columns. Its southern end terminated in an apse-like semi-circular wall that extended the central hall into the space of the southern wing and also formed an entrance to it. Between the northernmost columns of the hall was a statue of Mountstuart Elphinstone, Governor of the Bombay Presidency 1819–27, in a standing position. Elphinstone played a central role in the consolidation of the Bombay Presidency. To the east, the central hall opened onto a terrace. Beyond the eastern row of columns in the central hall, was a room in the southern wing, which led to the elliptical-shaped darbar room. Certainly until 1882, the sequence that led to and including the darbar room itself formed the public space of the building. The darbar room received this name as it was used for state purposes before the completion of the Secretariat in 1874. Undoubtedly, by 1909, it functioned as the Collector of Bombay's "personal office." Although their location was not specified, the Town Hall also contained rooms for the "personal offices of the Income Tax Collector and his deputy, and the Presidency Surgeon, first district."[22] This indicates that the public spaces of the Town Hall shrunk over time, and it is unlikely that the darbar room would have been used for public assembly once it became a "personal office."

The use of the term "darbar" for the name of the room is noteworthy and is intimately tied to British imperial rule in India. Modeled on imperial Mughal court practices that were then used, or more likely translated, by Hindu and Muslim rulers in the eighteenth century, these darbars were "meetings, with large numbers of Indian princes, notables and Indian and British officials, at which honours and rewards were presented to Indians who had demonstrated their loyalty to their foreign rulers during the uprisings of 1857–58."[23]

In the Town Hall, staircases were not only places for movement, but also spaces for viewing and display. For example, the statue of Sir Charles Forbes, initially located in the north wing, was only moved to the circular vestibule in the south wing in 1873.[24] This statue was first raised in 1822, more than a decade before the completion of the Town Hall. Forbes was the head of Forbes and Company, and as the first English firm to be established in Bombay in 1767, the firm "for many years transacted agency and mercantile business without a rival." One can get a sense of the firm's prestige from the fact that it "also financed the East India Company on various occasions."[25] Forbes may have played a role in the foundation of Bombay's town hall since Forbes and Company were involved in asking for the government's permission to hold lotteries to raise money for the building.

Despite the location of Forbes's statue in the south wing and of Elphinstone in the central hall, it was the space around the elliptical staircase of the northern wing that was the real repository of memorial statues. Through the portico on the north side one passed through a circular hall to enter a vestibule, which was lit by a skylight from where one moved up staircases. On reaching the first floor, according to the plan of 1885, along the center of the northern wall was a huge statue of the leader of the Parsi community in India, and the first native baronet, Sir Jamsetjee Jeejeebhoy (1783–1859) in Parsi dress and in a sitting position (Figure 8.6).[26] Directly in line with Jeejeebhoy's statue, between two columns was the standing figure of Sir John Malcolm (1739–1833), Governor of Bombay, 1827–30, lit by a shaft of light from a skylight, beyond which was the entrance to the central hall (Figure 8.7). This should be seen as two rectangular spaces divided by two columns. The larger rectangle contained the skylit stair in the center, whose corner niches held busts and statues of colonial officials: Stephen Babington (1790–1822), Lord John Elphinstone, Sir Bartle Frere, and Charles Norris (1791–1842) (see Figure 8.5). On the west side of the staircase, to the left of Jeejeebhoy's statue was the statue of Norris, who had "a long and distinguished career in the service of the East India Company." Opposite Norris's statue was the statue, sculpted in a sitting position, of Babington, the former "Judge of the Sadr Diwani Adalat of Bombay and President of a committee for the revision of the revenue and judicial codes." Statues of two governors of Bombay were located on the southern corners of this larger rectangle: Frere, shown in the sculpture in modern attire with left hand extended and right hand on hip, was the famous governor of Bombay from 1862 to 1867, whose urban transformations changed the city, occupied the western corner, while the standing statue of Elphinstone was located in the eastern corner.[27] Additional statues not marked in the plan were located in the corners. This section of the north wing would become the controversial site selected by native elites for the location of Shankarshet's statue in 1871. The circular staircase in the south wing also had semi-circular niches at its corners, which were not used to house statues, perhaps because they housed government offices and were not considered to be sufficiently public spaces.

Figure 8.6
Statue of Sir Jamsetjee Jeejeebhoy and British worthies, Town Hall, Bombay. Photograph by the author, 1998.

City Halls and Civic Materialism

Figure 8.7
Statue of Sir John Malcolm to the right and Lord John Elphinstone's statue in the background to the left, Town Hall, Bombay. Photograph by the author, 1998.

THE ASSERTION OF LOCAL ELITE CONTROL

The native public's belief in their ownership of the Town Hall is exemplified in the controversy that broke out in 1871 over the placement of the statue of the late Jagannath Shankarshet (1802–65) in the building. Shankarshet, a wealthy banker, was one of the most prominent citizens of Bombay. Sonar (goldsmith) by caste, he was long considered head of his own community as well as Bombay's Hindu community. He was a leading patron of education, President of the Bombay Association between 1852 and 1857 and member of the Bombay Legislative Council between 1862 and 1865.[28] Only "public buildings" and "public spaces" that were under the control of the state could belong in some sense to the entire public. The native elites' success in placing Shankarshet's statue in the Town Hall was a victory for native elites and an assertion of local elite control over public buildings that were often constructed with their financial help.

Shankarshet's statue was voted for at a public meeting of the inhabitants of Bombay held in the Town Hall on March 12, 1864, a year before his death.[29] A letter dated February 21, 1871 addressed to the government and signed by many prominent *shetias* (heads of castes or trading bodies, and distinguished by great wealth) announced the arrival of the statue, and requested permission to erect it at a site they had selected. In their opinion the best site for it was "opposite to, and facing the statue of the late worthy Baronet Sir Jamsetjee Jeejeebhoy and Sir Charles Forbes Baronet" at the entrance to the rooms of the Asiatic Society. According to them, this would not "interfere with the arrangements of the room, but will fill the gap and adorn it with statues."[30] At this time Forbes' statue was in the north wing and when it was moved to the south wing in 1873, the statue of Sir Bartle Frere took its place (see Figure 8.5).[31] The site was considered suitable by the *shetias* as it would set up a clear spatial relationship between the statues of three wealthy and prominent merchants and citizens of Bombay – two native and one British.

The government issued instructions to select a site in the Town Hall for the statues, in response to which a report was submitted to Colonel J. A. Fuller. The authors of the report received instructions from Mr Jacomb, who wrote his own opinion in April 1871 before or after the report. It is difficult to read the writing but what is clear is that Mr Jacomb considered the suggestion of the *shetias* for the location of Shankarshet's statue and concluded that there was no suitable location for the statue in the Town Hall: "Sir Jamsetjee's statue is placed in an alcove in the north wall but if Jugannath Sunkersett's were placed in the present position adjacent to Sir John Malcolm, it would not be similarly [illegible word, perhaps "located," "backed" or "bracketed"] but in an related position which [?] is not in my opinion suited to a statue in a sitting position on a high pedestal."[32] The two authors of the report, dated April 21, 1871, proposed that if the Government decided on placing the statue in the Town Hall then the statue of Sir John Malcolm be removed to the niche currently occupied by the bust of Sir James Carnac (not shown on the plan), which could be moved elsewhere. In that case, the statue of

Shankarshet could be placed in the position of that of Sir John Malcolm, facing "his friend and contemporary the first Sir Jamsetjee Jejeebhoy." Both these statues were in the sitting position. The statue of Sir John Malcolm was standing and would, in their opinion, "balance admirably the statue of Sir Charles Forbes."[33]

Even though the report indicated that it was possible to locate Shankarshet's statue in the Town Hall, the government replied to Sir Jamsetjee Jeejeebhoy, second baronet (1811–77) and others, that after consulting with their architectural engineer they were unable to agree on its placement. They offered no reasons.[34] Inserting Shankarshet's colossal statue between Malcolm's and Jeejeebhoy's statues, or replacing Malcolm's statue, may have been objectionable to British authorities. The two colossal statues of native *shetias*, each dressed in native costume, and placed in a central position, would have made the colonial officials appear like subsidiary planets in a solar system dominated by these two suns. Meanwhile Malcolm's image, a statue after all of a former governor of Bombay, either displaced or placed in an ambiguous position in line with the *shetias*, may have been even more objectionable.

The Bombay *shetias* remained undeterred by the government's refusal and in 1872 requested the government's permission to place Shankarshet's statue in the Victoria and Albert Museum in Bombay, which too was denied by the Governor in Council in a letter from 1872, because of the limited space available in that building.[35] In response, Sir Jamsetjee Jeejeebhoy wrote to Mr. Tucker (in 1872), and repeated his request that Shankarshet's statue "voted … by his native and European friends" be placed in "some conspicuous building." Jeejeebhoy made a few important arguments in his letter. First, that the native public had been major subscribers to the Victoria Museum and the late Shankarshet "was the chief source of the foundation of the Victoria Museum." Second, that the Government's refusal was "a very great reproach to the native community that the statue of one of their public spirited townsmen is refused to be placed therein."[36] In 1872, a subsequent petition from Bombay's leading *shetias* to the government reiterated that the statue had been raised by "public subscription" in honor of Shankarshet's "public services." They also pointedly observed, "one who has rendered long, faithful and valuable service both to Government and his country should be erected in some fit public building." The letter reminded the Government that Shankarshet was one of the "originators" of the museum and the public believed that his statue was "entitled" to a place in the building, "which owed its commencement, in a great measure to his exertions and to the support of the Public." Furthermore, the public expected the government to fulfill arrangements agreed upon at the public meeting.[37] In summary, the argument by the *shetias* was that a place had to be found for Shankarshet's statue in a public building.

A public building is a building owned by the state and housing a state institution; however, in the case of the Town Hall, the "public" was interpreted in some quarters as belonging to the public. The Parsi paper the *Rást Goftár* of March 31, 1872, wondered why the Governor had refused permission to house

Shankarshet's statue in the Town Hall or Victoria Gardens, and asked whether the Town Hall belonged to the public? And if it did, had the public not a right to use it for whatever purpose it thought fit?[38] Both in the letter from the Bombay *shetias* and the quote from *Rást Goftár*, the public being referred to was the "native community," and one can infer that the government was seen as "British." The Bombay *shetias*, who represented large sections of the native public, and thereby the majority of Bombay's population, could confidently speak in the name of the public and draw attention to the native community's perceived insult by the [British] government in its refusal to find a place for Shankarshet's statue in a public building.

In 1873 the government was forced to consent to the erection of Shankarshet's statue in the Town Hall, in the ground floor vestibule opposite the entrance to the north wing, where it still resides (Figure 8.8).[39] The same year Forbes's statue was relocated to the center of the circular vestibule in the Darbar-Room end of the hall.[40] In an undated later document from the twentieth century, its location is described as "First floor, South end."[41]

Why did the placement of the statue of Shankarshet pose problems? On the one hand, the matter could have simply been one of size. The colossal statue of Shankarshet was hard to accommodate. On the other hand, perhaps the issue was rather more political. At the time of the 1857 Sepoy Revolt, many prominent Indians were under suspicion for treason and one of those accused was Shankarshet. While many influential Englishmen considered him guilty, the Governor, Lord Elphinstone, did not. Charles Forjett, the Police Commissioner, was instructed to investigate the matter and found Shankarshet to be entirely innocent of any wrongdoing. Suspicion of Shankarshet's connection with the mutineers in Bengal had arisen because of the large number of wandering Brahmin mendicants who found accommodation in a *dharamshala* in the garden of Shankarshet's mansion. Forjett himself had placed spies there as these mendicants brought information from Bengal and the upper Provinces. In the middle of this situation, rumors had spread that Shankarshet was acting in conjunction with Nana Saheb, who the British considered to be a traitor.[42] Even though Shankarshet's innocence had been proved, there may have been many British members of Government who remained unconvinced.

CONCLUSION

The struggle to locate Shankarshet's statue in a public building was a claim made by a section of Bombay's native elite in the name of the public and in honor of Shankarshet's public services and the contribution made by the public to a public building. In a sense they saw the Town Hall as owned by the Government and the public. Even as it housed statues of British worthies and two Indian worthies, the Town Hall supported many diverse populations. Unless refused permission by the government, the Town Hall in Bombay accommodated a variety of public meetings.

Figure 8.8
Jagannath Shankarshet's statue, Town Hall, Bombay. Photograph by the author, 1998.

Many different classes of people drawn from various religious, racial, and ethnic groups would have attended these meetings even though members of the elite would probably have organized them and dominated the proceedings. The Town Hall was a middle ground between the British and Indians. The British set the rules and Indians believed that if they followed the rules – conducted public meetings, and wrote petitions to the government – they would, over time, be given a greater voice in governance. As far as the British were concerned, they had no plans to cede control to the Indians.

The importance of the Town Hall for Indian elites waned from the late 1890s, as many other public spaces in the city became sites for conveying the native public's opinion to the government and for the anticolonial struggle. The Town Hall was eclipsed by other institutions, such as the Municipal Corporation in the 1860s, and by new ways of rallying public opinion, such as through public festivals by Bal Gangadhar Tilak in the 1890s, and meetings held in a variety of spaces such as Madhav Baug. These showed that it would be the unbound spaces, rather than contained institutional spaces such as the Town Hall, and a new way of conducting politics that would become increasingly important in the twentieth century (Figure 8.9). The locus of political significance would move as well. From 1917 to 1934, Mani Bhavan on Laburnam Road in the Gamdevi district in the so-called "native town" in Bombay City would become the headquarters of the nationalist leader Mohandas Karamchand Gandhi when he visited the city. It would be from this two-storied residence of his friend Shri Revashankar Jagjeevan Jhaveri that Gandhi launched the Civil Disobedience, Satyagraha, Swadeshi, Khadi, and Khilafat movements.[43] Now a memorial to Gandhi, and museum, library, and research center, Mani Bhavan attracts visitors from all over the world, its fame and importance in the postcolonial era eclipsing that of the Town Hall and the memory of the limitations of the political space that it once embodied.

Figure 8.9
Madhav Baug, Bombay.
View from inside,
looking towards gate.
Photograph by the
author, 1998.

NOTES

1. An early version of this chapter was presented at the International Planning History Society Conference, July 12–15, 2010, at Istanbul, Turkey. I am grateful to Swati Chattopadhyay and Jeremy White for encouraging me to write on the Bombay Town Hall. Their insights, prompts, and thoughtful editing have been invaluable. I thank Madhu Kumar and M. B. Ravikumar for generously allowing me the use of their office for the preparation of drawings for this chapter. Charles Hallisey helped me coin the title and focus my arguments. Stella E. Nair patiently read and commented on multiple drafts and made substantial improvements each time. I thank my colleague Uli Schamiloglu for his support of my research. I would also like gratefully to acknowledge the support of the Middle East Studies Program, the Wisconsin Alumni Research Foundation (WARF), and the Graduate School at the University of Wisconsin–Madison.
2. For the purposes of this chapter, it is important to keep in mind that when one speaks of the Government of Bombay, one is speaking of the Government of the Bombay Presidency. By 1687, the command center of the Western Presidency shifted from Surat to Bombay. This would become the Bombay Presidency, with Bombay as its capital. See Lt Col. H. A. Newell, *Bombay (The Gate of India): A Guide to Places of Interest with Map*, second edition (n. p., 1920), 13–14. In the seventeenth and eighteenth centuries, the presidency would consist of some small and scattered possessions on the west coast of the subcontinent. In the decades after 1803 it expanded from the coastline to the interior to become a substantial province under British control.
3. *The Gazetteer of Bombay City and Island,* 3 vols., compiled by S. M. Edwardes (Bombay: Times Press, 1909–10), 3 (1910): 297–8, 373–4 (hereafter cited as *City Gazetteer*).
4. *City Gazetteer* 2 (1909): 144. The quote included is from the *City Gazetteer,* although the original source of the quote is not given.
5. An early example of the Town Hall's use for public entertainments is the farewell ball and supper held here for the Earl of Clare, Governor of Bombay from 1834 until his retirement in March 1835. See *City Gazetteer* 2 (1909): 142, including note 2.
6. Quote from Robert Tittler, *Architecture and Power: The Town Hall and the English Urban Community c.1500–1640* (Oxford: Clarendon Press, 1991), 9.
7. Letter from John Nugent, Acting Secretary to the Government of Bombay to E. C. Buck, Secretary to the Government of India, Revenue and Agricultural Department, no. 4045 of 1882, General Department (henceforth GD), October 11, 1882, Maharashtra State Archives (henceforth MSA), GD, 1882, vol. 107, comp. no. 788: 167–70.
8. *City Gazetteer* 3: 331.
9. Murali Ranganathan, *Govind Narayan's Mumbai: An Urban Biography from 1863* (London: Anthem Press, 2008), 9
10. Hugh Chisholm, *The Encyclopædia Brittanica: A Dictionary of Arts, Sciences, Literature & General Information,* vol. 4, 11th edition (New York: The Encyclopædia Brittanica Company, 1910), 185–9.
11. Sten Nilsson, *European Architecture in India 1750–1850* (London: Faber and Faber, 1968), 117.
12. Colin Cunningham, *Victorian and Edwardian Town Halls* (London: Routledge & Kegan Paul Ltd, 1981), 1–7.
13. Ibid., xiii.
14. Letter from Clerk, Municipal Commissioner's Office, to A. D. Robertson, Secretary to Government, GD, no. 3777 of 1861, December 10, 1861, MSA, GD, 1862–64, vol. 5, comp. no. 112: 3–11.
15. Jürgen Habermas, *The Structural Transformation of the Public Sphere: An Inquiry into a Category of Bourgeois Society,* trans. Thomas Burger and Frederick Lawrence (Cambridge, MA: MIT Press, 1989), 1–2.

16 *City Gazetteer* 3: 374.
17 Letter from John Nugent, Acting Secretary to the Government of Bombay to E. C. Buck, Secretary to the Government of India, Revenue and Agricultural Department, no. 4045 of 1882, GD, October 11, 1882, MSA, GD, 1882, vol. 107, comp. no. 788: 167–70.
18 *City Gazetteer* 2: 160.
19 It was then proposed to exchange the current Municipal Offices for the Town Hall and house the Asiatic Society there. See Letter from John Nugent, Acting Secretary to the Government of Bombay to E. C. Buck, Secretary to the Government of India, Revenue and Agricultural Department, no. 4045 of 1882, GD, October 11, 1882, MSA, GD, 1882, vol. 107, comp. no. 788: 167–70.
20 In 1883, the Secretary to the Government of India responded to this proposal by asking whether the Bombay Royal Asiatic Society were agreeable to the transfer, stating that their consent was "desirable if not necessary." The Society was not happy with the new accommodations offered in the building "now occupied as the Municipal Office." They found problematic "the whole style of the building, its situation, lighting, ventilation, door and window spacing rendering it unfit for their requirements." Finally, the transfer did not take place. See letter from the Secretary to the Government of India, Home Department (Municipalities), no. 31, February 13, 1883 in response to letter from John Nugent, Acting Secretary to the Government of Bombay, no. 4045, October 11, 1882; letter from the Secretary, Bombay Branch Royal Asiatic Society, March 10, 1883, with reference to Government letter no. 669, February 24, 1883, and letter from Secretary, Asiatic Society, April 30, 1883, in continuation of his earlier letter; and Resolution of Government in the Public Works Department, no. 557-C.W.-1245, August 14, 1883 in GD document, August 21, 1883, MSA, GD, 1883, vol. 127, comp. no. 788: 107.
21 *City Gazetteer* 3: 130–31.
22 Ibid: 374.
23 Bernard S. Cohn, "Representing authority in Victorian India," in Eric Hobsbawm and Terence Ranger, eds., *The Invention of Tradition* (Cambridge: Cambridge, University Press, 1983), 165–209; quote from p. 167, information from pp. 167–8.
24 See Resolution no. 49 C.W.-137 of 1873, P.W.D., January 21, 1873, MSA, GD, vol. 75, comp. no. 116: 139.
25 *City Gazetteer,* 1: 451 including note 1 on the same page.
26 Parsis were Zoroastrian by religion and migrated to the subcontinent from Persia in the eighth or tenth century and thrived under British rule. Colonial Bombay was a product of joint enterprise; one aspect of which was the collaboration of Indian philanthropists with the colonial state to found institutions for the general public. Jeejeebhoy was a foundational figure of these collaborations and a model colonial rulers hoped that other Indian elites would emulate. For an elaboration of this argument, see Preeti Chopra, *A Joint Enterprise: Indian Elites and the Making of British Bombay* (Minneapolis: University of Minnesota Press, 2011).
27 *City Gazetteer* 3: 345. At the time of the publication of the city gazetteer, the location of the statue of Sir Charles Forbes is described as being "on the north side of the custodian's room."
28 Christine Dobbin, *Urban Leadership in Western India: Politics and Communities in Bombay City, 1840–1885* (London: Oxford University Press, 1972), 274.
29 Letter from leading Bombay *shetias* to Mr. H. E. Ravenscroft, Acting Chief Secretary to Government, General Department, July 15, 1872, MSA, GD, 1872, vol. 70, comp. no. 169: 191–7.
30 Letter from several prominent Bombay *shetias*, including Jamsetjee Jeejeebhoy, Framjee Nasserwanjee, Byramjee Jeejeebhoy, Cowasji Jehangir, Rustomjee, Dinshaw Manockjee Petit, Vurjeevandas Madhavdas, Premchand Raichand, Bhugwandas Purshotumdas and

others to T (or F.). S. Chapman, Chief Secretary to Government, February 21, 1871, MSA, GD, 1871, vol. 61, comp. no. 398: 407–10.
31 See Resolution no. 49 C.W.-137 of 1873, P.W.D., January 21, 1873, MSA, GD, vol. 75, comp. no. 116: 139.
32 Minute by Mr. Jacomb, dated (day unclear) April 1871, in MSA, GD, 1871, vol. 61, comp. no. 398: 415–16.
33 Report signed by two gentlemen (perhaps G. W. Terry and Griffiths, but it is not clear), April 21, 1871, in response to instructions received by Government through Mr. Jacomb to Colonel J. A. Fuller, R. E., Architectural Executive Engineer and Surveyor, Bombay Presidency, MSA, GD, 1871, vol. 61, comp. no. 398: 419–21. See Resolution no. 49 C.W.-137 of 1873, P.W.D., January 21, 1873, MSA, GD, vol. 75, comp. no. 116: 139.
34 Letter from Chief Secretary to Sir Jamsetjee Jeejeebhoy, Bart and others, no. 1225 of 1871, GD, May 11, 1871, MSA, GD, 1871, vol. 61, comp. no. 398: 423–4.
35 Letter from leading Bombay *shetias* to the Mr. H. E. Ravenscroft, Acting Chief Secretary to Government, GD, July 15, 1872, MSA, GD, 1872, vol. 70, comp. no. 169: 191–7.
36 Demi-official letter from Sir Jamsetjee Jeejeebhoy, Bart to Mr. Tucker, July 8, 1872, in ibid., 181–3.
37 Letter from leading Bombay *shetias* to Mr. H. E. Ravenscroft, Acting Chief Secretary to Government, GD, July 15, 1872, in ibid., 191–7.
38 *Rást Goftár*, March 31, 1872, in the *Report on Native Papers Published in the Bombay Presidency* for the week ending April 6, 1872: 6, para. 41.
39 Government Resolution no. 2,994, General Department, July 30, 1872, MSA, GD, 1872, vol. 70, comp. no. 169: 187.
40 Resolution no. 49 C.W.-137 of 1873, PWD, January 21, 1873, MSA, GD, 1873, vol. 75, comp. no. 116: 139.
41 British Library, *List of Statues and Busts in the Town and Island of Bombay*.
42 See S. M. Edwardes, *The Bombay City Police: A Historical Sketch, 1672–1916* (London: Oxford University Press, 1923), 45–6.
43 http://www.gandhi-manibhavan.org/aboutus/aboutus_introduction.htm (accessed June 18, 2011).

Chapter 9: Los Angeles City Hall

Space, Form, and Gesture

Jeremy White

The scene is downtown.

November 30, 2011, early in the morning, still dark.

We are in front of Los Angeles City Hall, at the foot of that structure, once the tallest in the city. Ordinarily at this hour the place is quiet and the space around the building void of people, but this morning hundreds are here and more are trying to crowd in (Figure 9.1).

The building occupies an entire block, just enough space leftover to leave a lawn-covered park between the plinth and the street, but this morning there is scarcely room to sit down. There are tents. Police dismantle those the campers do not, as the municipal government asserts its sovereignty over this place. The scene is loud with voices, but many people are also capturing it in photographs, and the images are on the internet already.

Figure 9.1
Occupy LA evicted, November 2011. Source: Lucy Nicholson/Reuters.

177

There is an inside and an outside to this roofless urban space. The dividing line is a shifting cordon of uniformed police bodies in armor and yellow barricades. There is tear gas. Police are herding people out of that space, pushing back the people trying to get in, clarifying the space's edge. Everyone wants to save this space, the police and the protestors, but they do not share the same idea of that space. They are not saving the same thing. The police enact the mayor's ultimatum: evict the squatters and thus restore the public space. The damage to the grass is nearing half a million dollars, according to the Department of Parks and Recreation. The protesters worry that if they empty the space, the protest movement will end. The campers have been there for two months, calling themselves "Occupy LA," but they are leaving now, some carried away by police, arrested, but most walking away. Some are injured, and some say they will be back.[1]

There is irony: in the coming weeks the municipal Government will offer those arrested a chance to avoid prosecution if they take a course that teaches the First Amendment of the Constitution, the amendment guaranteeing freedom of speech and the right of assembly.[2]

The Los Angeles City Hall and the brief sojourn by protesters in the fall of 2011 remind us that architectural space is both physical and intangible. Occupying space is not merely an act of putting one's own body in a specific place; it is not a simple *physics* problem. Perhaps we should also think in terms of linguistics, or dramaturgy; the choice of stage was integral to the statement expressed. Put another way, without a stage, no statement could have been "seen," or "scened." Space and speech are integral and the implication here is that the Occupy squatters were not the only actors gesturing on that politically charged stage. Setting up tents under the shadow of that monument and its 452-foot tall tower also shone the spotlight on the state and its actions, creating a frame of dual visibility encompassing both citizen and government.

From its inception some 80 years earlier, Los Angeles City Hall was designed to be an eye-catching public building (Figure 9.2). Perhaps the contentious scene of eviction down on the grassy plaza in 2011 seemed disrespectful, but protesters had encamped there because of that building's monumentality, not in spite of it. The design and construction of that building and the policing of incongruous behavior are not separate problems; the one is integral to the architectural character of the other. Monumentality is a form of visibility, achieved by size, iconography, and the relationship of a building's form to neighboring forms. Iconography is a mode of expression and the size and configuration of the architectural form modulates iconography's clarity. The building was designed to be functional and tasteful, beautiful in some people's estimation, while the Occupy LA encampment was motivated by a contrary aesthetic. Contrariness was the point; the encampment's clarity of message would have been degraded had the protesters selected a less visible building to encamp alongside. The two spaces were visually incongruous, one carefully designed by professionally trained architects tasked with the problem of representing municipal government in three-dimensional form, the other an instantaneous construction bypassing municipal building inspectors and their codes, a transitory project intended to command attention for a variety of social, economic, and political motives. The architectural order of the building was a model of clarity, the product of a collaboration between the largest architecture firm in town, run by John C. Austin, president of the city's Chamber of Commerce, his engineer Albert Martin, and the venerable John Parkinson who was nearing the end of his career but had penned the master plan of the University of Southern California, the Memorial Coliseum, and would soon be asked to design Union Station. In contrast, the architectural order of the camp was muddled, suitably expressing the complexity of the political message voiced by its "builders" and residents.

Figure 9.2
City Hall: the building captured shortly after construction was completed. Originally published in Hales, *Los Angeles City Hall*, 1928.

City Halls and Civic Materialism ■

The Occupy LA episode at the foot of City Hall brought forth the didactic quality of that building, but not for the first time in its history. It is an attractive building, almost magnetic in its allure, the pull of protesters merely a small indication of that allure. It is one of the most visible buildings in America, and chances are you have seen it, whether you have been to Los Angeles or not. Even if you haven't scrutinized the images in this chapter, there is a pretty good chance you have seen parts of this building already. For decades television and film crews have pictured it in their cinematic frames, especially favoring the Greco-Roman inspired east portico and its steps that connect the building to Spring Street (Figure 9.3). That marble flight of stairs has played the role of Washington's Capitol Hill steps for much of the twentieth century in movie theaters and on television sets, and its portico has played visual placeholder for the courthouses of numerous towns in myriad films, making LA's City Hall one of the most familiar government buildings in the world. One of the municipality's motives for evicting the squatters when it did was to free the steps for a crew filming *The Gangster Squad*.[3]

Figure 9.3
Spring Street steps: a familiar prop in advertisements, television shows and movies. Photograph by the author.

180

This essay explores the visual and didactic character of Los Angeles City Hall, a building completed as a celebration of 50 years of dizzying urban growth, housing what had become a sizeable and powerful municipal body. It was meant to be a bold testament to the city's unique modernity. Like so many of its sister buildings constructed in the nineteenth and early twentieth centuries, as historian Mary P. Ryan has demonstrated, Los Angeles City Hall is a monument that visually stands in for municipal government, and as such has a rhetorical and didactic role to play.[4] It is both space and symbol. It can operate merely as a backdrop, or wallpaper (in the anachronistically virtual or cyber-sense of the word), against which a citizen can "act" in public, her actions read not merely as a soliloquy about her individuality but as a statement about government. This gestural quality is not ancillary to the building's function, it remains just as important as shelter.

City Hall was intended to contour the municipality's interface with citizenry. From the very beginning contact between municipal body and individual citizen was proscribed, the building's didactic architectural quality shaping the meaning of that contact. Even before the building came into being, public gatherings at that site were controlled. Since 1901, political speeches without a permit were banned downtown, and since 1908 non-Anglos and Socialists in particular were kept out (Figure 9.4). The local police force was the grantor of permits, guided by the Mayor's Office, which often denied permits to communists, anarchists, suffragists, and other politically motivated groups.[5] In 1928, City Hall was constructed in that no-speech zone, the heart of the white-collar area of downtown. By the end of the twentieth century the area would commonly host protesters, but not squatters. The latter were tolerated elsewhere, in a discrete area of the city called "Skid Row," an unofficially sanctioned urban space. Out of the way, out of public view, and yet in public space, peripheral, unmediated, squatting shoved aside so that it remains scarcely visible to the public eye.[6] By contrast, City Hall revels in its visibility. It is monumental; it gestures. Squatting next to that building is akin to engaging in conversation.

Funded by a bond measure and sited on the northern edge of downtown, the building was certainly an urban focal point – a gigantic white exclamation mark – hailed at its dedication as a "monument to [the] city's progress."[7] As a space of contact between citizen and government, Los Angeles City Hall has two primary functions: to accommodate the apparatus of bureaucracy, and to stand before the eye of the public as a representation of municipal government and its community. It is a tangible expression of the public while also functioning as a public space. As a monument its auxiliary function was to define place through the imaginative assemblage of historical fragments, some stretching back as far as antiquity, artfully composed as a unified whole. This essay focuses on that auxiliary function. The building's architectural and iconographic character was carefully designed to assert a very particular history. As a didactic building, its walls are stippled with iconographic and textual expressions intended to make claims about itself and the city it represents – what it is, who it was built by, and for whom. This essay is premised on the idea that monuments such as Los Angeles

City Halls and Civic Materialism

Figure 9.4
Location of City Hall in relation to the earlier no speech zone. The 101 and 110 freeways, as well as the area now known as "Skid Row," came decades after City Hall. Drawing by the author, adapted from Mark Wild, *Street Meeting: Multiethnic Neighborhoods in Early Twentieth-century Los Angeles*, 2005.

City Hall present a view of the city's past, not as a banal backdrop but as an active agent in the construction of civic identity. The building was intended to house representative government and to represent the city, but as a visual presentation of the city and its history, whom does that historical construction represent? If that building gestures, what stories does it tell?

BIGNESS

The building is supported on a steel-reinforced concrete frame clad in white California granite and terracotta blocks. The shape of its telescoping tower capped by a ziggurat roof was inspired by buildings in New York City. Its peak was installed with a rotating beacon, a "Lindbergh light," intended to alert approaching planes and blimps, a lusty feature in expectation of the age of airships and helicopters. The reference was to Charles Lindbergh, the first pilot to fly an airplane across the Atlantic Ocean.[8] That skyscraper-inspired tower made a great viewing platform too, an ideal spot from which to impress important visitors. Under that ziggurat four years after the building's completion, local organizers kicked off the Olympic Games of 1932 by hosting executive officials of the International Olympic Committee in the sumptuous aerie at the top of the tower. Twenty-foot high windows provided a 360-degree panorama. Limited only by the haze of the automobile city, itself a new phenomenon, the building offered a sublime sight of sun and land. The hazy edges of development spied from that loft signified the promise of vast growth and prosperity.[9]

City ordinance restricted buildings to a miserly height of 150 feet, but the enthusiasm for tallness was so acute in this civic project that City Hall was permitted to breach that limit, more than doubling it.[10] Despite this mandate for bigness, by the standards of LA's competitor's, New York and Chicago in particular, the City Hall tower was actually quite short. Ground would soon be broken on the Empire State Building and the Chrysler Building in New York City, and both would rise over 1,000 feet. Inspired by a recent trend replacing the ubiquitous domes of government buildings with dizzying towers, the architects of Los Angeles City Hall internalized the dome by installing a rotunda inside the tower at its base. The gleaming granite tower would be the language of its exterior massing, an "American perpendicular style," but tradition would rule on the inside.[11]

Height was thus an aesthetic, a style, but it could not materially compensate for shortness. This was made painfully evident earlier in 1932 when the dirigible *Akron* floated over town. What might have been a grand triumph for local boosters eager to demonstrate the city's technological modernity instead turned out to be an embarrassment. The dirigible worked its way up the coast but could not stay for long over Los Angeles. There was no structure suitable for it to anchor to, not even the new City Hall. As one Chamber of Commerce executive lamented after the *Akron* veered north shortly after its arrival: "[that is] the saddest kind of a report I ever hope to read. The biggest city on the coast has to ask for the biggest airship to circle over it because we have nothing here for it to tie to."[12]

For the Chamber of Commerce and other boosters, the importance of bigness could not be overstated. Promoters of Los Angeles habitually reveled in their city's impressive size. Vertically challenged, boosters exulted over the horizontal expanse. Since the late nineteenth century, in partnership with local government, capitalists had created a vast horizontal city beyond downtown's perimeter of density. Not a vertically oriented industrial metropolis so familiar back east, but a new kind of landscape where the distinction between the city and the country blurred. It was a big city; in terms of population it was the biggest west of the Mississippi River, and in square area it was by far the largest in the United States. Except for Detroit, it had the most automobiles and the most automobile roads anywhere in the country.[13] In terms of tonnage passing through its harbor or across its freight yards, Los Angeles had become one of the busiest commercial nodes in the western hemisphere. Although the city was enormous, its municipal boundary spanning 441 square miles in 1928, it lacked height, which happened to be the most visual form that bigness can take.[14]

City Hall was designed to fill that void in the sky, a modern-day menhir announcing the city's claim to progress and civic respectability. It would not only mark downtown, it would accentuate the sublime horizon of the sprawl around it. And for some, it certainly had the capacity to thrill. A contemporary architectural booster wrote that the "campanile-like structure … serves to produce a striking silhouette against the sky, and an impressive landmark of glistening whiteness when viewed from any point of the compass."[15] Inspired by the towers of town halls in Northern Italian towns, that Renaissance architectural form offered a legitimizing allusion that took the mind's eye across continents and the Atlantic Ocean, and across the centuries, invoking a historical context. Inspired by that "glistening whiteness," a local columnist and amateur historian later proclaimed that "Los Angeles is an epic – one of the greatest and most significant migrations in the long saga of the Aryan race."[16] The building was not only crafted to compensate for the city's diminished height, it tackled the problem of its diminutive local history.

REFERENCE

While the building's height reflexively connoted a zeal for bigness, the hue of the exterior and the iconography adorning it spoke of the city's matrix of race and history. A mark of the building's iconic value was the quick utilization of its image in the *Los Angeles Times*, a local newspaper published by Harry Chandler, a zealous booster of the region. A cartoon published in the *Times* in 1929 was intended to promote continued public investment in projects such as the newly completed City Hall (Figure 9.5).[17] It depicts in perspective a cluster of buildings representing downtown Los Angeles, and although the object depicted may be the city, its subject is less tangible for it depicts Los Angeles not so much in space as in time.

The buildings occupy the lower third of the drawing. City Hall, completed a few months before the cartoon was published, is featured in the prominent "front" position, centered in the image. Receding to the vanishing point beyond and to the left can be seen the lines of a tall office building, a generic example of those common in LA at the time. There are more structures there as well. Beyond that cluster of buildings, beyond the downtown of the present, looms a big, almost bilious mountain. It is not a depiction of the San Gabriel Range north of Los Angeles, at least not a very good one; this cartoon version is too steep and too close, and it seems to sprout right out of downtown itself. Geographic verisimilitude was not the point. That mountain is a pedestal of time supporting yet more buildings on its slopes and cliffs, structures planned or dreamt but not yet realized.

Height signifies greatness, but along with distance it signifies relative states of time. The buildings on the mountain are the city of the future; a vision of what might be, lending tangible expression to the booster's ambition. The mountain is partly illuminated in the center and partly dim on the left and the right. The illuminated center practically glows, if that is possible in a black-line ink drawing, and by 1929, the year of publication, this was an old visual trick signifying enlightenment progress.[18] The glowing part signifies legitimacy, grandeur, wisdom, rationality, progress, and so on. The darker areas of the mountain are vital too, because they signify plenty and abundance. There is still dark-space left for the light to conquer and civilize, or in booster's parlance, to "develop."[19]

Los Angeles City Hall

Figure 9.5
Miss LA: City Hall is depicted at the foot of the mountain representing the promise of growth. Originally published in the *Los Angeles Times*.

While the mountain in the background represents the future, and the cluster of buildings with City Hall in the middle ground signifies achievement in the present, the past was represented as well – as a human figure. Her name is "Miss Los Angeles" and she is whimsically denoted by the costume of a Spanish maiden. By 1929 she was an expected *Times* caricature, a common feature of its political and promotional cartoons since the end of the first decade of the twentieth century.[20] She plays the role of civic cheerleader, her expression of adoration – feet together, the umbrella of her pleated skirt billowing out, arms outstretched, back arched, poised maybe for a pirouette – is directed at the glowing mountain. She seems wowed by the five airplanes and three dirigibles circling the city on the mountain. As the city's pre-Anglo-American incarnation, her role was to witness and to make tangible the emotions of approval and amazement. The story of progress is one where the past is amazed by the present.

The juxtaposition of the antiquated past with the modern present was ensconced in the very landscape itself. City Hall was constructed just two blocks from the old Spanish plaza, founded in the late eighteenth century as the heart of a Laws of the Indies town.[21] A quaintly designed lane juts off from the plaza called

Olvera Street, which had been imaginatively preserved as a tourist attraction the very same year City Hall was completed. "Preserved" is a generous term. The bricks it was paved with were new, the first time in its history that bricks had ever paved that street, and many of the modest buildings were newly built, designed to look old.[22] From Olvera Street the tower of City Hall looms just over the quaint skyline, and the juxtaposition of signifiers is remarkable – modern and premodern, American and pre-American, of "glistening whiteness" to motley asymmetry – and continues to evoke comments about a historical trajectory. In the words of its late twentieth-century curator, "el pueblo seems perched on the edge of another world."[23] The edge signified a limit between past and present as well as present and future, as an assertion about the city's history. City Hall was constructed to invoke and shape this temporal edge, an edge crossed by the trajectory of progress.

By 1928, more than any other city in the United States, Los Angeles had a larger majority of those who were referred to at the time as "native Americans," Caucasians born in the United States. It was promoted as the whitest city in the country, an economic landscape unfettered by powerful unions. Fourteen percent of the city's population in 1930 was classified as non-white, double that of New York and Chicago, and yet only 15 percent of the population was foreign-born, half the number of foreign-born in New York and two-thirds those in Chicago.[24] Paradoxically, it also had the largest population of Mexicans and Mexican-Americans in the United States. This particular non-white demographic was so large, that there were more Mexicans in Los Angeles than in any city in Mexico, apart from Mexico City itself. Boosters tended to view that segment of the population in Los Angeles as guests or transitory workers, preferring to believe that the city's identity was derived entirely by the white majority. In terms of identity and the construction of the public body, the Mexican was relevant only as a signifier of a pre-American past. The Mexican of the present was important as a source of labor, and as a historical reference point. Like the Indian, the Mexican was conceptualized as a vestige of a defeated race, and could therefore be subsumed under such romantic categories as "the sons of Montezuma."[25] White capitalists and boosters promoted their city as an "open shop" where labor unions were weak or nonexistent, a condition facilitated they said by the presence of guest workers who supposedly had no roots here in the community. Even as late as the 1960s historian Robert Fogelson would describe the Mexican community as "maladjusted."[26]

ICONOGRAPHY

As bold as its formal characteristics were, the building's iconography was equally forthright. Inscribed on each of the four facades of the tower were short quotes by classical and classically inspired authors. The four entrances were also marked by inscriptions above the doors. The words of James Russell Lowell above the north entry: "The Highest of All Sciences and Services – the Government." Words by

Cicero over the south entrance: "He that Violates his Oath Profanes the Divinity of Faith Itself." Quotes such as these map points in the history of law and philosophy, linking the present to a very specific past. From early-American thinkers to post-Enlightenment English philosophers, back to the humanists of the Italian Renaissance to Christian theologians and the Old Testament, and even further back to Imperial and Republican writers of ancient Rome, and ultimately, to the men of Greece.

The principal or ceremonial entrance was from the west on Spring Street. White granite steps led up to a colonnade of paired columns that wrapped a forecourt on three sides, the back wall a sheer cliff of white granite that transitioned neatly to beige terracotta, a vantage point that cranes the neck to appreciate when standing in the forecourt. The colonnade supported a series of groin vaults, an architectural element intended to evoke images of Romanesque Europe, of cloisters, cathedrals, and other majestic masonry institutional buildings. The walls under the colonnade and on two sides of the forecourt were subdivided into panels that matched the rhythm of the columns, each panel a frame for a tile pattern, each pattern depicting one of the city's industries: motion pictures, machinery, automotive, oil production, building construction, shipping, airplane, and printing (Figure 9.6).

The lower block of City Hall was roofed by terracotta tiles, which complicated the aesthetic program by referencing an imagined local history. Although in Europe such tiles were prevalent from Rome to Stockholm, in Los Angeles they symbolized a particularly Hispanic cultural memory, and thus constituted a visual component to what has come to be thought of as the "Spanish fantasy past."[27] Architectural historian David Gebhard has shown, however, that the style to which such allusions belonged was thought of not as a narrow "Spanish" aesthetic but as a "Mediterranean Revival style."[28] The latter could reference old

Figure 9.6
The forecourt is enclosed by a colonnade sheltered by groin vaults, each bay punctuated by a mosaic representing industry (e.g. movie studios). Photographs by the author.

Spain, the pre-American past, and the Italian Renaissance without contradiction. The didactic references asserted continuity to a culture carried west by "native Americans" on their march to the sea from Atlantic shores and Pilgrim origins.

The actual entrance is at the back of the forecourt, a classically inspired architrave, pediment, exaggerated consoles, and steps that elevate the experience of entrance. The cornice was a form ultimately derived from ancient Greek and Roman temples, and inscribed on the wall above it were the words of Solomon: "Righteousness exalteth a people." And above that, "Let us have faith that right makes might," by Abraham Lincoln (Figure 9.7). The decorative bas relief in the pediment was described at the time as "richly carved," inspired not so much by Aegean muses, as much by a then fashionable taste for Art Deco: the swirls alluded

Figure 9.7
Forecourt: the tower wall above the doors are adorned with a pediment and inscriptions. Photograph by the author.

Los Angeles City Hall ■

more to a Mayan fantasy, or Toltec perhaps, or maybe Aztec. The pseudo-Indian architectural fantasy such as this had its most flamboyant and persuasive moment in rival San Diego during the Panama California Exposition of 1915.[29] The architectural command over the historically charged eclecticism of City Hall was an important and empowering aspect of what the architects meant by the term "American Modern style."[30] It could allude to ancient Greece, the Sons of Montezuma, French cathedrals, Old Abe, and old Spanish California, all without fear of inconsistency.

The double-doors in that entry were made of bronze and ornamented by a gridded composition of six square panels, offering perhaps the most coherent history of place in the building (Figure 9.8). Each door-leaf was relieved by three square, indented panels, one on top of the other, and in turn each panel was decorated with a scene and inscribed with a date. Taken together, the six panels depicted six moments of city-building – 1769, 1781, 1846, 1854, 1913, 1915 – thus presenting a chronological pattern. Framed, or rationalized, by the imposition of the grid, the rectilinearity of the doors further organized the six panels geometrically. The frame had as much to do with ideology as with geometry, and the inscriptions of Lincoln and Solomon above the door roped the six dates into a larger framework of manifest destiny, finished by the deft hands of sculptor Henry Lion. The six panels tell a confident story of ambition, pride, and invention on an

Figure 9.8
Entry doors: each of the six panels depicts a moment in the city's history. Originally published in Hales, *Los Angeles City Hall*, 1928.

189 □

epic scale. It was the story of a new city willed into being by the imagination and know-how of the latecomers, and the selection of those six dates plotted a neatly edited history of that invention. The relieved panels serve as temporal points used in the construction of that imagined reality. They are the "mile-posts of destiny," to borrow from one of the city's great boosters.[31]

The top two cells of the grid represent the city's Spanish eighteenth century, the middle two the American nineteenth century, and the bottom two the modern twentieth century. Taken as a whole the grid "reads" from left to right and top to bottom, each panel inscribed with a title that included the date, just in case the scenes and figures in low-relief were otherwise unrecognizable. The first two panels commemorate 1769 and 1781, the discovery, naming, and founding of el pueblo. The next two commemorate the years 1846, the moment of American conquest, and 1854, the founding of a public school in the town, a key moment in the Americanization process. The 1846 panel expresses masculinity: it commemorates not a peace treaty, not California's admission to the Union, nor the city's incorporation in 1850, but invasion and conquest. The founding of the first public school was a placeholder for a more complex historical contest. Statehood and municipal incorporation were followed by a transitionary decade marked by violence and vigilante terror. After conquest a white minority sought to impose its dominance backed by the power of law courts that meted out asymmetrical justice; murders by "Americans" against working-class Mexicans, referred to as "Sonorans," often went without conviction. The most alarming episode occurred in 1856 after an American was exonerated for killing a Sonoran. For days afterward Americans were ambushed, prompting gangs of vigilantes to organize in response. This first race riot in Los Angeles' history, as late twentieth-century historians have dubbed it, was put down ultimately by an alliance of Americans and upper-class Mexicans, the famed "Californios" whose ranchos depended upon the rule of law.[32] The founding of a public school signified Americanization, the amalgamation and disciplining of non-American cultural forces into a capitalist public, and institutionalization of that public.

The bottom two panels commemorate the technological triumph over the inherent limitations imposed by the finite resources of the natural landscape, a key component of the construction of the booster's identity in Los Angeles. The panels marked the opening of the Owens Valley aqueduct in 1913, and completion of the breakwater off the San Pedro harbor in 1915, two crucial moments that ensured the city's continued commercial and suburban expansion across the landscape. The Owens Valley was 200 miles to the north of downtown, up high in the mountains, and that engineering project was funded by voters who approved $23 million worth of bonds to build it, a 225-mile aqueduct that allowed Los Angeles to drink from a river. The panel commemorating the year 1915 referenced the completion of the breakwater at San Pedro. It made that small town into a world-class port capable of accommodating even the largest merchant vessels. Los Angeles had annexed San Pedro and its port in 1908 as part of the city council's ambitious expansion of its municipal boundaries.[33]

There is no panel commemorating 1885, the year Los Angeles was plugged into the transcontinental railroad system. There is no panel commemorating 1821 either, the birth of the Mexican Republic, nor 1834, the secularization proclamation that divested the missions of half of its lands and established the geographic boundaries of the rancho system, that would guide the dividing and subdividing of the landscape during the real estate booms of the late nineteenth and early twentieth centuries. Like any history, the one presented by these doors is selective.

On the other side of the bronze double doors is the rotunda, its concave ceiling finished in a glazed-tile mosaic, the floor elegantly marbled with a medallion at its center depicting a Spanish galleon, and marble dark-colored Corinthian columns framing the corridors that lead away to the three other entrances (Figure 9.9). The mosaic depicts eight human figures, each generically clad in robes,

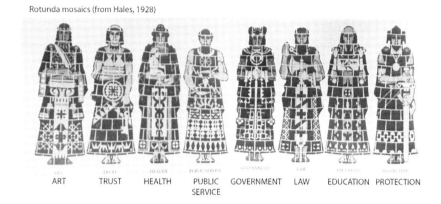

Figure 9.9
Under the rotunda: the two principal corridors intersect under the rotunda, its walls, floor and ceiling adorned in iconography.
Photographs by the author; mosaic drawings adapted by the author from Hales, 1928.

sandals and moccasins evocative of missionary or Indian attire. Each figure symbolizes a virtue: art, law, health, and so on, humanistic virtues embodied in colonial figures. Two of the eight figures are female, health and art, and the masculinized figure of law and justice are depicted holding a sword and large axe, respectively. Health holds a white baby in its dark arms. A pair of vaulted corridors leads away from the rotunda, each ceiling richly tiled and ornamented with lily-white depictions of classical figures. Just a few feet from the rotunda can be seen the image of plenty, a panel depicting a toga-clad blonde loosening her garment to let spill fruits and vegetables. Not a basket-sized amount, the image evokes the likeness of a river or an avalanche, for the flow down onto the landscape is impressive. The eclectic imagery that moves the mind's eye from pre-Columbian American in one corner to ancient Greece around the corner, back to Spain's conquest, might seem jarring, yet it is congruous with the architectural eclecticism on the exterior. Such iconography and historical arrangement of the decorative program constructs a tight story, and thereby represents the community without necessarily incorporating the entire past. By cropping out the secularization proclamation of 1834, for example, the story omits the Mexican Republic's move to divest the missions of land, handing it to the ranchos. That omission leaves the story of *civitas* entirely in Anglo-American hands, relegating the pre-Anglo past to a pre-civic chapter in the story.

ACCESS

Today, the most striking feature of the central space under the rotunda-dome is not the architectural drama of its surfaces, but its emptiness. It serves no function except the intersection of two main circulation paths. No longer is the forecourt leading down the steps to Spring Street, City Hall's principal entrance. An architecturally less-prominent entrance on the other side of the building, one floor down, equipped with metal detectors, has that honor. Even the double-loaded corridors leading away from the rotunda are also empty, lined with doors, their nameplates enumerating a zoology of municipal departments. Their Romanesque-inspired vaulted ceilings and painted ribs neatly dissect the building into four distinct quadrants. Each quadrant is organized around its own light court, dedicated to a particular municipal function. The building was thus intended as something of a map of the municipal bureaucracy (Figure 9.10). In the southeast quadrant was the mayor's office. In the southwest, across the main corridor, was the city council. Councilman's offices were located on floors above the main floor, but the council chamber was on the main floor reached at the end of a semi-private corridor that bent away from the main hallway. It was decorated in an eclectic style that could pass as either Romanesque or as Spanish Revival, and with its central aisle and long proportions it looks like a mission sanctuary. The other two quadrants belonged to the Board of Public Works and the City Clerk's office, which included the early Department of Motor Vehicles before its expansion necessitated larger quarters.

Los Angeles City Hall

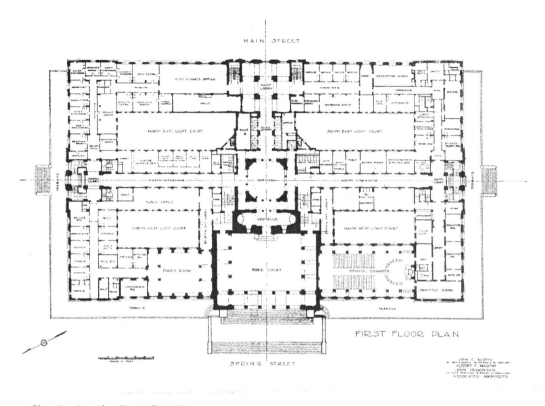

Plan: Los Angeles City Hall, 1928

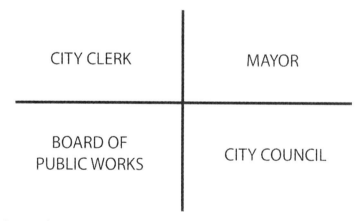

Figure 9.10 Plan. Source: Hales, 1928.

City Hall is a building stocked full of people, of course, but the vast majority is sequestered behind closed doors, removed from the public space of the ornamented hallways. In these spaces, the public is an intruder encountering the cavity of public space, before making contact with lesser-ranked municipal bureaucrats, incapable of coming face to face with elected officials. The layered building insulates mayor and city council from the public, while allowing for the experience of contact, the City Hall building playing the prosthetic role of an augmented limb. Technically public, the majority of the building remains paradoxically off-limits.

Engaging with this municipal government was a matter of negotiating a bureaucracy facilitated and augmented by its building. Local government had come a long way since the days of the Mexican *Ayuntamiento* (city council) of the nineteenth century. City Hall was now a portal lodged between the people and its government, with gatekeepers stationed at key junctures insulating government officials. The role of this building was to ornament those points of contact, to dramatize and ennoble, and to impose a cultural memory that really had more to do with reinforcing and legitimizing the dominant social group rather than representing the rich breadth of the city's history.

Built as a visual landmark and representation of community and its government, City Hall included imagery of nearly the full matrix of LA's population, but in a structured way. Images of Indians, Spanish ships, and Indo-Mexicans appeared in tiles, medallions, and mosaic patterns, visually represented but as culturally empty icons. Inscriptions of philosophy pertaining to law and social order were not derived from Pre-Columbian North America, Mexico, or Catholic Spain, but from another ethnic tradition. It is ironic that at the time of writing the Mayor occupying that building is Mexican-American, as are a number of City Councilmen, housed in the "gleaming tower of whiteness." As a system of signs and significations, City Hall is not really static, of course. The squatters of the Occupy LA movement were only part of the latest episode to engage with the building and its meaning, capitalizing upon and challenging its gesture as a public building.

NOTES

1. Kate Linthicum and David Zahniser, "Repairing Occupy L.A. damage to City Hall lawn could cost $400,000," *Los Angeles Times*, October 19, 2011. See also City Councilman Richard Alarcon's press release: "Councilmember Richard Alarcón Issues Statement Regarding Occupy Los Angeles Developments," November 30, 2011.
2. Kate Linthicum, "Some Occupy L.A. protesters may get a lesson in free speech," *Los Angeles Times,* December 21, 2011.
3. Richard Verrier, "On Location: Occupy L.A. upstages film production at City Hall," *Los Angeles Times*, November 30, 2011.
4. Mary P. Ryan, "'A laudable pride in the whole of us': City halls and civic materialism," in this volume.
5. Mark Wild, *Street Meeting: Multiethnic Neighborhoods in Early Twentieth-century Los Angeles* (University of California: Berkeley, 2005), 157.

6 For several years the area referred to as "Skid Row" has been a space of large-scale homelessness in Los Angeles. The documentary film screened in 2011, "Lost Angels: Skid Row is My Home," by director Thomas Napper, was a rare attempt to expose the invisible landscape of homelessness to public view.
7 "City Hall three-day program of dedication ceremonies," *Los Angeles Times*, pt. 2, p. 1, April 26, 1928.
8 *Los Angeles City Hall* by George P. Hales, Board of Public Works, City of Los Angeles, California, 24 c. 1928.
9 The Committee of the Games of the Xth Olympiad 1932 Ltd., *The Official Report of the Xth Olympiad, Los Angeles, 1932*, Los Angeles: Wolfer Printing Co., 1933.
10 Hales, *Los Angeles City Hall*.
11 The phrase "American perpendicular style" belongs to architectural historians David Gebhard and Harriet Von Breton, *Los Angeles in the Thirties: 1931–1941* (Los Angeles: Hennessey & Ingalls, Inc., 1989), 35. For a study of the city hall building type and the popularity of the dome and the tower, see William L. Lebovich, *America's City Halls* (Washington, DC: The Preservation Press, 1984). For the monumentality of the "skyscraper city hall" type, see Dell Upton, *Architecture in the United States* (Oxford: Oxford University Press, 1999), 218.
12 Los Angeles Chamber of Commerce, "Meeting Minutes and Stenographer's Notes: January 28, 1932," in *Chamber of Commerce Papers*, Western Regional History Center, Special Collections, University of Southern California. A few weeks later a man plunged to his death as he attempted to secure the Akron's tie-ropes to a mast over Seattle.
13 The statistics on the city's growth in population, square footage, and automobile ownership is well established. The urtext on this is Robert M. Fogelson, *The Fragmented Metropolis: Los Angeles, 1850–1930* (Berkeley: University of California Press, 1967). Other scholars have followed, most notably Scott L. Bottles, *Los Angeles and the Automobile: The Making of the Modern City* (Berkeley: University of California Press, 1987), and Greg Hise, *Magnetic Los Angeles: Planning the Twentieth-Century Metropolis* (Baltimore: Johns Hopkins University Press, 1997).
14 Fogelson, citing census figures for commerce, and city engineering files for municipal expansion.
15 Hales, *Los Angeles City Hall*, 17.
16 Harry Carr, *Los Angeles: City of Dreams* (New York: Grosset & Dunlap, 1935), 5. The racist tenor of that line has recently drawn attention. Carr has been quoted by William Alexander McClung, *Landscapes of Desire: Anglo Mythologies of Los Angeles* (Berkeley: University of California Press, 2002), 72; and William Deverell, *Whitewashed Adobe: The Rise of Los Angeles and the Remaking of its Mexican Past* (Berkeley: University of California Press, 2005), 36.
17 "Miss Los Angeles Contemplates a Brilliant Future," *Los Angeles Times*, 31 December 1928, II–1.
18 Patricia Hills, "Picturing progress in the era of westward expansion," in William Truettner, ed., *The West as America: Reinterpreting Images of the Frontier, 1820–1920* (Washington: Smithsonian Institution Press, 1991), 97–147.
19 Historian and lawyer, Carey McWilliams, surveyed the language of boosters in the 1940s in his frequently reprinted book, *Southern California: An Island on the Land* (Layton: Gibbs Smith, 1973).
20 The caricature of a Spanish maiden for the *Los Angeles Times* was the creation of that newspaper's political cartoonist, Edmund Gale, who penned her from 1907 to 1934.
21 The Laws of the Indies was proclaimed by the Spanish king in 1573, intended to govern the planning and administration of colonial settlements in the Spanish empire. It was organized around a plaza, although the original location of Los Angeles's plaza was actually a few blocks from the space recognized as the plaza in the early twentieth

century. John W. Reps, *The Making of Urban America: A History of City Planning in the United States* (Princeton: Princeton University Press, 1965); and "The Laws of the Indies," in Jean-Francois Lejeune, ed., *Cruelty and Utopia: Cities and Landscapes of Latin America* (New York: Princeton Architectural Press, 2003), 18029.

22 Christine Sterling, *Olvera Street: Its History and Restoration* (Los Angeles: Old Mission Printing Shop, 1933).

23 Jean Bruce Poole and Tevvy Ball, *El Pueblo: The Historic Heart of Los Angeles* (Los Angeles: Getty Conservation Institute, 2002), 1.

24 As Kevin Starr notes, editor and booster Charles Fletcher Lummis boasted that "the ignorant, hopelessly un-American type of foreigner which infests and largely controls Eastern cities is almost unknown here." Kevin Starr, *Inventing the Dream: California through the Progressive Era* (Oxford: Oxford University Press, 1985). And Mike Davis noted how scientist and Nobel laureate Robert Millikan toured the country promoting the city as having a "population which is twice as Anglo-Saxon as that existing in New York, Chicago or any of the other great cities of this country." Mike Davis, "Sunshine and the open shop: Ford and Darwin in 1920s Los Angeles," in Tom Sitton and William Deverell, eds., *Metropolis in the Making: Los Angeles in the 1920s* (Berkeley: University of California Press, 1999), 116. Census figures are quoted in Fogelson, *Fragmented Metropolis*.

25 Montezuma was the Anglicized name of Moctezuma, the Aztec ruler defeated by Cortez in 1521. The phrase "the sons of Montezuma" was employed to refer to Mexicans and Indians. See for example, Harry Carr, *Los Angeles*.

26 See George Sanchez, *Becoming Mexican American: Ethnicity, Culture and Identity in Los Angeles, 1900–1945* (Oxford: Oxford University Press, 1993). See also, Davis, "Sunshine and the open shop." The phrase "native American" has changed, but in the 1920s it referred primarily to Anglo-Americans born in the United States, and excluded non-white ethnicities. Also see Fogelson, *The Fragmented Metropolis*.

27 For explorations of the concept, see Phoebe Kropp, "Citizens of the past? Olvera Street and the construction of race and memory in 1930s Los Angeles," *Radical History Review* (Fall 2001), 35–60; and Deverell, *Whitewashed Adobe*.

28 David Gebhard, "The Spanish colonial revival in Southern California, 1895–1930," *Journal of the Society of Architectural Historians* 26, no. 2, (May 1967), 131–47.

29 Phoebe S. Kropp, *California Vieja: Culture and Memory in a Modern American Past* (Berkeley: University of California Press, 2006).

30 Hales, *Los Angeles City Hall*.

31 Carr, *Los Angeles*, 5.

32 Details of the episode can be found in Lawrence E. Guillow, "Pandemonium in the Plaza: The first Los Angeles riot, June 22, 1856," *The Southern California Quarterly 77* (Fall 1995), 183–97.

33 Details of these two engineering projects can be found in Fogelson, *The Fragmented Metropolis*.

Re-forming public space

Chapter 10: Politics, Planning, and Subjection

Anticolonial Nationalism and Public Space in Colonial Calcutta

Swati Chattopadhyay

In 1998 the Calcutta Town Hall was restored and turned into a museum (Figure 10.1). A tableau of Calcutta's history and a visual narrative of anticolonial nationalism came to occupy much of the lower-floor hall, while a library was located to the left of the entrance foyer (Figure 10.2). The upper-floor hall and surrounding rooms were designated for conferences and state celebrations. In a poignant way the museumification of Town Hall returned the space to its original function. The Town Hall was first proposed in 1792 with the objective of providing a public space for the city's residents. The idea was taken up in earnest in 1804 when a building was found necessary to display the marble statues of two preceding Governor Generals of the East India Company, Lord Cornwallis and Lord Wellesley, that had just then arrived from England.[1] Other statues of notable

Figure 10.1
Calcutta Town Hall.
Photograph by the author.

Figure 10.2
Exhibits in the Lower Floor of Town Hall, Calcutta. Photograph by the author.

residents were added in due course. Although not intended, the display cases of the contemporary exhibition housing the historical mannequins provide an interesting counterpoint to the marble statues from the nineteenth century that continue to adorn the foyers.

The Calcutta Town Hall's purpose, location, and ultimately the contestation over its use during the first hundred years after its inauguration, were deeply political, but for much of its existence it was not meant as a space of representative politics – it was about the denial and bitter contestation of that privilege of self-representation and citizenship. If city halls are always about representation – whom do they represent and in what capacity? – what indeed is the relationship between the city hall's function as public space, its architectural vocabulary, and the planning ethos in which it is embedded? Who constitutes the legitimate public? And how does the city hall inflect the answer to that question? Calcutta's Town Hall helps us understand the limits of self-representation in a colonial milieu and the impact of those limitations on the larger scale of the city as political space. The spatial lessons here, I would argue, need not be limited to the colonial context. In a more important sense, the history of Calcutta Town Hall as public space, suggests something critical about the changing spatial imaginary of representative politics.

THE CONTEXT OF REPRESENTATION

The need for a respectable establishment, more polite than the taverns and coffee houses of the city, was part of an emerging early nineteenth-century British vision of Calcutta, capital of British India until 1911, that sought to impress the power of the ruling elite on the landscape. In the late eighteenth century, in the absence of a town hall and because of the smallness of the erstwhile residence of the Governor General, most state celebrations and important entertainments organized by the British community in Calcutta were held in the Old Court House. The latter's demolition in 1792 left the city without any "grand halls for public suppers or dances."[2] That and the Governor General Lord Wellesley's penchant for ceremonial pomp meant that several new buildings, including the Town Hall and a new Government House, would be erected in the city center on Esplanade Row. The location of Calcutta's Town Hall was exceptionally privileged. It faced the vast open expanse of the Esplanade or the Maidan, and Fort William, and stood in line with the Supreme Court and the new grand pile of Government House, the residence and office of the Governor General (Figure 10.3). Together they constituted the front row of the administrative center, and this view was faithfully recorded in contemporary depictions of the city. Visitors arriving by ship in the nineteenth century were routinely impressed with the solemnly organized row of public buildings facing the Esplanade.

The city center itself was a heady combination of government offices, warehouses, churches, large agency houses, taverns, markets, petty shops, and residences. The police headquarters on Lall Bazaar Street was just a block away, so was the Writers' Building, the administrative headquarters of the East India Company. Wellesley pursued a plan to buy the properties behind Government House, so that the grandeur of the imperial center could be extended over a larger space. But the proprietors of these buildings did not comply with his vision. So ceremonial activities turned towards the Esplanade in the nineteenth century.

The buildings on Esplanade Row worked as an aesthetic and social ensemble with the green space of the Esplanade, which included the Course (for drives) and Respondentia Walk. Special celebrations in the Governor's mansion concluded with fireworks in the Esplanade, which the guests could observe from the porticoes and balconies of the buildings on Esplanade Row. While Indian gentlemen crowded the Course in search of fresh air, in 1831 both the Course and Respondentia Walk were made exclusive European preserves from five to eight in the mornings and evenings.[3] Such exclusionary measures were considered necessary to prevent natives from disfiguring a valued social event. The Town Hall was considered part of this privileged landscape. The landscaping in front of Town Hall explicitly linked it to the ceremonial space of the Esplanade and Government House. In Fredrick Feibig's mid-nineteenth century depiction we see the copper statue of Governor General Lord William Bentinck by Richard Westmacott placed across the street from Town Hall's front entrance around 1830 (Figure 10.4).[4]

The building itself, designed by Colonel John Garstin of the Engineers, was grandiose, in excess of even the typical palatial scale of public and private buildings in the city. The lower floor was 23 feet tall and the upper floor another 30 feet high.[5] A wide flight of stairs leading directly from the street to a double-story portico framed by non-fluted Doric-style columns made for an impressive entrance. The fund for the construction of the building was raised by a public lottery,[6] and the government provided the cost for its initial interior furnishing.[7] Its grandiosity,

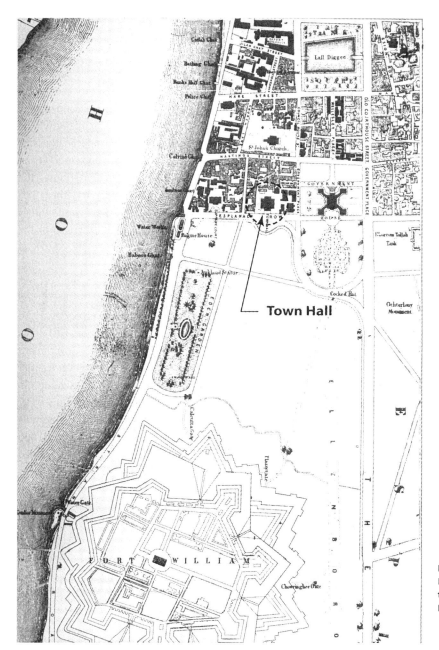

Figure 10.3
Map of Calcutta showing the location of Town Hall.

Politics, Planning, and Subjection

Figure 10.4
The Town Hall in Calcutta by Fredrick Fiebig. Tinted lithograph, Calcutta c. 1845. Copyright British Library Board.

and the fact that the building showed signs of structural failure soon after it was completed generated sarcastic commentaries from contemporaries:

> ... that far-famed hall.
> In which there of Graecia's school the traces,
> But by its cracking predisposed to fall.
> Till patched up, and well tried by many a festive ball.[8]

In 1818 Garstin undertook the necessary structural remediation at his own cost. Subsequently, the steward, William Hastie, undertook to furnish it at his own expense in exchange for the privilege of supplying provisions for dinners and other social events. While the steward was responsible for daily supervision, the Town Hall was placed under a committee that set the conditions of use and enforced the rules. Accordingly, the public could visit the lower floor hall housing the statues from 8 am to 4 pm Monday to Saturday, and merchants and other individuals who wanted space for business purposes were allocated one of the southern rooms by the steward. The use of the upper floor hall was restricted for meetings and entertainments for public occasions for which one needed to apply to the Town Hall Committee. The responsibility and maintenance of Town Hall underwent periodic changes after 1824 when the initial committee was dissolved. The government did not wish to support the costs, and transferred the responsibilities to the Justices of the Peace in 1865, instituting a new rule of charging Rs 100 for general use such as dinners, entertainments, and professional meetings.[9] Town Hall could be used for free only for charitable or public purposes. In 1867 the property was transferred to the Calcutta Municipality.

The centerpiece of the building plan was the transverse hall on each floor, the entry to the building being located perpendicular to their long sides (Figure

10.5). Such an arrangement was uncommon as a planning device in colonial Calcutta, where the norm was to build the central hall on axis with the entry. The balcony that overlooked the rear portico acted as a gallery and provided an impressive view of the administrative center of the city and the river. The main hall on the upper floor with its teak floor was conceived of as a ballroom with a music gallery on the west end and a raised platform on the east end. The rooms on the north were used as card and supper rooms, and the ground floor rooms next to the foyer were rented out for business meetings. Both its interior and exterior were designed with a certain elite performativity in mind. Although not architecturally distinguished, the largeness of the central hall allowed the space to be suitably dressed for events. Jeremy Losty gives us the description of such an interior decoration scheme from William Prinsep's unpublished journal. The occasion was a fancy-dress ball to welcome back Lady Hastings from England:

> [W]e [William and his brother James, newly arrived in Calcutta] were both on the decorating committee. It was to be done regardless of expense. Between each pillar a shield was suspended by wreaths of evergreens with the name of some Indian victory on it. The ceiling was made to represent the interior of a tent by the tinted muslin festooned from the centre to the capitals of the pillars. At one end was a splendid tent of open drapery looped on to a group of tilting lances and a shield with the armorial bearings of the Loudoun and Moira arms. On the other end under the orchestra we made with the cheap white muslin of the

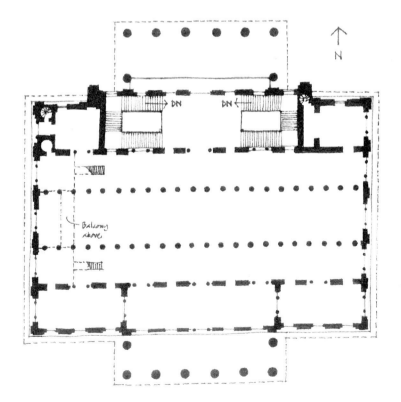

Figure 10.5
Plan of Upper Floor of Town Hall, Calcutta. Drawing by author based on drawings courtesy of Calcutta Town Hall and plan by Sivashish Bose.

country a temple to Hymen with fluted columns looking like a Doric peristyle with flowers at the capitals, the only colour about it. It had the most elegant light appearance.[10]

The production of imperial elegance by transforming the neoclassical interior with symbols of conquest was typical of such celebrations, and invited the participation of the guests, both British and Indian, in the performance of imperial glory. But this participatory terrain remained uneven.

When James Prinsep died in 1840, a "great meeting" was held in the Town Hall on August 6, chaired by Sir Edward Ryan, to determine the best manner in which his contribution to India and Calcutta ought to be commemorated. We do not know what transpired at that meeting, but William noted that "the natives in the meanwhile held a meeting among themselves and formed a subscription of their own to build a ghaut [stepped landing] to his memory." William, partner with William Carr and Dwarakanth Tagore in the firm Carr, Tagore and Company, did not mention who these natives were, despite his closeness to the elite Indian community. He continued:

> A site was given them by the Gov General at the Coolie Ghaut just below the Fort and the erection of a very neat Palladian Porch at the head of a flight of steps was entrusted to our friend Fitzgerald an officer of the Engineers. It is an ornament to the river, and mostly used for the landing of troops arriving by sea which before mostly had to jump out of the boats on to a very muddy shore. It bears the name of James Prinsep on the architrave in four different languages – English, Bengallee, Hindi, and Persian. My last act in India was to add 2 stone recumbent lions to slope off the stairs which I got well done in Buxar for 700 rupees, but I did not remain long enough to see them in place. It is called Prinsep's Ghaut so that our name cannot easily be forgotten in India.[11]

It appears from William's recollection that except for providing the funds to erect the structure, the Indian community had little to do with the decisions that went into the making of the memorial; that is, if the Indian elite were involved in the planning process, it is not acknowledged. This was not the only instance of cooperation between the European and Indian communities in public matters in the first half of the nineteenth century. There are several instances of meetings in which both Indians and Europeans participated. A joint meeting of Europeans and Indians was convened in 1836 to commemorate John Palmer. The same year, 200 Indians gathered in Town Hall to express their gratitude towards Charles Metcalfe, the officiating Governor General, and in an earlier meeting they had pledged to raise money to build a Hall to memorialize his name. William's narration, which mentions and at the same time de-emphasizes the role of the Indian community, is characteristic of the colonial context in which public buildings and public places in the city acquired meaning as sites of the triumph and "contribution" of British colonialism, and the asymmetry of social relations between the British and the Indian communities that marked the process. In political terms, under colonialism, Indians could only be subjects, not citizens.

"MAKING UNEQUALS EQUAL"

A large repertoire of events was held in Town Hall in the nineteenth century: apart from the usual banquets, balls, dinner receptions, and memorial meetings, there were concerts, theaters, art and photography exhibitions, examinations, prize distribution, and convocation ceremonies for schools and colleges, and meetings of several elite associations such as the Landholder's Association and Calcutta School Book Society. And, of course, it was the site of political and "protest meetings," long before any form of representative governance was introduced. The vast majority of events that took place in Town Hall until the 1870s was under the auspices of the European community. While members of elite Indian families participated in many of these events, they were sharply aware of the racial difference insinuated every time some government decision was seen as infringing upon the privileges of European citizens. And yet, until the 1850s at least, elite Indians continued to work in support of the British government and the European community on the assumption of mutual benefit. It was, however, the response of the European community to Thomas Macaulay's proposal of trying British-born subjects under the jurisdiction of civil courts of the East India Company, followed by the second round of Acts passed in 1849 (proposed by John Drinkwater Bethune), collectively known as the Black Acts, that began to change the attitudes of Indians towards the possibilities of Town Hall as public space.

The British community met on December 29, 1849, in Town Hall, to protest the degradation of Englishmen to "the present level of natives." The Black Acts, they claimed, made "unequals equals."[12] The racist objections voiced in this meeting produced a spirited response from the Indian community. In 1851 this same group of elite Indians who had contributed to the commemoration of previous Governor Generals and James Prinsep, formed the British Indian Association to press demands on their behalf, and in an 1853 meeting the Association demanded inclusion of Indians in the civil service. Importantly, this was not the first time that matters related to racial prejudice were voiced in Town Hall: in 1831 the Anglo-Indians headed by Henry Derezio held a meeting in Town Hall to protest the prejudicial treatment meted out to the "mixed races" by the government.[13] While the British Indian Association formed by the Indian comprador class remained loyal to the British government, individuals in the Association were beginning to see the political landscape differently. In a public meeting called in Town Hall in 1857, Kissory Chand Mitra, referring to the protests against the Black Acts, repudiated the "false doctrine put forth by the exemptionists" seven years ago, that "unequals cannot be equals."[14]

The effect of the disagreement between the elite sections of these two communities was significant. As early as 1842, and shortly after the meeting in which the decision to commemorate James Prinsep was made by the Indian community, Ramgopal Ghose, in a private letter to a friend, mourned the absence of a town hall in the "native part of town," in which "we could hold our meetings, and place our libraries, our pictures, our statues."[15] Ghose suggested that there were concerns that were peculiar to the Indian community and that there was an Indian public whose opinion could not be freely expressed and accommodated in the present Town Hall. The Indian community was acutely aware that a proposal for a meeting in Town Hall could be easily denied by the Sheriff. In 1827 a petition by Raja Radhakanta Deb and Raja Rammohun Roy to use the Town Hall to protest the Stamp Act was denied by Sheriff T. Plowden on the pretext that the government was not informed beforehand.[16]

Amid a growing sentiment for a separate space in the northern part of the city for public meetings, in 1840, Radhakanta Deb began construction of a Natmandir within his own palatial premises. This was an early move to create a "public" building in the city that served as an alternative to Town Hall. Its location within Deb's residential premises, however, tied it to a particular early nineteenth-century tradition of elite Indian patronage of public events, both secular and religious.

Deb's residential complex consisted of a series of buildings formed around courtyards and divided into inner private compartments (andar-mahal) and the outer public compartments (bahir-mahal). The western part of the complex consisted of a large garden with a tank and summer house. Public festivities, including important religious festivals, were held in the spacious courtyard of the outer compartments. The Natmandir was added adjacent to the public courtyard, and set away from the entrance in the garden, so that the open space in front would provide an opportunity to appreciate its Doric-style façade (Figures 10.6 and 10.7). Approached through the double-story carriage port, the central feature of the plan was a large hall with a raised stage on one end. Paired rows of columns created an aisle on the periphery of the hall and supported balconies above. The

Figure 10.6
Natmandir of
Sobhabazar Rajbari.
Photograph by the
author.

City Halls and Civic Materialism ■

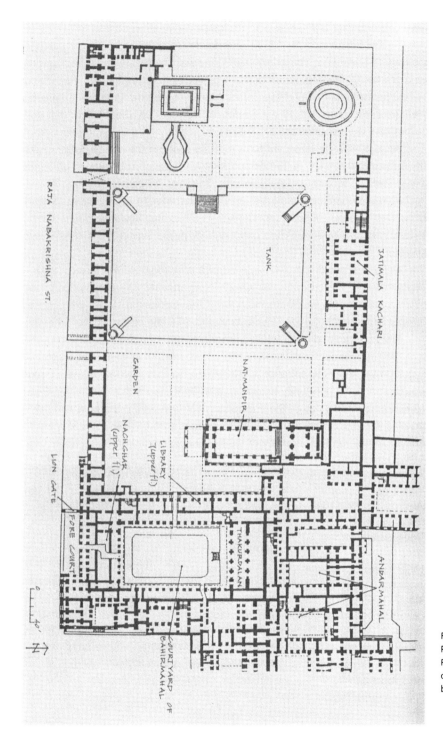

Figure 10.7
Plan of Sobhabazar Rajbari showing location of Natmandir. Drawing by the author.

counterpoint of the neo-classical façade was a *nava-ratna* (nine-jeweled or nine-pinnacled) temple roof over the stage at the rear. The architectural vocabulary was strategically signaling access to two cultural spheres – classical western and a princely Indian.[17] The building was used for a variety of public events, including meetings of the School Book Society, Dharmasabha, British Indian Society, literary and political gatherings, religious festivities, as well as balls and suppers to which Europeans were invited.[18] Part temple, part public hall, part theater, the Natmandir was a substitute for Town Hall, where Deb could perform his role as the patron of the Indian community, and set the terms of social and political discourse.

In the second half of the nineteenth century, two venues, Deb's Natmandir, and from 1868, the newly constructed British India Association Hall became popular venues for political meetings of the Indian community. One of the most famous of these was held in Deb's Natmandir in 1861 to protest the collusion between the state, the judiciary, and British civil society over the publication and translation into English of a Bengali play by Dinabandhu Mitra, titled *Nildarpan* (Mirror of Indigo). The play was a commentary on the revolt of the Indian peasantry against the indigo planters in Bengal. Lt. Governor John Peter Grant wanted the play translated, and the translation was entrusted to writer and playwright Madhusudan Dutt (his name was not published) and published by the Reverend James Long. The British planters sued Long for libel. In a public display of the Indian community's support for the cause, Long's bail was paid by Kaliprasanna Sinha. As Partha Chatterjee has pointed out, neither the author nor the translator were even considered for libel, demonstrating that the only people who counted as part the legitimate public in European eyes were members of the European community. Members of the Indian community, no matter what their contribution to public institutions and the public sphere did not register as members of the public sphere of the city.[19] In the meeting held at Deb's Natmandir the leaders of the Indian community demanded a recall of the officiating judge from office for his "frequent and indiscriminate attacks on the characters of the natives of the country with an intemperance … not compatible with the impartial administration of justice."[20]

Town Hall continued to be used for meetings by Indians, however. Indeed in the Indian elite conception of the city's topography, Town Hall became the hallowed site of early nationalist agitation because of the fiery speeches delivered by the likes of nationalist leader Surendranath Banerjee. It remained the most sought-after venue for voicing critiques of government policy into the first two decades of the twentieth century, simply because it was the most symbolically charged public venue for the British.[21] Its location on Esplanade Row made it the most visible, and for the British authorities, the most threatening platform for political discourse held among Indians.

An important change in the expansion of political space in the city came in 1883, when in the wake of the Surendranath Banerjee's imprisonment following the Ilbert Bill agitation, the Indian Association under the leadership of Anandamohan Bose planned a protest meeting in Town Hall.[22] On the morning of the meeting he was informed that the Town Hall would not be available. The

Indian elite balked at the idea of allowing such a protest meeting within their own residential premises. The meeting was held in open air in Beadon Square in the northern part of town, with an attendance of 20,000 people, including a large number of students. This move from the interior space of the Town Hall, Natmandir, theaters, and private mansions to open air parks and squares began a process of "democratizing" political space in the city that would be concretized during the *swadeshi* (indigenous self-sufficiency) movement that was launched to protest the 1905 Partition of Bengal.[23] The necessary logic of a mass agitation meant that politics spilled beyond the spaces, and often control, of the erstwhile elite constituency.

SWADESHI AND THE REIMAGINATION OF POLITICAL SPACE

The 1905 Partition of Bengal was about territory and the imagination of Bengal as an integral community – a powerful political space. While the official reason provided for partitioning Bengal into two provinces was to ease the burden of administering so large a territory,[24] confidential reports and private communication among senior government officials confirm that it was done to curb the political ambition of the Bengali community by separating the Hindu-majority western districts from the Muslim-majority eastern districts. As the nationalists put it, it was a method of "divide and rule." Sporadic protests against an impending partition had been voiced in meetings and newspapers since December 12, 1903, when the proposal for transferring Chittagong and Dacca divisions to Assam were published in the *Government of India Gazette*.[25] The Inspector-General of Police's Confidential Report emphasized that the modes of agitation were directed from the "center" of leadership in Calcutta, and that by the beginning of January 1904, "what is generally accepted as public opinion ["opinion of the Bar and of schoolmasters"] in Bengal has been roused to strong opposition against the Government of India."[26] Viceroy Lord Curzon penned his view of the political advantage of partitioning Bengal despite these protests:

> The Bengalis who like to think of themselves a nation, and who dream of a future when the English will be turned out, and a Bengali Babu will be installed in Government House, Calcutta, of course bitterly resent any disruption that is likely to interfere with the realization of this dream. If we are weak enough to yield to this clamour now, we shall not be able to dismember or reduce Bengal again, and you will be cementing and solidifying on the eastern flank of India, a force already formidable.[27]

Even those British officials who thought the lack of public consultation on Partition was inadequate, agreed about its political advantage to colonial rule, and believed that while there would be protests ("What Howls they will be!"), "the native will quietly become accustomed to the new conditions." The official calculations misjudged the depth of discontent against the government's decision. The movement against the partition, particularly during its initial stages, gathered widespread support among the Bengali community, departed from previous methods of agitation, and broadened into a demand for *swaraj* (self-rule).[28] International events – British losses in the Boer War and the Japanese victory against Russia – boosted the confidence of the Indian community protesting the partition. The most significant change was the transformation of city space as sites of protest.

Two concerns were central to the strategy of the antipartition movement: to present the movement as having mass appeal cutting across class, caste, and religion, and to create an emotive, didactic space from which the Bengali "public" could learn to value their *swadesh* (own country) and draw moral sustenance.[29] The need to formulate a new form of public gathering to initiate a larger public was clearly recognized, and such gatherings were marked by an effort to sacralize the secular/profane realm of politics and urban experience. *Swadeshi* leaders were faced with the formidable challenge of wresting the spatial imagination of the city, and in extension, the province, and thus the command over space, from British colonial authorities. This was also the first time a concerted effort was made to connect the city with the provincial towns and villages as sites of political agitation. The reimagination of Calcutta as political space became of central importance. The leaders of the movement felt compelled to find sites of protest other than Town Hall, to initiate a spatially dispersed movement, and to accommodate the large numbers that were expected to attend these meetings, because of the desire to change the mode of conducting such assemblies. Protest meetings were held in Albert Hall, the Star Theater, the Grand Theater, and mansions of the Indian elite.[30] Speeches and the passing of resolutions had become associated with a borrowed "western" vocabulary of civil gatherings and political "mendicancy." Now there was a new attempt to discern those modes that could be more clearly identified as "Indian" or "Bengali." Rituals, initially connected to religious rites, such as the *rakhi* ceremony (sisters tying a sacred thread on the wrist of brothers wishing them long life), were plucked out of context and secularized: the leaders of the movement asked men as well as women to tie *rakhis* on the wrists of friends and strangers alike as a mark of national solidarity. The emotional appeal of the meetings was extended beyond stirring speeches, now increasingly delivered in Bengali rather than in English, to include Bengali nationalist songs, a first for political rallies in the city. The city, the *Sanjivani* claimed, had metamorphosed into a sacred space (*punya bhumi*) by the fire of *swadeshi*:

> The sacred flame of love for native land has been lighted in every quarter of Calcutta. Last week we noticed meetings at College Square, Beadon Square, Shyambazaar and Raja's Bazaar. This flame has now spread from the center to the outskirts of town.[31]

Bengali-edited papers took on the task of publishing the name of every meeting site, producing long lists of place names – parks, squares, temples, meeting halls, schoolhouses, residences, theaters – through which Bengal was territorialized as *swadesh*.[32] The holding of public meetings and the presence of *swadeshi* agitators awaiting *darshan* (devotional gaze) of leaders in public places were seen to render these sites with a superior ambiance that transcended their everyday meaning.[33]

There were several meetings held in the Town Hall leading up to the Partition. A section of the Bengali community, however, preferred more radical forms of protest and viewed the meetings in Town Hall, including the meeting on August 7, 1905 (considered a watershed in anticolonial nationalism) as a continuation of political mendicancy. In physical terms, however, the meeting of August 7 forebode the future. It was at this meeting that the resolution to boycott British-manufactured goods was taken. Preparatory meetings for the boycott were held in district towns and at the Government Eden Hindu Hostel prior to the August 7 meeting. Surendranath Banerjee who presided over the meeting recalled:

> The young men of Calcutta marched in solemn procession from College Square to the Town Hall … A huge crowd gathered. They came rushing up the steps filling the upper and lower hall, flowing out into the portico and the grounds beyond. We decided to have three meetings, two in Town Hall, upper and lower floor, and the third in the *maidan*, near the Bentinck statue. I made the announcement from the steps of the Town Hall.[34]

The Statesman noted the constituencies that made up the assembled multitude:

> The floor was packed, and the window spaces, staircase, and corridors swarmed with people vainly attempting to hear the far-off speakers … A careful observer would have remarked that a large majority of the immense audience upstairs were mature men, and that of the lower floor also there was a noticeable proportion of such men than is customary at Town Hall demonstrations … The student community was, of course, in evidence, but it was mainly on the edge of the crowd and outside on the Maidan, with a huge number of the processionists assembled, to be reinforced after five o'clock by hundreds of men from the city offices … The official apologist would have found it difficult, in the face of this eager and enthusiastic and indignant multitude, to speak of simulated opposition or artificial agitation. Among those present were over five hundred delegates from the various districts of Bengal.[35]

Permission for this meeting was secured from the Police Commissioner by Surendranath and Bhupendranath Bose, and the route to be followed was decided upon and adhered to by the processioners. For a similar march to a meeting on September 22, 1905, no permission was secured and the "students proceeded by a variety of routes to the Town Hall and were addressed both within the Town Hall by the Hon'ble Babu Lal Mohun Ghose and on the Maidan in front of the Town Hall by the Honbl'e Mr Bhupendra Nath Bose." The Commissioner of Police wrote to Surendranath and Bhupendranath and prohibited further political meetings in the Maidan.[36]

Soon after, the Calcutta Municipal Commissioner decided to prohibit *swadeshi* meetings in the Town Hall, and later, in all "public" places – open-air parks and squares under the jurisdiction of the Municipality. The Bengali newspaper *Hitavadi* noted with satisfaction the impact of "monster meetings," and claimed that the government is mistaken if it expects such measures to end meetings and public rallies.[37] Others questioned the legitimacy of such an order itself: "Is the Town Hall … Mr. Allen's paternal inheritance? Is it not public property?" the editor of the *Sandhya* of February 13, 1906 asked.[38] The prohibition was treated as a challenge to intensify the agitation, and a cue to expand the notion of public space. In the absence of a town hall, all open-to-sky space would become "public" space, the *Hitavadi* claimed.[39] In response to the government's claim that the movement against Partition had lost steam, on March 3, 1906, seventeen meetings were held in Calcutta on a single day, with the *Bengalee* publishing beforehand a list of 57 speakers.[40] Picketing, mostly by school and college students, in the city's shops selling foreign goods, meant the movement had to be encountered in the streets and markets, linking these commercial venues with those of educational institutions. Contemporary police reports considered the educational institutions (mostly founded and patronized by the Indian community) and the Bar (with a powerful coterie of Bengali lawyers) as the breeding ground of agitation against the Government.[41]

In 1907 after the Risley Education Circular had forbidden teachers and students to take part in political agitation, the *Sanjivani* responded by suggesting that as soon as the "political" is marked off bounds, all that is religious and social will become the domain of political unrest:

> You wish to stop this agitation by forbidding meetings? Impossible. Bengalis have ever so many religious festivities, which are the occasions for drawing large crowds, and which may be made use of to preach the boycott of things British. Will these gatherings be forbidden?[42]

The newspaper went on to cite all such socio-religious occasions – christenings (*naamkaran*), weddings, funerals, as well as popular performances (*jatras*, *kathakatha*s, *barwaris*), and fairs. The *baithakkhana*s (salons) of the Bengalis, it noted, draw large numbers of people every evening, "who would use the occasion to talk of the boycott of things British."[43]

All these forms of getting together implied a continuity with traditional practices of the Bengali community, and involved both "private" and "public" spaces. The attributes of *swadeshi* space were, however, not framed in terms of a private/public distinction. Demarcated as "sacred," it was codified in a manner that made it inaccessible to those seen as "outsiders." Such sanctity was understood differently by each constituency within the Indian community. While there were those who preferred not to invoke religion at all, a strong tone of Hinduism was inserted into the movement by others as a mode of reaching the masses. The Hindu religious invocation was considered necessary precisely because of the need to restrict access to "outsiders." The strategic decision to underline the religious tone of the agitation was an invitation to the colonial state to violate the sphere and spaces now marked "sacred." Protest marches intentionally chose routes that either touched "holy" sites such as the river *ghats* and temples, or went past key colonial edifices in the administrative district, and most importantly, the police stations, thus challenging the state's claim to city space.[44] The *Swadeshi* movement had not only changed the size of meetings and the content and language of protest, the movement had produced a different spatial understanding of the city. While Town Hall continued to occupy a prominent place in the nationalist agitation into the 1940s, its significance now had to be deciphered in relation to a larger network of political venues in the city, and not merely those on Esplanade Row.

The desire to have an alternate site that could be called "one's own," that Ramgopal Ghose had yearned for, led to the proposal of building a Federation Hall on Circular Road in the northern part of the city. The foundation stone was laid on October 16, 1905, as the culminating event of the day's protest. When finally built in 1955, Federation Hall would only host the memories of a bygone era of nationalist agitation. After independence from British rule, political space was bifurcated: open air political meetings with the possibility of showing the strength of numbers became the norm, and the everyday power of city politics and management based on bureaucratic governmentality moved to the Calcutta Corporation building on a street that would be renamed after Surendranath Banerjee.[45]

NOTES

1   Basudeb Chatterjee, *The Townhall; A Short History* (Calcutta: Homage Trust, 2004), 12.
2   J. P. Losty, *Calcutta: City of Palaces* (London: The British Library and Arnold Publishers, 1990), 91.
3   Swati Chattopadhyay, *Representing Calcutta: Modernity, Nationalism, and the Colonial Uncanny* (London: Routledge, 2005), 91.
4   Ibid., 120.
5   It was not unusual for buildings in colonial Calcutta to have ceilings 16 feet high.
6   Ibid., 94.
7   Chatterjee, The townhall 17.
8   Losty, *Calcutta*, 91.
9   Ibid., 17–20.
10 Ibid., 92.
11 Ibid., 112.
12 Chatterjee, Townhall 36.
13 Ibid., 26.
14 Ibid., 38.
15 Ibid., 39.
16 Town Hall Record of Events, 2007, Collection of Town Hall Archives.
17 For a more detailed analysis of the architectural vocabulary and the use of the Nat-mandir see Chattopadhyay, *Representing Calcutta*, 150–67.
18 Radhakanta Deb had inherited vast property from his father Nabakrishna Deb. Learned in Persian and Sanskrit, he was a leading member of the Dharmasabha (founded as an institution to defend the values of Hindu caste society), and served on several secular associations: the British Indian Association, Board of the Hindu College, as the secretary of the School Book Society, and Sanskrit College.

19 Partha Chatterjee, *The Nation and its Fragments: Colonial and Postcolonial Histories* (Princeton: Princeton University Press, 1993), 23.
20 Ibid.
21 Criticism of government policy became increasingly strident after the mid-1870s: 1876 marked the beginning of representative municipal politics, as well as the passing of a series of laws that attempted to curb the power of Indian public opinion in the form of the Indian Vernacular Press Act and the Dramatic Performances Act.
22 The Bill was designed to amend the Code of Criminal Procedure on February 2, 1883. Named after Law Member Courtney Ilbert, it would have given Indian judges the authority to try British subjects.
23 While the idea of partitioning Bengal went back to the nineteenth century, it was taken up in earnest under the Viceroyalty of Lord Curzon. On July 19, 1905, the Government of India announced the decision to set up a new province of "Eastern Bengal and Assam" by appropriating districts from the Bengal province, and the decision was put into effect on October 16, 1905. The Bengal partition was annulled in 1911, but at the same time the decision had been made to move the capital of British India from Calcutta to New Delhi in response to the political environment of Calcutta. For a detailed analysis of the Partition and Swadeshi Movement that followed, see Sumit Sarkar, *The Swadeshi Movement in Bengal* (New Delhi: People's Publishing House, 1973).
24 Sarkar, *The Swadeshi Movement,* 11–12.
25 Report on the Agitation Against the Partition of Bengal, C. J. Stevenson-Moore, Inspector-Genl. Of Police, L.P. and F.C. Daly Special Assistant to the Inspr. Genl. of Police, L.P., POL (Pol) F. No. (J)/1905, in *Bengal Partitioned: Selections from Confidential Records* (Calcutta: West Bengal State Archives, 2007), 27.
26 Ibid., 31.
27 Curzon to Brodrick, 17 Feb 1904, Curzon Collection MSS Eur F111/163, vol 8, cited in Sarkar, *The Swadeshi Movement,* 19-20.
28 Sarkar, *The Swadeshi Movement,* 21.
29 The public – *janasadharan* – here was supposed to represent all Bengalis. That this was not the case in practice is demonstrated both by numerous reports of Muslims and lower castes refusing to boycott foreign goods, as well as by the exaggerated enthusiasm with which some reports emphasized the participation of disparate groups in boycott meetings.
30 One of the most important was a meeting in the mansion of Pasupatinath Bose in which the idea of a National Fund for education was proposed.
31 The *Sanjivani*, September 14, RNP of Bengal, week ending September 16, 1905.
32 For example, *Sanjivani,* 31 August, 1905, RNP ending September 19, 1905; *Sri Sri Vishnupriya-o-Anandabazar,* September 28, 1905, RNP week ending September 30, 1905.
33 *Hitavadi*, February 14, RNP week ending February 17, 1906.
34 S. N. Banerjea, *A Nation in Making* (Bombay: Oxford University Press, 1963).
35 "Partition of Bengal: Demonstration in Calcutta, procession and mass meeting," *The Statesman,* August 8, 1905, in *Bengal Partitioned*.
36 Report on the Agitation Against the Partition of Bengal, in *Bengal Partitioned*, 85.
37 By 1907 the British administration had banned all *swadeshi* public meetings, the public singing of "Bande Mataram" and *sankirtan*, all public advertisement of *swadeshi* meetings and plays, had successfully cracked down on picketers, and secured significant advantages in suppressing the Bengali press.
38 The RNP of Bengal week ending February 17, 1906.
39 *Hitavadi,* September 5, 1905, RNP week ending September 9, 1905.
40 Sarkar, *The Swadeshi Movement*, 277.

41 "It would be idle to deny that the partition of Bengal excited very strong feelings in a certain section of the Bengalee community. The section was an important one, as it comprised a very considerable part of the educated classes and, especially in Calcutta, practically the whole of the Bar." From R. W. Carlyle, Offg Chief Secretary to the Government of Bengal to the Secretary to the Government of India, Home Department, Calcutta, January 25, 1906. POL (Pol) F. No 86 (J)/1905.
42 *Sanjivani,* May 16, 1907, RNP week ending May 25, 1907.
43 Ibid.
44 *Sanjivan*i, February 1, 1906, RNP of Bengal, Week ending February 10, 1906.
45 As this chapter was going to press I learned that only recently, in the last year, the Chief Minister of West Bengal has begun the practice of holding cabinet meetings and meetings with ministers and secretaries of the different ministries in the Town Hall, thus bringing the Town Hall once again into the direct political control of the state. I am thankful to Gautam Bhadra for bringing this to my attention.

Chapter 11: Transformation of Public Space in Fascist Italy

Lucy Maulsby

In 1923, the year after Mussolini was appointed prime minister of Italy, the National Fascist Party (Partito Nazionale Fascista) purchased a stately eighteenth-century palazzo on the venerable Corso Venezia in Milan, the commercial and financial center of Italy and birthplace of Fascism, to serve as the center of its operations in the province (Figure 11.1). The late-eighteenth-century Palazzo Serbelloni, one of the city's most notable neoclassical buildings (which had once been the temporary residence of luminaries such as Napoleon Bonaparte and Victor Emanuel II) stood a short distance away; and located just two doors down was the early-twentieth-century Palazzo Castiglioni designed by Giuseppe Sommaruga in the Liberty style, an example of how wealth produced by recent industrial expansion promoted artistic patronage in Milan. On the day of the inauguration, flags and garlands of flowers hung from buildings along Corso Venezia and crowds lined the sidewalks hoping for a glimpse of the procession as it made its way toward the palazzo for the mid-afternoon ceremony. To maintain order, military police (*carabinieri*) and Fascist paramilitary squads (*militi nazionali*) closed surrounding streets. Twenty musketeers stood guard. Mussolini, who had made a special trip from government headquarters in Rome, led the procession and was joined by government officials, local luminaries, Fascist leaders, and relatives (especially the mothers and widows) of those who had sacrificed their lives for Fascism. Two hours later, as the inauguration drew to a close, the highest ranking local Fascist official stood on the balcony, joined by Mussolini's brother and confidant Arnaldo, and celebrated the party's "beautiful and architecturally aristocratic" new provincial headquarters to the crowds still gathered on the street below.[1] The event and its architectural backdrop provided evidence of Fascism's recent political triumphs (Mussolini was invited by King Victor Emmanuel III to be prime minister in October 1922) and provided an early indication of the ways in which the Fascist Party would use architecture to assert its presence and undermine traditional centers of social, religious, and civic life.

Benito Mussolini's Fascist regime imposed its national rule on local communities in Italy during the 1920s, '30s, and early '40s, via a broad strategy

Figure 11.1
The Provincial Fascist Party headquarters, 1923–27 on Corso Venezia, Milan. *La Rivista Illustrata del Popolo d'Italia*, 2, no. 4 (1924), 27. The Wolfsonian-Florida International University, Miami Beach, Florida, The Mitchell Wolfson, Jr. Collection.

that included devoting significant time and expense to the design and construction of public buildings that housed the institutions through which it sought to secure its position and transform Italian life. The state sponsored the construction of buildings – schools, hospitals, town halls, train stations, and sports arenas, among others – intended to shape the character, habits, and attitudes of Italian citizens.[2] The Fascist Party, which was legally subordinate to and independent of the state (unlike the Nazi Party in Germany or the Communist Party in Russia),[3] built headquarters (*case del fascio*) from which it organized and controlled its base and administered a variety of programs in order to make Italians Fascist. These programs included job training, medical assistance, economic relief, and services according to the needs of local communities, that often replicated those run by state agencies, philanthropic organizations, mutual aid societies and other workers groups, as well as the Catholic Church.[4] In this respect *case del fascio* represented the Fascist interpretation of a larger European social and architectural phenomenon that aimed to bring about social and political change. The party's organizational structure paralleled that of the state and, following this logic of doubleness (*doppiezza*), the duties and responsibilities of the local head of party operations (*federale*) corresponded to those of the provincial prefect (*prefetto*) but also encompassed those of the head of the municipal government (*podestà*).[5]

In large population centers such as Milan, there was a provincial headquarters in the city's center in addition to numerous neighborhood outposts, somewhat like the hierarchy of a Catholic cathedral and the parish churches within its jurisdiction.[6] The provincial headquarters was at first called a *casa del fascio* but later was more often referred to as a *sede federale* or *palazzo del littorio*; it housed the offices of the highest-ranking local officials and a variety of ceremonial spaces, supervised the activities of neighborhood groups, organized parades, celebrations to mark Fascist anniversaries, exhibitions sporting events, and other collective events, and served as a direct link to the central administration in Rome. Intended to be more than just a bureaucratic center, *case del fascio* were likened to churches, town halls and medieval castles, all recognizable symbols of authority.[7] The formal character, urban position, and program designated for these buildings reinforced associations with these building types. Party headquarters played a central role, as the historian Emilio Gentile has shown, in advancing Fascism as a lay religion by providing a setting for the party's most important rituals and (after about 1927) each held a memorial chapel or *sacrario* dedicated to so-called Fascist martyrs. In the second decade of Fascist rule, the formal language and urban location of newly designed buildings, as Diane Ghirardo argues in her analysis of Giuseppe Terragni's celebrated *casa del fascio* in Como (1932–36), evoked Northern Italian town halls in an effort to reinforce the civic authority of the Fascist Party through legible associations with Italy's noble past.[8] An analysis and discussion of the Fascist Party's provincial headquarters in Milan from 1923 to 1943 (an arc of time that begins with the establishment of the Fascist Party's headquarters on Corso Venezia and concludes with the official dissolution of the Fascist Party) clarifies the changing role of these buildings with the aim of better understanding how the Fascist Party drew upon and manipulated established symbols of power and prestige to find a symbolic language for its own institutions (Figure 11.2).

The Fascist Party made its first significant claim on the urban fabric of Milan when it purchased the stately eighteenth-century palazzo on Corso Venezia in 1923. The new provincial headquarters provided visual evidence of Mussolini's recent political accomplishments; he now led the national government as prime minister, and his supporters controlled Palazzo Marino (Galeazzo Alessi, 1557–63), which had served as Milan's town hall since the unification of Italy in 1861. By virtue of its location, the headquarters fostered associations with the city's late-eighteenth- and late-nineteenth-century histories, periods of cultural and commercial growth in which Milan benefited from the rise of a civic-minded bourgeoisie. The party capitalized on its connections to business and industrial leaders to finance the new headquarters, a strategy that would become routine in the following decades. Contemporary accounts called attention to the building's neoclassical character and its formal rooms on the second floor *(piano nobile)*, which held Corinthian columns, glass chandeliers, patterned wallpaper, and furniture in "antique Venetian" style (Figure 11.3).[9] The party also planned extensive renovations in order to create a space for concerts and lectures, a restaurant with a veranda, a fencing hall, a library, and offices for the Fascist Institute of High Fascist Culture (Istituto di Alta Cultura Fascista).[10] The building and its interior appointments compared favorably to the social clubs frequented by local elites, groups to which the party's base aspired and whose political and financial support Mussolini's brother actively cultivated as Fascism sought to expand its influence by penetrating local civic, economic, and cultural institutions.[11]

Mussolini's growing political power (he established a dictatorship in 1925) helped to solidify the Fascist Party's authority. The following year the Fascist dictator abolished opposing political organizations and did away with local elections.[12] The city's first Fascist-appointed *podestà* – a position that replaced that of the

City Halls and Civic Materialism ■

Figure 11.2
Map of Milan from 1932 showing the approximate location of the Fascist Party's provincial headquarters, 1923–43. a) Corso Venezia, b) Piazza Belgioioso, c) Piazza San Sepolcro, d) Piazza Diaz. Map from Ferdinando Reggiori, *Milano, 1800–1943* (Milan: Edizioni del Milano, 1947), 16. Graphics by author.

democratically elected mayor[13] – reorganized municipal offices, turned many public functions over to private interests, and endorsed projects that appealed to middle-class interests.[14] That same year the newly appointed *federale*, who was likely being directed by Mussolini's influential brother, began to gather resources to construct the Fascist Party's first provincial headquarters in the city. As with the earlier headquarters on Corso Venezia, the location of the new building communicated the party's effort to position itself within the symbolic structure of the city. In a scheme that suggests collaboration between municipal and party leaders, the party purchased property in an area of the city slated for significant redevelopment. The site stood along the quiet residential Via Nirone (later renamed Via Fascio) in a district to the west of the city's symbolic and commercial center.[15] The city planned to construct a new Palace of Justice opposite the new headqarters

Transformation of Public Space in Fascist Italy ■

Figure 11.3
Office of the Secretary of the Provincial Federation, Corso Venezia. From *La Rivista Illustrata del Popolo d'Italia*, 2, no. 4 (1924), 31. The Wolfsonian-Florida International University, Miami Beach, Florida, The Mitchell Wolfson, Jr. Collection.

(on what had been an army barracks) and introduce two new roads that, had they been built, would have substantially altered the character of the narrow street. The plan for the proposed new roads included a sizable open space in front of the headquarters and placed the *casa del fascio* adjacent to a projected major east-west artery linking two significant areas of central Milan: Piazza Cordusio and Piazza San Ambrogio Laid out in the late nineteenth century, Piazza Cordusio was only a short distance from the Duomo and was the location of several of Milan's leading financial institutions, including the stock exchange. The large, L-shaped Piazza San Ambrogio had as its principal monument the plain brick Basilica of San Ambrogio. Founded in the late fourth century, the complex was one of the most important sites of early Christian Milan. Behind the basilica, the octagonal marble Monument to the Fallen (Monumento ai Caduti, 1924–28), designed by Milanese architect Giovanni Muzio and others, was under construction.[16] Party leaders anticipated that the provincial headquarters would not only claim a prominent position in this redesigned urban fabric but also that it would be viewed within a visual sequence that presented Fascist institutions within the context of established symbols of cultural, religious, and civic authority.

The party hired the Milanese architect and engineer Paolo Mezzanotte (1878–1969), whose social connections to the *podestà* and Mussolini's brother helped him to gain the commission, to design the building. Mezzanotte's *casa del fascio* showed how an updated interpretation of the traditional neoclassical Milanese palazzo might be reworked to serve the needs of the Fascist Party (Figure 11.4). The overall proportions, as well as details such as engaged composite pilasters, a central balcony, and a crowning pediment, reinforced connections with

City Halls and Civic Materialism ■

local adaptations of this architectural type, themselves based on Renaissance models. At the same time, Mezzanotte's project showed the party's desire to create a building that would be distinct from earlier architectural examples. The new building on Via Nirone had a bold and robust character, a consequence of Mezzanotte's handling of the details and materials – brick and travertine. Indeed, Mussolini had criticized an earlier version of the project for not being sufficiently "simple and severe."[17]

Mezzanotte's final version accorded with Mussolini's desire to present the party as a forceful and vigorous organization and to make this headquarters a local manifestation of his command. Design decisions also responded to the practical needs of the party. The long central balcony provided a platform from which party officials could address crowds gathered in the street below during public rallies. Fasces, placed on each of the obelisks set between the lateral pairs of composite pilasters on the second story, made explicit the political function of the building;

Figure 11.4
Casa del Fascio, Paolo Mezzanotte, Via Nirone, Milan, 1926–27.
Architettura e Arti Decorative 2, no. 7 (1928): 321.

and the bundles of shields and arrows beneath the fasces served as a reminder that the headquarters also served as a base for the organization's paramilitary action squads (*squadre d'azione*).[18] The adoption of an architectural vocabulary that borrowed elements from local neoclassical examples reinforced officials' efforts to make the party appear legitimate during a period of rapid political change; it also emphasized the bourgeois character of the party's base and buttressed party leader's efforts to attract the local industrial, business, and social elite.[19] Paired with symbols of the new political order, these architectural associations presented Fascism as both part of a continuous Milanese tradition and as a force of change.[20]

In designing the interior plan, Mezzanotte again turned to the palazzo as a model, modifying this typical locus of secular authority to serve the particular needs of the Fascist Party. He organized the first two stories around a double-height atrium (Figure 11.5).[21] The spatial arrangement recalled the open courtyards of *palazzi* throughout Milan and recent commercial adaptations of this architectural type.[22] While the opulent atriums of banking halls and department stores glorified the individual as a consumer in a capitalist economy, Mezzanotte's

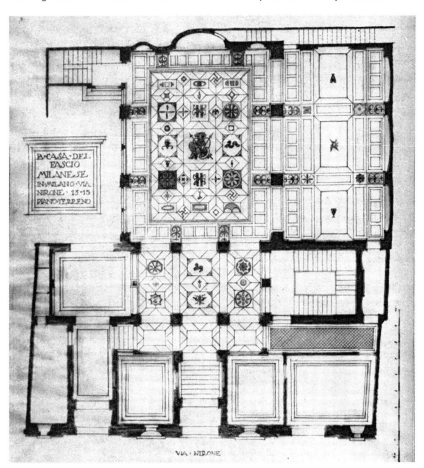

Figure 11.5
Plan of ground floor,
Casa del Fascio,
Mezzanotte.
Architettura e Arti Decorative 2, no. 7 (1928): 320.

atrium drew attention to the collective nature of Fascist participation. The narrow raised platform and shallow niche at one end of the hall served as a visual reminder of the hierarchy of party life and recalled the historic use of the inner courts of Italian *palazzi* as a space of assembly. As an essential feature of party buildings, large halls or auditoria were used for lectures, films, ceremonies, rallies, and other collective events. On the ground floor, Mezzanotte placed the membership office (conveniently located near the main entrance) and offices for the Association of Mothers and Widows of Fallen Fascists (Associazione Madri e Vedove dei Caduti Fascisti) and the Organization of Fascist Women (Fascio Feminile). To the right of the entrance hall, the stairway to the second floor used to lead to the Room of Honor (Salone d'Onore) and other rooms, including the office of the local party secretary, for more restricted audiences. Upper floors contained additional offices for the Milan Federation and space for various other affiliated organizations, including the Federation's newspaper *Il Popolo di Lombardia* and the Institute of Culture (Istituto di Cultura).[23] The emphasis on offices and meeting rooms (and the absence of informal gathering spaces such as a restaurant, library, or game room) clarified the provincial headquarter's elite status as the authority responsible for implementing Fascist policy at the local level.

The central atrium not only provided an enclosed area for large meetings and gatherings but also suggested how architecture could be used to communicate the symbolic and practical needs of the party. In order to enlarge the hall, initially conceived as a smaller single-height space, Mezzanotte added galleries along its perimeter, apparently following a suggestion made by Mussolini.[24] He further expanded the flexibility of the atrium by using glass to physically separate but visually connect distinct spaces within the palazzo. On the ground floor, glass doors separated the atrium from the vestibule and could be opened to accommodate larger numbers of people during popular events. On the second floor, similar glass doors divided the upper-gallery level from the Room of Honor, the most important meeting room within the building (Figure 11.6). The glass doors leading from the Room of Honor to the balcony on the front façade encouraged a similarly fluid relationship between the interior and exterior of the building and facilitated the pageantry of party gatherings. The extensive use of glass, a material associated with modern architecture, gave the interior of the building a contemporary feel and linked its ceremonial spaces. It also suggested that Fascist politics – in contrast to the often corrupt and opaque bureaucracies of the preceding liberal government – were inclusive and transparent. Indeed, the strategy anticipated the fluid visual and spatial character of Terragni's Casa del Fascio in Como and Mussolini's claim that "Fascism is a glass house into which all can look."[25]

The Room of Honor, which held sturdy wooden furniture with neoclassical details and potted plants, provided access not only to the most public areas of palazzo – the atrium and the balcony – but also a room holding a large marble plaque honoring soldiers who died in World War I and Mussolini's supporters killed during the rise of Fascism.[26] Since the early 1920s *case del fascio* had served as the

Figure 11.6
Room of Honor (Salone d'Onore), Casa del Fascio, Mezzanotte. The room opens onto the gallery surrounding the atrium. The plaque commemorating the first Fascist martyrs (installed in 1927) is visible just beyond the glass doors at the end of room. *Architettura e Arti Decorative* 2, no. 7 (1928): 323.

setting for services and ritual events in honor of deceased party members. Simultaneously evoking the symbolic role of the church and state, the first so-called Fascist martyr, Armando Morgani, lay in state in the provincial headquarters before his funeral in 1920 and branch offices typically incorporated memorial elements, such as plaques, photographs, and portrait busts, in remembrance of those who died fighting for the party or nation.[27] In 1926 the party ratified a new statute that defined Fascism as "fundamentally a faith," a declaration that triggered the proliferation of ceremonies and altars dedicated to Fascist heroes throughout Italy.[28] However, the impetus for the creation of this memorial space came directly from Arnaldo Mussolini, who specifically requested its addition after touring the building two weeks before its inauguration.[29] Following Arnaldo's instructions, Mezzanotte placed a marble slab – illuminated by a candelabrum – that listed the names of each of the first thirteen Fascist martyrs in the room adjacent to the Room of Honor.[30] This appears to be the first instance in a *casa del fascio* of a memorial chapel (or *sacrario*), a physical reminder of the party's effort to establish a civic religion and an architectural element that became a defining feature of this building type by the early 1930s.

Three years after officials inaugurated the Casa del Fascio on Via Nirone, the Fascist Party relocated the regional headquarters to the neoclassical Napoleonic-era Palazzo Besana (Giovanni Battista Piuri, 1819) in Piazza Belgioioso (Figure 11.7). The press once again cited the inadequate size of the current headquarters as the reason for the move.[31] However, the Via Nirone site had failed to achieve the kind of urban prominence anticipated by party leaders when they embarked on the project. A number of factors, including fiscal mismanagement in the mayor's office, forced the city to set aside plans for the new network of roads and to build a new Palace of Justice in that district. In addition, scandals involving the highest-ranking local party and city officials tainted the project as a reminder of a corrupt administration. In December 1928 Mussolini had dismissed the head of the Milan Federation for "profiteering" and dispatched the powerful National Vice-Secretary of the Fascist Party Achille Starace (who would be named Secretary in 1931) to "normalize" party operations, a process that resulted in the removal of all but a few mid- and lower-level officials from office in Milan.[32] The imperial aspect of the Palazzo Besana's massive colonnade communicated Fascism's resilience in the face of significant upheaval. To claim the building the Federation emblazoned its façade with a bronze *fascio* surrounded by a laurel wreath and "P.N.F. Federazione Provinciale Milano," a gesture that mirrored the Italian government's strategy of renovating and converting palaces for government functions. The architectural setting, tied to the party through symbol and text, presented an image of triumph as the party attempted to repair its image in the Lombard capital.

The new location also reinforced the Federation's connections to Fascism's origins and suggests that it sought a more aggressive role in directing local affairs. The building occupied the long side of Piazza Belgioioso; adjacent to the Casa di Manzoni, the residence of the late-nineteenth-century Italian author Alessandro Manzoni, and opposite Giuseppe Piermartini's Palazzo Belgioioso (1772), a celebrated example of Milanese neoclassicism. Maintaining the strategy employed in the selection of the Via Nirone site, the party positioned itself in proximity to reminders of Milan's venerable past. However, the Piazza Belgioioso, in contrast to

Figure 11.7
Provincial Fascist Party headquarters, 1931–40. Palazzo Besana, Piazza Belgioioso, Milan, early nineteenth-century. From Osvaldo Lissone and Siro della, *La Milano voluta dal Duce e la vecchia Milano* (Milan: Officine Grafiche 'Esperia,'1935).

those earlier sites selected by the party, carried Fascist associations. After the party's electoral defeat in 1919, Mussolini had addressed his supporters in the piazza, and it served as a meeting point for Fascist groups participating in political demonstrations throughout the following decade.[33] The piazza also positioned the party in relation to existing centers of power. On one end, the piazza opened on to Corso Littorio (1928–30, now Corso Matteoti), an arcaded street that was one of the first important urban projects directed by the Fascist government. It connected the recently expanded Piazza San Babila, a key feature of the urban plan for Milan being developed in the same years, with the new Piazza Crespi (opened in 1926, now Piazza Meda), where several local banks as well as luxury office and residential buildings were located. Even more important, the plaza was steps away from the Piazza della Scala, onto which faced the sixteenth-century Palazzo Marino, the seat of the municipal government. Situated between two poles of local authority – the city government and the business and commercial interests that drove Milan's economy – the Palazzo Besana communicated Fascism's reliance on local systems as a practical route to power and its progressive effort to undermine centers of civic authority and influence.

The Milan Federation restructured the building's interior to meet the needs of the organization. The entrance atrium – the walls of which were faced with donated marble – led to several meeting rooms, an elaborate memorial chapel (Cappella dei Caduti), and a lecture hall capable of accommodating a thousand people. Also included on the ground floor were offices for serving the general public (such as membership and public assistance) and for managing the operations of the Federation (including the technical and bursar's offices). The second story, reached by a "monumental staircase," held the offices and reception rooms for the highest-ranking local officials.[34] Local reports emphasized the grandeur of the interior spaces and appointments and gave particular attention to the memorial chapel. The chapel, described as "the mystical temple where the spirit of the unforgettable thirteen [first Fascist martyrs] will be exalted in silent meditation," had as its focal point the marble plaque that had been created for the old Via Nirone headquarters.[35] Above the plaque hung a bronze crucifix and beneath it a marble base, in front of which stood a censer, two roman lamps, and a kneeling stool. Black marble accented by green stripes ornamented the floors, heavy red-and-gold cloth covered the walls and a luminous gold ceiling completed the ensemble.[36] The incorporation of the marble plaque from the earlier headquarters created a degree of continuity between the buildings, but its location on the ground floor, where it was accessible to all who entered, and the material richness and ecclesiastical character of its setting, suggested a fundamentally new approach to memorial spaces within party buildings. Mussolini paused here in silent prayer during the inauguration of the building, a demonstration of its particular importance.[37]

The appointment of Starace as national party secretary (a post he occupied until 1939) had far-reaching consequences for the Fascist Party. Starace campaigned aggressively to expand Fascism's influence, particularly among Italian youth in the wake of Fascism's confrontation with Catholic Action youth groups (in 1931), and to make the party an organization of the masses.[38] In 1930 the roster of party members in Milan held 13,217 names; in 1933 the number grew to 39,004; and by 1936 membership had reached 56,117.[39] The increase in membership did not necessarily correspond to a surge of popular support for the party, but was due to the fact that Starace reopened membership subscriptions in 1932 and made party affiliation a requirement for all public-service officials, including teachers, after 1934. Membership also provided access to numerous benefits and was thus a practical necessity for many Italians.

In order to better carry out the party's mission, Starace encouraged the construction and refurbishment of *case del fascio*. This initiative resulted in the construction of a new provincial party headquarters in Milan. For the new headquarters, the Federation purchased the Palazzo Castani, a modest Renaissance building on Piazza San Sepolcro owned by the Provincial Union of Shopkeepers (Unione Provinciale dei Commercianti), and the adjacent residential properties. The Federation hoped to broker a deal in which it would exchange the Palazzo Besana, the current home of its headquarters, for the Palazzo Castani, and party leaders anticipated that the municipal government would help underwrite the purchase of the adjoining buildings.[40] The city proved reluctant. It was only after continued pressure from party officials, including Starace, that the *podestà* approved the expropriation of the property abutting Palazzo Castani.[41] The municipal government justified the expropriation by using some of the land to widen adjacent roads in order to ease movement through this area, which preserved a medieval street pattern. However, the city ceded the majority of the property to the Federation, an example of the tensions between local party and municipal officials as they each sought to advance their own, sometimes conflicting, agendas.

The Milan Federation's acquisition of Palazzo Castani and adjacent properties for the Sede Federale, the new provincial party headquarters, represented not only an opportunity to reclaim one of the principal sites associated with Mussolini's rise to power but also repositioned the headquarters within the city as it was being transformed by the new master plan, a process facilitated by the appointment of a new *podestà* who had personal ties to Mussolini and Starace (Figure 11.8).[42] One of the rooms in the Palazzo Castani, where Mussolini had gathered his base of support and founded the Fascist movement in 1919, was known among Fascists as the Room of the Sansepolcristi (Sala dei Sansepolcristi). This room was regularly evoked in recollections of Fascism's early years in Milan; a simple marble plaque surrounded by electric lights adjacent to the entrance recorded the building's pivotal role in the party's history, and the party occasionally used Piazza San Sepolcro for commemorative rallies. On the opposite side of the square is the venerable Ambrosian Library (Biblioteca Ambrosiana) and the medieval brick church of San Sepolcro. The square also marks the location of the city's ancient Roman forum. In the first phase of the project, the Federation renovated Palazzo Castani and joined the Renaissance building to new construction on three of its four sides.

In a second phase of construction, which was never completed, the party planned to build an independent but related structure behind the Palazzo Castani block. This second building was to be separated from the first by Via Sacrario (today Via Ardeatine) and to face an expansive new cross street (*trasversale*) that replaced the narrow and irregular Via San Maurilio and connected Largo Cairoli and Piazza Missori. The project architect, Piero Portaluppi, took advantage of the historical associations of Piazza San Sepolcero and as well as the modern implications of the broad new Via San Maurilio with a building designed to address both urban conditions.

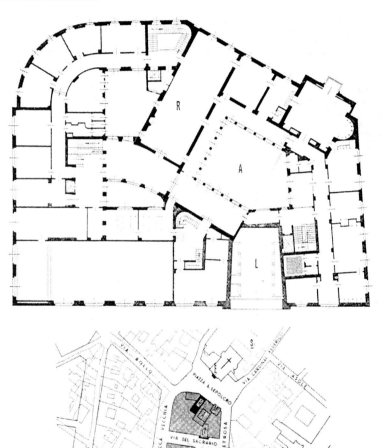

Figure 11.8
Ground floor and site plan for the Sede Federale, 1940. The plan is labeled to show: P the open courtyard, E the theater, L the *sacrario*, R the Room of the San Sepolcristi (Sala San Sepolcristi), and M the tower. From a.c.r. [Antonio Cassi Ramelli], "Una Villa a Merate, il Palazzo dei Fasci e una casa di abitazione a Milano," *Rassegna di Architettura* no. 10 (1940): 296.

Portaluppi made a six-story tower with a balcony the defining feature of the curved front along Piazza San Sepolcro (Figure 11.9).[43] A politically savvy designer who had already completed several buildings for the party, he positioned the tower such that it was framed by the narrow and winding Via Valpetrosa; the primary route for visitors approaching from the city center.[44] The corner placement of this vertical accent ensured the building's visual prominence and reinforced associations with other contemporary examples of this building type that likewise referenced Northern Italian town halls (particularly those constructed from the late thirteenth to fifteenth century). These medieval buildings typically had an unornamented tower (commonly placed on a corner and unbroken by windows), a balcony (or *arengario* from which speeches or proclamations were delivered), and spaces for assembly (often in the form of a large hall or interior courtyard) to set them apart from other important civic structures.[45] The strategic position and the vertical openings at the top of the Sede Federale's tower also implied that it might be used as a tool of surveillance and control, a theme that would become increasingly dominant as Italy advanced toward war in the late 1930s. Within the context of Piazza San Sepolcro, the tower confronted the modest bell towers of the facing brick Church of San Sepolcro, recalling the juxtaposition of sacred and secular command found in medieval towns throughout Italy and therefore calling attention to the party's civic authority.

Via Sacrario, the street that separated the Palazzo Castani block and the block facing the new artery, also joined the buildings by visually uniting the ritual functions housed in each. The Palazzo Castani block held the tower as well as office space, two large meeting halls (the Salone Sansepolcristi and another larger room capable of accommodating 1,200 people), and a mortuary chapel or

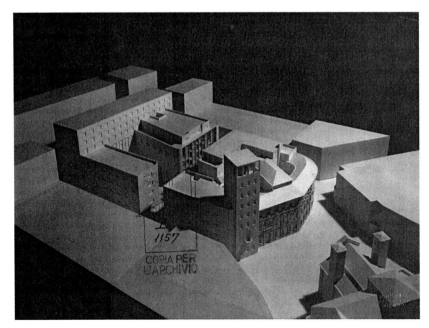

Figure 11.9
Portaluppi, model of
Sede Federale, 1939–40.
Fondazione Piero
Portaluppi, Milan.

sacrario, located at the rear of the block which faced the second phase of the project – the block extending toward via San Maurilio. Portaluppi anticipated placing a theatre – the major feature of this building – designed to hold up to 5,000 people diagonally opposite the chapel along the dividing street.[46] Blurring the boundaries between architecture and urbanism, Portaluppi intended to unite the two independent structures through exterior spatial sequences and visual associations.[47] A tripartite opening in the main façade of the Via San Maurilio block permitted passage from the proposed thoroughfare to an internal courtyard that tapered to direct the viewer's attention to the glass-fronted memorial chapel, the culmination of this calibrated sequence.[48] Portaluppi used a glass wall for the rear of the theatre to expose a system of stairs that would have served members of the party hurrying to and from meetings and rallies. The use of glass to suggest and reveal movement within buildings repeated an established motif in modernist architecture. However, Portaluppi directed this modernist interest in circulation, transparency, and efficiency to the Fascist commitment to collective service. Specifically, the theater and the chapel reinforced the shared struggle of the living and dead members of the Fascist Party by their visual connection in location and materials. Thus the narrow Via Sacrario physically separated but symbolically joined the two blocks of the party headquarters and drew the ritual performance of the party into the public space of the city. This act suggested that the street and piazza, traditional venues for diverse social interaction and political participation, could be reconfigured to serve the specific ritual functions of Fascism. At the same time, the absence of a clear architectural and urban hierarchy suggests a degree of resistance to the totalitarian strictures of Fascism.

Two years after the Milan Federation moved its offices to Piazza San Sepolcro, local officials began to take steps to make a new regional headquarters part of the proposed redevelopment of Piazza del Duomo, the monumental and ceremonial heart of the city.[49] This urban initiative included the refurbishment of the southern and western edges of the piazza and the development of Piazza Diaz. Located to the south of Piazza del Duomo and adjacent to the *manica lunga* (long sleeve) of the Palazzo Reale, the seat of the municipal government in the Middle Ages and the locus of political life in Milan until the unification of Italy, this square had attracted controversy since the municipal planning office proposed its creation in the late 1920s.[50] Portaluppi's Palazzo dell'Istituto Nazionale delle Assicurazione (1932–37) filled out one side of the large opening but the interface between the new square and Piazza del Duomo remained unresolved. Plans approved in 1939 showed that Piazza Diaz would open directly on to the Piazza del Duomo and face the soaring glass vaults of the Galleria Vittorio Emanuele II (Giuseppe Mengoni, 1862–77) on the opposite side of the piazza. To mediate between the squares Giovanni Muzio proposed two pavilions (1939–56) composed of superimposed arches (Figure 11.10). The eastern pavilion functioned as a speaking rostrum or *arengario* for Mussolini and as a new center of political operations and thus as secular counterpoint to the Duomo; today it is the city tourist office and exhibition space (Palazzo del Tourismo).

Archival records show that Portaluppi prepared a study for a new provincial party headquarters (Palazzo del Fascio) in Piazza Diaz; unfortunately no visual evidence of the project remains.[51] The new structure would likely have been contiguous with Muzio's *arengario* and thus adjacent to the Palazzo Reale. The party's interest in constructing a new headquarters in the symbolic center of Milan, the birthplace of Fascism, suggests that party's officials sought to reassert the organization's importance at a time when its influence was in decline; a consequence of Mussolini's appointment of a series of ineffective or incapable party secretaries following the dismissal of Starace in 1939.[52] The project might also be seen in light of some Fascists' interest in a new "totalitarian and extremist initiative," a strain within Fascism that had deep roots and, with its proposals for a fundamental renegotiation of the relationship between party and state, foreshadowed the Republic of Salo (Italian Social Republic, 1943–45).[53]

As these examples demonstrate, the strategies used by the Fascist Party to insinuate itself into the urban fabric and to challenge established centers of authority changed over time. In the early 1920s, the period in which Mussolini sought to obtain power through legitimate channels and cultivate the support of the local elite, the Fascist Party made architectural and urban choices that helped to mitigate the unsettling aspects of the significant social, cultural, and political upheavals brought about by Fascism. The elite associations of the regional headquarters on Corso Venezia complemented Mussolini's efforts to downplay the radical origins of the Fascist Party and penetrate the local establishment as he pursued power through an established political structure. Indicative of Fascism's rapid ascent, only a few years later the Fascist Party had the confidence and connections to make its new headquarters part of the proposed redevelopment of the area around San Ambrogio. The headquarters on Via Nirone, like the Fascist Party's later headquarters on Piazza Belgioioso, strategically positioned the party alongside the political and economic institutions whose power and influence it hoped to command as it reached deeper into the structure of Italian life. The Piazza

Figure 11.10
Model of proposed reorganization of Piazza del Duomo showing Giovanni Muzio's Arengario exhibited at the VII Triennale, Milan, 1940. From *Emporium* 5 (May 1940): 212.

Belgioioso headquarters also points to a new interest in celebrating Fascism's beginnings, a narrative that would be reinforced through the preservation of places associated with Fascism's origins and given a mythic dimension at the Exhibition of the Fascist Revolution (Mostra della Rivoluzione Fascista, 1932) in Rome.

In the second half of the *ventennio nero*, the Fascist Party – propelled by changes in party leadership at the national level and a need to respond to the changing political, economic, and cultural complexion of the nation – participated in a more aggressive reordering of the urban fabric. Portaluppi's provincial party headquarters in Piazza San Sepolcro projected the significant redevelopment of a large swath of central Milan and made public spaces – traditional venues for social engagement, commercial enterprise, political discourse, and political activism – a permanent stage for the enactment of Fascist rituals. At the same time, it refused the kind of monumental classically derived architectural and urban formulas typically associated with totalitarian regimes and acknowledged the more circumstantial order of the traditional city. Indicating that the party again sought to adjust its image, the Piazza Diaz project made the headquarters part of a geometrically regular and aesthetically coordinated urban square that was to replace the Piazza del Duomo as the symbolic and ceremonial center of Milan.[54]

NOTES

Some of the material included in this essay appears in my book *Fascism, Architecture and the Claiming of Modern Milan, 1922–1943* (Toronto: University of Toronto Press, forthcoming). I would like to thank the editors for comments on earlier drafts of this essay and for the opportunity to first work through some of this material at the Society of Architectural Historians Annual Conference (2006).

1 "Bella e anche architettonicamente aristocratica." "La nuova Casa del Fascio Milanese," *Il Popolo d'Italia*, October 30, 1923.
2 See Augusto Rossari, "Ideologia e tipizzazione," in Cesare Stevan, Sergio Boidi, Cecilia Colombo, Augusto Rossari, and Angelo Torricelli, *Architetture sociali nel Milanese, 1860–1990* (Milan: Touring Club Italiano, 1994), 57–105.
3 Emilio Gentile, *La via Italiana al totalitariismo: Il partito e lo Stato nel regime fascista* (Rome: La Nuova Italia Scientifica, 1995), 137.
4 Franco Biscossa, "Dalla casa del popolo alla casa del fascio," in Marco De Michelis, ed., *Case del popolo un architettura monumntale del moderno* (Venice: Marsilio, 1986), 177–94.
5 Gentile, *La via Italiana al totalitariasmo,* 172–75; Biscossa, "Dalla casa del popolo alla casa del fascio," 197.
6 For a survey of *case del fascio* see Flavio Mangione, *Le case del fascio in Italia e nelle terre d'Oltremare* (Rome: Ministero per i beni e le attività culturali direzione generale per gli archivi, 2003); Paolo Portoghesi Flavio Mangione and Andrea Soffitta, eds., *L'architettura delle case del fascio: Catalogo della mostra, Le case del fascio in Italia e nelle terre d'Oltremare* (Florence: Alinea, 2006). For a more comprehensive history of these

buildings in Milan see my *Fascism Architecture and the Claiming of Modern Milan, 1922–1943* (Toronto: University of Toronto Press, forthcoming).
7 Carlo Savoia, "La Casa del Fascio," *L'Assalto*, May 26, 1932.
8 See Diane Ghirardo, "Architecture and the State: Fascist Italy and New Deal America" (PhD diss., Stanford University, 1982), 47–91, as well as later articles including "Terragni, conventions, and the critics," in William J. Lillyman, Marilyn F. Moriarty, and David J. Neuman, eds., *Critical Architecture and Contemporary Culture* (New York: Oxford University Press, 1994), 93–6.
9 "La nuova Casa del Fascismo Milanese," *Il Popolo d'Italia*, October 25, 1923. See also Piero Parini, "La Casa del Fascio a Milano," *La Rivista Illustrata del Popolo d'Italia* 2, no. 4 (1924): 27–31.
10 "La nuova Casa del Fascismo Milanese," *Il Popolo d'Italia*, September 5, 1923.
11 Ivano Granata, "Il Partito Nazionale Fascista a Milano tra 'dissidentismo' e 'normalizzazione' (1923–33)," in Maria Luisa Betri, Alberto De Barnardi, Ivano Granata, and Nanda Torcellan, eds., *Il fascismo in Lombardia: Politica, economia e società* (Milan: Franco Angeli, 1989), 14–23.
12 Ivano Granata, "PNF: Organizzazione del consenso e società Milanese negli anni trenta," in *Storia di Milano*, vol. 18, pt. 1 (Rome: Istituto della Enciclopedia Italiana, 1995-96), 631–5.
13 The title *podestà* was also the name given to the head of local governments in Italian medieval city-states. For the reorganization of municipal and provincial governments under Fascism see Ettore Rotelli, "Le trasformazioni dell'ordinamento comunale e provinciale durante il regime fascista," *Storia Contemporanea* 1 (March, 1973), 57–121.
14 Maurizio Boriani, "La costruzione della Milano moderna," in Maurizio Boriani, Remo Dorigati, Valeria Erba, Marina Molon, Corinna Morandi, eds., *La costruzione della Milano moderna* (Milan: Clup, 1982), 89.
15 The city renamed the street when the party relocated the regional headquarters to the Palazzo Besana in 1930. "La sede del Fascio trasferita in Piazza Belgioioso," *Corriere della Sera*, March 29, 1930. The building later housed offices for the city's welfare organization (Ente Comunale d'Assistenza). Ferdinando Reggiori, *Milano, 1800–1943* (Milan: Edizioni del Milano, 1947), 396. In the immediate post-war period the building served as the Milan headquarters for the Christian Democrat Party (Democrazia Cristiana, DC), a party of the center-right. The building has recently been restored and is part of the nearby Catholic University (Università Cattolica).
16 Throughout the interwar period San Ambrogio played an important role as the representative symbol of Milan. The city bulletin *Milano* featured San Ambrogio on its cover in 1934 and made San Ambrogio and the Monument to the Fallen the subject of its cover in 1939. Osvaldo Lissone and Siro della Morte made both a feature of the cover for their book *La Milano volutoa dal Duce e la vecchia Milano* (1935). For the Monument to the Fallen see Fluvio Irace, *Giovanni Muzio 1893–1982* (Milan: Electa, 1994), 91–102.
17 "Semplice e severo." "La nuova Casa del Fascio in via Nirone," *Il Popolo d'Italia*, June 18, 1926.
18 These replaced the four pairs of freestanding obelisks and fasces placed along the edge of the central balcony in an early design criticized by the Building Commission (Commissione Edilizia). Sindaco to Sig. Consigliere Delegato della Società Immobiliare Casa del Fascio, March 22, 1926, Archivio Storico Civico Milano, Ornato Fabriche, serie II, c. 1201.
19 Granata, "PNF: Organizzazione del consenso e società Milanese negli anni trenta," 631–5.
20 As evidence of the growing interest in architectural models from Roman antiquity, some critics claimed that Mezzanotte had been inspired by Roman models, including recent

excavations at Ostia. "La nuova Casa del Fascio Milanese," *Il Popolo d'Italia*, October 9, 1927. "La nuova Casa del Fascio," *Il Popolo d'Italia*, June 18, 1926.

21 Richard Etlin provides the best post-war account of this project and notes the similarities between Mezzanotte's building and Giuseppe Terragni's Casa del Fascio, Como (1933–36). Richard Etlin, *Modernism in Italian Architecture, 1890–1940* (Cambridge, MA: MIT Press), 463–6.

22 Etlin, *Modernism in Italian Architecture,* 462.

23 Mezzanotte also provided offices for the Gruppo degli Studenti Universitaria Fascisti, Gruppo dei Postelegrafico, Gruppo dei Ferrovieri Fascisti, Commando degli Avanguardisti, Balilla, Direzione dell'Ente Provinciale Sportivo. "La nuova Casa del Fascio," *Il Popolo d'Italia*, October 9, 1927.

24 Il battistrada [Raffaello Giolli], "La Casa dei Fasci Milanesi," *Problemi d'Arte Attuale* 1, no. 3 (November 1927): 29. "La nuova Casa del Fascio," *Il Popolo d'Italia*, October 9, 1927.

25 "Il Fascismo è una casa di vetro in cui tutti possono guardare." From Mussolini's address to party leaders in Milan in July 1929, reproduced in Giuseppe Terragni, "La Costruzione della Casa del Fascio di Como," *Quadrante* 35–36 (October 1936; repr., Como: Tipografia Editrice Cesare Nani, 1994): 6.

26 "La visita di Arnaldo Mussolini alla nuova Casa del Fascio," *Il Popolo d'Italia*, October 11, 1927.

27 "La nuova Casa del Fascio," *Il Popolo d'Italia*, October 9, 1927. Aldo Pasetti, "Gloria delle camicie nere, gli squadristi del Fascismo Milanese caduti per la rivoluzione," *Milano*, March 1939, 112.

28 "Il Fascismo … è sopratutto un fede." "Statuto del PNF" (1926), reproduced in Mario Missori, *Gerarchie e statuti del PNF: Gran consiglio, direttorio nazionale, federazione provincial* (Rome: Bonacci, 1986), 355.

29 "La visita di Arnaldo Mussolini alla nuova Casa del Fascio," *Il Popolo d'Italia*, October 11, 1927.

30 "In questa casa aperta alle glorie e alle fortune del Fascismo Milanese i camerati ricordano con orgoglio riconoscente e memore i gloriosi caduti Fascisti che nel nome d' Italia suggellarono nel sangue la grandezza e la nobilita della fede comune." The thirteen were: Aldo Sette, Franco Baldini, Ugo Pepe, Eliseo Bernini, Edoardo Crespi, Emilio Tonoli, Cesare Melloni, Paolo Grassigli, Enzo Meriggi, Vittorio Agnusdei, Loris Socrate, Blce Avignone, and Giuseppe Ugolini. "I segni tangibili della Vittoria," *Il Popolo d'Italia*, October 30, 1927.

31 "La Sede del Fascio trasferita in Piazza Belgioioso," *Corriere della Sera*, March 29, 1930.

32 Granata, "Il Partito Nazionale Fascista a Milano tra 'dissidentismo' e 'normalizzazione,'" 31–9.

33 "La sede del Fascio trasferita in piazza Belgioioso," *Corriere della Sera*, March 29, 1930. See for example, *Il Popolo d'Italia*, October 29, 1924.

34 "Scalone monumentale." "La nuova sede della Federazione Fascista," *Il Popolo d'Italia*, May 18, 1930.

35 "Il tempio mistico ove gli spiriti dei Tredici indimenticabili verranno esaltati in muto raccoglimento." "La nuova sede della Federazione Fascista," *Il Popolo d'Italia*, May 18, 1930.

36 "La nuova sede della Federazione Fascista," *Il Popolo d'Italia*, May 18, 1930.

37 "L'inaugurazione della Casa del Fascio," *Il Popolo d'Italia*, May 21, 1930.

38 Albert C. O'Brian, "Italian Youth in Conflict: Catholic Action and Fascist Italy, 1929–1931," *The Catholic Historical Review* 68, no. 4 (1982), 625–35.

39 Ivano Granata, "PNF: Organizzazione del consenso e società Milanese negli anni trenta," 637.

City Halls and Civic Materialism

40 Ravasco to Marinelli, October 31, 1935. Archivio Centrale dello Stato, Rome, Partito Nazionale Fascista (ACS, PNF), Servizi Varie, Serie II, b. 1197.
41 Ravasco to Marcello Visconti di Modrone, February 5, 1935; Ravasco to Visconti di Modrone, March 2, 1935; Starace to Visconti di Modrone, June 18, 1935. ACS, PNF, Servizi Varie, Serie II, b. 1197. Ravasco to Marinelli, June 4, 1935. ACS, PNF, Servizi Varie, Serie II, b. 1197.
42 Daniele Bardelli and Pietro Zuretti, "L'amministrazione comunale del periodo podestarile," in *Storia d'Italia* (Roma: Istituto della Enciclopedia Italiana, 1995–96), 659.
43 For a brief history of the project see Ferruccio Luppi, "Sede della Federazione dei Fasci Milanesi," in Luca Molinari, ed., *Piero Portaluppi: Linea errante nell'architettura del novecento* (Milan: Skira, 2003), 132–3.
44 For more on Portaluppi see Paolo Nicoloso, "Il contesto sociale, politico e universitario di Portaluppi," in Molinari, ed., *Piero Portaluppi,* 241–9.
45 See note 8.
46 "La nuova sede della Federazione," *L'Ambrosiano*, February 23, 1939. Ferdinando Poch, "La nuova sede del Fascio Primogenito," *Città di Milano*, March 1930, 122.
47 Earlier plans had indicated that this memorial chapel would be part of or adjacent to the restored Room of the Sansepolcristi on the opposite side of the building and on axis with the nave of San Sepolcro. a.c.r., "Una Villa a Merate – il Palazzo dei Fasci e una casa di abitazione a Milano," *Rassegna di Architettura* 10 (1940), 269. Ferdinando Poch, "La nuova sede del Fascio primogenito," *Milano*, March 1930, 120. "La storica Sala dei Sansepolcristi è stata oggi simbolicamente consegnata alla Federazione Fascista," March 1939, in *Archivio Storico Civicio*, Milan, Archivio Giuseppe Rivolta, c. 61.10.
48 Portaluppi left the design of this memorial space to his students (Gianni Albricci, Mario Tevarotto, Marco Zanuso, Luigi Mattoni, Gianluigi Reggio Mario Salvedè). "Generazioni nate e maturate nel solco lasciato e segnato dagli Eroi scomparsi." a.c.r., "Una Villa a Merate – Il Palazzo dei Fasci e un casa di abitazione a Milano," 303.
49 Capo dei Servizi Giovanni Montefuseo to Sede Federale Milan, October 3, 1942. ACS, PNF, Servizi Vari, b. 1197.
50 See Massimiliano Savorra, "Piazza Duomo," in *Portaluppi*, 134–7. Fluvio Irace, *Giovanni Muzio, 1893–1982* (Milan: Electa, 1994), 124–32. Marta Petrin, "L'Arengario a Milano, 1935–1943," in Paolo Nicoloso, ed., *Architetture per un'identita Italiana* (Udine: Gaspari, 2009): 169–84.
51 Portaluppi spent 17 hours working on designs for the Palazzo del Fascio in 1942, Fondazione Piero Portaluppi.
52 Emilio Gentile, "The problem of the party in Italian Fascism," *Journal of Contemporary History* 19, no. 2 (1984): 271. For a discussion of the party's building activity in Rome in the final stages of the regime see: Vittorio Vidotto, "Palazzi e Sacrari," Roma Moderna e Contemporanea 11, no. 3 (2003): 583–99.
53 Gentile, "The problem of the party in Italian Fascism," 273.
54 This strategy owed much to Marcello Piacentini's reworking of the historic center of Brescia (1932) and became an effective means to both preserve and displace traditional centers of power. Another example (and one that is often overlooked) is Giuseppe Samonà's reworking of the Messina harbour which included a new provincial headquarters for the Fascist Party adjacent to that city's town hall.

Chapter 12: Moving Beyond Colonialism

Town Halls and Sub-Saharan Africa's Postcolonial Capitals

Garth Andrew Myers

INTRODUCTION

The architectural state of affairs for town halls across postcolonial Sub-Saharan Africa is richly symbolic of colonial and national government relationships to municipalities in the region. Colonial-era town halls or city halls have often been disregarded or demolished, while postcolonial regimes in most cases have spent as little money renovating the old municipal buildings as they have constructing new ones. The second colonial occupation, a term for the postwar European investments in Africa aimed at shaping allies out of colonies clamoring for independence – and then independence itself – did initiate construction of some new town halls across the continent between the 1950s and early 1970s. Most notable among these were the town halls built for the new capitals that a number of countries established, such as in Lilongwe, Malawi.[1] New municipal buildings also appeared in older cities – Nairobi, Kenya gained an impressive city council building in the 1950s, while Lusaka, Zambia, had a new one built after independence. But besides these and a few other cases, the general terms one might use to describe the state of most African town halls would be *peripheralization* and *disrepair*.

In this chapter, I examine the causes of this peripheralization and disrepair, and the parallel inability of most postcolonial African states to move beyond colonial legacies of disregard for municipal buildings, with a case study focus on Tanzania's two former capital cities, Dar es Salaam and Zanzibar, and its current, explicitly postcolonial one, Dodoma.[2] I argue that colonialism generally denied the right to the city to the colonized majorities, leaving the vast majority of urban residents disenfranchised and urban local government insignificant even where it did exist. In architectural terms, colonial regimes used buildings to emphasize and accentuate the power of the colonial state rather than the local municipality. Postcolonial regimes often outdid their colonial predecessors in underfunding, or even eliminating, urban local government, and in using public architecture to symbolize instead starkly nationalist aims.

Sub-Saharan African urban hierarchies still display extraordinarily high primacy ratios and capital-city dominance. As of 2010, the capital city was not only the largest city but was so by a ratio of more than two-to-one in 43 of 49 Sub-Saharan countries; in many of these cases, the capital city remains the only city of any significance demographically. In two of the six exceptions, Nigeria and Tanzania, the former colonial-era capital is the overly-primate city (Lagos and Dar es Salaam, respectively), despite the shift of capital status.[3] Hence it is often in capital (or former capital) cities like Dar es Salaam, Zanzibar, and Dodoma where we find the "barometer of new [or old] ideological approaches" made manifest, "in the capital's architecture, in its public monuments, and the names of its streets and public spaces."[4] At the same time, ordinary residents remade these spaces, often more effectively than the dominant order that had created them in the first place. These claims are amply displayed in the spatial stories of Dar es Salaam, Zanzibar, and Dodoma.

In the chapter's next section, I survey the status and the literature, such as they are, for town halls in Sub-Saharan Africa. This survey contextualizes the main section's discussion of the peripheralization and disrepair of Tanzanian public municipal architecture, as part of the Sub-Saharan region. My aim is to show that the Tanzanian examples fit comfortably within the general parameters of contestation over the right to the city enmeshed in the stories that surround the town halls of Africa. A massive literature has arisen analyzing the idea of the right to the city, and a thorough review of debates within this literature is beyond the scope of the chapter. Moreover, it is a concept, or a slogan, with multiple possible interpretations. I generally take its origins to have been in the work of Henri Lefebvre, as a "cry and a demand."[5] Peter Marcuse clarifies this as a "demand by those deprived of basic material and legal rights, and an aspiration for the future [from] those discontented with life."[6] As John Friedmann once put it, "a city can truly be called a city only when its streets belong to the people."[7] The fact that urban governments are in many parts of the world seen as increasingly important agents for answering the cry and demand means to me that the spaces the state claims, the physical and social architecture of its power, and the public access to or control over these matters are fundamental, symbolically and materially, to the right to the city.[8] What we see in much of Africa under colonial and postcolonial rule is predominantly the denial of that right, spatially embodied in municipal buildings and socially expressed in weak representative local government frameworks.[9]

TOWN HALLS IN SUB-SAHARAN AFRICA IN CONTEXT

This book seeks a global history of town halls, looking at the building not simply as a spatial type but as a manifestation of spatial practices and symbolization of the social relations of the public sphere. I contend that to appreciate the marginalization of town halls in Sub-Saharan Africa, it is necessary to document the marginalization of cities and of municipal government at the expense of national government. We can even see this marginalization with the continent's three recognized megacities, Johannesburg, Lagos, and Kinshasa. For instance, there is the peripheralization of Johannesburg's impressive old City Hall, which grew so "underutilized" that by the late 1990s the post-apartheid regime converted it into – tellingly – the Gauteng Provincial Legislature.[10] From the time when City Hall's "crowded" conditions in the 1950s led to construction of a nearby Civic Center (completed in 1972) until today's Unicity (the post-apartheid multi-racial urbanism), Johannesburg's "town hall" has never been much of a central feature of broader architectural attention.[11] Even this city, which Achille Mbembe and Sarah Nuttall proclaim as "the premier African metropolis, the symbol par excellence of the 'African modern'," Africa's richest city, home to Africa's largest stock market, still suffers from more than a century of the marginalization of municipal governance: after all, its majority of citizens were only included in the municipality's governance in the 1990s.[12]

Lagos had at least somewhat more substantial municipal government than most non-settler African cities under European colonialism; but even here the city council was circumscribed soon after independence; one of Africa's greatest storehouses of trained modern architects found their foci elsewhere than city government buildings; soon enough the national government voted to move the capital to Abuja, precipitating the "neglect of metropolitan Lagos by the federal government."[13] The elite of Lagos surely benefited from Nigeria's postcolonial oil boom, and they built a forest of skyscrapers to showcase their wealth – while leaving the modest 1968 city hall to rot, until it was devastated by fire in 1998. Grand plans for a new city hall were delayed for over a decade by mismanagement, including a period when the central government seized all funds for the city council itself; the fancy new building was only completed in 2010 with the funds of the Lagos State Government, whose high-profile, ambitious governor had in effect taken over the municipal government.[14]

Kinshasa, by most estimates the second largest city in Sub-Saharan Africa (ranking behind only Lagos) had, as of 2010, a municipal government budget of US $23 million, meaning something near to two dollars per resident. "National legislation granting Kinshasa the power to generate and retain its own finance was only passed in 2008."[15] Filip de Boeck has traced the peripheralization and disrepair of Kinshasa – here, not of its municipal buildings, but of the very city itself. After decades of disinterest and laissez faire where the city's governors announced plans for "cleaning up the city" and proceeded to do no such thing, the contemporary regime seems to mean business in its effort to "rewrite the city's public spaces."[16] Yet its grand ambitions do not rest on representative governance, and its new cityscape vision is full of "conference centers, five-star hotels, and skyscrapers" (most resplendently in the plan for *La Cite du Fleuve* to be fashioned from land reclaimed from the Congo River) – without a new city hall at the center.[17]

There are some historic exceptions to what might seem to be generalizations about Sub-Saharan African town halls in the above paragraphs that should be noted. For example, in some of West Africa's historic city-states, we might consider the still-grand palaces of local emirs as "town halls" in some senses, or in the settler cities and towns of South Africa – but even there vestiges of my argument remain. Moreover, South Africa's white minority apartheid regime (1948–94) took the (dis)investment in municipal governance and town halls into a new realm of the bizarre with construction of capitals for its "bantustans" through which it sought to divide the black majority by "tribal" identities into puzzle-piece territories it tried to call independent. Two of these even became provincial capitals in the post-apartheid order, in part by rededicating the "capital" buildings as provincial government headquarters, but many town halls are sidelined in the new metropolitan municipality governance structures.[18]

Unsurprisingly, then, the academic literature analyzing the municipal buildings or town halls of Sub-Saharan Africa is strikingly limited. Even for the region with the longest influence of the European style of municipal architecture that gave rise to the centrality of town halls, the Cape region of South Africa, scholarship directly focused on architecture seldom spends much time on the town halls.[19] Even a rare example of an African city hall that draws tourists for its architecture, that of Durban's 1910 building designed by Stanley Hudson with direct inspiration from the City Hall of Belfast (to my untrained eyes, it is an exact copy), no relevant architectural scholarship exists that I have been able to locate. The excellent, architecturally oriented edited volume on *Capital Cities in Africa* has only limited reference to town or city halls as major manifestations of the local or national state's symbolic or representative power in either colonial or postcolonial times.[20] The chapter by Goerg on Conakry, Guinea, cites the national People's Palace as its major site of power in the city, with no note on any town hall in its history.[21] A similar story pertains for Diop's chapter on Dakar, Senegal, that bemoans the central government's "monopoly" over the capital city such that it "manages local urban affairs with the involvement neither of local authorities nor of community groups."[22]

There are some understandable political reasons behind the fact that many colonial-era town halls were torn down or allowed to slip into disrepair after independence, or why post-independence (and post-apartheid) scholarship has left these structures disregarded. Most major cities in Sub-Saharan Africa were influenced substantially by colonial rule, and "buildings devoted to government or bureaucratic functions embody the colonial state's efforts to impose control, as they provide settings for managing the local population through legal and military means as well as symbolizing the colonizers' power."[23] As Aidan McQuillan put it, "if the historic townscape is the product of imperial rulers, then justification for its preservation may be difficult."[24] Phillipe Gervais-Lambony noted that in Lomé, Togo, not only did the postcolonial regime demolish the colonial town hall, but it also made sure that "the municipality no longer has great power or great importance."[25]

In most African cities, a colonial (or apartheid) legacy of the underdevelopment and underfinancing of municipal governance metastasized in the postcolonial (or post-apartheid) era. It would be implausible to expect a grand architectural statement for democratic municipal governance, and a concerted effort to maintain that statement, out of their town halls. Even in Kenya's audacious recent Nairobi Metro 2030 plan for making the capital city into a "world-class city region," the entire effort was centralized in a new national Ministry for Nairobi Metropolitan Development, and not the Nairobi City Council.[26] At least Nairobi has its still fairly grand 1950s-era City Hall, replete with a substantial annex finished in 1981. Most city governments in postcolonial Africa operate from unimportant, poorly maintained and unimpressive colonial-era physical structures (typically dwarfed by nationalist and modernist monumental architecture) that have been allowed to decay, and are now characterized by atrocious plumbing and leaking roofs.

TOWN HALLS OF TANZANIA

Tanzania exemplifies the arguments I have outlined above. I document this here, beginning with its primate city and former capital of Dar es Salaam, moving to its secondary capital of the semi-autonomous polity of Zanzibar, and ending with its new postcolonial capital of Dodoma. Even in a relatively recent burst of scholarly enthusiasm for analysis of architecture in all three cities, we find a strikingly limited interest in town halls; this parallels the broad deformity of Tanzanian municipal governance, and the ways the cities' public spaces have been reframed from below.

At first pass, some elements of the latter two Tanzanian cases might seem to offer contrasts with Dar and other African cases. Both Zanzibar's colonial-era Ng'ambo Civic Center and the postcolonial plan for a new Tanzanian capital are examples of attempts to make grand architectural statements with urban public buildings, and to frame these attempts in terms of popular democratic governance. That both attempts failed is not as interesting as the manner by which both attempts were reframed by the populace that was the intended audience for the statements. In Lefebvrean terms, if the Ng'ambo Civic Center and the new capital at Dodoma are conceived representations of space, then the popular reframing took the form of lived representational space.[27] Since Lefebvre intended for us to see these two forms of urban space "in relation to one another," it follows that we can see both Ng'ambo Civic Center and the Master Plan of Dodoma as "spatial contradictions, where the manner in which a space is routinely used by one social group may actually subvert or disrupt the dominant or controlling rhythm."[28] Hence the peripheralization and disrepair we see at first pass might be even more a part of an alternative spatial rhythm remaking cities in Tanzania than what I suggest for Dar in the first sub-section here below. I return to this premise in my conclusion.

Dar es Salaam

Dar es Salaam began as a mainland outpost of the Omani Sultanate of Zanzibar in the 1860s, became a German military site in the 1880s, and eventually was designated the capital of German East Africa in 1891. Its first site of colonial administration was a fortress, or *boma*, that subsequently served as a prison.[29] Even when a successor building was created by the colonial authorities, it retained the look of a fort (opposite the original *boma* of the *Omani* sultan), and its location was proximal to the only thing that mattered to the colonial regime, the port where it secured customs.[30] Africans were not supposed to be there, and their increasing presence in the city as a whole alarmed colonial authorities intent on seeing detribalization and other outcomes of urbanization as vestiges of a criminal, civilizational decline that threatened their control and order in the territory.[31]

The postcolonial socialist regime actually continued "colonial style planning under a colonial style planning law" while taking "a heavy-handed, insensitive and bullying approach to the exercise of powers against the urban poor" who made up the vast majority of residents.[32] Urban local government was eliminated entirely from 1972–79 under the ironically entitled "decentralization" policy of President Julius Nyerere's regime. Meanwhile, Nyerere's government voted to relocate the country's capital to a new site at Dodoma, turning its back on Dar es Salaam even as a potential national symbol. Subsequently, Dar es Salaam's City Hall has remained in a dilapidated state. Even though it serves a city of more than three million people whose civic leaders have now spent more than 20 years espousing the United Nations' notion of the "inclusive city," the municipal building itself has highly controlled access, and the citizens scarcely consider themselves "included" in much that is done there.[33]

Dar es Salaam was the pilot city for the UN's Sustainable Cities Program (SCP) in the 1990s, and the head of its city commission, Charles Keenja, earned a place on the UN Habitat's Scroll of Honor for planning efforts he led from 1996 to 1999. Yet the ironies run deep. The SCP was built around rhetorical tactics of participatory, decentralized, democratic planning. Not even a year passed after Tanzania's first multi-party democratic elections in 1995, though, before the national government dissolved Dar es Salaam's first democratically elected representative City Council. The Council was replaced by a City Commission, the entire membership of which was appointed by the Prime Minister. Keenja's dictatorial, centrally appointed Commission did oversee a successful re-planning of solid waste management, reorganization of public transportation, and privatization of downtown parking. The 2000 reorganization of local government did return a modicum of local representative democracy by carving Dar into three municipalities, each with its own, now-being-completed headquarters and council of elected representatives which appoint five of their respective members to the 15-seat Dar es Salaam City Council. But in no way did the Commission represent an implementation of the democratized or participatory inclusion Habitat espoused, and the post-2000 urban governance was barely an improvement.[34]

Dar es Salaam's version of the SCP was scaled up to the national level and an Urban Authorities Support Unit was created to coordinate a multi-city engagement – from a virtually inaccessible, cramped, top-floor back office of the city building in Dar.[35] In 2010, Habitat's Tanzanian Executive Director returned home from Nairobi to become Minister of Lands and Human Settlements in the national government, but she proceeded to carry out policies of demolition and slum clearance in Dar based on colonial-era planning laws, moving about as far as possible in practitioners' terms from inclusivity.

Dar es Salaam has had little experience, then, with representative municipal governance, as a city managed from the central national government or regional and local units controlled by it. The spatial and architectural marginality of its town hall fits that narrative of governance perfectly. And yet it is important not to lose sight of how Dar es Salaam's ordinary residents reframe the city, remaking its architecture, literally and figuratively. While acknowledging Lefebvre's claim that "an architecture of pleasure and joy, of community in the use of the gifts of the earth, has yet to be invented," I argue that there are ways, even in a city like Dar es Salaam, that we can see popular striving for such an architecture.[36] Some might see it in the Dar es Salaam buildings of the city's most celebrated architect, Anthony Almeida. After a successful decade of private practice in the colonial era, Almeida served the postcolonial socialist regime by designing numerous public buildings – yet he deliberately eschewed grand political statements, so that "people, instead of the building, took a central place."[37] Others might point to the long career output of Tanzanian architect Beda Amuli, such as his market building for the pulsing heart of Dar, the historic African CBD of Kariakoo.[38] But the clearest articulation of the reframing of the public sphere comes in the everyday life of the informal settlements where more than two-thirds of Dar's citizens live, in the houses its people "erect and keep with pride," in the open spaces they reclaim as public places, and in the de facto town halls that the gathering spots on their streets become.[39]

Zanzibar

The contemporary city of Zanzibar grew out of an indigenous fishing village with the arrival of Omani overlords on the island in the 1690s. It rose to the status of the "island metropolis of Eastern Africa" amid the expansion of Oman's economic might along the coast, particularly after the Omani Sultan moved his capital to Zanzibar early in the 1800s and jumpstarted a period of clove plantation agriculture and caravan trading for slaves and ivory.[40] Britain ultimately gained ascendancy with the Sultanate and, in 1890, declared Zanzibar a Protectorate. It remained a British colony from then until December 1963, with its only major town as the colony's capital. From its independence-era population of less than 50,000, the city rapidly expanded, and it is now a metropolitan area with 450,000 people. But it essentially has no town hall.

The only building that was ever really purpose-built to (sort of) fulfill that role is very hard to see.[41] It lies behind the broadcast studio and offices of Radio Tanzania Zanzibar, a gaudy red and white building on the downslope from the highest point in the older section of Ng'ambo, Zanzibar's historic "Other Side." Radio Zanzibar's two-story building, with its quirky central spiral, red metal visor strips, smoky glass windows and significant footprint on the main central route out of Zanzibar's downtown, stands out uncomfortably from its surroundings (Figure 12.1). The curious office was built by engineers from the People's Republic of China in the late 1990s, under the guidance of Qian Kequan; it lies adjacent to the eight-story, 300 meter-long apartment blocks in the area known as Michenzani (Figure 12.2). The Michenzani apartment complex, built at Ng'ambo's center and highest elevation in the early 1970s, took its social and architectural inspiration from the communist East German planners, led by Hubert Scholz, who had completed the city's first Master Plan of the revolutionary era in 1968 and a model socialist village in the nearby Kikwajuni neighborhood of southern Ng'ambo.[42] Between them, the Michenzani blocks and the Chinese Radio Tanzania Zanzibar building shadow the crumbling remnants of what was once the Ng'ambo Civic Center, the colonial-era town hall for Ng'ambo's Town Council.

Figure 12.1
Radio Zanzibar headquarters, Raha Leo, Zanzibar, 2012. Source: Iddi Ali Haji, photograph taken for the author.

Figure 12.2
The ten Michenzani apartment blocks dominate the Ng'ambo skyline, 1991. Source: author.

The Ng'ambo Civic Center was given the name Raha Leo (Happiness Today) by the orchestrator of its construction, the British Protectorate's Chief Secretary from 1941–52, Eric Dutton. It served, rather unsuccessfully, as the physical home of British attempts to introduce heavily circumscribed democratic politics in the 1940s and 1950s in Zanzibar's highly fractured society. It is most remembered, however, for the roles its radio station and grounds played in the January 1964 Zanzibar Revolution: the revolutionaries broadcast their terror from the radio station and gathered their prisoners and corpses in its courtyard. Thus it came to symbolize anything but "happiness."

Yet the building itself (Figure 12.3) was a major achievement for its leading designer, the Punjab-born Zanzibari architect Ajit Singh Hoogan – Raha Leo was "Ajit Singh's Masterpiece," in the words of German architect Erich Meffert, and the "peak of [his] design work":[43]

> Restricted to a mere cubus with a center part slightly protruding, it offers an image linked to Zanzibar's historical roots. The rhythm of front and side elevations is masterly [sic] accentuated at roof level in the common manner of Ajit Singh, i.e. by means of acroterions, corner and center ones, which still fulfill their role today in a state of deplorable decay ... Raha Leo is a genuine national monument and deserves better treatment.[44]

Following on Meffert's final sentence above, it is pertinent to note that considerable attention and donor financing has been directed at the historic preservation of Zanzibar's architectural heritage over the last 30 years, and the most notable institutional manifestation of this is the Stone Town Conservation and Development Authority (STCDA) that Meffert helped to create and lead. Stone Town lies to the west of Ng'ambo, across the city's main downtown north-south road, once known as Creek Road, because it covered the creek, Pwani Ndogo, that historically separated Stone Town and Ng'ambo. Under colonial rule, Stone Town

Figure 12.3
Raha Leo Civic Center, 1947. Source: from the papers of Ajit Singh Hoogan, used by permission of Parmukh Singh Hoogan.

was "Zanzibar Town," with a separate Town Council, a separation that STCDA reproduced.[45] That Town Council of the colonial era met in the Victoria Hall in the Vuga section of Stone Town, as did the Legislative Council of the colony.

After colonialism ended, a new combined town council (Stone Town and Ng'ambo together) met in Stone Town in what is known as the Bharmal Building (originally a private residence, then the provincial commissioner's office in the colonial era), which also houses the current manifestation of the Zanzibar Municipal Council. That Municipal Council was disbanded between 1972 and 1984 in Zanzibar. As it grew again in significance after its 1984 reinstatement, the ZMC was allocated additional office space in Vuga's Victoria Hall. Although STCDA and a United Nations planning effort in the early 1980s had drawn attention to the collapsed state of the Bharmal Building, neither it nor the Victoria Hall have received any significant renovation or rehabilitation, despite their architectural significance as products of Zanzibar's only other important official town architect, John Sinclair. Indeed, between them, Ajit Singh and John Sinclair are responsible for nearly every major public building of the colonial era in the town.[46] Yet none of the buildings that they built that might be considered town halls have ever been restored – although Meffort's influence did, in 2012, finally lead to modest repair work on Raha Leo (seen while underway in Figure 12.4).

After the revolutionary cooptation of Raha Leo and its grounds for the consolidation of the revolution itself, the building began its slow decline into a functional existence as just another asset of the Ministry of Communications. I had to have my photograph taken there as a part of the process of registering my Zanzibari residency in 1991, and Radio Zanzibar occupied the building until the new Chinese headquarters were completed a few years later. Prior to 2012, the building had been untouched by the rhetorical zeal for both architectural preservation and democratization (Zanzibar's main opposition party has won all

Figure 12.4
Raha Leo Civic Center under repair, 2012.
Source: Iddi Ali Haji, photograph taken for the author.

four national multi-party elections [1995, 2000, 2005, and 2010] by winning the majority of city constituencies, only to have the Zanzibar Electoral Commission manipulate the results to retain power in the hands of the Revolutionary Party[47]). But the reframing of the building's surroundings is more profound in symbolic terms than in architectural ones. Along every edge of Raha Leo's former public spaces, extending into what was the colonial regime's Ng'ambo Girls School and grounds next door, one finds informal sector businesses and alternative urban spaces, in a mall made of former ship containers, in a strip of kiosks selling building materials of all kinds, and in a street of homes that house spirit possession groups which see in the neighborhood many sites of connectivity with Giningi, the spirit underworld. The streets and alleys of this quarter of the city are alive at all hours with people of all ages. A constantly evolving array of activities, experiments, and makeshift gatherings makes Raha Leo just one of dozens of moving spaces that belong to the Zanzibar public, despite a long run of quasi-disenfranchisement. It is in the public streets, and on the domestic verandahs of Ng'ambo, where the lived "town hall" of Zanzibar can be found.

Dodoma

Among his many bold achievements, Tanzania's first President, Julius Nyerere, is remembered for having led the government's decision to relocate the national capital from Dar es Salaam to Dodoma in the 1970s. The move was meant as a powerful postcolonial symbol of Tanzania's new order. In 1967, in the Arusha Declaration, Nyerere's government had made *ujamaa* the philosophy that would guide national development. Often translated as "socialism," *ujamaa* literally means family-hood. Under *ujamaa*, the government deliberately de-emphasized urban areas to deconcentrate and ruralize industrial growth. Dar es Salaam was the main victim of this de-emphasis, largely because it "remained for Nyerere a reminder of a colonial legacy;" instead, Nyerere sought to "construct his own personal vision of an African socialist state" in a new capital city nearer to the country's agricultural heartlands.[48]

Dodoma's designed layout and plan were in keeping with the ideals of *ujamaa* philosophy. The 1976 Master Plan had "proposed nothing less than the first nonmonumental capital city."[49] What the city now calls Nyerere Square was to have been *Ujamaa* Square. It would not have had a towering statue of Nyerere in it, as it now does; the Master Plan envisioned a large sculpture of an acacia tree, to follow the traditional gathering place of Tanzanian villagers and townspeople in the shade of a tree.[50] Its Master Plan was "modest and people oriented."[51]

Although there was a small settlement there by the 1890s, Dodoma was a rather small regional center until the 1970s.[52] Tanzania's decision to relocate its capital there came in a vote by the 1973 Biennial Conference of the ruling party, Nyerere's Tanganyika African National Union.[53] The Master Plan was commissioned the next year and published in 1976.

Dodoma's spatial plan was designed to "enable the open space of the landscape to flow through it."[54] As Hess has written, "the architecture of Dodoma was intended to embody Nyerere's belief in the equalization of urban and rural development," emphasizing "the village as the means to 'the brotherhood and equality of man.'"[55] In between the plan's pods of housing, since planners avoided placing the communal areas on higher quality farm and pasture land, the idea was to foster agricultural development for food self-sufficiency, along with afforestation and recreational green spaces. There was no place on the plan for a city hall, as its Master Plan was produced and approved during the years when Tanzania's "decentralization" policy had eliminated municipal government.

Dodoma has grown from a dilapidated, dusty settlement with less than 50,000 people at the time of the Master Plan to a city of more than 300,000. Most of the growth has been in informal settlements.[56] Municipal government operates out of the Dodoma Local Authority Headquarters; by far the more powerful local city government entity has been the Capital Development Authority (CDA), appointed and run by the national government – yet even its offices are decidedly non-monumental.

It could be easy to dismiss Dodoma as a failed postcolonial urban vision. It is certainly not the green city of urban communal foresters, farmers, and herders Nyerere idealized. Most significantly, the government itself did not really move its seat of operations – parliament meets there most of the time, but no ministerial headquarters are there, and neither are the main offices of the President or Prime Minister. Government housing construction fell far short of what had been planned. Amenities, infrastructure, and services that the Master Plan expected either have not materialized or were far more limited in number or scope. The planning practices of the Capital Development Authority were often repressive toward residents and building control, hardly in step with ideas of "negotiation, dialogue and consensus building" which one might think could form the basis of a city built to symbolize "family-hood" and "self-reliance."[57]

Yet Wilbard Kombe and Volker Kreibich's study of Dodoma's Chang'ombe informal settlement reveals the ways in which community leaders, including ruling party activists and the ruling party's ten-house cell leaders "worked tirelessly as a pressure group to mobilize [informal] settlers against" attempts by the CDA to evict them.[58] The active collaboration and collusion of the majority of settlers with local party and government leaders created "spatial orderliness" in the "informally regularized" settlement during the first ten years of its development (1976–86). Kombe and Kreibich argued that there had been a steady decline in community cohesion, and a corresponding rise in "apathy" toward socialist goals among residents, both of which followed a 1986 central-government directive that limited the CDA's capacity for demolition and enforcement of strict building controls.[59] The orderly and regularized dimension of Chang'ombe's subsequent expansion decreased, but Kombe and Kreibich nonetheless saw great potential at the grassroots for "collaborative initiatives" in future planning.[60]

In the years since their study was published, the formal capital relocation re-emerged as a serious idea, particularly under the leadership of Nyerere's protégé, Benjamin Mkapa, during his second term as President (2000–05), and then continuing with the election of Jakaya Kikwete as Tanzania's President in

2005. Despite predictions that multi-party politics, which emerged in Tanzania after 1992, would lead to the capital relocation being "scrapped altogether," in fact since opposition politicians first came to the Dodoma parliament in 1995 they often pushed the government to speed up the process of relocating the capital, particularly in the last decade, with an emphasis on nation-building rhetoric.[61] As a result the government's budget and aid moneys have gone toward many improvements in Dodoma. Dodoma is becoming more than a "singular precedent for the amalgamation of moral vision and architectural planning"[62]: it is becoming its own city. It has done so without anything we might really call a city hall.

The way in which that city's residents live their lives is hardly in tune with the socio-spatial ideals of *ujamaa*, but one might argue that the residents often work toward their own *ujamaa* (as in its literal translation: family-hood) framework of development. We see this, for instance, in the de facto CBD of Dodoma, where row upon row of plastic-covered market stalls and plain small shops teem with people buying and selling cheap, imported basic goods, in a space the Master Plan of 1976 had set aside for a ministerial office (Figure 12.5).[63]

CONCLUSION

In the early twenty-first century, Tanzania is having an odd neoliberal economic takeoff, with substantial foreign direct investment, led by its mineral sector and spurred on by the "new scramble for Africa."[64] Some renewed enthusiasm for urban development, and some conscious coordination of planning between its cities may be beginning. New satellite towns are in the works from Arusha to Zanzibar. Yet the primary, central buildings in all of these efforts are hotels, conference centers, central government buildings, or sports stadiums – with nary a new town hall to be found.[65] Parallel to this, when the recently formed Tanzania

Figure 12.5
Street scene in downtown Dodoma, 2008. Source: author.

Cities Network launched an effort to produce a *State of Tanzania's Cities* report, the keynote address from the Deputy Permanent Secretary in the Prime Minister's Office for Regional Administration and Local Government blamed "local government leaders and mayors" for their "failure" and "laxity" in implementing "laws and regulations" to shape urban development. This is what he told the representatives of municipal governments that his office had steadfastly underfunded for 50 years: "you are the ones causing all these problems."[66] Representative governance at the municipal level in Tanzania, it seems, only exists to provide the national government with units to blame for the unjust, corrupt, and ineffective state of affairs in urban governance in the country. The makeshift, ever-changing, peripheral, and dilapidated locations of municipal governance in these cities speak with space to document that claim.

Cities in Africa, whether they emerge from a more organic milieu, or from a formal plan, do not typically create a structure akin to the town halls of European or North American municipalities, at least in terms of the socio-political role or power of such buildings. Some reasons for this certainly lie with the postcolonial regimes that have consolidated power at the national level at the expense of the local/municipal level. Tanzania provides a prime example of this. Yet other reasons lie with European colonial rule. First, colonial regimes set the trend in motion for that postcolonial enfeeblement of municipalities, through the general marginalization of cities in the colonial order and of municipal government specifically. Even larger cities on the continent lacked representative urban government until the last decade or so of colonial rule, and even when it was introduced, participation in it was carefully circumscribed. Postcolonial regimes continued or even expanded upon the peripheralization of urban local government, leaving city governments utterly at the mercy of central government financing and political control, and making the democratic character of city government ever more precarious. The architecture of urban government often manifests this precarious and peripheral position.

A second colonial legacy, then, is explicitly architectural. Where colonial powers built something of a "town hall," it was to serve the municipal interests of a small colonial elite – for example in settler colonies, where representative urban government and citizenship belonged to white (and to some extent Asian) minorities to the exclusion of African majorities. It is not surprising to see how often such municipal town halls were shunted aside, demolished, or repurposed after independence. While postcolonial regimes invested heavily in new national government buildings, in doing so they frequently eschewed any architectural reference to colonial styles (albeit with nods to Western modernism). To be sure, colonial-era buildings of national government often remained central to the architecture of postcolonial rule, but such endurance was less common for municipal town halls. It is my contention that these buildings, more directly than the national buildings, often symbolized everything wrong with colonialism in tangible, everyday ways – racial segregation, despotic rule, inequality in citizenship and access to urban services – to both postcolonial regimes and their citizens.

What John Allen has called a "spatial contradiction" arises from the clash in African cities between the conceived representations of space that this governance-and-town-hall trend above embodies and the lived representational spaces of the urban majority who are busy remaking the streets of these cities. From Johannesburg to Lagos, Lomé to Kinshasa, or Dakar to Dar, the streets do not, at least in Friedmann's sense of things, "belong to the people." Colonial and postcolonial regimes have set about restricting the rights of ordinary residents to their own cities. What this has led to, however, is a circumstance in which, in the absence of a representative town hall, the people refashion those "streets" (or alleys, verandahs, or market stalls) that *do* belong to them in informal, often illegal spaces, to take the place of the town halls that would otherwise mark the public sphere.

NOTES

1   Garth Myers, *African Cities: Alternative Visions of Urban Theory and Practice* (London: Zed Books, 2011).
2   Zanzibar was a separate colony from Tanganyika; it gained independence in December 1963 and united with Tanganyika to form the United Republic of Tanzania in April 1964, but its capital city, also called Zanzibar, retains some capital city functions for the semi-autonomous Government of Zanzibar (and it is home to an alternative Parliament building for the United Republic). Dar es Salaam was Tanganyika's colonial and independent capital, and the United Republic's capital until the creation of the new capital of Dodoma in the 1970s; even with the formal shift to Dodoma, Dar retains most capital city functions for Tanzania, as home to all government ministries, the President, and the Prime Minister.
3   UN Habitat, *The State of African Cities 2010: Governance, Inequality and Urban Land Markets* (Nairobi: UN Habitat, 2010).
4   Simon Bekker and Goran Therborn, "Introduction," in Simon Bekker and Goran Therborn, eds., *Capital Cities in Africa: Power and Powerlessness* (Cape Town: HSRC Press, 2012), 1.
5   Henri Lefebvre, "The right to the city," in Eleanore Kofman and Elizabeth Lebas, eds., *Writings on Cities*, (London: Blackwell, 1996 [1967]), 158.
6   Peter Marcuse, "Whose right(s) to what city?," in Neil Brenner, Peter Marcuse, and Margit Maye, eds., *Cities for People, Not for Profit: Critical Urban Theory and the Right to the City* (New York: Routledge, 2012), 30.
7   John Friedmann, "The right to the city," in Richard M. Morse, Jorge Satterthwaite and J. Hardoy, eds., *Rethinking the Latin American City* (Baltimore: Johns Hopkins University Press, 1993), 139.
8   Christian Schmid, "Henri Lefebvre, the right to the city, and the new metropolitan mainstream," in Brenner, Marcuse and Mayer, eds., *Cities for People,* 54.
9   Susan Parnell and Edgar Pieterse, "The 'right to the city': institutional imperatives of a developmental state," *International Journal of Urban and Regional Research* (2010), 146–62; UN Habitat, *State of the World's Cities 2010/2011: Bridging the Urban Divide* (Nairobi: UN Habitat, 2008).
10 Martin Murray, *City of Extremes: The Spatial Politics of Johannesburg* (Durham: Duke University Press, 2011), 257.
11 Keith Beavon, *Johannesburg: The Making and Shaping of the City* (Pretoria: University of South Africa Press, 2004).

12. Achille Mbembe and Sarah Nuttall, "Introduction: Afropolis," in Sarah Nuttall and Achille Mbembe, eds., *Johannesburg: The Elusive Metropolis* (Durham: Duke University Press, 2008), 1.
13. Laurent Fourchard, "Lagos," in Bekker and Therborn, eds., *Capital Cities in Africa*, p. 75; G. Egbo, "Debate review: Lagos... mega city or crisis city?," *ArchiAfrica Newsletter* (Sep 2010) 2–4.
14. Martin Green, "The making of a megacity," *FT Weekend*, (August 8–9, 2009), 1–2.
15. AbdouMaliq Simone, *City Life from Jakarta to Dakar: Movements at the Crossroads* (London: Routledge, 2010), 127.
16. Filip de Boeck, "Spectral Kinshasa: building the city through an architecture of words," in Tim Edensor and Mark Jayne, eds., *Urban Theory Beyond the West: A World of Cities* (London: Routledge, 2012), 319.
17. Ibid., 320; see also F. de Boeck, "Inhabiting ocular ground: Kinshasa's future in the light of Congo's spectral urban politics," *Cultural Anthropology* 26 (2011), 263–86.
18. Aaln Mabin, "South African capital cities," in Bekker and Therborn, eds., *Capital Cities in Africa*, 168–91.
19. Hans Fransen, *Old Towns and Villages of the Cape* (Cape Town: Jonathan Ball Publishers, 2006).
20. Bekker and Therborn, "Introduction."
21. Odile Goerg, "Conakry," in Bekker and Therborn, eds., *Capital Cities in Africa*, 12.
22. A. Diop, "Dakar," in Bekker and Therborn, eds., *Capital Cities in Africa*, 40.
23. Anne Lewinson, "Viewing postcolonial Dar es Salaam through civic spaces: a question of class," in Fassil Demissie, ed., *Postcolonial African Cities: Imperial Legacies and Postcolonial Predicaments* (London: Routledge, 2007), 45.
24. Aidan McQuillan, "Preservation planning in postcolonial cities," in Thomas Slater, ed., *The Built Form of Western Cities* (Leicester: Leicester University Press, 1987), 394.
25. Philippe Gervais-Lambony, "Lome," in Bekker and Therborn, eds., *Capital Cities in Africa*, 49.
26. Samuel Owuor, and Teresa Mbatia, "Nairobi," in Bekker and Therborn, eds., *Capital Cities in Africa*, 120-140; in my interview with Tom Odongo, Director of City Planning, Nairobi City Council, 28 July, 2012, he indicated that the new Ministry for Nairobi Metropolitan Development was likely to be eliminated in a then-ongoing round of constitutional reforms.
27. Henri Lefebvre, *The Production of Space* (Oxford: Blackwell, 1991); Edward Soja, *Postmetropolis: Critical Studies of Cities and Regions*, (Oxford: Blackwell, 2000).
28. John Allen, *Lost Geographies of Power*, (Malden, MA: Blackwell, 2003), 161.
29. James Brennan and Andrew Burton, "An emerging metropolis: A history of Dar es Salaam, circa 1862–2000," in James Brennan, Andrew Burton, and Yusuf Lawi, eds., *Dar es Salaam: Histories from an Emerging African Metropolis*, (Dar es Salaam: Mkuki na Nyota Publishers, 2007), 24.
30. Lusugga Kironde, "Race, class and housing in Dar es Salaam: the colonial impact on land use structure, 1891–1961," in Brennan, Burton, and Lawi, eds., *Dar es Salaam*, 100.
31. Andrew Burton, *African Underclass: Urbanization, Crime and Colonial Order in Dar es Salaam*, (Oxford: James Currey, 2005), 70–1.
32. Patrick McAuslan, "Law and the poor: the case of Dar es Salaam," in Andreas Philippopoulos-Mihalopoulos, ed., *Law and the City*, (London: Routledge-Cavendish, 2007), 175 and 178–9.
33. UN Habitat, *State of the World's Cities*; Garth Myers, *Disposable Cities: Garbage, Governance, and Sustainable Development in Urban Africa* (Aldershot, UK: Ashgate Press, 2005).
34. Myers, *Disposable Cities*.
35. Ibid.

36 Lefebvre, *The Production of Space* 379.
37 Pieter Burssens, "The (non)political position of the architecture of Anthony B. Almeida between 1948 and 1975," *Proceedings of the ArchiAfrika Conference on Modern Architecture in East Africa around Independence*, (Utrecht: ArchiAfrika, 2005), 124.
38 Kanywanyi S. Kanywanyi, "The story of the boy from Tanganyika who went to Israel to study architecture," *Anza* 1 (2012), 6–7.
39 Abella Mutalemwa and Comfort Mosha, "Making a model of Dar es Salaam," *Anza*, 1 (2012), 10; Eileen Moyer, "Not quite the comforts of home: searching for locality among street youth in Dar es Salaam," in Piet Konings and Dirk Foeken, eds., *Crisis and Creativity: Exploring the Wealth of the African Neighborhood* (Leiden: Brill, 2006), 163–96.
40 Garth Myers, *Verandahs of Power: Colonialism and Space in Urban Africa* (Syracuse, NY: Syracuse University Press, 2003).
41 The revolutionary postcolonial regime did start out to build a town hall, but as soon as it was finished it was immediately repurposed to be the headquarters of Television Zanzibar, Sub-Saharan Africa's first national television station.
42 Myers, *Verandahs of Power*.
43 Erich Meffert, *Ajit Singh, Architect: 1910–1986* (Zanzibar: Von Heute auf Morgen Publishers, 2010), 28.
44 Ibid.
45 William Bissell, *Urban Design, Chaos, and Colonial Power in Zanzibar* (Bloomington: Indiana University Press, 2011).
46 Dean Sinclair, "Field note: 'memorials more enduring than bronze:' J. H. Sinclair and the making of Zanzibar Stone Town," *African Geographical Review* 28, 71–97; Meffert, *Ajit Singh, Architect*; Myers, *Verandahs of Power*.
47 Alexander B. Makulilo, "The Zanzibar Electoral Commission and its Feckless Independence," *Journal of Third World Studies* 28 (2011), 263–83.
48 Janet B. Hess, *Art and Architecture in Postcolonial Africa* (Jefferson, NC: McFarland & Company, 2006), 123.
49 Lawrence Vale, *Architecture, Power, and National Identity*, 2nd edition, (London: Routledge, 2008), 179.
50 Ibid., 181.
51 Nnamdi Elleh, "Examining the aspirations of modern architecture in East Africa around independence, 1950–1975," *Proceedings of the ArchiAfrika Conference on Modern Architecture in East Africa around Independence* (Utrecht: ArchiAfrika, 2005), 32.
52 Wilbard J. Kombe and Volker Kreibich, *Informal Land Management in Tanzania* (Dortmund: University of Dortmund), 2000.
53 TANU subsequently became *Chama cha Mapinduzi* (CCM, the Revolutionary Party) four years later, after uniting with the ruling party of Zanzibar.
54 Capital Development Authority, *National Capital Master Plan: Dodoma, Tanzania* (Toronto: Project Planning Associates, 1976), 69.
55 Hess, *Art and Architecture in Postcolonial Africa*, 124.
56 Kombe and Kreibich, *Informal Land Management*.
57 Ibid., 135.
58 Ibid., 132.
59 Ibid., 147.
60 Ibid.
61 J. Kironde, "Will Dodoma ever be the new capital of Tanzania?," *Geoforum* 24 (1993), 435.
62 Hess, *Art and Architecture in Postcolonial Africa*, 126.
63 Myers, *African Cities*.
64 Padraig Carmody, *The New Scramble for Africa* (Malden, MA: Polity Press, 2001).

65 J. Mikaili, "Arusha to get Sh 20bn shopping mall," *Guardian on Sunday* (online), September, 25, 2011, http://www/ippmedia.com; Lusekelo Philemon, "Arusha city plans new satellite town," *The Guardian* (online), August 17, 2011, http://www.ippmedia.com.
66 Felister Peter, "PS attacks lazy, negligent local govt politicians," *The Guardian* (online), September, 30, 2011, http://www.ippmedia.com.

Chapter 13: Jakarta's City Hall

A Political History

Abidin Kusno

The City Hall, a crucial feature of the European transformation of social space and of the emergence of urban modernity,[1] did not always represent civic identity, especially when situated in a colonial context. In the colony, the City Hall enacted practices that contradicted its ideal form as an institution of civic pride. There is thus a discrepancy of meaning between the City Hall in Europe and that in the colony even though they refer to the same building type and even though they might share an architectural style. An essay about the City Hall could therefore not be anything other than an inquiry into power relations within a specific context.

The significance of the City Hall in Jakarta would need to be understood within the socio-political relations of colonialism, postcolonial nation-building, and democratic transformation in the current era. This chapter outlines a loosely chronological history of the City Hall in Jakarta starting from the early formation of Batavia under the Dutch East India Company (VOC) and the colonial state to the era of decolonization, the subsequent authoritarian regime, and the present time of democratic reform. It traces a journey of Jakarta's City Hall from its status as the stadhuis of European merchant-administrators-turned-colonial state to its postcolonial incarnations. Along the way, I interpret the City Hall's symbolic elements in the urban setting to create what Laura Kolbe calls "a narrative element in the townscape" central to the justification of political rules, and reveal its contradiction by addressing the questions outlined below.[2]

Importantly, the story of the city hall in Jakarta is not of one, but of at least three buildings (Figure 13.1). The city hall as a site of governance has been moved several times and has been charged with new meaning to suggest the political ambitions of changing regimes, from the colonial era to the present. But the inscribed meaning has not always been stable. This chapter is an inquiry into the instability of the meaning of the city hall as public space, giving particular attention to the changing significance of architectural and spatial representation of power over time.

How did the City Hall contribute to the development of the political cultures of the state? What is the position of the City Hall within the broader dynamics of power relations between the city and the nation? How has the City Hall developed

City Halls and Civic Materialism

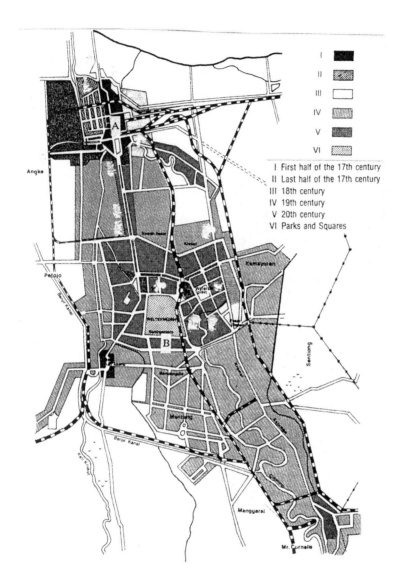

Figure 13.1
Analytical map of Jakarta (1938) indicating the locations of the city halls discussed in the chapter: (a) The *Stadhuis* of Batavia (1710); (b) The *Balai Kota* – City Hall – complex (1945, 1972) and the Governor's Office (1954); based on A. Surjomihardjo's Pemekaran Kota, Jakarta: Djambatan, 1977.

its inherited structures, leadership styles, and mission to address the challenge of the new times? In the context of shifting power, what kind of new socio-political spaces has the City Hall tried to open up? What can the symbolism of the City Hall tell us about old and the new political practices?

Such questions are framed around the idea that the City Hall is a symbol of civic autonomy embodied in the urban "public" space in critical relation to the authority of the state and private capital. While adorned with iconographic and symbolic elements to represent political idealism, the City Hall also bears the burden of an audience: as Chattopadhyay and White point out, City Hall "is more than a shell or a stage."[3] Instead, it is "the most public of public space." Yet, "its ability to accommodate the 'public' has yet to be explored."[4] Such ability has to be understood within the historical context of the formation and transformation of the City Hall in a particular place.

The colonial foundations of the City Hall in Batavia/Jakarta, along with its centralized mode of state governance, continued to structure the meaning of the City Hall in much of the postcolonial era. The attachment of the city to the nation-state has given the image of the City Hall as the citadel of authority rather than as the space for interplay between citizens and officials. With governors and council members appointed by the government and its ruling party (instead of being elected by citizens) throughout the twentieth century, the City Hall thus offered only limited access to the public. Such practices have contributed to the insulation of the City Hall from the general population. This is the main story of this paper, and it ends by addressing the weakening of national authority in the midst of neoliberal urbanization at the turn of the twenty first century, that has turned the City Hall into an arena of urban conflict as well as a space of hope in Jakarta today. Since the origin of Jakarta's City Hall is embedded in the ideology of the Netherlands East Indies Company, which itself evolved into a colonial state, I shall start with the stadhuis of Batavia.

VOC AND THE STADHUIS OF BATAVIA, EIGHTEENTH CENTURY

In 1770 the Danish painter Johannes Rach (1720–83), a member of the Royal Dutch East Indies Army, made a drawing of the stadhuis, the town hall of Batavia (Figure 13.2). Rach drew the Stadhuis 60 years after it was built. The building in his painting serves as a background to the square (known as the stadhuisplein), flanked on two sides by a row of tropical *kanari* trees. On the right, behind the trees, stand a fence and the New Dutch Church (Niew Hollandschekerk). On the left is the Tiger River (Tigergracht) and the houses of the wealthiest Batavians.

Figure 13.2
Johannes Rach's
Stadhuis, 1770.

City Halls and Civic Materialism

The stadhuis of Batavia was located at the center of Batavia *intramuros*, enclosed and surrounded by a deep moat and high coral rock walls, all forming a VOC (Dutch East India Company) town with a physical size of about 2,250 meters in length and 1,500 meters across.[5] The stadhuis is a two-story edifice, surmounted by a cupola-tower in a seventeenth-century Baroque style (Figure 13.2). Originally, the building housed "most of the attributes of Dutch municipal administration: the Board of Aldermen, trustees of the orphanage, civil court and jail, the Board of Marriage Registration."[6] The total building area is about 1,300 square meters with two main wings, and is today a museum with a collection of artifacts from Jakarta history since precolonial times. As a tourist location (Figure 13.3), every year the stadhuis offers a variety of festival events, such as the Jakarta Old Town Art Festival and the Coastal Tourism Festival 2011, which displayed a multicultural carnival of cultures.[7]

The circumstances that had led to the building of a stadhuis in 1710 are uncertain but it was built to replace an earlier, smaller, and perhaps unofficial building meant for the administration of the company.[8] Constructed under the rule of Governor General Abraham van Riebeeck (1709–13), the stadhuis was completed in three years (1707–10) by the VOC's craftsman W. J. van de Velde under the leadership of chief carpenter J. Kemmer. It is not clear if the style of the Batavia stadhuis was authorized by the VOC or suggested by the Governor General, but every social group in the town was coerced to contribute to the cost of construction. According to historian Leonard Blusse, the Chinese, an important minority group, "paid three times as much as did all other groups together."[9]

The monumental building and its square have obviously an important story to tell, as evidenced by Rach's work. The artist located the building and the square at the center of the picture, as a conspicuous statement of Dutch colonial rule and

Figure 13.3
The Stadhuis of Batavia, now Museum of Jakarta, January 2011.
Photograph taken by the author.

cultural dominance. The stadhuis and its square stand for the Company's authority and also its relation with its population, internally within the wall and externally with the surrounding populations. On a larger scale it represents the VOC's regional or global role and its relation to the Dutch Republic, the architectural style being modeled on that developed in the Netherlands. For some, it recalls the Paleis op de Dam, the erstwhile Town Hall of Amsterdam designed by Jacob van Campen in the seventeenth century.[10] One could also say that the neoclassical architectural style of the Batavia stadhuis, belonging to the age of enlightenment, sought to reflect the liberal values of the Dutch Republic. Johannes Rach's Batavia stadhuis seems to capture such a spirit (see Figure 13.2).

The square occupies the center of Rach's lithograph. In the figures that populate the square, the painter has skillfully captured the social structure of Batavia. There is a horse carriage carrying officers to the stadhuis; ladies accompanied by servants carrying an umbrella; slaves bringing water from the fountain at the center of the square; a merchant or vendor wandering around the square. After all, Batavia was a multiethnic town the occupants of which were brought together by the Company from different parts of Asia and the Indonesian archipelago.[11] From Rach's depiction we can imagine the square as a secular "civic center" or even a place of "civic pride" where the diverse population of Batavia met with or without interaction. It may well be a kind of "public space" with a sense of common good as represented by the water fountain and the patterns of trees providing the shade. But such appearances are deceptive. Batavia remained a slave town until Rach's death.

The slaves in Batavia were kept not merely for mills and households, but also for "retinues to flaunt the wealthy who were mostly Europeans."[12] In a town where "slaves stood out as the single largest population group,"[13] some of them must have found their way into the public square of Rach's painting. Abraham van Riebeeck, the Governor General under whom the stadhuis was built, embodied the complete contradiction of an eighteenth-century enlightenment man. He was said to be a "hater of all pomp" but he too took advantage of his wealth and position to indulge a passion for race horses, and he liked to be followed, when he rode, by a "great train of slave women on donkeys."[14]

As a colony, Batavia was run by the oligarchic barons of a corporation that recognized no civil rights. The Governor General acted like a local king, approving or disapproving decisions of the municipal board. Historian of VOC, Leonard Blusse, notes that the Dutch burghers were not given political power and were thus unable to form any real town community. The governing body of the Company had made clear that "we must remain the masters of the enterprise, even if that means the disposal of the Batavian citizenry."[15] The Company nevertheless protected its "citizens." It made efforts to create conditions that would prevent the Dutch from becoming the target of revolt or social unrest. For instance the wall that separated Batavia and its surroundings prevented an uninvited population from staying inside the town. From the beginning, the Company had banned Javanese (whose Kingdoms the Dutch subdued) from living within the walls.[16] The different ethnic groups that populated Batavia were divided through their separate kampongs, each organized by its pacified officer.[17] They were allowed to cultivate their diverse customs, religions, and languages to a degree, and within those confines. This early socio-spatial strategy of "divide and rule" continued throughout the history of Batavia, thus creating multiple affiliations and different quarters in the segregated city. In each of the separate kampongs, for instance, each ethnic group formed a relatively autonomous kampong quarter under the supervision of its own leaders with different scales of connections to the European power. For the "Indonesians" the stadhuis stood as symbol of the VOC's absolutism: it ruled not only by force and domination but also by preventing its population from forming a town "community." In this circumstance, the stadhuis did not represent the principle of civic government that its architectural style gestured.

As far as the colonized are concerned, much of the history, or better memory, of Batavia Town Hall and its square, would not be that of civic engagement. Instead what have prevailed are stories of people put in the underground jails, or torn to pieces, beheaded, hanged, and whipped under conditions of public spectacle. As a symbol of colonial absolute authority, one would imagine that the stadhuis would be the target of unrest, demonstrations, and revolts, but this did not happen. The only serious threat took place in 1740 and it came from Chinese peasants and coolies who, after suffering from oppression, marched to the town after hearing of the Company's plan to deport them to Ceylon, and the rumors of throwing them overboard on the trip.[18] Alarmed by the possibility of revolt from the sizeable numbers of Chinese who lived inside the wall, Europeans and Indonesians "spontaneously" attacked and burned 6–7,000 Chinese homes and massacred about a thousand of their inhabitants. While the Governor General did not order the massacre, he did nothing to stop the violence. The killing even took place in the jails of the stadhuis where 500 Chinese were brought out and killed, one by one.[19]

THE COLONIAL STATE AND THE NEW CITY OF THE NINETEENTH CENTURY

Johannes Rach's painting could be seen as both a parody and an idealized depiction of an unsustainable socio-political life of the colony in the eighteenth century. The painting was made three decades after the massacre of 1740 and three decades before the collapse of the VOC and the defeat of the Netherlands by the French army. The New Governor General, Wilhem Daendels (1808–11), sent by Louis Bonaparte, dismantled Batavia's *intramuros* and demolished the Company's fort. He used the rubble to build a new center of power at Weltevreden, some ten kilometers south of Batavia[20] (see Figure 13.1). With the European exodus to the south, to the healthier and drier Weltevreden, old Batavia was left crippled from the lack of resources. The "new Batavia" belonged to the age of the nineteenth-century colonial state and was centered on the suburban environment surrounding two major squares: the Koningsplein (the Kings's Square) and Waterlooplein (the

Waterloo Square). The vast field in the south allowed the space of colonial power to be born anew through the building of monumental government structures around the two squares that were designated as the new seat of colonial administration in Batavia. The pseudo Greek façades, which historian Handinoto calls the "Empire style," gave an air of authority to the palace, the gentlemen's club, the Schouwburg, officers' houses, military barracks and hospitals around the area.[21] Wealthy Europeans followed suit by building spacious bungalow-style residences, known as the Indies woornhuis, around the squares. The architecture and space of Weltevreden replaced the old company town of Batavia and gave an impression that "everything in Batavia is spacious, airy and elegant."[22]

In this new public architecture and the squares in the Weltevreden there was no new town hall to register the urban consciousness of the inhabitants. The old stadhuis of Batavia in the north continued to serve as the home of municipal government, and as a court that handled civic and criminal cases, all through the nineteenth century. As the stadhuis entered the nineteenth century, it shifted from being the town hall of a Company to being an apparatus of the colonial state. It remained, however, an institution of the *ancien regime* that provided no space for civic engagement. It remained a symbol of the centralized power of the Governor General. The burghers of Batavia, the European citizenry, were not even influential. They were "small in numbers and without leadership, representation, influence, money or prestige," and throughout much of the eighteenth and nineteenth centuries they were subordinated to the government.[23] It was only in the early twentieth century that the urban citizenry (mainly Europeans) emerged as an important force. The sign of their emergence came with the issuing of the Law of Decentralization by the King in the Netherlands, looking for ways to minimize the cost of governing the colony.

THE CITY COUNCIL IN THE LATE COLONIAL TIME

On July 23, 1903, the Law of Decentralization was passed allowing Batavia to assume autonomy over the city and, for the first time, establish a municipality.[24] The creation of the Batavia city council was the result of at least two factors. First was the attempt to minimize the city's financial burden on the Netherlands as decentralization would prompt the local government to generate its own revenues. Second was the Dutch liberal conscience and concomitant awareness of their neglect of the Indonesians who constituted a majority of the urban population.[25] The creation of the urban municipality was thus a mixture of colonial benevolence and entrepreneuralism, and not a product of popular pressure.

In a valuable study of the origin of urban municipality in colonial Indonesia, Peter Nas has shown how the institution was formed from "above," mainly for the interest of the Netherlands and the colonial state. Only later did it evolve, unofficially, into a relatively autonomous institution for the European (burgher) communities in the colony.[26] We thus have an instance where an urban municipality in colonial times was initially formed without the primary aim being local representation. It started out as an apparatus of the Netherlands Indies Government, with the Resident as the head of the municipality, and council members appointed by the colonial state. Nothing could be more telling of this intricate reform within the structure of the colonial state than its spatial representation in the architecture and urban setting. The office for the city council and the palace of the Governor General were located respectively on the South and North ends of the Koningsplein (the King Square). At the symbolic level, an axis was formed which linked the King (at the center) with the Governor General (at the North) and the City Council (at the South) (Figure 13.7). This configuration has survived decolonization. Today, the Koningsplein has been transformed into Independence Square with the National Monument at the center, and the palace of the Governor General has become the palace of the President of the postcolonial state. Meanwhile, the site for the city council building has been converted into the *Balai Kota* (City Hall) of Jakarta (see the section below).

With the structure of command dominated by the office of the Governor General, a municipal meeting could be nothing more than a meeting of state officials that, as Nas points out, eschewed political discussion.[27] This state-dominated city council remained largely intact throughout the colonial era, although dramatic changes nevertheless occurred behind the scene. Peter Nas succinctly summarizes the internal restructuring over the years:

> While political meetings were still forbidden, the municipal councils and local election associations offered the possibility of discussing local affairs officially and trying to realize fruitful ideas. The domination of the Netherlands Indies Government became restricted in the course of time. In 1908 the requirement that officials should constitute the majority of the appointed Europeans in the municipal council was abolished; after 1916 the place of the Assistant Resident heading the municipality was taken over by the more independent – council-nominated though government-appointed – mayor; after 1917 all the members of the council were elected; and after 1926 collegial executive councils (colleges van wethouders) were introduced. So, step-by-step the concept of administrative decentralization was redefined as the strengthening of the local autonomy of the European citizenry.[28]

From the 1920s onwards, with the "Indonesianization" of the civil service, "a small Indonesian elite served in the municipal councils … and even a few Indonesian mayors were appointed."[29] This new arrangement, altered from within the body of the state-dominated municipality, may well have been a response to the rise of an Indonesian elite and anticolonial sentiment in the colony, but it was also a reflection of the increasing power of the municipality to autonomously manage the city.

Throughout the remaining days of Dutch colonialism, the municipality gained more legitimacy as an agent of change for European communities.[30] The benefits for the Indonesian population, however, remained scant. The participation of Indonesians in the council, while affecting some policies, did not contribute much to the improvement of their communities.[31] The improvement of the indigenous Kampung in the mid-1920s was more a result of concern over the built environment inhabited by Europeans. This initiative had also not been entirely successful for it lacked the support and political will of the central government. In 1925, an Indonesian representative on the council, Dr. Soetomo, resigned. Other Indonesian members of the Council such as M. H. Thamrin and Abdoel Muis became famous only for their role in voicing criticism of the Euro-centricity of the municipality.[32] In their eyes, the municipality was formed to promote the primary interests of the European community. The urban municipality had nevertheless helped produce a circle of Indonesian nationalist elites who, after decolonization, took over the colonial government and the municipality.

THE SYMBOLIC POWER OF "INDIES WOONHUIZEN"

Decolonization can be understood as both a rupture and a continuation of power relations. It entails the appropriation of symbols and the investment of meanings into the architecture of the colonial era. The name of Batavia was changed to Jakarta, whereas the building for the Batavia City Council ("staadsgemeente raadhuis") was renamed "Balai Kota – the City Hall (Figure 13.4). In 1954, the Mayor of Jakarta, Sudiro, integrated the neighboring building for the Dutch Resident into the City Hall complex and used it as his office (Figure 5). This office has since become the office of the Governor of Jakarta, and it soon became the representative icon of Jakarta's City Hall. Since these two buildings (Figures 13.4 and 13.5) shared a similar architectural style, and one of them (see Figure 13.5) has survived until today as the office of the Governor and the icon of the City Hall, some thoughts about the building style and its symbolism are in order.

Figure 13.4
The Stadgemeente Raadhuis of the Dutch colonial era became the "Balai Kota" (City Hall) in 1945. The picture above is dated 1956. This building was demolished in 1972 and replaced by "Blok G," a 24-floor office of the municipality (see Figure 13.8).

City Halls and Civic Materialism ■

Figure 13.5
The office of the Governor, first used in 1954 and today the icon of the City Hall (next to it, on the right, is the high-rise Blok G [see Figure 13.8], which replaced the "Balai Kota" of Figure 13.4). Photograph by the author.

Both the "Balai Kota" City Hall and the Office of the Governor adopted what is called the style of "Indische woonhuizen" (Indies empire-style house). One might argue that the Indies house was inspired by the idea of the British colonial bungalow, but in colonial Indonesia it was known more as the "free-standing" house style of the Jakarta suburb in contrast to the densely packed row buildings of old Batavia. The Indies house thus emerged only in the nineteenth century following the European exodus to the suburbs of Batavia.[33] Susan Abeyasekere indicates that, in the nineteenth century:

> the Europeans built in a very different manner from that of the lower town, adopting the colonial empire style: uniformly white-painted, simple single-storey buildings with colonnaded galleries. Here the Europeans lived in a relaxed fashion in airy rooms overlooking potted plants, palms, sweet smelling frangipani and massive tamarind, kenari and other tropical trees.[34]

The Indies empire-style house encouraged not only leisure activities and social gatherings, but it also displayed power, social prestige, and government rank.[35] The elevated veranda often sustained by a series of columns (normally in Doric style) and small steps under a roof extended from the main building. The veranda at the front was the sign of a respectable urban house. With a slightly raised floor, like a stage, it makes the owner of the house an object to be seen from the street. It is a device for the expression and enactment of a respectable and thus powerful self.

Architectural historian Cor Passchieur points out that the colonial state incorporated the Indies "empire style" house into its repertoire of rank.[36] The Indies empire-style house of the Dutch Resident is thus part of the architectural order of power, but what is more important to us is that this building style is also favored by Indonesian elites. Photographs from the late nineteenth and early twentieth centuries often show the Indies house of the Dutch Resident and Javanese Regents. We can also see both Dutch and Javanese elites posing in front of their verandas. The Indies house is a symbol of authority to the Dutch as much as it is to the Indonesian nationalist elites. As an ambiguous and hybrid cultural product, the Indies house is open for appropriation and claims to ownership.

The office of the Jakarta Governor is today the "face" of the City Hall, and has become its icon (see Figure 13.5).[37] The front yard is adorned with pots of plants and a "welcoming" fountain. The house appears modest and open to public, but its veranda serves only as a platform for receptions, welcoming dignitaries, and launching municipal events. The whole complex is fenced off from the street. The building itself is registered as a heritage building, an amalgam of neo-classical and indigenous *Betawi* architecture. It has received several renovations especially in 1995, when the preservation effort was most "thorough, systematic and planned," but the façade has been kept "according to the original."[38]

Through its façade, the building projects a certain ethos. Its veranda is a symbol of elite dignity or at least, a desired self-image of the occupant. From there the body of the Governor is framed in a ritualized performance in relation to the interior space, which is divided into three core areas along an axis line: the Governor's Room, the Balairung (the royal audience hall), and Balai Agung (the grand hall).[39] The Balairung, located in front of the Governor's office, is adorned with additional pillars to resemble a Javanese *pendopo* (pavillion). The 1995 renovation placed much attention on calibrating the sequences of spaces, by way of elevation and decoration in order to emphasize the hierarchy.

THE NATIONALIST MUNICIPALITY (1950–98)

By the end of Mayor Sudiro's term in 1960, the municipality of Jakarta had been upgraded to *Pemerintah Ibu Kota Jakarta* (the capital city of the Indonesian Government's Capital City) headed by a Governor.[40] By then Jakarta had already been launched by President Sukarno as the "beacon of the newly emerging forces" of the decolonized nations of Asia and Africa. The Koningsplein was renamed *Lapangan Merdeka* (Independence Square), and Sukarno ordered a design of the National Monument and placed it at the center of the square. As a capital of the newly decolonized nation-state, the city could not be left autonomous. Instead, it was given the burden of representing the nation. It was expected to play the distinctive role of symbol of national unification and progress.

The subordination of the city to the nation is symbolized by the emblem of the municipality which shows the image of the National Monument at the center (Figure 13.6). The site plan of Independence Square also reflects the order of power (which is consistent with the layout of the colonial era), as shown in Figure 13.7. At the north is *Istana*, the President's Palace (ex-palace of the Dutch Governor

City Halls and Civic Materialism

Figure 13.6
The emblem of the municipality of Jakarta with the national monument at the center. Photo taken at the City Hall by Yudi Bachrioktora and author.

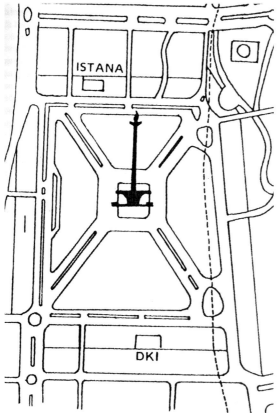

Figure 13.7
The site plan of Independence Square indicating the *Istana* (the President's Palace) on the north and *DKI* (the City Hall of Jakarta) on the south. Source: pamphlet for visitors to Jakarta in 1977, author's collection.

General) and at the south is City Hall (previously the seat of the stadgemeenten raadhuis), noted as *DKI,* both constituting a north-south axis with the National Monument at the center. Spatially, the City Hall complex does not have a public square of its own. It shares the Independence Square of the National Monument with the palace. The south side of the square thus "belongs" to the City Hall, and the north part is reserved for activities related to the palace of the President. While this is seemingly a form of power sharing between the city and the nation, this configuration (as I will discuss shortly) soon shows the power of the President over the Governor.

From the memories of five postcolonial governors of Jakarta under Sukarno from 1945–66, it has become clear that the interests of the centralized nation-state have dominated the city.[41] All through the subsequent Suharto period (1966–98), the capital city was under the direct control of the central government with the President appointing the governors, all of whom came from military backgrounds. With such a structure of command, the City Hall only represents the agenda of the nation with no need to justify its policies and actions in front of the public – a condition which has contributed to the formation of what urban historian Jo Santoso called "*Kota Tanpa Warga*" (a city without citizens), or to put it more mildly, a city with restricted citizen participation.[42] The City Council, the members of which were elected via political parties, is a collaborator, rather than a critic, of the Governor's policy. All the governors during the Suharto era worked within a social regime which demanded that the Governor be responsible to the head of state rather than the urban citizenry.

This is not to say that the Governor and the City Council have not shown concern for the citizenry. They have carried out government development programs to ensure that the living standards of the citizens have been improved. But with the appointment of a Governor and key members of the City Council at the discretion of the President and his ruling party, it is unlikely that the city hall could speak to power. Safely guarded by the authority of the state, the City Hall is not politically accessible to the public. It is located in front of the heavily guarded presidential palace across Independence Square, and it is unlikely that public protests could be mobilized near it.

While the national agenda structured the priorities of the city, the Governor of Jakarta was not always a passive agent. Governor Ali Sadikin, (1966–77), perhaps the most independent-minded Governor of the Suharto era, demonstrated how he could work for the city by empowering the citizens of Jakarta to voice their concerns about social justice.[43] This was conducted primarily through his support of what he called "free and responsible" journalism.[44] He also proposed a centralized communication unit to make the City Hall appear transparent and to prevent conflicting messages coming from the government to the public. He established connections with the public especially via the popular annual folk festival known as the "Jakarta Fair" held on the southern part of Independence Square facing the City Hall. He was able to increase the revenue of City Hall and establish a budgetary right to develop urban programs.[45]

Sadikin is remembered today as a Governor who (to a certain degree) promoted public participation and encouraged journalists to put forward critical comments on the city's performance. He is perhaps an exceptional case, as he worked during the formative period of Suharto's New Order when his personal leadership was much needed to register the authority of the City Hall and help modernize the physical space of the capital city. Sadikin nevertheless worked within the context of the state's pursuit of order and stability with almost zero tolerance for mass protests against the ruling regime. During his administration he monitored the workings of every social organization, making sure that these associations would never evolve into entities capable of political protest.[46] He enjoyed some freedom of maneuver and established his idealism, even though his mandate was to promote the agenda of the national government. As a backdrop to these activities, however, has stood an administration dominated by the military-supported central government. Assessing in the 1980s the difference the postcolonial City Hall had made for Jakarta, Susan Abeyasekere concludes that "as far as the Municipal Council is concerned, a big difference is that in the colonial period there was outspoken public criticism of the urban executive of a kind which does not exist today."[47]

In 1972, Sadikin expanded the office space of the municipality by constructing a 24-floor high-rise, "international-style" building known as Blok G. Seen as an architectural wonder at the time of its construction, even today it serves as a landmark (Figure 13.8).

For Sadikin, Blok G was a representation of national development and urban administrative reform. He believed that the City Hall needed a building that would symbolize modernity, innovative capacity, and the integrity of the administration. In addition such a building would contribute to the beautification of the city.[48] He considered the construction of Blok G a historic moment, for it replaced the building of the Dutch city council (see Figure 13.4).[49] Blok G, planned and constructed by Indonesian engineers, was intended to showcase the national engineering capacity and become the model for all subsequent high-rise buildings in Jakarta; it became synonymous with the modernization of the city administration. Along with the construction of Blok G, officially opened by President Suharto on April 28, 1976, a series of administrative buildings was built around the office of the Governor, all named by blocks, such as Blok C, D, E, H and in 1982, the building for the People's Representative for the Local Government (DPRD). Each of these buildings contains a complex inter-connected system, identified by nameless administrative blocks, in this way leaving an impression of a well planned cluster of impersonal bureaucracy (Figure 13.9).

Yet, for Indonesian urban scholars and activists, the City Hall during the Suharto era was merely a client of governmental and business patrons.[50] This sense has been particularly strong since the 1980s when the state liberalized the Indonesian economy and encouraged the city to privatize urban development. By the end of the 1980s, large-scale private urban development projects, such as shopping malls, office spaces, and "new towns" began to encroach massively into urban parks and displaced settlements of low-income neighborhoods in the city. In

Figure 13.8
The 24-floor Blok G, constructed in 1972 to replace the demolished "stadgemeenten raadhuis" used as "Balai Kota," 1950–72 (see Figure 13.4). Photograph by the author.

this (public-oriented) private space, the management office of developers could set up its own rule and in several instances violated city bylaws. The pervasive "privatization" of land in both the city and the peri-urban has further diminished the authority of the City Hall. While large scale new towns are located outside the territory of the Jakarta administration, several of them are in the city. In this self-contained town, autonomous township developed without any relation with the City Hall. What this means to the residents of these private estates is that the developer's management office is more relevant to their lives than the City Hall.

City Halls and Civic Materialism

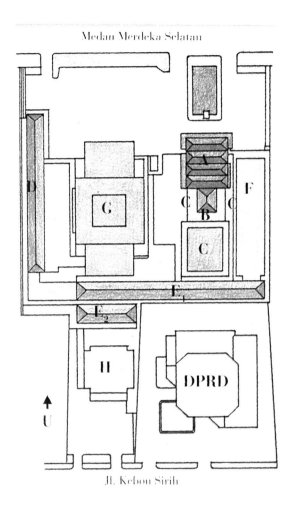

Figure 13.9
The cluster of the City Hall is identified by a series of "blocks." Block G and Block A (the Governor's Office) are at the front.

THE RETURN OF CITY HALL?

In 1999, a year after the fall of Suharto, the new government of Indonesia (through a consultation process with the World Bank and the IMF) introduced legislation conferring regional autonomy. As part of the efforts to dismantle the centralized authoritarian system of the country, regional autonomy set in motion a condition that has allowed the City Hall for the first time to play a leading role in urban development. For some this is a "neoliberal" withdrawal of the state and the promotion of the city as an "autonomous" entity to release its entrepreneurial spirit to compete over resources from both domestic and foreign investments. The 1999 legislation is basically an initiation of the transfer of power and resources from the state to the city (*kota*) and districts (*kabupaten*). By 2001, city and district administrations found themselves in the position of controlling their own political and economic affairs. While the idea behind this decentralization of power is to enhance productivity and economic recovery by an increased privatization of public services at the local level, it also ushers in a new era of more efficient government and greater public participation.[51]

The city government in Jakarta, while empowered by the new policy, is also subjected to unprecedented pressures from its residents who bring to the streets socio-economic issues almost on a daily basis. Unlike in the past, today the target of demonstrations includes the City Hall.[52] Governor Sutiyoso, who was appointed Governor during the authoritarian regime and survived the post-Suharto era, witnessed what he called the "time of madness" and "people's changing behavior." He was shocked to note that, during his first term between 1997–2002, "4,538 demonstrations were staged by Jakartans against me … from small-scale rallies to ones that led to anarchy."[53] For many Jakartans, the local autonomy program was not working well. The Governor was still appointed by the ruling party and President whereas the City Council, the only institution controlling the Governor, in the words of a critic, "does not exercise its authority properly as the councillors do not really serve as the people's representatives."[54] Instead, "the views of the public were often ignored by the City Council as corrupt councillors frequently colluded with the Governor or other executive leaders."[55] The legacy of excluding the public in the policy-making process continues to mark the City Hall of the post-Suharto era, but it encounters today an increasingly aggressive public that demands "democracy," "accountability," and the "rights to the city" by staging protests right in front of the City Hall.

In 2002, as protests against policies of the cities and the reappointment of Sutiyoso as Governor heightened, Sutiyoso decided to fence Independence Square with a four-meter high fence to prevent the site from becoming a ground of protests. The City Hall itself had been barricaded leaving protesters with a limited space for demonstration. Meanwhile, as if to anticipate the challenge of protests and demonstrations, the five supporting administrative centers, the offices of the mayors (*kantor Walikota*), have been rebuilt in a new location. Located relatively far from Independence Square, thus at a distance from the secured area, these buildings are carefully designed to prevent easy access by the public. The design of the building complex is not only monumental and intimidating but it also resembles a fortress which is protected by moats that run around the building complex.

Sutiyoso was the last appointed Governor of Jakarta. In 2007, for the first time a Governor was elected by residents of Jakarta. Candidates sought support from political parties, which in turn find Jakarta to be an important base for the mobilization of their ideologies. City Hall thus has further registered its presence as the site of struggles between different political parties. In the 2007 election for instance, candidate Adang Dorodjatun was supported by Partai Kesejahteraan Sosial (PKS), an influential Islamic Party. Alerted by the possibility that Jakarta might implement Sharia law if Dorodjatun won, 14 political parties came together to support Fauzi Bowo, today's Governor of Jakarta.[56] City Hall thus matters today, as urban politics becomes more relevant to the daily life of people in Jakarta. As an important arena for a struggle to define urban citizenship, the City Hall today has become the target of protests from a variety of emerging social movements in the city.

Unlike the rallies at the national institutions, which often address more general issues, protests in front of City Hall put forward more concrete grievances. For instance, in December 2008, a group of residents of Jakarta coastal areas staged a protest in front of City Hall demanding that the administration deal with ecological disasters, such as regular floods and heavily polluted seawater, which have affected their livelihoods.[57] In October 2009, around 100 drivers of three-wheeled "bemo" public transportation vehicles rallied in front of City Hall demanding a halt to raiding them. They parked some 50 old rusty bemo along the green strip of the street in front of the City Hall. They argued that the raids meant the loss of livelihood.[58] In the same month, a rally was also staged by the Street Parliament Alliance in front of the City Hall to push the newly elected councilor to sign "pro-poor" political contract. Toward the end of 2009, hundreds of labor unions and thousands of workers across Jakarta rallied outside City Hall to demand a higher minimum wage.[59] Contract teachers too staged a protest at the City Hall demanding an increase of their salary. They hurled plants, garbage, and tomatoes at the City Hall after having been denied a meeting with high-ranking administration officials.[60] In March 2010, over a thousand chicken vendors staged a series of protest against the plan to relocate poultry slaughterhouses from the inner city. The plan was drafted in response to the spread of avian influenza but vendors feared the plan would put them out of business.[61] In the same month, dozens of protesters representing progressive NGOs, such as the Urban Poor Consortium (UPC), the Jakarta Legal Aid Institute, the Indonesian Women's Coalition, and the Urban Poor Network forced entry to the City Hall to meet the Governor to demand retraction of the 2007 law on public order which had allowed the public order agency to act repressively.[62] Meanwhile, hardline ethnic organizations too, such as the Betawi Brotherhood Forum, staged protests in front of the City Hall to demand the review of public order.[63]

All the above instances show that the position of City Hall has become increasingly important in post-authoritarian Jakarta. The legislation and plan for the city is still laid down by the City Hall without public consultation, but its meaning has become the object of argument especially by those who are affected. The City Hall continues to maintain its authority by supporting the cultures of the middle class who would vote for the Governor, empowering certain values and practices while excluding others. However the politics of City Hall today is neither singular nor stable. With a relatively democratic election in place, the Governor would have to defend his position to a public who are increasingly aware of the importance of urban politics and social movements. The figure of Governor and the City Hall matter today. Jakarta's residents are increasingly engaged in municipal affairs via electoral politics as well as protests in front of the City Hall.

NOTES

1 See Mary P. Ryan, "'A laudable pride in the whole of us': city halls and civic materialism," in this volume.
2 Laura Kolbe, "Symbols of civic pride, national history or European tradition? City halls in Scandinavian capital cities," *Urban History* 35, no. 3 (2008), 413.
3 Swati Chattopadhyay and Jeremy White, "City halls: Civic representation and public space," this volume, 2.
4 Chattopadhyay and White, ibid.
5 Leonard Blusse, "An inane administration and insanitary town: The Dutch East India Company and Batavia (1619–1799)," in Robert Ross and Gerard J. Telkamp, eds., *Colonial Cities: Essays on Urbanism in a Colonial Context*, (Dordrecht: Martinus Nijhoff Publishers, 1985), 72.
6 Susan Abeyasekere, *Jakarta: A History* (Singapore: Oxford University Press, 1987), 19.
7 Tasa Nugraza Barley, "Putting the spotlight on Jakarta's Old Town," *Jakarta Globe*, 2 September 2011.
8 S. J. Heuken, *Tempat-tempat Bersejarah di Jakarta*, Jakarta: Cipta Loka Caraka, 1997.
9 Leonard Blusse, "Batavia, 1619–1740: The rise and fall of a Chinese colonial town," *Journal of Southeast Asian Studies* 12, no. 1 (1981), 166.
10 Pradaningrum Mijarto, "Paleis op de Dam dan Stadhui Batavia," Kompas.com, Juni 9, 2010. http://www1.kompas.com/readkotatua/xml/2010/06/09/2144562/paleis.op.de.dam.dan.stadhuis.batavia
11 Abeyasekere, *Jakarta*, 14.
12 According to Abeyasekere, by the beginning of the nineteenth century, slave owners include Chinese, Arab, Indian, and even Indonesians. Ibid., 22.
13 Ibid., 21.
14 Jean Gelman Taylor, *The Social World of Batavia: Europeans and Eurasians in Colonial Indonesia* (Madison: University of Wisconsin Press, 2009 [1983]), 57.
15 A statement in a letter from the Company dated 1651, as cited in Blusse, "An inane administration," 75.
16 Blusse, "Batavia," 169.
17 Ibid., 169.
18 Ibid., 176.
19 Abeyasekere, *Jakarta*, 26.
20 Blusse, "An inane administration," 75.
21 See Handinoto, "Indische empire style," *Dimensi* (20 December 1994), 1–14; see also Handinoto, "Daendel dan Perkembangan Arsitektur di Hindia Belanda Abad 19," *Dimensi* 36, no. 1 (2008), 43–53.
22 Abeyasekere, *Jakarta*, 57.
23 Peter Nas, "The origin and development of the urban municipality in Indonesia," *Sojourn*, 5, no. 1 (1990), 89.
24 Ibid., 86.
25 Ibid., 90–2.
26 Ibid., 101–5. Nas describes the complex linkage and negotiations between the top level (consisting of the King and his ministry in the metropole), the middle level (the Governor General and his Residents in the colony), and the lower level (i.e. the European citizenry in Batavia) that led to the formation of the municipality. Each of these levels had different interests and even assumed different issues and contexts. In the end, the middle level took the lead and defined what "local authority" really meant in the colony, that is "bureaucratic decentralization in order to reduce the burden of the governmental apparatus." Ibid., 101.
27 Ibid., 102.

28 Ibid., 102.
29 Ibid., 103.
30 The increasing legitimacy of the municipality allowed architects at the time, such as Thomas Karsten, to design in 1937 a Raadhuis (a building for the city council) at the center of Koningsplein. Karsten had in mind a new form of governance with the municipality above the authority of the state. His plan however never got beyond the drawing board, as the Dutch surrendered to the Japanese military government in 1942. For a discussion of Karsten's design, see Abidin Kusno, *The Appearances of Memory*, (Durham: Duke University Press, 2010), Ch. 7.
31 Nas, "The origin," 107.
32 Ibid., 107; see also Abeyasekere, *Jakarta*, 108; Susan Abeyasekere, "Colonial urban politics: The Municipal Council of Batavia," *Kabar Seberang* 13–14, (1984), 17–24.
33 Historian of Jakarta, Adolf Heuken, calls the style of the Indies house "tropical classicism" for it brings together both European classical and Javanese/Betawian references. The veranda recalls the *pendapa* (pavilion for welcoming guests) of the traditional Javanese house, and the architectural language, especially the Doric columns, offers the authority of the West. See Adolf S. J. Heuken and Grace S. T. Pamungkas, *Menteng: "Kota Taman" Pertama di Indonesia*, (Jakarta: Yayasan Cipta Loka Caraka, 2001).
34 Abeyasekere, *Jakarta*, 54.
35 See Handinoto, "Indische empire style."
36 According to Cor Passchier: "In 1854 for reasons of both hierarchy and economy, the central government felt the need to regulate the different types of housing for diverse higher- and lower-ranking governmental officials, and later on (in 1870) decreed standard designs for the housing of the indigenous regents (*bupati*), followed (in 1879) by standards for the European district officers (resident and controlleur)." See "Colonial architecture in Indonesia: References and development," in Peter Nas, ed., *The Past in the Present: Architecture in Indonesia*, (Rotterdam: NAi Publishers, 2006), 103.
37 See Sudiro, "Sudiro" in Soedarmadji Damais, ed., *Karya Jaya: Kenang Kenangan Lima Kepala Daerah Jakarta 1945–1966*, (Jakarta: Pemerintah Daerah Khusus IbuKota Jakarta, 1977), 124.
38 Soedarmadji Damais, ed., *Gedung Balai Kota Jakarta: Jalan Merdeka Selatan No. 8*, (Jakarta: Pemda DKI, 1996), 19.
39 Damais, ibid., 23.
40 Jakarta was only formalized in 1964 by President Sukarno as the capital city of the nation, ending several discussions and debates since 1955 about whether the capital city should be in Palangkaraya to be less "Jakarta-centric." Sudiro, "Sudiro," 94.
41 Soedarmadji Damais, ed., *Karya Jaya: Kenang Kenangan Lima Kepala Daerah Jakarta 1945–1966* (Jakarta: Pemerintah Daerah Khusus IbuKota Jakarta, 1977).
42 See Jo Santoso, *Kota Tanpa Warga* (Jakarta: Gramedia, 2006).
43 Suryono Herlambang indicates that as the city moved forward to embrace the global economy in the 1990s it also left behind the legacy of Ali Sadikin which sought to establish a public (middle class) participatory urban life. See Suryono Herlambang, "Kisah Lapangan Monas, Politik Kota dan Hak Atas Kota," in Chri Verdiansyah, ed., *Politik Kota dan Hak Warga Kota* (Jakarta: Kompas, 2006), ix–xxii.
44 Ali Sadikin, *Gita Jaya: Catatan H. Ali Sadikin, Gubernur Kepala Daerah Khusus Ibukota Jakarta 1966–1977* (Jakarta: Pemda Khusus Ibu Kota Jakarta, 1977), 109.
45 For urban planner and critic Suryono Herlambang, the demise of the City Hall in the Suharto era was marked by the removal in 1991 of the Jakarta Fair (started in 1968 by Ali Sadikin), from the site in front of the City Hall to the ex-airport land of Kemayoran where the Fair was turned into a corporate "trade exhibition." Herlambang, "Kisah Lapangan Monas," xiii–xiv.

46 Sadikin noted that "many social organizations were connected to the interest of political and mass mobilization." Sadikin, ibid., 141.
47 Abeyasekere, "Colonial urban politics," 25.
48 Sadikin, ibid., 87.
49 Ibid., 88.
50 Manasse Malo and Peter Nas indicate the dominance of "strategic groups" that comprised governmental and business groups in directing urban development in Jakarta. "The military and the administration form one governmental strategic group that is very dominant in administrative affairs and urban planning. The business community, including the banks, industry, and large developers also has strategic resources at its disposal, and in co-operation with the government strategic group it effectively determines the development of Jakarta by the construction of offices, malls and houses." See Manasse Malo and Peter J. M. Nas, "Queen City of the East and Symbol of the Nation: The Administration and Management of Jakarta," in Jurgen Ruland, ed., *The Dynamics of Metropolitan Management in Southeast Asia* (Singapore: ISEAS, 1996), 130. See also Robert Cowherd,"Planning or cultural construction? The transformation of Jakarta in the late Soeharto period" in Peter J. M. Nas, ed., *The Indonesian Town Revisited* (Singapore: Institute of Southeast Asian Cities, 2002), 17–40.
51 World Bank, *Cities in Transition: Urban Sector Review in an Era of Decentralization in Indonesia*, East Asia Urban Working Paper Series, Dissemination Paper No. 7, Urban Sector Development Unit, Infrastructure Department, East Asia and Pacific Region, World Bank, 2003: 78–84.
52 The ground of protests in Jakarta is often associated with national symbols (such as the Thamrin-Sudirman corridor), such as the presidential palace, the ministries' offices, the parliament, the central bank and the Supreme Court, but the City Hall today has also increasingly become the target of protests especially for issues related to local legislation. For a discussion of protest movements in Jakarta, see Merlyna Lim, "Transient civic spaces in Jakarta demopolis," in Mike Douglass, K. C. Ho, and Giok Ling Ooi, eds., *Globalization, the City and Civil Society in Pacific Asia: The Social Production of Civic Spaces* (New York: Routledge, 2008), 211–20.
53 As cited in "Sutiyoso: Most maligned governor?," *Jakarta Post*, November 11, 2002.
54 Andi Mallarangeng as cited in Bambang Nurbianto, "Undemocratic Jakarta makes mockery of local autonomy implementation," *Jakarta Post*, November 19, 2002.
55 Mallarangeng as cited in Nurbianto, ibid.
56 "Upaya Menerapkan Hukum Syariah: Jakarta Target Utama PKS," *Berita Kota*, August 5, 2007.
57 "Come on shore," *Jakarta Post*, December 17, 2008.
58 "Bemo dan Bajaj Serbu Balai Kota DKI," *Warta Kota*, July 20, 2010; Indah Setiawati, "Include us in decision-making," *Jakarta Post*, October 31, 2009; see also "Contract teachers throw tomatoes at City Hall," *Jakarta Post*, July 1, 2010.
59 "Hundreds protest for minimum wage increase," *Jakarta Post*, December 9, 2009.
60 "Guru PNS Berunjuk Rasa," *Warta Kota*, March 27, 2010; "Pendemo ancam duduki Balai Kota," *Berita Kota*, July 1, 2010; "Guru DKI Tuntut Tunjangan Kerja Daerah," *Media Indonesia*, June 22, 2010.
61 Indah Setiawati, "City administration tells sellers to find new jobs," *Jakarta Post*, March 24, 2010.
62 Hasyim Widhiarto, "NGOs rally for public order agency dismissal," *Jakarta Post*, March 13, 2010.
63 "FBR stages protest demanding review of public order agency after deadly clash," *Jakarta Post*, April 15, 2010.

Chapter 14: Seoul Spectacle

The City Hall, the Plaza and the Public

Hong Kal

On May 24, 2012, after three years of construction and $256 million of expenditure, the new Seoul City Hall was finally unveiled to the public. The thirteen-story glass-walled building looms over the historic old city hall, a neo-classical stone building erected in 1926, during the Japanese colonial period (1910–45) (Figure 14.1). The contrast between the old and the new designs surely contributes to the spectacle of the new building. It shows the new era of Seoul as a world-class city. The image of progress under capitalist growth is sustained by the image of a better public architecture.

The new city hall is part of a series of urban renewal projects undertaken by municipal authorities in the last decade or so to make Seoul a competitive world city. The mega projects launched include the Cheonggye Stream Restoration (2005), the Seoul Plaza (2004), the Han River Renaissance Project (2006–13), the Gwanghwamun Square (2009), the new Seoul City Hall (2012), and the Dongdaemun Design Plaza and Park (2013). In all these projects, the notion of "public" is foregrounded: it is both a justification and an effect.

Figure 14.1
The new Seoul City Hall built in 2012 behind the old City Hall. Source: reprinted from *Yonhap News*.

In Korea, until the 1990s, the term "public" (kong gong) was hardly used and it was only associated with state institutions. Not until the last decade has the idea of the public become a crucial part of popular discourse. The new "public" seems to carry a double meaning. First, it emphasizes the sphere of civil society and its association with citizenship, democracy, communication, participation, and openness that would challenge both the forces of the neoliberal market and the undemocratic state.[1] Second, it reveals the crisis of the public as the nation's ongoing economic liberalization since the 1990s has led to problems of massive lay-offs, labor flexibility, privatization, and increasing class division.[2] The Seoul City Hall materializes this double meaning of the public. Its new architecture and the Seoul Plaza in front of it are part of the city government's strategic plan to brand Seoul as a world-class civic entity. They are also attempts to come to terms with an ever-worsening socio-economic polarization and the pressure from members of civil society who claim their rights to protest in public space. This essay analyzes the recent debates and conflicts around the City Hall and shows how they represent a contestation over the meaning of the public in Korea today.

The essay focuses on the creation of Seoul Plaza in 2004 and its concomitant construction of the new City Hall. I examine how they both serve as a stage of spectacle to unite the urban population, which has been increasingly fragmented by deepening socio-economic division. By spectacle I mean the constitution of society through images of new public architecture at the time of a major economic transformation, in this case the post-1997 financial crisis.[3] The spectacle was not uncontested. People took to the City Hall plaza to demonstrate their resentment over government policies. The City Hall thus symbolizes at once democracy, insurgency, and spectacle. It is a crucial element in the struggle between the Korean state and its citizenry to frame a new identity amid the changing economic, political, and social milieu.

COLONIAL ORIGINS

Seoul's City Hall is a historical document of modern Korea. In 1910, the colonial government opened the Seoul City Hall (Kyŏngsŏngbu ch'ŏngsa) in the building originally constructed in 1896 for the Japanese Consulate in downtown Seoul. In 1926, the city hall was moved to a new building built to administer the growing colonial capital (Figure 14.2). The building was designed by a group of Japanese architects as a four-story reinforced-concrete structure designed in an early-twentieth-century Beaux Arts style with a total floor space of 8,272 square meters. It sought to integrate the latest construction technology with a received academic vocabulary considered suitable for state institutions. As an important part of the colonial administrative apparatus, the City Hall was located strategically, at the junction of two main boulevards: the north-south boulevard running from the Government General of Korea through Seoul Train Station down to Chosŏn Shinto Shrine, and the east-west boulevard, which served business establishments downtown.[4] Standing at the intersection of the political and economic axes of

City Halls and Civic Materialism

Figure 14.2
The Seoul City Hall built in 1926 during the Japanese colonial period.

power, the tall structure dwarfed nearby traditional buildings, such as the Deoksugung Palace of the Chosŏn dynasty where the Korean king, Kojong, resided until his death in 1919.

The space in front of the City Hall contains historical memories of modern Korea. The area was originally created in the late 1890s by King Kojong as part of the expansion of the Deoksugung Palace. The king intended to build a site for public gatherings as part of his effort to modernize the country at a time when foreign imperial powers increasingly threatened his rule. Despite his reform effort, Chosŏn was annexed by Japan in 1910. When Kojong died on January 21, 1919, Koreans assembled in front of the Deoksugung Palace to mourn the king's death. On March 1, 1919, on the same spot, Koreans staged a mass uprising against Japanese colonial rule. Despite the military police's attempts to contain them, the protests that followed rapidly spread to the whole country, gathering over two million participants. These first public displays of resistance resulted in a major change in the colonial strategy of governing Korea: the government's approach towards the colonized population shifted to a more subtle policy, known as Cultural Policy, intended to change the military image of colonial rule.

In 1926 the City Hall was built adjacent to the site of the anticolonial popular uprising. The building of the City Hall thus could be seen as a strategy of the colonial state to erase public memory of resistance and to contain further popular resistance by creating an officially controlled public space. The strategy of colonial pacification was reflected in the building's design. Compared to the Government General building that was constructed in the same year, the City Hall was lower in height, smaller in size, and simpler in design. According to Iwatsuki Yoshiyuki, one of the architects involved in the building design, the City Hall was intended to be more functional and less intimidating to the public.[5] As the first government building dedicated to the management of the city and its population, the city hall could be seen as an ultimate symbol of colonial service to the public. This concept, however, was not entirely new. During the Chosŏn dynasty, "public" (공, 公) as a counterpart of "private" (사 私), connoted the ethical norms that applied to the ruling class. In other words, the "public" was associated with the ruling elite and was not applied to ordinary people. After Chosŏn was forced to open doors in 1876, the term became more widely applied, but not until the colonial period did it extend to ordinary people. This broader application came about, in particular, through the expansion of public spaces such as public schools, public parks, and public buildings. In all of these, the city hall was an ultimate symbol of colonial service to the public. As historian Hwang Byoung-joo points out, the idea of the public was an essential part of the ideology of colonial rule.[6] Japanese colonial rule, he stresses, was not simply exploitation but the production of the modern colonial Korean subject, which was coeval with the production of the Korean public. However, it should be noted that this colonial promotion of the idea of the public did not mean that Koreans were given political rights. Excluded from political participation, they comprised the public of the non-political sphere governed by the "benevolent" colonial state. It is in this sense that Hwang refers to "colonial public." During the colonial period, the space in front of the City Hall was emptied of political assemblies.[7] It served only as a traffic circle. This view of the public as a sphere of the state was carried over into postcolonial Korea, with the city hall serving as a representation of the state-controlled public body. In the postcolonial era, however, the public has become more critical towards the state and the City Hall, too, has become the site for contestation over the definition of the public.

THE SPACE OF RESISTANCE

After independence in 1945, the City Hall building continued to serve for the capital of the Republic of Korea. Even though the space in front of the City Hall remained a traffic circle, it became a focal site for mass rallies. For instance, in 1960, students gathered around the City Hall in protest against government corruption, resulting in the resignation of Rhee Syngman (1948–60), the first President of the Republic of Korea. One year after Rhee's forced resignation, Park Chung-hee (1963–79) took power in a military-led coup. He built the national economy through state programs of modernization. Highways, paved roads, high-rise buildings, and mega-industrial facilities rose as monuments to national productivity, progress, and industrialization. In the 1960s and 1970s, Korea's phenomenal economic development was achieved by the state's active role in industrialization. The Park Chung-hee government intervened in the economy through policies that tightly controlled and protected domestic businesses, industries, and markets. However, President Park was also responsible for the authoritarian rule of the country. Throughout his tenure, political assemblies were forbidden and the government did not hesitate to crack down on them. Perhaps for fear of being used by anti-government protesters, no open public spaces were created in downtown Seoul.[8]

Even under close police surveillance, however, people took to the streets to protest against the authoritarian regime, confronting the riot police. In the 1980s with the advent of the new military rule led by Chun Doo-hwan (1981–87), street struggles became more radical and spread to the urban middle class. The climax was reached in the summer of 1987 when hundreds of thousands of people assembled in front of the City Hall and demanded a constitutional amendment requiring a direct presidential election system which led to the democratic transition of the country in the 1990s. The gathering at the City Hall occurred not only because the area could accommodate a large number of people, but also because it contained historical memories as the site of public resistance. The "power of place," which recalled mass uprisings in the past, seems to have contributed to the making of the area around the City Hall as a symbolic political center of the city.

In Korea, the process of democratization has taken place during the transition to neoliberalism. The popular democracy movement of 1987, as Byung-doo Choi points out, was a turning point in the nation's political and social changes "from a military authoritarian developmental state to a relatively more democratic neoliberal state."[9] The importance of the City Hall and the eventual creation of Seoul Plaza in front of it, came in the context of the nation's transformation towards democratization which coincided with the state's adoption of neoliberal policies since the 1990s. President Kim Young-sam (1993–98) proclaimed globalization, translated as "segyehwa," as a necessity for national survival, which meant reforming every aspect of Korean society. In his globalization drive, Kim pushed financial liberalization and the capitalist market, along with a series of deregulations to facilitate international capital flow. In the end, Kim's globalization drive "turned out to be a dismal failure with the financial crisis in 1997."[10]

When Kim Dae-jung (1998–2003), a long-time opposition party leader, was elected President in 1997, he faced the urgent task of coping with the crisis. His solution was to follow the neoliberal reforms demanded by the International Monetary Fund (IMF). With the financial bail-out arranged by the IMF, the government implemented restructuring programs towards further financial and trade liberalization, labor-market flexibility, public sector privatization and corporate reorganization, all of which are the core tenets of neoliberal reform around the world. The subsequent Roh Moo-hyun government (2003–08), known for its progressive politics, continued to support the neoliberal economy and initiated a Free Trade Agreement with the US. Despite the allocation of more funds for social security and public assistance, democratic governments of the period embraced neoliberal ideas. Democratization in Korea has an ambivalent relation with neoliberalization. For instance, during the democratization period, any attempt to transform old institutional arrangements, including neoliberal reforms, appeared to be a radical departure from the developmental authoritarian state.[11] The conservative Lee Myung-bak government (2008–13) more explicitly carried out neoliberal policies towards further labor-market flexibility and privatization of public sectors. As a result, economic inequality, accompanied by serious social and spatial polarization, has been exacerbated.[12] In this context, the "public" emerged as a central subject of debate. As pointed out earlier, it used to refer largely to the realm of state authority such as government, military, and police during the state development era in Korea. What is noticeable in the last decade is an explosion of the term, ranging from public welfare to public art. The growing attention to the "public" indicates the contestation over its meaning. For instance, civic groups have called for an alternative notion of the public that is based on democracy, justice, communication, participation, and openness, detaching it from its association with an undemocratic state. Lee Myung-bak as the Mayor of Seoul (2002–06) was quick to co-opt the idea of the public. He promoted the new image of "public" via urban redevelopment projects where citizens would be allowed to assemble in newly created "public spaces" and to participate in the celebration of Seoul becoming a world-class city. Central to this new approach was the creation of Seoul Plaza in front of the City Hall, the first public plaza in downtown Seoul.

THE PLAZA AND THE NEW PUBLIC

Mayor Lee's idea of constructing Seoul Plaza was not an instance of state benevolence. Rather, it was a case of the state being compelled to respond to a series of spontaneous public gatherings. In June 2002 a crowd of people gathered in front of the City Hall to cheer for the Korean soccer team during the FIFA World Cup soccer tournament. The cheering crowds were not mobilized by political vanguards such as students, activists, or workers but brought together by internet communication. The participants of the mega global sports entertainment collectively cheered "Taehan min'guk" (Korea), all wearing red t-shirts (Figure 14.3). A few months later, in December 2002, people spontaneously gathered again. This time they held a candlelight vigil to protest the death of two schoolgirls

Figure 14.3
The crowd gathered in front of the City Hall to cheer for the Korean soccer team during the FIFA World Cup soccer tournament in June 2002. Source: reprinted from *Yonhap News*.

killed by a US military vehicle on military exercise. The vigil culminated in front of the City Hall. A majority of ordinary citizens including young school students, homemakers, and office workers assembled there waving lighted candles, transforming the traffic circle into a public space for grievance and hoping to deliver their political messages to the government.

Witnessing the political potential as well as threat of the new form of popular assemblies that have moved "from street corners to plaza" in Cho Myungrae's term,[13] Mayor Lee formally designated the space as a public plaza.[14] On May 1, 2004, Seoul Plaza was opened with Hi Seoul Festival, an annual official festival, redesignating what was once a space of insurgency as a space of festive spectacle under the theme of "refreshing, exciting and dynamic."[15] Declaring, "Seoul Plaza is open for 24 hours. Please, everyone, enjoy to the full," Mayor Lee seemed intent on making the plaza a public celebration for the city to pursue new urban life.[16] Yet the new plaza, promoted as an open, vital, and pedestrian-centered public space, soon became a focal site of conflicts between authority and people. To keep political protesters off the ground, one month after its opening, the city government enacted the Seoul Plaza Ordinance that limited the use of the plaza to "citizen's wholesome leisure and cultural activities" and required the Mayor's official permission for any event that took place in it.[17] The underlying rationale is that for the plaza to become a civic space it should be subject to rules that protect its function. Civic groups, however, criticized the ordinance for violating the principle that a public space should be open, free, diverse, and interactive without any coercion by powerful institutions. Despite the criticism, the city council, composed of a majority of members from the conservative Grand National Party, passed the ordinance. Only cultural events and official ceremonies were then allowed in the plaza.[18]

Despite the effort to ban political activities, the plaza became a central venue for popular protests with even greater participants. In April 2008 when the Lee Myung-bak government agreed to reopen the market to US beef imports that were previously banned after a cow infected with mad cow disease was found in the US, hundreds of thousands of people took to the streets of downtown Seoul carrying candles to express their concern for food safety and opposition to the government's ratification of FTA with the US. The candlelight demonstrations lasted over three months. They were concentrated in Cheonggye Plaza, located at the entrance to the redeveloped Cheonggye waterfront, and later in Seoul Plaza to accommodate the increased number of participants (Figure 14.4).[19] The events outlined above underline the irony that these two plazas were created by Lee during his mayoral term as his signature projects to make Seoul a culturally vibrant, environmentally pleasant, and pedestrian-centered city. In those public plazas emblematic of his achievement, protesters challenged the President, chanting "No FTA" and "Lee Myung-bak, Out."

The city hall plaza by then had fallen into the hands of the public. During the candlelight assemblies, people turned the plaza into a festive space by organizing music concerts and other events.[20] While using the plaza as a space of resistance,

Figure 14.4
A huge crowd of candlelight protesters gathered in front of the City Hall in 2008. Source: photo by Yu Sŏng-ho.

they also used festivities as an integral part of their protest and subverted the authorities' claim on the plaza as spectacle. In response, large numbers of riot police were deployed to disperse protesters and keep them off the plaza. A year later the plaza was again turned into a battleground between people and the city government. On May 2, 2009, a group of people who wanted to celebrate the first anniversary of the candlelight campaign against US beef imports clashed with the police in the plaza during the opening event of the Hi Seoul Festival. A few weeks later, on May 27, a huge crowd gathered again in the plaza grieving the death of the former president Roh Moo-hyun who killed himself on May 23 amid an intense investigation of an alleged bribery case against him, leaving the government vulnerable to the criticism that the politically motivated investigation might have caused his suicide. Out of the fear that it might develop into another mass protest, Mayor Oh Se-hoon (2006–11) banned the mourners who tried to set up a memorial service in the plaza. In accordance with the city government's ban, the riot police chased protesters out and established a blockade by lining up buses around it. The scene of the plaza blocked by police was taken as visible evidence of the undemocratic nature of the central and city governments (Figure 14.5).

In June, 2009, civic groups such as People's Solidarity for Participatory Democracy claimed the plaza for the public. This time, they launched a grassroots campaign to amend the ordinance so that people might be allowed to use the plaza for political assemblies and demonstrations as guaranteed by the constitution. In March 2010, with 85,000 signatures collected from city residents, they submitted a motion to amend the ordinance to the city council. As the motion was voted down in the city council, they soon organized a campaign in the election in June against those council members voting against the motion. As a result, the opposition, the Democratic Party, for the first time won a majority of seats in the city council and the amendment was passed.[21]

City Halls and Civic Materialism

Figure 14.5
Seoul Plaza blocked by lining up police buses, 2009. Source: photo by Kwon U-sŏng.

There was much more at stake in the city hall plaza than the issue of securing it. The struggles over the plaza raised the question of how to define both "public" and "public space." As Don Mitchell points out, "By claiming space in public, by creating public spaces, social groups themselves become public"; the Seoul city hall plaza becomes a public space when people claim their rights to be part of the public by making themselves visible to other members.[22] One may speculate that the significance of the discourse of public, which has rapidly gained importance in the last decade in Korea, along with the terms citizenship, participation, and accessibility, seems to have emerged out of the struggles over the city hall plaza. The ideas of the "public" and "public space" find most explicit expression and contestation in the spectacles of the city hall plaza. It is in this context that the city government tried to restore its legitimacy in the eyes of the public through building a new city hall.

ARCHITECTURE OF CONTAINMENT

In 2005, before ending his mayoral term, Lee Myung-bak announced a plan to construct a new building for the Seoul City Hall. This project would complete his series of urban spectacles, which have included the Cheonggyechon waterfront and Seoul Plaza. The plan for a new City Hall building was not new but this time it was proposed to be built right behind the old City Hall building. A design competition was held with a guideline that the new City Hall building ought to represent "the place's history and symbolism, a harmony between tradition and technology, and a space for citizens."[23] The selection process was far from smooth. The chosen design, featuring a 22-story building by Samsung Corporation Consortium, was rejected by the Cultural Heritage Committee of the Cultural Heritage Administration. The main criticism was that the high-rise building was not in harmony with nearby low-rise traditional buildings such as the Deoksugung Palace. The design was revised several times in six meetings between June 2006 and October 2007.[24] Yet the negotiation with the Cultural Heritage Committee did not lead to a resolution. For Mayor Oh, who took over the project from Lee, the revised final design looked too plain and not spectacular enough. The Mayor held a new competition with four invited architects and selected the design of architect Yu Köl in 2008.

The winning design features a building (comprising five stories underground and thirteen stories above the ground with a total floor space of 80,254 square meters on a site covering 12,709 square meters), embodying the key concepts, "tradition, citizens and future." The building was intended to blend design aspects

Figure 14.6
The Eco Plaza inside the new City Hall. Source: photograph by the author.

City Halls and Civic Materialism

of traditional Korean architecture, such as protruding curved eaves and horizontality, with contemporary expression.[25] Yet the building looks radically modern and futuristic as it is enclosed in 7,000 glass wall panels and built with eco-friendly cutting-edge technologies. What is most significant is not only the spectacular appearance but also its interior space. In its front section, it has a huge, vertical space, named Eco Plaza, seven stories high and covered with glass walls. It was meant to be a vertical extension of the plaza outside (Figures 14.6 and 14.7). The architect describes the idea as follows: "When entering the building, one will first encounter the vertical open garden. It is designed to be like a plaza where the grass climbs up the walls."[26] The new City Hall indeed shows an explicit reference to Seoul Plaza. The concept of the plaza as an open space is repeated throughout the space. For instance, other small plazas are designed "for citizens to walk up to the end of the building."[27] The new City Hall built with the concept of an open space symbolizes transparency, connectedness, and accessibility as if to replace the controversial and uncontrollable plaza outside.

DEBATING THE OLD CITY HALL

Meanwhile, in the process of remaking the City Hall's new identity, the question of what to do with the old City Hall building became a focus of debate. The city government was determined to remove the old building from its original site. To justify its position, the city government even mobilized the claim raised by anticolonial nationalists that when seen from the aerial view, the City Hall forms the second character of "Japan" (本 of 日本) and it supposedly complements the former Government General building built in the shape of the first character of "Japan" (日 of 日本). The reason for this formalist reading is that the old City Hall would then follow the fate of the former Government General building, which was demolished in 1995. Invoking the public sentiment of anticolonialism and also potential safety problems of the old building, the city government campaigned for

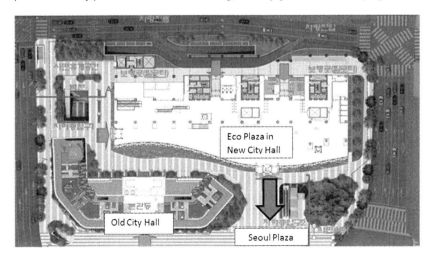

Figure 14.7
A plan of the new City Hall and the old City Hall. Source: reprinted from Seoul metropolitan government official website, accessed May 2011.

the removal of the old City Hall. The proposal was opposed, however, by civic groups, professionals, and the Cultural Heritage Committee. For them, the proposal was tantamount to vandalizing a historical building.[28] The building, a Registered Cultural Property, represents the architectural and technological development of that time and also houses the history of 32 mayors of Seoul in postcolonial Korea.[29] The conservationists strongly advised the city government to preserve the entire old City Hall building on its original site. Confronted by this criticism, the city government agreed that some parts of the building, such as its dome and central Peace Hall, would be preserved.

On August 26, 2008, however, the city government took a surprise action. It tore down large parts of the building without any notice. On the same day, shocked by the surprise demolition, the Cultural Heritage Committee hurriedly called an emergency meeting and designated the building as a Historical Property that legally protects it from further destruction. The new status forced the city government to stop the demolition.[30] Mayor Oh blamed the committee for "insisting unconditionally on original preservation of the old building" and delaying the construction of the new landmark.[31] The preservation of the old City Hall building was indeed an obstacle to his ambition of creating a new architecture of spectacle. After 40 days of negotiation between the city government and the committee, the construction was resumed and a thin layer of the old City Hall facade was retained in front of the new City Hall (see Figure 14.7). The mayor was hopeful that with its completion in 2012 the new City Hall would "remain for 100 years as a proud symbol of Seoul."[32] The mayor's aspiration, however, lends prominence to the creative destruction embedded in the ongoing urban redevelopment.[33]

DESIGNING SEOUL AS SPECTACLE

In 2007 the International Council of Societies of Industrial Design, an organization that promotes progress made by cities through design, appointed Seoul the World Design Capital of 2010. To showcase Seoul as the World Design Capital, Mayor Oh launched a project named Design Seoul and set up its headquarters under his direct supervision.[34] Early in 2006 during his inaugural ceremony, Mayor Oh made a pledge that "I will create Seoul a competitive world-class city with its own brand value." In particular he highlighted the significance of design: "In the twenty-first century, design is everything. From this moment, we are designers who will create a top-notch Seoul in the world."[35] Under the vision of "Soft Seoul," the city government carried out a series of urban projects including the Han River Renaissance Project, the Namsan Renaissance Project, the Street Renaissance Project, the City Gallery Project, the Dongdaemun Design Plaza and Park, and the Seoul Design Olympiad. The spectacular appearance of the new City Hall belongs to the Design Seoul project. However, Mayor Oh's drive to recreate Seoul, with $100 million of the city budget annually dedicated to it, was heavily criticized for marketing the city as a "luxury brand" that aimed largely to attract tourism, business, and capital from outside, while ignoring pressing issues such as the growing number of urban poor and their worsening living conditions.[36] In addition, the revitalization projects were accompanied by forceful evictions as most evident in the deadly clash on January 20, 2009 between tenants protesting against the city's redevelopment plan and police in the Yongsan district, which led to six deaths. In 2010, Oh narrowly won a second term in the mayoral election but his Design Seoul project did not survive.[37]

The idea of urban renewal by way of "design" reflects Korea's turn to neoliberalism. During the developmental era, the city was extended as a platform for manufacturing and industrial production.[38] With the advent of neoliberalism, Seoul, as elsewhere, has been compelled to become "entrepreneurial" by reinventing itself as innovative, high-tech, eco-friendly, and culture-oriented.[39] Mayors Lee and Oh, enthusiastic advocates of neoliberal ideas, urged that Seoul ought to have not only the technological and cost competitive edge but also the competitive edge in attractiveness. During their terms, Seoul was increasingly participating in the spectacle of city branding which caters to capital in global inter-city competition for resources.[40]

In this chapter I have examined how the city hall plaza and its new architecture are not only part of the branded built environment but are the site for the spectacle of the public. As shown earlier, the public appeared as a key discourse with an emphasis on the ideas of openness and accessibility, and the crowds assembled in the plaza displayed public participation. Joined in both protest and celebration, such spectacle also enacted a sense of uniformity in the body of the public. As such the City Hall and its plaza frame the public as spectacle. A space is needed to concentrate the crowd of people who can become part of spectacle. Such a space needs a material object to unify feelings. The City Hall, filled with historical memories, is such an object. The concentration of the crowd creates an imagined community of the "public," members of which do not know each other but find themselves "united" by the shared symbolic space of the City Hall. The City Hall seeks to represent them as the public. My contention is that the idea of the public in its critical and reified form is enacted through the built environment and social memory of the City Hall. The spectacle of the public and the City Hall operates within the ongoing neoliberalization of the city and the nation. With the new mayor, Park Won-soon (2011–present), a former civil activist and lawyer elected as an independent candidate, what role the City Hall takes in the future and what kind of critical public it produces remain to be seen.

NOTES

1 For the concept of the public (kong gong) in the Korean context, see Cho Hee-yeon, "Saeroun sahoe undongjŏk hwadu, konggongsŏng ŭi sŏnggyŏk kwa wisang," [The topic of new social movements and the characteristic and status of the public], *Simin kwa segye*, 11 (2007), 54–69; Hong Seong-tae, "Simin jŏk konggongsŏng kwa han'guk sahoe ŭi paltchŏn," [The civil publicness and development of Korean society], *Minju sahoe wa chŏngch'aek yŏn'gu*, 13 (2008), 72–97; Kim Sang-gon, "Konggong pumun

minyŏnghwa wa sahoe konggongsŏng t'ujaeng," [The privatization of public sectors and struggle for social publicness], *Nodong sahoe* (June 2008), 10–16; Lee Sang-bong, "Taeanjŏk konggong konggan kwa minjujŏk konggongsŏng ŭi mosaek," [A search for the alternative public space and the democratic public], *Taehan chŏngch'ihak hoebo* 19, no. 1 (2011), 23–45; Shin Chin-uk, "Konggongsŏng kwa han'guk sahoe," [The publicness and the Korean society], *Simin kwa segye*, 11 (2007), 18–39; and Youm Chirl-ho, Cho Jun-bae, and Sim Kyung-mi, *Kŏnch'uk tosi konggan ŭi hyŏndae konggongsŏng e kwanhan kich'o yŏn'gu* [A study on the contemporary publicness of architecture and urban space], Seoul: Kŏnch'uk tosi konggan yŏn'guso, 2008.

2 For neoliberalism in Korea, see Choi Byung-doo, *Chabon ŭi tosi* [*The City of Capital: Neoliberal Urbanization and Urban Policy*] (Seoul: Hanul, 2012); Choi Byung-doo, "Developmental neoliberalism and hybridity of the urban policy of South Korea," in Bae-Gyoon Park, Richard Child Hill, and Asato Saito, eds., *Locating Neoliberalism in East Asia: Neoliberalizing Spaces in Developmental States* (Chichester, West Sussex: Wiley-Blackwell, 2012), 86–113; Lee Kwang-il, "Han'guk esŏ sinjayujuŭi kyŏngjaeng kuka ŭi kyebo wa hyŏnjae," [The genealogy and the present of neoliberalism in Korea], *Munhwa/kwahak*, 2008, 28–51; Lee Kwang-il, "Sinjayujuŭi, Lee Myung-bak chŏngkwŏn kwa minjujuŭi," [Neoliberalism, the Lee Myung-bak regime, and democracy], *Simin kwa sahoe* 14 (2008), 333–53; Lim Wun-taek, "Han'guk sahoe esŏ sinjayujuŭi ŭi palchŏn tangye wa hegemoni chŏlyak e taehan inyŏmhyŏngjŏk punsŏk," [An analysis on the development of neoliberalism and hegemonic strategy in Korea], *Kyŏngje wa sahoe* 88 (2010), 300–76; and Yoon Sang-wu, "Oehwan wigi ihu han'guk ŭi palchŏnjuŭijŏk sinjayujuŭihwa," [The developmental neoliberalism in Korea after the financial crisis], *Kyŏngje wa sahoe* 83 (2009), 40–68.

3 The idea of spectacle, which was put forward by Guy Debord and has been later modified, addresses the social relation dominated by "images" which conceal the real contradictions of society in the rise of capitalism, state-led modernization, mass media, and consumerism. See Guy Debord, *The Society of Spectacle*, trans. by David Nicholson Smith, (Cambridge, MA: MIT Press, 1994 [1967]).

4 The Government General of Korea building was built in 1926 right in front of the Gyeongbokgung Palace, the royal palace of Chosŏn, and demolished in 1995. Seoul Train Station was built in 1925 and remains. Chosŏn Shinto Shrine was built in 1925 and burned down in 1945.

5 See Sohn Jŏng-mok, *Ilche kangchŏmgi tosi sahoesang yŏn'gu*, [A social history of the city during the Japanese colonial period], Seoul: Iljisa, 1996, 561–87, and Shin Ye-kyeong and Kim Jin-kyoon, "20 segi ihu Sŏul tosim ne chuyo konggong kŏnch'uk ŭi hyŏngsŏng mit kongganjŏk t'ŭksŏng," [The formation and spatial characteristics of public architecture in Seoul since the 20th century: In case of Seoul City Hall, Seoul Central Post Office Building and Seoul Metropolitan Railway Station], *Taehan kŏnch'uk hakhoe* 25, no. 4 (2009), 107–18.

6 See Hwang Byoung-joo, "Singminji sigi 'kong' kaenyŏm ŭi hwaksan kwa chaegusŏng," [The diffusion and reconstruction of the idea of 'kong' during the colonial period], *Sahoe wa yŏksa* 73 (2007), 5–44.

7 See Kim Baek-yŏng, "Singmin kwŏllyŏk kwa kwangjang konggan," [The colonial power and the square space], *Sahoe wa yŏksa* 90 (2011), 271–311.

8 Instead, the government created the 5.16 Square (later renamed Yŏŭido Square) outside the crowded downtown and held official ceremonies and pro-government rallies such as military parades and anti-communist assemblies.

9 Choi Byung-doo, "Developmental neoliberalism and hybridity of the urban policy of South Korea," 96.

10 Lim Hyun-chin and Jang Jin-ho, "Between neoliberalism and democracy: The transformation of the developmental state in South Korea," *Development and Society* 35, 1 (June 2006), 11.
11 Ibid., 1–28.
12 Yoon Sang-wu, "Oehwan wigi ihu han'guk ŭi palchŏnjuŭijŏk sinjayujuŭihwa," [The developmental neoliberalism in Korea after the financial crisis], *Kyŏngje wa sahoe* 83 (2009), 40–68.
13 Cho Myungrae, "From street corners to plaza: the production of festive civic space in central Seoul," in Mike Douglass, K. C. Ho, and Giok Ling Ooi, eds., *Globalization, the City and Civil Society in Pacific Asia: Social Production of Civic Spaces* (London and New York: Routledge, 2007), 194–210.
14 As soon as he took the mayoral office in 2002, Lee formed the Citizen's Square Preparation Committee, an advisory committee composed of professionals and civic groups, and opened a design competition for the plaza which would be "a shelter for citizens." The winning design was the Plaza of Light by Sŏ Hyŏn, who used the concept of light shedding from the ground. The city government however suddenly aborted the design without any consultation with the committee or the designer and instead made a plaza covered with grass. See Kim Chin-ae, "Sŏul sich'ŏng ap chandi tokjae, munhwa tokjae," [Lawn dictatorship, cultural dictatorship in front of Seoul City Hall], *Inmul kwa sasang* 89 (2005), 104–15.
15 Hi Seoul Festival is an annual street festival. It was launched by Mayor Lee in 2003 to promote the city's identity as a cultural center. Until its scale was expanded in 2007, the main site was Seoul Plaza.
16 "Lee Myong-bak, Sŏul kwangjang, mosun ŭi chŏngch'I," [Lee Myong-bak, Seoul Plaza, politics of contradiction], *Kyunghyang Shinmun* (June 4, 2009)
17 Lee Jae-keun, "Kwangjang ŭl yŏrŏra minjujuŭi rŭl yŏrŏra," [Open the plaza, open democracy: the process and meaning of Seoul Plaza ordinance amendment movements], *Simin kwa segye*, 16 (2009), 174.
18 For controversies around the Seoul Plaza Ordinance, see Hwang Jin-tae, "Tosikwŏn ŭi ch'ŭngmyŏn esŏ parabon kwangjang ŭi chŏngch'I," [The politics of agora in the right of the city], *Konggan kwa sahoe* 21, no. 1 (2011), 42–69; and Lee Jae-keun, "Kwangjang ŭl yŏrŏra minjujuŭi rŭl yŏrŏra," [Open the plaza, open democracy: the process and meaning of Seoul Plaza ordinance amendment movements], *Simin kwa segye* 16 (2009), 167–84.
19 For candlelight protests in the Seoul Plaza, see Kang Chun-man, "Sŭpektŏkŭl losŏ ŭi ch'otbul siwi," [The candlelight protests as spectacle], *Inmul kwa sasang* 124 (2008), 46–59; Ko Pyŏng-kwŏn, Kim Se-kyun, Park Yŏng-kyun, Wŏn Yŏng-jin & Kang Nae-hi, "T'ŭkjip chwadam: chwapa, 2008 nyŏn ch'otbul chiphoe rŭl malhada," [Special talk: The leftist, talking about the 2008 candlelight protests], *Munhwa/ kwahak* (2008), 15–65; Hwang Jin-tae, "2008 nyŏn ch'otbul chiphoe siwi ŭi konggansŏng e kwanhan koch'al," [The analysis on the spaciality of the 2008 candlelight protests in Korea], *Kyŏngje wa sahoe* 90 (2011), 262–89; Lee Tong-yeon, "Ch'otbul chiphoe wa sŭt'ail ŭi chŏngch'I," [The candlelight protests and the politics of style], *Munhwa/sahoe* (2008), 150–67; and Seung-ook Lee, Sook-jin Kim, and Joel Wainwright, "Mad cow militancy: Neoliberal hegemony and social resistance in South Korea," *Political Geography* 29 (2010), 359–69.
20 See Lee Tong-yeon, "Ch'otbul chiphoe wa sŭt'ail ŭi chŏngch'i."
21 Mayor Oh Se-hoon, from the Conservative party, requested the council to reconsider it but the council chair declared the amendment.
22 Don Mitchell, "The end of public space? People's park, definitions of the public and democracy," *Annals of the Association of American Geographers* 85, no. 1 (1995), 115, 108–33.
23 Seoul metropolitan government official website, http://smih.seoul.go.kr/appli/appli01.html (accessed May 2011).

24 Ibid.
25 Seoul metropolitan government official website, http://smih.seoul.go.kr/appli/appli01.html (accessed May 2011).
26 "Sŏul sich'ŏng sinch'ŏngsa sŏlgye han kŏnch'ukga, Yu Kŏl," [Yu Kŏl, the architect who designed the new Seoul city hall," Chosun.com (February 18, 2012).
27 Ibid.
28 "Sŏul sich'ŏng pon'gwan pojon moksori nopa," [Loud voices for the preservation of the Seoul City Hall building], *Han'gyŏre* (June 9, 2008).
29 "Oh sijang i hŏrŏbŏrin kŏsŭn," [What Mayor Oh destroyed is], *Han'gyŏre* (August 31, 2008).
30 "Sae ch'ŏngsa chikkettago munhwajae hŏrŏbŏrin Sŏulsi," [The Seoul city government demolished the historic property in order to build a new city hall building], *Han'gyŏre* (August 26, 2008). The building became a Registered Cultural Property in 2003 but there was no legal protection from demolition.
31 Oh Se-hoon, "Sŏulsich'ŏng ch'ŏngsa sajŏk kajijŏng kwallyŏn simin kogaek yŏrŏbun kke dŭrinŭn malssŭm," [The statement to citizens regarding the designation of the Seoul City Hall as Historic Properties], *Saengsaeng Seoul Report* (August 28, 2008), from Seoul official blog, http://blog.seoul.go.kr (accessed May 2011).
32 Ibid.
33 David Harvey, "Neoliberalism as creative destruction," *Annals, AAPSS*, 610 (March 2007), 22–44.
34 For the Design Seoul Project, see Choi Chang-sik, Choen Yu-ri, Chung Na-ri, and Chung Tong-yoel, "Kamgakjŏgin kŏt ŭi nanum ŭl t'onghae pon tijain Sŏul," [The Design Seoul viewed from 'sharing of the sensational'], *Han'guk sahoehakhoe*, 12 (2008), 960–75; Kang Nae-hi and Yoon Ja-hyoung, "Tijain Sŏul kwa konggan ŭi munhwa chŏngch'I," [The Design Seoul Project and its cultural politics of space: A semiotic analysis], *Marŭkŭsŭ juŭi yŏn'gu* 7, no. 4, 188–216; Kim Hyŏn-u, "Oh Se-hoon ŭi myŏngp'um tosi," [Oh Se-hoon's luxurious city], *Munhwa/ kwahak*, 6 (2008), 278–89; and Hwang Jin-tae, "Sinjayujuŭi tosi esŏ tosi e taehan kwŏlli ŭi sirhyŏn," [Realizing the right to the city in the neoliberal city], *Konggan kwa sahoe*, 34 (2010), 33–59.
35 Choi Chang-sik, Choen Yu-ri, Chung Na-ri, and Chung Tong-yoel, "Kamgakjŏgin kŏt ŭi nanum ŭl t'onghae pon tijain Sŏul," 962.
36 Kim Hyŏn-u, "Oh Se-hoon ŭi myŏngp'um tosi," 287.
37 Hwang Jin-tae, "Sinjayujuŭi tosi esŏ tosi e taehan kwŏlli' ŭi sirhyŏn," 53.
38 Choi Byung-doo, "Developmental neoliberalism and hybridity of the urban policy of South Korea," 95, 107.
39 For neoliberal entrepreneurial city, see David Harvey, "From managerialism to entrepreneurialism: The transformation in urban governance in late capitalism," *Geografiska Annaler* 71, no. 1 (1989), 3–17.
40 For "branding" as the contemporary reconfiguration of spectacle in the neoliberal context, see Shiloh Krupar and Stefan Al, "Notes on the society of the spectacle (brand)," in C. Greig Crysler, Stephen Cairns, and Hilde Heynen, eds., *The Sage Handbook of Architectural Theory*, (Los Angeles: Sage, 2012), 247–263.

Epilogue

Chapter 15: Public Space and Public Action

A Note on the Present

Jeremy White

As we are in the final stages of editing this book, Taksim Square in Istanbul has emerged as the site of confrontation between protestors – mostly young adults, and the police. Tayyip Erdoğan, Turkey's Prime Minister, was out of the country on a diplomatic assignment when the protests started at the end of May, but he is back now: calling the protesters "provocateurs and terrorists," he has stated that the confrontation will be over by the weekend."[1] The demonstration started when environmentalists attempted to halt the government's tearing down of trees on the edge of the square in Gezi Park to make way for new construction. Police attacked the environmentalists with tear gas, rubber bullets, and stun grenades, injuring many with batons and sparking a spontaneous civil action that had the square filled night and day. Ankara, the capital city, now has a parallel protest as do cities and towns throughout the country, 78 of them at last count, and one of the nation's trade unions has declared solidarity with this new "marginal group," as Erdoğan dubbed them. Media analysts and bloggers are already calling this the "Turkish Spring." Four people have died including one police officer; some protesters wield molotov cocktails and fireworks, and wear gas masks. Others just stand in silence in a defiant performance of non-violent objection to the authoritarian actions of the state.[2] While the Prime Minister was away, the Deputy Prime Minister offered an apology for the state's initial use of "excessive force," but now Prime Minister Erdoğan claims that the square and the park are for promenading, not occupying.[3]

Gesture and counter-gesture, the people occupying space and turning it into a scene of self-representation, the state attempting to control that space in response: it has become a referendum on the Prime Minister's rule. While this battle over spatial-civil order transpires, both parties conduct a fragmented conversation on the internet through journalists and bloggers. The screen now accompanies the plaza, the coffee house, and the street as categories of public venue. The Prime Minister has said he will meet with protesters, but not at Gezi Park or in Taksim Square. Analysts have been quick to raise questions about this offer, because those highly visible public spaces were filled spontaneously, without the direction of leadership. Which protesters will he meet? And for whom will they speak? Removing a few protesters from those spaces, isolated from the rest by sequestering them out of public view, seems a tactical move on the state's part. The voice of the protester is activated by the occupation of public space, and this would seem an attempt to take the voice out of the protest.

Consider the interesting situation 3,000 kilometers to the southeast, on the outskirts of Abu Dhabi in the United Arab Emirates. A city is under construction there, called Masdar, and it is designed to be the most aggressively sustainable human settlement in the world. Intended as a research and development site for green technology companies, it has forged relationships with universities such as the Massachusetts Institute of Technology. The city is far from complete and is inhabited mostly by college students, interns, and technology professionals, as well as the labor needed to sustain them, although most low-wage labor commutes from Abu Dhabi, that labor pool ultimately drawn from Asia and Africa. When completed, Masdar City will accommodate around 50,000 dwellers, not including the low-wage commuters.[4]

At the heart of this new settlement is a high-tech building called Masdar Headquarters, and it plays the role of city hall. Nested inside Masdar City, it too is under construction, designed by former Skidmore Owings and Merrill's principal architect Adrian Smith, the master-technician of the tallest building in the world in nearby Dubai, the Burj Khalifa. Masdar HQ will be a seven-story, 134,000-square-meter, mixed-use corporate building at the heart of a business park masquerading as a city. Much attention has been given to its flat roof, an enormous photovoltaic-covered umbrella casting shade over the construction site while providing the electricity needed for its construction as well as its use after completion. That marvelously green building would seem to be a poster-child for the cradle-to-cradle flow of technical nutrients: re-usable structural elements that can be dismantled after the building is demolished when it has outlived its usefulness, not to mention the horizontal-axis wind turbines under the roof, and the cool towers and gardens underneath. That building has been a story about rain capture and recirculation of water, the natural flow of ventilation, zero waste... etc. But notice the name of the building: Masdar *Headquarters*.

Masdar HQ will be a de facto governmental center, the space where decisions will be made that affect the new city as a whole, reducing that city to an enterprise run by a corporation, the Abu Dhabi Future Energy Company. The municipality of Abu Dhabi itself might seem to be run in a similar way, as a department of a larger corporation, ruling not citizens but "customers," to use the term that appears on the municipality's website. Abu Dhabi does not have a city hall either; instead it has a Department of Municipal Affairs, a symmetrically organized building situated at the end of a large flagpole-studded plaza. This ornamental space is an extension of the pomp of the Municipal Headquarters, a civic space of questionable social or political discourse. In 2006 when construction workers protested low wages and poor working conditions, they did not gather in front of that irrelevant building. They took to the streets, marching, chanting and damaging parked cars, demanding equitable treatment and higher pay. Were they customers or laborers, members of the public or "guests" inhabiting the outside of civic life? Approximately 85 percent of the United Arab Emirates population is foreign residents, mostly from South Asia and Africa, low wage "guest workers" barred from citizenship and most unable to remain in their host country for more than a few years, the consequence of a deliberate government policy intended to preserve the ethnic identity of the nation. According to the Minister of Labor, "We want to protect the minority, which is us."[5] That "us" did not include "guests."

Of all the problems dealt with in this anthology of essays about city halls, identity, and nationalist identity in particular, features prominently. The city hall is intended to represent, or comes to represent over time, the public, and this public is understood to be the dominant ethnic community and in extension the imagined community of the nation. Representations of the state are situated at the confluence of ethnicity and national identity. The city hall building as a space and an urban landmark establishes an ethnic mirror reflecting the society it governs. As an icon it expresses the "who" of the governed, and the nation, embodying in image and word the deeds and precepts of the nation's history, and yet, in a society where more than three-quarters of the population are foreign, what does the mirror reflect? When city hall is an absent building and institution, as at Abu Dhabi and its new satellite, Masdar, its absence has lasting consequences. But "absence" is not always widely perceived. A city hall might feel imposing and regal constituting a profound presence for one person, while for another its nation-signifying role may be alienating, entirely outside of personal and civic experience, or irrelevant, if not absent. The contributors in this volume who study city halls in colonial contexts have offered us parallel examples of civic-material disenfranchisement.

Just last month, in May 2013, ethnic youth in the suburbs of Stockholm took to the streets with rocks and incendiaries, setting ablaze automobiles and buildings, even attacking police stations. It started in the neighborhood of Husby where 80 percent of the residents are first- and second-generation immigrants, where unemployment is double the city's average, and where 12 percent of residents receive social benefits. The rioters were representatives of the 15 percent of the population born in a foreign country, mostly from war-ravaged places such as Iraq, Somalia, the former Yugoslavia, Syria, and Afghanistan. Nine suburbs saw rioting, more than 100 automobiles torched, and when fire department workers were on the scene they too were attacked with stones and laser pointers, an unexpected weapon of the twenty-first century.[6] One fireman posted a letter directed at rioters who threw stones at him: "Why are you treating me like this?"[7]

Riots and protests in Abu Dhabi and Istanbul, or in the many public spaces of the Arab Spring of 2011, might seem less surprising than what took place in the low-rent districts on Stockholm's periphery, and yet it was not the first time ethnic youth exploded in frustration there. To dwell in a place and a nation and yet not be fully of that nation, has its social as well as political implications. According to Rami-al-Khamisi, founder of a non-profit organization called Megafonen based in

Husby and dedicated to assisting and enriching Stockholm suburbs, the riots had as much to do with the perceived second-class status of immigrants as with the high unemployment rate. During the upheaval some police officers allegedly directed racial slurs at rioters – "rat," "monkey," and "nigger" – and even at bystanders seeking to help maintain order during the conflict. According to Sweden's Integration Minister, the violence could be attributed to unemployment as well as social exclusion.[8] As we saw with Laura Kolbe's essay on Scandinavian city halls, the iconography may be remarkably open to all classes, but when a Somali gazes at the walls of Stockholm's magnificent building, does she see herself reflected as part of the national story? This begs the larger question of political relevance – a simple question of who belongs? To occupy public space is to assert one's own political relevance.

The HQ model of city hall is a corporate scheme where citizens are either customers or merely laborers. Power is wielded by an "enlightened leadership" (to borrow again from Abu Dhabi's municipal website), with more interest in safeguarding the profits of investors than the rights of its "customers." The protest and riots in Istanbul and Stockholm took place in a different political geography, but there, in very different ways, protester/rioters staked claim to rights, and that claim began with establishing the actors' visibility and exercising their voice. To assign civic rights to a citizen presupposes the citizen, and for a municipal government (or any other jurisdiction) to refuse to "see" citizenship in its customers, no such rights need be granted let alone protected. The status of citizenship may be taken for granted in some geographies, but it is elusive in others. In Stockholm, the riots made the immigrants visible. As one rioter told a Swedish reporter, "at least everyone is listening to us now."[9] And the guest workers in Masdar's futuristic city may seem to anchor one end of the RIGHTS – NO RIGHTS spectrum, but recent developments elsewhere would seem to stretch that spectrum even further.

According to economist Edward Castronova, a new continent has been discovered and is rapidly being populated. He calls it the "synthetic world," and it is popularly known as the virtual world of massively multiplayer online gaming (MMOG). As trivial as it may seem, an unlikely debate over avatar rights has emerged out of that world, as a consequence of the exodus of millions of players who prefer it to the real world.[10] This synthetic world already has a very real economic presence, so it is not surprising that it takes on a political character as well. People in the real world spend money to purchase virtual swords and virtual gold in the synthetic world. There are currency exchange markets and very real exchange rates where real people spend real dollars to purchase virtual real estate – islands and castles and other virtual creations encoded onto servers. The tally in 2007 of the synthetic world's net worth exceeded $30 million – in real money – and millions of players spend as much time mucking about gathering gold in that strange virtual world as they do in the real one.

Castronova refers to the dividing line between that new continent of the synthetic world and this real one as a "membrane," and already he and others have identified political activity, even protest movements, occurring on the strange side of that wall. In 2000 Ralph Koster, the chief architect of one of the pioneering online worlds, posted a "Declaration of the Rights of Avatars."[11] It was fashioned after the first ten amendments to the United States Constitution, the 1789 Declaration of the Rights of Citizens, and the more recent United Nation's Charter of Rights and Freedoms. And avatars, those representations of gamers in the synthetic world, have even mounted a crude political movement – stripping naked and vomiting in protest over a change in game programming.[12]

What is the spatial component of this? The server is not an extension of public space into cyberspace, those machines are owned and operated by private companies doing so for profit, but by virtue of creating the rules, or the laws of nature of these synthetic worlds, those companies play the role of god and government. Real people access the "space" of the synthetic world by remaining at home or at work in real space, often private space. There are no city halls in the synthetic world that function as we expect them to on the real side of the membrane. The stripping and vomiting may not have happened in a cyberspace version of Taksim Square or the grassy plaza in front of a city hall, but it did happen in a king's throne room, and that "room" was viewable by the public. There have been sit-ins, marches, mail campaigns, and petitions, but the most effective recourse against dictatorial "coding authorities," the administrators and programmers that establish the rules of a synthetic world, has been to beseech them outside of the world itself in online "forums." In Masdar and wherever a municipal government is aloof from citizens, we might find the hollowness of the city hall to be problematic, or at least symptomatic of the government's lack of responsiveness to the public, but this is taken to an extreme in the synthetic world where the very laws of gravity are encoded by the corporation and its programmers.

To suggest avatar rights and to ponder what might be the role of city hall in cyberspace may seem frivolous, but until recently the notion of an Arab Spring – and the unprecedented successful pairing of physical space and cyber space that it demonstrated – also seemed unlikely. If an Avatar Spring seems ludicrous, what about a Scandinavian Spring? Decades ago Isaac Asimov envisioned a Robot Spring in his science fictions, although he never called it by that phrase.[13] But the world is now populated by aeronautical drones in the skies, robotic surgical arms in hospitals, and California's legislature recently passed a law allowing self-driving cars on state roads.[14] Is it too early to ponder what rights an artificial intelligence might have in future public discourse? How would it (?) "occupy" public space? And what becomes of civic space, political rights, and the traditions of spatial imagination and spatial types when virtual and real domains interpenetrate and artificial life is not merely human prosthetic but autonomous? What would our explorations of viewing city hall at the edges of its political identity have to teach us for this next spatial move?

NOTES

1. Associated Press, "Four dead and 5,000 injured during anti-government protests in Turkey," *Daily News*, June 11, 2013, http://www.nydailynews.com/news/world/riot-police-eject-protesters-taksim-square-istanbul-article-1.1369092?localLinksEnabled=false (accessed June 11, 2013).
2. "Quiet New Hero for Protesters: Standing Man," *Wall Street Journal*, June 19, 2013, A10.
3. Dorian Jones, "Turkish Deputy PM Apologizes to Protesters," Voice of America on-line, June 4, 2013, http://www.voanews.com/content/turkey-protests-reach-5th-day/1674659.html (accessed June 10, 2013).
4. Abu Dhabi Future Energy Company, Sustainability Report, September 2012, Smith & Gill, Masdar Headquarters, http://smithgill.com/work/masdar_headquarters/ (accessed June 11, 2013).
5. Jason DeParle, "Emirates making peace with migrant workers," *New York Times*, August 5, 2007.
6. "Stockholm riots throw spotlight on Sweden's inequality," BBC, May 24, 2013; "Stockholm restaurant torched as riots spread," BBC, May 23, 2013; "Riots grip Stockholm suburbs after police shooting," BBC, May 22, 2013; "Riot police 'resorted to racial slurs' in Husby," *The Local*, May 20, 2013.
7. "Stockholm Riots: Sweden's 'Urban Underclass' demands attention," *Spiegel* Online International, May 24, 2013.
8. "Rioters continue to battle police in Stockholm," Al-Jazeera, May 24, 2013.
9. "Stockholm Riots," *Spiegel* Online International.
10. Edward Castronova, *Exodus to the Virtual World: How Online Fun is Changing Reality* (New York: Palgrave, 2007). An avatar is a movable icon representing a player in the space of a game or online "world."
11. Ralph Koster, "Declaring the Rights of Players," August 27, 2000, http://www.raphkoster.com/gaming/playerrights.shtml
12. Elizabeth Kolbert, "Pimps and Dragons," *The New Yorker*, May 28, 2001, p. 88.
13. Asimov first penned the now famous three laws of robotics in a short story: "Runaround," *Astounding Science Fiction*, March 1942 (famous among science fiction enthusiasts, that is). The laws were the basis of several subsequent stories, adopted by other writers, and have made their way into novels, films, television shows, and popular imagination.
14. Ashley Vance, "Google's Self-Driving Robot Cars Are Ruining My Commute," *Bloomberg Business Week*, March 28, 2013.

Index

Locators in *italics* indicate a figure.

Aachen, Germany, 80–82, *80*, *81*, *82*
Aborigines, Australia, 122
Abu Dhabi, 296–297
access to public space, 5, 9
   Bombay Town Hall, 161, 163–166
   Los Angeles City Hall, 192–194
   Morelia, Mexico, 138
   New York, 30–31, 37–38
   San Francisco, 43–44, 51
   Scandinavian city halls, 67–70
   Sydney Town Hall, 119–120
accountability, 143, 147–154
administrative uses, 83, 106–107. *see also* self-administration
African capitals, 237–251
Akron airship, 183
Allen, John, 251
Almeida, Anthony, 242
Almonester y Roxas, Don Andres, 21
Alvord, William, 42
American Modern style, 189
Amess, Samuel, 124
Amsterdam, 259
Amuli, Beda, 242
Anzac Day, 122–123
apartheid, 240
Art Deco, 9
artificial intelligence, 299

Asiatic Society of Bombay, 163–166
assemblies. *see* gatherings
Austin, John C., 179
Australia, 115–133
   Melbourne Town Hall, 123–128, *124*
   Sydney Town Hall, 116–123
   Toodyay Town Hall, 128–132
avatar rights, 298–299
ayuntamiento, 136–137, 149

Babington, Stephen, 167
Balai Kota, Jakarta, 262, *263*
balconies, 22, 222
Band, Karl, 84
Banerjee, Surendranath, 209, 212, 214
Baroque style, 80–82
Batavia (Jakarta), 257–261, *257*, *258*
Bavaria, 85
beef imports, 282
Bell, Edward, 117
Bém, Pavel, 109
Bengal, 210–214
Berlin, Germany, 88–91
Bharmal Building, Zanzibar, 246
bigness, 182–184, 201, 203
Black Acts, Calcutta, 206
Blok G, Jakarta, Indonesia, 268, *269*, *270*

Blunt's visitors' guide, 35
Bohemian Renaissance, 104, 107
Bombay Town Hall, 158–173, *159*
Bond, Albert, 117
Bose, Anandamohan, 209
Bose, Bhupendranath, 212
bourgeoisie, 7–8
   Germany, 86–87
   Mexico, 152
   New Orleans, 27
   Prague, 101, 103
   Scandinavia, 59
Bowo, Fauzi, 271
brick architecture, 65
British Indian Association, 206–210
British influence. *see* Bombay Town Hall
British town halls, 4, 161
budget. *see* funding
Burauen, Theo, 84
bureaucracy, 46, 192, 194
Burr, Aaron, 50
bushfires, 132

Cabildo, New Orleans, 20–24, *20, 22*
Calcutta Town Hall, 199–214, *203*
California, 42–48
capital cities
   in Africa, 237–251
   in Australia, 116, 123, 128
   in Czech Republic, 97-98, 103, 106-108
   in Germany, 80, 85, 86
   in India, 161, 200
   in Indonesia, 265, 267–268
   in Korea, 277
   in Mexico, 136–138
   relocation, 247–249
   in Scandinavia, 10, 56-75
Capital Cities in Africa, 240
Casa del Fascio, Milan, 218–219, 221, *222*
Cederborg, Allan, 56

Centennial Hall, Sydney, 118–119, *119*, 123
centrality, 59. *see also* location
ceremonies, 45–46
Charlottenburger Rathaus, 88, 90
Cheonggye Plaza, South Korea, 282
Chicago City Hall, 42
Chinese in Batavia, 260
Christer, Steve, 60, 63
circulars, *142*
citizenship, 5, 11,19, 27, 52, 61, 119, 137, 144–145, 152–153, 200, 205, 271, 277, 296, 297–298
City Hall, New York, 28–36, *30, 33, 34*
City Hall Park, New York, 52
civic decline, 49
civic identity. *see* identity
civic pride, xix, 5, 8, 17, 29, 35, 42, 46, 71–72, 81, 255, 259
class division, 27
Cologne, 82–85, *84*
colonialism, 3–5
   African postcolonial capitals, 237–251
   Bombay Town Hall, 158–173, *159*
   Cabildo, New Orleans, 22
   Calcutta Town Hall, 199–214
   decolonization, 5, 255, 262–263, 265
   Jakarta, 255–272
   Korea, 277–279
   Mexico, 153
   Shankarshet's statue, 169–171
Common Council, New York, 28–36
Communist Party, 108–109
community engagement, 130–131, 133
concrete, 65
conflict, 116
contestation, 10, 200
Copenhagen City Hall, 56–72, *58*
   access to public space, 67–70
   banqueting hall, 72
   decoration, 67

design of, 64
inauguration, 56
location, 57–58
planning stage, 60, 61
Rådhushallen, 71
Cornwallis, Lord, 199
corruption, 40, 42, 48–51
Corso Venezia, Milan, 217, *218*, 219, *221*, 232
County Courthouse, New York, 36–41
Cowper, Colonel Thomas, 158
Cremer, Fritz, 89
"cultural landscape," Dell Upton, 18
Culture of Cities, The, Lewis Mumford, 7
Cursetjee, Manackjee, 160–161
Curzon, Viceroy Lord, 210
Czech Republic, 97–110

Daendels, Wilhem, 260
Damus, Martin, 86–87
Dar es Salaam, Tanzania, 238, 241–243
Deb, Raja Radhakanta, 207, 209
decolonization, 263, 265
decoration. *see also* façades; iconography
    in Germany, 81, 82, 85, 87, 89
    Los Angeles City Hall, 188–192
    New York, 32, 38, 45
    Scandinavian city halls, 65, 67–68, 70–73
democracy, 8, 46–47, 51–52, 280–284
Democratic Republic of Congo, 239
demonstrations
    Jakarta, Indonesia, 270–272
    Seoul, 279–284, *283*
    Stockholm, 296–297
    Sweden, 296–297
    Turkey, 295–296
Design Seoul, 287–288
destruction, 80–82
Díaz, Porfirio, 137–138
dirigibles, 183

disrepair, 237, 241
Dodoma, Tanzania, 238, 241, 247–249, *249*
domes, 183
doors, 189–191, *189*
Dorodjatun, Adang, 271
Durban, 240
Dutch East India Company, 255–260
Dutton, Eric, 245

East India Company, 160, 199
Eidlitz, Leopold, 37–38
electoral meetings, 130
elite, 7–8, 143. *see also* bourgeoisie
Elphinstone, Lord John, 167, *168*, 171
"empire style" house, 263–265
employment, 47
England, 4
Erdoğan, Tayyip, 295
ethnic divisions. *see also* racism
    Batavia (Jakarta), 260
    Los Angeles, 186
    New Orleans, 24
    Prague, 98
European influence
    Bombay Town Hall, 158–164
    Los Angeles City Hall, 187
    Scandinavian city halls, 64–66, 71–72
exclusion, 10, 47
    Africa, 242–243, 250–251
    Australia, 120–122, 126–127
    India, 201, 203–205
    Indonesia, 259–260, 262
    Mexico, 144–145
    South Korea, 279
    Sweden, 298
    US, 47, 181

façades
    Jakarta, Indonesia, 265
    Milan, Italy, 222–223
    Old Town Hall, Prague, 101–102
    Scandinavian city halls, 67–68

Fascist Party, Italy, 217–233
Federal Hall, New York, 28
Federation Hall, Calcutta, 214
Fieberg, Fredrick, *203*
Fischer, Helmut, 85
Fišer, Jaroslav, *109*
Fitzgerald, Shirley, 116
flags, 122–123
floor plans. *see* plans
Forbes, John, 166, 171
fountains, *41*
Frayne, Beth, 129
French style, 124
Frere, Sir Bartle, 167
Fridtjof Nansen's Square, Oslo, 69
funding
    Bombay Town Hall, 160
    Calcutta Town Hall, 201
    Sydney Town Hall, 117, 118
    US city halls, 21, 29, 36, 40, 50
furnishings, 32

Gallier, James, 24–25
Gallier Hall, 49
Gandhi, Mohandas, 173
Garstin, Colonel John, 201
gatherings
    Bombay Town Hall, 162
    Municipal Palace, Morelia, 142
    Toodyay Town Hall, 129–130
    union meetings, 121–122, *122*, 126–127
Germany, 78–94
    Aachen, 80–82
    Berlin, 88–91
    Cologne, 82–85
    Hannover, 91–92
    Munich, 85–86
    nationals in Prague, 106–107
    Stuttgart, 92–93
Ghose, Ramgopal, 206–207, 214
Gilded Age, US, 41, 42, 49, 51
Giuliani, Rudolph (Mayor), 51
glass, 224, 231, 286

Glockenspiel, Munich, 85
Gocár, Josef, 104, *105*
Gothic style, 80–82, 83, 85–86, 90, 99–100
government structure
    in Africa, 238–241
    in Australia, 116–117, 121–122
    in Czech Republic, 97–98
    in Indonesia, 265–269
    local government, 59–60, 115–116
    in Mexico, 150–151
    municipal, 136–137, 143–144, 238–241
    state control, 164–165
    ujamaa, 247–249
    in US, 194
Guggenheim, Michael, 6
Guinea, 240
Gustav V, King of Sweden, 56, 67

Habermas, Jürgen, 7–8, 27, 163
halls, 70–73, 124–126, *125*, *126*
Hannover, 91–92, *91*
Hansasaal, Cologne, 83
Hardardottir, Margret, 60, 63
Harper's Weekly, 40–41
Harris, Mayor, 118
Hastie, William, 203
Helsinki City Hall, 56, 60, 62–63, 69
Heyerdahl, Hieronymus, 62
Hillebrecht, Rudolf, 92
Hitavadi, 213
Hodler, Ferdinand, 91
Hoffman, Ludwig, 89, 90
Hoogan, Ajit Singh, 245
human rights, 121–122

iconography. *see also* decoration
    Germany, 87
    Los Angeles City Hall, 181, 186–192
    Prague, 101–102
identity
    civic pride, 138, 182
    colonial, 4

Los Angeles City Hall, 182
Morelia, Mexico, 138
national, 94, 102
vecino identity, 153
illiteracy, 146
Illustrated Australian News for Home Readers, 124
imperialism, 3–5. *see also* colonialism
inclusion, 10, 119
Independence Square, Jakarta, 265–269, *266*, 271
India, 158–173
Indies Houses, 263–265
Indonesia, 255–272
Batavia stadhuis, 257–260
interior space
Cabildo, New Orleans, 21
City Hall, Calcutta, 204–205, 210
New York City Hall, *31*, 35
Jakarta, 265
Los Angeles City Hall, *191*
Milan, 219, 224, 227, 230
modern, 63
Municipal Hall, New Orleans, 25, *26*
Municipal Palace, Morelia, *141*
San Francisco City Hall, 44–45, 46
Seoul City Hall, 286
Istanbul, 295
Italianate style, 90
Italy, 4, 217–233

Jackson Square, New Orleans, 20–24
Jakarta, Indonesia, 255–272, *256*
Japan, 277–279
Jeejeebhoy, Sir Jamsetjee, 167, 170
Jensen-Klint, Peter Vilhelm, 64
Jewish Town, Prague, 103
Johannesburg, South Africa, 239
Josephson, Ragnar, 64
Justice statue, New York, 32

Kearney, Denis, 43
Keenja, Charles, 242
Kellum, John, 37–38

Kenya, 237, 241
Kequan, Qian, 244
Kikwete, Jakaya, 248–249
Kim Dae-jung, 280
Kim Young-sam, 280
Kinshasa, DRC, 239
Klett, Arnulf, 93
Kojong, King, 278
Korea, South, 276–288
Koster, Ralph, 299

Lafayette, General, 23
Lafayette Square, New Orleans, 24, *25*
Lagos, Nigeria, 238, 239
Lambert, W.H., 123
Latrobe, Benjamin, 29, 31
Laver, Augustus, 43
Lee Kyung-bak, 280, 282
Lefebvre, Henri, 241, 242
Leitenstorfer, Hermann, 85
L'Enfant, Pierre Charles, 28
"lettered city," 146–147
Liberec (Reichenberg), 107
Liberty statue, *41*
Liebermann, Max, 91
limestone, 93
Lindbergh, Charles, 182
Lion, Henry, 189
literacy, 145–146
local government, 59–60, 115–116. *see also* government structure
location, 19, 59
Bombay Town Hall, 162–163, *162*
Calcutta Town Hall, *202*
Los Angeles City Hall, *182*
Milan, Italy, *220*
Old Town Hall, Prague, *99*
Scandinavian city halls, 65–66
Sydney Town Hall, 116
Lopate, Phillip, 29
Los Angeles City Hall, 177–194, *179*, *185*, *187*, *188*
Lupfer, Gilbert, 93
Lyons, Joseph, 120

Macintosh, Sir James, 160
Madhav Baug, *173*
Magnussen, Arnstein, 60
Malawi, 237
Malcolm, Sir John, 167, *168*, 170
Mangin, Joseph François, 29
Mani Bhavan, 173
marginalization, 238–241
Marshall Plan, 79
Martin, Albert, 179
Masdar City, 296–297, 298
massacre, Batavia, 260
McBeath, David, 117
McComb, John Jr., 29, 32
Mediterranean style, 187–188
meetings. *see* gatherings
Meffert, Erich, 245
Melbourne Town Hall, Australia, 123–128, *125*, *126*
memorial chapel, Palazzo Besana, Milan, 227
Menzies, Robert, 120
Mexicans, Los Angeles, 186
Mexico, 136–154, 192
Mezzanotte, Paulo, 221–225
Michenzani apartments, *244*
Milan, Italy, 217–233
Milan Federation, 224, 227, 231
Miller Lane, Barbara, 64
Mirror of Indigo play, 209
Mkapa, Benjamin, 248
modernism, 65, 87–88, *93*, 231
monarchy, 97–98
monumentality
  Los Angeles City Hall, 178, 181, 183–184
  Scandinavian city halls, 70–73
Morelia, Mexico, 136–154, *139*, *140*
Moses, Robert, 50
Muis, Abdoel, 263
Mumford, Lewis, 7–8
Munich, 85–86, *86*

municipal government, 136–137, 143–144, 238–241. *see also* government structure
Municipal Hall, New Orleans, 24–27, *26*
Municipal House, Prague, 106–107
Murdoch, Walter, 115
Mussolini, Arnaldo, 217, 219, 225
Mussolini, Benito, 217–233
Muzio, Giovanni, 221, 231

Nairobi, Kenya, 241
national identity, 4, 73, 94, 102, 297
nationalism, 4–5, 56–73, 98, 102, 133, 199, 209–210, 212, 265–269
nationalist, 4, 10, 73, 101, 173, 209–214, 237, 241, 263, 265, 286, 297
Nationalist Socialism, 10, 78, 85
Natmandir, *207*, *208*, 209
Nazis, 78–79, 81, 87–88, 108
Nesbitt, Thomas, 123
Netherlands, 255–262
New Council House, Prague, 106–107, *107*
New England, US, 4
New Orleans Picayune, 27
New Orleans, US, 17, 20–27, *22*
New York Preservation Society, 52
New York Times, 37, 40
New York Tribune, 36
New York, US
  City Hall, 28–36
  County Courthouse, 36–41
Ng'ambo Civic Center, 243–247
Nigeria, 239
Nildarpan play, 209
Nobile, Peter, 100
Nobile's Town Hall. *see* Old Town Hall, Prague
Nordic city halls, 56–73
Norris, Charles, 167
notaries, 146
Nyerere, Julius, 242, 247–248
Nyrop, Martin, 60, 61, 72

Occupy movement, 177–179
O'Dwyer, Paul, 52
Oh Se-hoon, 283, 285, 287–288
Old Town Hall, Prague, 97–110, *101, 102, 105*
Old Town Square, Prague, *100*
Olvera Street, Los Angeles, 186
Olympic Games, 182
Oman, 243
orchestras, 128
Oslo City Hall, *66*
  access to public space, 69
  decoration, 67, *68*
  Det Lange Galleriet, 73
  European influence, 66
  inauguration, 56
  location, 58, 68–69
  planning stage, 60, 62
  Rådhushallen, 71
Östberg, Ragnar, 60, 61

paintings, 91–92
Palacio Municipal, Morelia, Mexico, 136–154
Palazzo Besana, Milan, Italy, 225–228, *226*
Palazzo Castani, Milan, Italy, 228–229
Park Chung-hee, 279
Park Won-soon, 288
Parkinson, John, 179
parks, 68–70
patrimony, 143, 153–154
peripheralization, 238–241
petitioning, 137, 147–152
Petrasová, Tatána, 102, 103
Philadelphia, US, 42
Piazza del Duomo, Milan, 231–232, *232*
Piazza Diaz, 232, 233
Place d'Armes, New Orleans, 20–24, *20*
plans, 19
  Bombay Town Hall, *163–164*
  Calcutta Town Hall, *204*
  Casa del Fascio, Milan, *223*
  Dodoma, Tanzania, 248
  Los Angeles City Hall, *193*
  Scandinavian city halls, 60–64
  Seoul City Hall, *286*
police, xx, xxi, 52, 65, 67, 87, 90, 126–128, 145, 161, 177–178, 181, 201, 210, 212–214, 217, 278, 280–281, 283, 288, 295, 297–298
political context. *see also* democracy; petitioning
  Cabildo, New Orleans, 23–24
  Jakarta, Indonesia, 270–272
  Mexico, 136–138
  Prague, 103, 108–110
  San Francisco, 46–47
  Sydney Town Hall, 120–122
  Toodyay Town Hall, 130–131
  US, 19, 27, 41, 48–49, 51–52
Pontalba, Micaela Baroness de, 23–24
Porfiriato, 137–138, 143, 154
Portaluppi, Piero, 228–231, 232
power, 261, 270–272. *see also* government structure
Prague, 97–110
Pratt, Leonidas, 46
pride. *see* civic pride
Prince Alfred's Tower, Melbourne, 125
Prinsep, James, 204–205, *206*
Prinsep, William, 204–205
protest movement
  Calcutta, 210–214
  Los Angeles City Hall, 177–179
  Old Town Hall, Prague, 100
Prussia, 81, 88
public meetings. *see* gatherings
public participation, 268
public protection, 150–152, 154
public shame, 42
public space, 5–11 *see* access to public space
  Calcutta, 210–214
  Cologne, 84
  contestation, 200

differentiated, 158–159
Italy, 217–233
in Korea, 278–284
meaning of city hall, 255–256, 277, 278, 281
Scandinavian city halls, 68–71
social space, 162
public sphere, xxi, 7–8, 11, 27, 35, 43, 46, 137, 152, 209, 238, 243, 251

quotations in decoration, 186–187, 188

Rach, Johannes, *257*
racism. *see also* ethnic divisions
Calcutta, 206–210
Los Angeles, 190
New Orleans, 27
Sydney Town Hall, 119–120, 122
Radio Zanzibar, 244–247, *244*
Raha Leo, Zanzibar, *244, 245, 246*
Rama, Angel, 145
Rást Goftár, 171
Rathaus, Germany, 78–94
Reed and Barnes (architects), 123
representation, xx, xxi, 3–5, 7, 18, 29, 38, 47, 97, 103, 107, 108, 109, 153, 181, 194, 279, 297
Calcutta, 200–201, 203–205
Jakarta, Indonesia, 261, 262, 268, 272
Scandinavian city halls, 59, 62, 64–70, 73
self-representation, 7, 73, 200, 210–214, 295
Tanzania, 249–251
Rethel frescoes, 81, 82
revolt, 165, 171, 260
Reykjavik City Hall, *70*
inauguration, 56–57
location, 58
planning stage, 60, 63
public space, 71
Rhee Syngman, 279

Riebeeck, Abraham van, 259
rights. *see also* citizenship
avatar rights, 298–299
human rights, 121–122
right to the city, 238
Risley Education Circular, 213
Roh Moo-hyun, 280, 283
romanticism, Prague, 103
Room of Honor
Casa del Fascio, Milan, *225*
Milan, 224–225
Rosenthal, Anton, 143
Rotes Rathaus, Germany, *88*
rotunda, 191–192
Rowe, Peter, 18
Ruusuvuori, Aarno, 60, 62–63

sacred space, 213–214
Sadikin, Ali, 267–269
Saheb, Nana, 171
Samsung Corporation, 284–285
San Francisco, 42–48, *44, 45, 48*, 51, *52*
San Francisco Chronicle, 42–43, 47
"Sandlots," San Francisco, 51, *52*
sanering, 63
sanitation project, Prague, 103, 104
Sapsford, Thomas, 117
Scandinavian city halls, 56–73
Schmidt, Friedrich von, 103
Schudson, Michael, 52
scribe, public, *146*
Sede Federale, Milan, Italy, 228–231, *229, 230*
self-administration, 97–98, 99
self-representation, 200, 295. *see also* *Swadeshi*
Senegal, 240
Seoul, South Korea, 276–288, *276, 278, 285*
Seoul Plaza, 281–284, *284*
Sepoy Revolt, 165, 171
Shankarshet, Jagannath, 167, 169–171, *172*

Sholz, Hubert, 244
situation. *see* location
size
   Calcutta Town Hall, 201, 203
   Los Angeles City Hall, 182–184
   Scandinavian city halls, 70–73
slaves
   Batavia, 259
   New Orleans, 23
Smith, Adrian, 296
social justice, 267
social space, 162
Soetomo, Dr, 263
Sokol, Jan, 110
South Africa, 239, 240
South Korea, 276–288
space. *see also* public space
   conceptual mode, 9–10
   social space, 162
   spatial arrangement, 19
   spatial contradiction, 251
   spatial practice, xix, 7, 9–10, 238
   spatial type, 5–7
Spanish influence, 187. *see also* Morelia, Mexico
Sparrow, Jeff and Jill, 126–127
Sprenger, Paul, 101
Sprenger's frontage, 108
Spring Street steps, Los Angeles City Hall, *180*, 187
squares, 98, 106–107
   Independence Square, Jakarta, 265–269, *266*, 271
   Jackson Square, New Orleans, 20–24
   Lafayette Square, New Orleans, 24, 25
   Milan, Italy, 231–232, *232*, 233
   Old Town Square, Prague, 98, 109
   Scandinavian city halls, 68–70
   Seoul Plaza, 281–284
   St. Louis Cathedral, New Orleans, 20, *20*
Starace, Achille, 226, 227–228, 232

state control, 164–165. *see also* Fascist Party, Italy
statues
   Bombay Town Hall, 166–171
   Calcutta Town Hall, 199–200
   Cologne, 84–85
   Hannover, 91
   Justice statue, New York, 32
   Shankarshet's statue, 169–171, *172*
steps, 165, *180*, 187
Stockholm demonstrations, 296–297
Stockholm's City Hall, *62*
   access to public space, 70
   Blåa Hallen, 71, *72*
   decoration, 67
   European influence, 66
   Golden Hall, 72–-73
   inauguration, 56, *57*
   location, 58
   planning stage, 61
Stone Town, Zanzibar, 245–246
Street, Jessie, 121
Stuttgart, 92–93, *92*, *93*
sub-Saharan Africa, 237–251
Supreme Court, Australia, 132
sustainability, 296
Sustainable Cities Program (UN), 242
Sutiyoso, Governor, 270–272
Swadeshi, 210–214
Sweden, 296–297. *see also* Stockholm's City Hall
Sydney Morning Herald, 116, 117
Sydney Town Hall, Australia, 116–123, *118*
synthetic world, 298–299

Tanzania, 238–250
Thamrin, M.H., 263
The Argus, 124, 127
The Gangster Squad, 180
Third Reich, 88
Tickner, Robert, 122
Times, 184–185
Togo, 240

Toodyay Town Hall, Australia, 128–132, *129*
towers
    Cologne, 83
    Los Angeles City Hall, 182–183
    Scandinavian city halls, 66–67
    Sede Federale, Milan, 230
    Stuttgart Rathaus, 92–93
Townsville Daily Bulletin, 121
Tramm, Heinrich, 91
Trumbull, John, 32
Tweed, William M., 40–41
Tweed Courthouse, New York, 36–41, *38*, *39*

ujamaa, 247–249
Umbach, Maiken, 87
UN Sustainable Cities Program, 242
union meetings, 121–122, *122*, 126–127
United Arab Emirates, 296–297
Upton, Dell, 18
US
    exclusion, 47, 181
    funding, 50
    Gilded Age, 49, 51
    government structure in, 194
    history of city halls, 18–19
    New England, 4
    New Orleans, 17, 20–27, *22*
    New York, 28–41
    Philadelphia, 42
    political context, 19, 27, 41, 48–49, 51–52

vecino identity, 153
Via Nirone, Milan, Italy, 220, 222
Victoria, Australia, 123–128
Vienna, 103
Vogts, Hans, 83
Vybíral, Jindřich, 106

Wellesley, Lord, 199, 201
Weltevreden, Batavia, 261
Western Australia, 128–132
Wiehl, Antonin, *105*
Wilhelmine empire, 88
William II, 91–92
Willson, John Henry, 117
Wodon de Sorinne, Guillermo, 149–150
women, 34, 121, 158
Wood, Fernando, 36, 40
World War II, 78–79, 81–82. *see also* Nazis
writing, 145–146

Yemen, 161
Young, John (Mayor), 117
Yu Kŏl, *285*

Zambia, 237
Zanzibar, 238, 241, 243–247